THE EUROPEAN SPORTS HISTORY REVIEW

Volume 4

Editors and Advisers

Pieces appearing in this collection are abstracted and indexed in *Political Science Abstracts, Historical Abstracts and America: History and Life* and *Physical Education Index*

THE EUROPEAN SPORTS HISTORY REVIEW

Volume 4

REFORMERS, SPORT, MODERNIZERS
Middle-Class Revolutionaries

Editor

J.A. Mangan
University of Strathclyde

FRANK CASS
LONDON • PORTLAND, OR

First published in 2002 in Great Britain by
FRANK CASS PUBLISHERS
Crown House, 47 Chase Side
London N14 5BP

and in the United States of America by
FRANK CASS PUBLISHERS
c/o ISBS, 5824 N.E. Hassalo Street
Portland, Oregon 97213-3644

Copyright © 2002 Frank Cass & Co. Ltd.

Website: www.frankcass.com

British Library Cataloguing in Publication Data

Reformers, sport, modernizers : middle-class
revolutionaries. – (European sports history review ; v. 4)
1.Sports – Europe – Sociological aspects 2. Sports – Europe
– History – 19th century 3. Middle class – Europe – History
– 19th century
I. Mangan, J. A. (James Anthony), 1939–
306.4'83'08622'094'09034

ISBN 0-7146-5244 X (cloth)
ISBN 0-7146-8228 4 (paper)
ISSN 1462-1495

Library of Congress Cataloging-in-Publication Data

Applied for.

Printed in Great Britain by
Antony Rowe Ltd, Chippenham, Wilts

Contents

List of Illustrations ... vii

List of Tables ... viii

Preface ... *J.A. Mangan* ... ix

Prologue: Middle-Class 'Revolutionaries' in
Pursuit of Moral, Physical, Political and
Social Health ... *J.A. Mangan* ... 1

1. The Living Legacy: Classical Sport and
Nineteenth-Century Middle-Class Commentators
of the German-Speaking Nations ... *Ingomar Weiler* ... 9

2. A Tranquil Transformation: Middle-Class
Racing 'Revolutionaries' in Nineteenth-Century
England ... *Mike Huggins* ... 35

3. Unrecognized Middle-Class Revolutionary?
Michael Cusack, Sport and Cultural
Change in Nineteenth-Century Ireland ... *Joseph M. Bradley* ... 58

4. Missing Middle-Class Dimensions:
Elementary Schools, Imperialism and
Athleticism ... *J.A. Mangan and Colm Hickey* ... 73

5. Mostly Middle-Class Cycling Heroes:
The *Fin de Siècle* Commercial Obsession
with Speed, Distance and Records ... *Andrew Ritchie and Rüdiger Rabenstein* ... 91

6. 'Golden Boys' of Playing Field and Battlefield:
Celebrating Heroes – 'Lost' Middle-Class
Women Versifiers of the Great War ... *J.A. Mangan* ... 134

7. Modernizing Bulgaria: Todor Yonchev –
   Middle-Class Patriot and the Assertion   *Vassil Girginov*
   of a Nation   *and Lozan Mitev*   162

8. Radical Conservatives: Middle-Class
   Masculinity, the Shikar Club and Big   *J.A. Mangan*
   Game-Hunting   *and Callum McKenzie*   185

9. A Dark 'Prince' of Denmark: Niels Bukh,
   Twentieth-Century Middle-Class Propagandist   *Hans Bonde*   210

10. The Apostle of Italian Sport: Angelo Mosso
    and English Athleticism in Italy   *Gigliola Gori*   230

Epilogue: The History of Modern European
   Sport as a History of Modern European Ideas   *J.A. Mangan*   253

Notes on Contributors   257

Abstracts   260

Select Bibliography   265

Index   273

List of Illustrations

5.1 'Road-Riders of 1890' by George Moore   107

5.2 The first Bordeaux–Paris race, 1891   108

5.3 Advertisement for pneumatic tyre company, 1892   109

5.4 Charles Terront in an advertisement for Rudge Cycle Company, Ltd., 1893   110

5.5 The Dunlop cycling team, 1897   111

5.6 Robert L. Jefferson's *Awheel to Moscow and Back* (1895)   112

5.7 Map of the first Tour de France (1903) showing winner Garin   113

7.1 Todor Yonchev   169

7.2 The front cover of Daniel Blanchud's Complete Handbook of Gymnastics (1901)   178

List of Tables

5.1 Cyclists participating in the first German velocipede
    race in Altona, 10 September 1869   121

5.2 Occupations of 175 international bicycle racers before
    their sports careers   122

5.3 Occupations of 46 international bicycle racers after
    their sports careers   123

5.4 Analysis of a group of 353 international professional
    bicycle racers in 1916   124

7.1 Aspects of Bulgaria's social structure, 1885–1944   166

7.2 Main principles, aims and forms of delivery employed
    by Unak Union, 1895   179

7.3 Union Unak congresses and strategic decisions, 1898–1911   180

Preface

J.A. MANGAN

'Middle class and not ashamed of it' trumpeted the Business News Section of the *Daily Telegraph* in April 2001 of David Felwick, Chief Executive of Waitrose.[1] The assertion will serve as a statement of intent for *Reformers, Sport, Modernizers*.

This is the fourth volume of the well-received *European Sports History Review*. It uniquely records the role of selected middle-class individuals across Europe who made notable contributions to the early evolution of modern sport and who saw success in modern sport as an expression of human qualities to be admired, applauded and encouraged and who further viewed sport as a medium of personal, collective and national virtue. This volume represents the first general consideration of a selection of these innovatory pioneers and proselytisers who placed Europe at the forefront of major developments in contemporary world sport – now a phenomenon of global significance. Incidentally, its companion volume in Sport in the Global Society, *Freeing the Female Body: Inspirational Icons*, is a general consideration of various middle-class women who performed the same service in Europe and the rest of the world.[2]

In the extraordinary modern sports revolution of the late nineteenth century – considerably an English manifestation – European middle-class 'revolutionaries' were in the vanguard. There was not a major sport in which their influence was not felt – for better or worse. Virtually all minor sports felt their enthusiastic influence. These cultural 'revolutionaries' were not necessarily radicals, some were conservatives but all effected 'fundamental changes ... in some aspect of ... cultural ... life'.[3] Too few historians appreciate their importance to European culture.[4]

In recent years, the middle classes have suffered 'a bad press' in some academic quarters.[5] Compensatory apologists for other classes have set about them or set them aside. It is time for appropriate revisionism in the interests of balance, accuracy and impartiality.[6]

NOTES

1. The Kate Rankin Interview, *Daily Telegraph*, Saturday 21 April 2001, p.32.
2. J.A. Mangan and Fan Hong (eds.), *Freeing the Female Body: Inspirational Icons* (London and Portland, OR: Frank Cass, 2001).
3. *Longman Dictionary of the English Language* (Longman, 1984), p.1275.
4. A recent example is Norman Davies, *Europe: A History* (Oxford: Oxford University Press, 1996).
5. See Mike Huggins, 'Second-Class Citizens? English Middle-Class Culture and Sport 1886–1910: A Reconsideration', *International Journal of the History of Sport*, 17, 1 (2000), 1–35.
6. It is more than pleasing that the full significance of the role of the middle classes in the evolution of modern sport is at last being gradually recognized. Mike Higgins' superb *Flat Racing and British Society, 1790–1914* (London and Portland, OR: Frank Cass, 2000) won the North American Society for Sports History Book Prize for 2001.

Prologue:
Middle-Class 'Revolutionaries' in Pursuit of Moral, Physical, Political and Social Health

J.A. MANGAN

In *Scholastic Humanism and the Unification of Europe*, R.W. Southern wrote:

> Theology, Law, and the liberal Arts were the three props on which European order and civilization were built during the twelfth and thirteenth centuries – that is to say, during the period of Europe's most rapid expansion in population, wealth and world-wide aspirations before the nineteenth century.[1]

All three props owed their coherence and influence to the development of schools of European importance. Masters and pupils came from every part of Europe[2] and took the sciences which they had learnt back to their cities, towns and villages, and sometimes to places much further afield, where they applied them to the practical issues of life and death, to the advancement of their own well-being and to making a livelihood.[3]

A similar development occurred in Europe in the nineteenth century.[4] In European, and especially in English, schools in a similar period of rapid expansion in population, wealth and world-wide aspirations, props of gender, moral, social and political order were erected. Educationalists used modern sport as a central prop to support a structure of perceived moral superiority. This is no exaggeration.[5] Some of these educationalists feature prominently in *Reformers, Sport, Modernizers*.[6] They helped to change Europe – and the world – ideologically, recreationally and topographically.

As earlier in the early medieval period, there evolved 'an organised Christian society for which the schools were largely responsible'[7] and the influence of the schools was felt throughout society. Of course this was a period of defensive religiosity and assertive secularism. With reference to the Renaissance, John Hale has remarked that the word *rinascitor* (rebirth) was used to describe a new enlightenment yet, for all its secular content, it was a word of powerful religious resonance. *Rinascitor*, with its powerful two-pronged connotations, serves equally well to describe the Europe of the second half of the nineteenth century – it too was a time of moral rebirth.[8]

A system of thought concerning the body and its relationship to gender, politics, morality and society, as well as the body's physical well-being, was transmitted through the schools by innovative, committed 'missionaries' who worked to influence the nature of schooling, of morality, of masculinity and femininity, of education, of secular and spiritual values and of society itself. In English society beyond the schools, has been noted that middle-class 'missionaries', both political and professional, made their mark on entire communities. 'Since great structural transformations reflect profound changes in mental outlook, the professional social ideal – the professionals' ideal of how society should be organized and of the ideal citizen to organize it – began to infiltrate men's minds and replace the [earlier] entrepreneurial ideal.'[9] The comment has relevance to the whole of Europe.

There was a 'revolutionary' cohesion in attitudes to the exercise of the body across Europe, despite national, regional and local differences of emphasis, enthusiasm and involvement. Physical exercise for reasons of health – moral, physical and social – was formalized and promoted in schools. It was equally keenly, if more unevenly, promoted in societies although the structure was less formalized. Nations used sport to make militaristic masculinity, with the eventual result that at the outbreak of the Great War educated middle-class women stepped out of the shadows of convention and urged self-sacrificial heroism on schoolboys as they fought on the bloody battlefields of the Western Front. These women were also social 'revolutionaries', in their way, through their open display of patriotic assertion.

Of course, the revolution was not all cohesion. Nor was it all altruism. There was doctrinal confrontation between conservative and radical as well as gender repression and oppression and class prejudice and intolerance. It was not only in England that 'the middle class was riddled with ... divisions and ... snobberies; not only of income and geography but also religion' and divided vertically as well as horizontally.[10]

Nevertheless, whatever the imperfections involved, the second half of the nineteenth century saw more change than continuity in sport across

Europe: where it was played; when it was played; how it was played; who played it and why. Yet there was a core of consistency within a welter of contradictions, namely new attitudes, new actions and new venues.

As in the early Middle Ages, this consistency was the result of vastly more favourable material conditions which gave rise *inter alia* to an increasingly comfortably-off, confident and powerful European middle class: 'only occasionally did a professional man recognise the separate existence of his own class, and then only to emphasise its ineffable superiority'.[11] It was the start of a long cultural revolution with the middle classes in the vanguard *not* merely of the popular cultural revolution of Raymond Williams but of a global recreational revolution with confident moral overtones. Historians, generally, have been slow to appreciate this.[12]

What was true of Southern states of the Scholastic Humanism of the twelfth and thirteenth centuries, was equally true of the 'Sports Humanism' of the late nineteenth and early twentieth centuries. It is important to note and record the achievements, the extent of the associated benefits and the fact that, as in the early Middle Ages, 'the full development of these benefits (and abuses) lay in the future'[13] – in the structures and systems of sport in Europe and the world in the twentieth century. In the late nineteenth and early twentieth centuries, increasing systematization was established and an extensive and common practice of 'play' was eventually put in place across the world[14] – a practice essentially 'communicated to the whole world through a combination of preaching and teaching';[15] a substantial amount of this communication was by Europeans.[16]

If the end to which Western Christendom was moving at the end of the twelfth century was the creation of a scholastic system 'aimed at restoring to fallen mankind, so far as it was possible, that perfect system of knowledge which had been in the possession or within the reach of mankind at the moment of Creation',[17] no less was it the plan in the minds of some European middle-class 'missionaries' to take a system of morality encapsulated in sport to fallen members of mankind in the lower-classes of Europe and the 'lower strata' of humanity in various European empires of the nineteenth century. Historians have also been slow to recognize this.[18]

If the twelfth and thirteenth centuries were 'wonderful times for academically qualified men and their services were in great demand',[19] as influential arbiters of orthodoxy then, likewise, the late nineteenth and early twentieth centuries were marvellous moments for athletically-inclined educationalists who became influential arbiters of orthodoxy.[20] The teachers of both periods defined moral conduct and conveyed those doctrines which 'impinged on faith and practice'[21] and which were considered fundamental for the requirements of middle-class life. The universities provided continuity and stability for a 'flow of masters'[22] to the schools which then reproduced a 'systematic body of doctrine'[23] which then perpetrated a way of life. Both periods eventually experienced disintegration born out of disillusionment, opposition and confrontation due to an increasing prolixity of knowledge and changing interpretations of the value of this knowledge, yet in both cases the influence of both 'revolutions' has proved to be long lasting.

Throughout Europe in the late nineteenth and early twentieth centuries, the body, especially the male body, became an icon of bourgeois morality. It came to be represented by a set of attitudes and views and moral directives characteristic of its own time and place[24] – stimulated by economic transformation.

It has been observed of Western Europe as a whole, that:

> The forty years before 1914 were a period of extraordinary peace and prosperity. By 1914, although the population had risen very considerably, most people were fed, housed and generally looked after far better than before. Education progressed, to the point of virtually universal literacy in most countries ... In Europe, outside the Balkans, there were no wars after 1871; and European civilization swept over the globe.[25]

Peter Stearns has put the matter succinctly – Europe after 1850 was in unprecedented social upheaval: a new kind of society had been formed. From the eighteenth century onwards the population expanded rapidly and grew exceptionally mobile; it became urbanized; the economy was transformed; production hugely increased; new marketing and transport systems emerged and governments were characterized by new methods and policies. 'Demographic, economic, and political forces arose that were truly revolutionary in their intensity.'[26]

The term 'modernization' usefully summarizes the changes. It embraces industrialization, the widening of a market mentality, the growth of political consciousness, an active state and, most important of all, a changed outlook. Modern man is more secular, rational and progressive than pre-modern man.[27] In sporting terms, one by-product of modernization was an obsession with fitness, competition, records and performance. *Every* aspect of this modern life was affected and not only more associated with the body but with opportunities for exercising the body: 'Pre-modern society had a different notion of work from modern society. It had little sense of *specific leisure*; the notion of vacations and regular, off-the-job recreation was born into the nineteenth century.'[28] This adaptation was widespread, if not constant and uniform, throughout Europe. While there are quite a number of European civilizations, 'these civilizations are interrelated and overlap ... "No European can be a complete exile in any part of Europe"'.[29]

Of course, not all changes were positive – change, *inter alia*, is stressful: 'it is possible that the stress of modernization pushes more people to the brink of despair, or over it, than was true before'.[30] Nevertheless, the general view appears to be that modern society is better than pre-modern society. The reasons are easy to discern: better health, better standard of living, more personal freedom, greater social mobility and far more opportunities, more outlets, more time and more places to pleasurably exercise the body.

The concept of stratification is useful to better understand the shifting nature and extent of this adaptation. In terms of stratification, class is a key term. Here it is broadly defined to denote people with 'a roughly similar style of life and social status'[31] and, for obvious reasons, the concern here is with the so-called middle class commonly characterized by comfortable lifestyles and property ownership: 'by the nineteenth century ... groups with the same earnings could rarely stay apart too long [and] increasingly localised into single classes because of shared economic position'.[32] Thus, an extended middle class, divided into sub-groupings, became consolidated across Europe.

It has been argued that 'in taking class lines seriously, as the social historian must, to understand the impact of modernization, a fresh look is required at the upper levels of society'.[33] *Reformers, Sport, Modernizers* does just this.

> A society at any given stage of modernization can be understood in terms of certain general trends and institutions, such as technological levels and political structure. Its people, however, must be broken down by class and often by subgroup, by age level, and by sex. A complex arrangement, to be sure, but not indigestible and essential to grasp the way contemporary society came into being.[34]

Peter Stearns has neatly summarized the background to *Reformers, Sport, Modernizers*:

> It is increasingly recognized that essential aspects of the modernization process were taking shape in Western Europe from about 1750 onward, in the form of population increase and the spread of new forms of manufacturing. From this base flowed industrialisation itself, from about 1820 onward (a bit earlier in England). This second phase of modernization saw only a minority of the population touched by the factories directly, but it witnessed the most rapid urbanization. Together the first two stages of modernization, 1750–1820 and 1820–1870, constitute the period in which change was most bewildering and the institutions of society most severely challenged.[35]

James Joll makes the point that 'there have been years in which certain historical experiences were common to Europe as a whole ... and they were years in which the course of European history profoundly affected society in countries outside Europe.'[36] Joll echoes Stearns in his remarks that the last quarter of the nineteenth century 'for the wealthier classes of Europe ... was more comfortable than ever before and offered a greater possibility of choice in sorts of fields'[37] within a framework of urban improvement and expansion and the growth of consumption and leisure. All of this is relevant to middle-class sport in the Europe of the period and to the 'revolutionaries' who were involved in dramatic change both in and beyond Europe.

In the relative stability of the last quarter of the nineteenth century the European middle-class 'revolutionaries' of this volume took up their crusades and enthusiasms and carried them into the twentieth century, not only in pursuit of sectional indulgence but in pursuit of general health – physical, political, social and, not least, moral!

NOTES

1. R.W. Southern, *Scholastic Humanism and the Unification of Europe*, Vol.1 'Foundations' (Oxford: Blackwell, 1995), Introduction, p.1.
2. Ibid., p.2.
3. Ibid., p.5. See, for example, J.A. Mangan, *Athleticism in the Victorian and Edwardian Public School* (London and Portland, OR: Frank Cass, 2000) and J.A. Mangan, *The Games Ethic and Imperialism* (London and Portland, OR: Frank Cass, 1998).
4. Of course, as John Hale points out, there was yet another age of upheaval in the sixteenth century in which education played a critical part. See John Hale, *The Civilization of Europe in*

the Renaissance (London: Harper Collins, 1993), p.xix: 'No slice of historical time is self-contained. But what has usefully come to be referred to as the "long" sixteenth century does have a coherence of its own. It was the first age in which the words "Europe" and "European" acquired a widely understood significance. It saw the emergence of a new and pervasive attitude to what were considered the most valued aspects of civilized life. It witnessed the most concentrated wave of intellectual and creative energy that had yet passed over the continent, with the culture of Renaissance Italy reaching its apogee and being absorbed or rebuffed by other vigorously developing national cultures.'

5. See, for example, Mangan, *Athleticism* and *The Games Ethic*.
6. Only a few individuals and nations are considered in *Reformers, Sport, Modernizers*. Space precludes more extensive coverage.
7. Southern, *Scholastic Humanism*, p.4.
8. Hale, *The Civilization of Europe*, p.587.
9. Harold Perkin, *The Rise of Professional Society: England since 1880* (London: Routledge, 1989), p.xiii.
10. Perkin, *The Rise of Professional Society*, p.118.
11. As already mentioned (see Preface), a clear example is Norman Davies in *Europe: A History* (Oxford: Oxford University Press, 1996). Davies fails to fully appreciate the political, cultural, social and emotional role of modern sport in modern European history. His is a regrettable but not untypical myopia.
12. Southern, *Scholastic Humanism*, p.6. As regards abuses, what is so very different in the authoritarian manipulation between Coubertin and Samoranch?
13. See, for example, J.A. Mangan, *Europe, Sport, World* (London and Portland, OR: Frank Cass, 2001), *passim*.
14. See Mangan, *The Games Ethic*, *passim*.
15. A good example is Latin America, see J.A. Mangan and Lamartine P. DaCosta, *Sport in Latin American Society: Past and Present* (London and Portland, OR: Frank Cass, 2001), *passim*.
16. Southern, *Scholastic Humanism*, p.7.
17. Ibid., p.10.
18. A recent example of this cultural myopia is to be found in John M. MacKenzie (ed.), *The Victorian Vision: Inventing New Britain* (London: V & A Publications, 2000). Morality encapsulated in spirit was one of the strongest late Victorian Visions and resulted not only in the reinvention of middle-class masculinity in Britain, but also in the Empire of the English and Imperial public school athleticism which played such a significant part in socialization into imperial order, see Mangan, *Athleticism, The Games Ethic* and *The Cultural Bond* (London and Portland, OR: Frank Cass, 1993). MacKenzie and Cannadine are recent examples of a regrettably analytical myopia. David Cannadine in *Ornamentalism: How the British Saw Their Empire* (London: Allen Lane, The Penguin Press, 2001) also completely fails to connect the concern with the social class stratification of the British symbolized in imperial ornamentalism with the all persuasive and powerful myths, rituals and symbols in which the moralistic visionary nature of the Public School Games Cult in Empire is inexcusably overlooked.
19. See Mangan, *Athleticism*, Ch.6.
20. Ibid.
21. Ibid.
22. Ibid.
23. Ibid.
24. See Maria Ossowaka, *Bourgeois Morality*, trans. G.L. Campbell (London: Routledge and Kegan Paul, 1986), p.2.
25. Norman Stone, *Europe Transformed 1878–1919* (London: Fontana, 1987), p.1.
26. Peter N. Stearns, *European Society in Upheaval: Social History since 1750* (New York: Macmillan, 1975), p.1.
27. Ibid., p.2.
28. Ibid., p.4.
29. Michael Grant, *The Civilizations of Europe* (London: Weidenfeld and Nicolson, 1965), pp.3–4.
30. Stearns, *European Society in Upheaval*, p.4.
31. Ibid., p.5.

32. Ibid., p.6.
33. Ibid., p.7.
34. Ibid., p.8.
35. Ibid.
36. James Joll, *Europe Since 1870: An International History* (London: Weidenfeld and Nicolson, 1973), p.xi.
37. Ibid., p.31.

1

The Living Legacy:
Classical Sport and Nineteenth-Century Middle-Class Commentators of the German-Speaking Nations

INGOMAR WEILER

First, two preliminary points dealing with the term 'German innovators' and the employed chronology; the term 'German' refers to the 'German-speaking world' – which includes Switzerland and Austria – and those countries making a major contribution to European Winter Sports and Alpinism. Regarding the chronology, Reinhart Kosellek describes the period from 1789 to 1914 as the nineteenth century, which is followed by the short twentieth century which spans from 1914 to 1989.[1] For the historian primarily dedicated to political and constitutional developments, this suggested dating may appear sensible. Those considering the social and cultural, or economic phenomena of the nineteenth century, will find arguments for extending this period, as suggested by R. Kosellek, or for agreeing with Christiane Eisenberg and her remark that the long nineteenth century lasted 'not only to the First, but at least to the Second World War'.[2] However, for an understanding of the intellectual and social changes in the nineteenth century there remains an indispensable need to include in any consideration the empirical and rationalistic conceptions of the Age of Enlightenment ('le siècle des lumières') of the eighteenth century which preceded the Revolution of 1789. The fact that this Age of Enlightenment, with its pedagogical aims, itself in the Age of Humanism turned to the rediscovered philosophy and poetry of Antiquity should not be overlooked. The conventional chronological term for the nineteenth century thus requires modification in response to specific interests in the humanities and social history.

The polyvalent physiognomy of the nineteenth century in Europe is marked by the grave consequences of the Industrial Revolution, by colonialism and imperialism, by the polarization of capitalism and socialism, by nationalism and cosmopolitanism, as well as by democratic, monarchist and dictatorial systems. Significant innovation is also shown in education and in recreational cultures. The English (British) Sports Movement, the Games Movement, the Swedish Gymnastics Movement and the German *Turnen* of Friedrich Ludwig Jahn (1778–1852) collectively signify the relinquishing of traditional patterns of life marked by the aristocracy and religious institutions and the assumption of their powerful influence at various social levels. Of course, the new movements did not become established in the countries of Europe without friction.[3] *Turnvater* Jahn and his close colleagues, Ernst Wilhelm Bernhard Eiselen (1792–1846) and Karl Friedrich Friesen (1784–1814), for example, opposed the spread of the English (British) Sports Movement in the German-speaking world. History, however, reveals that the secular *Kulturkampf* between gymnastics and sport was decided in favour of the latter.[4] However, from the point of view of a global history of sport, the important impulse and its broad effect on sport in the twentieth century arguably takes its starting point from 'folk gymnastics' and, towards the end of the nineteenth century, from the expansion of winter sports, especially the Alpine varieties and Alpinism. There are comprehensive depictions of the history of Jahn's *Turnen*, European water sports and Alpinism available.[5]

While various processes of acculturation and diffusion have been comprehensively documented by the historians of sport, with regard to society, culture, lifestyles and leisure – through which industrial society formed its newly constituted middle class – there are two remarkable academic inquiries regarding the development of sport and physical education in the German-speaking world which have been insufficiently, and indeed superficially, analyzed. Both are concerned with the adoption of Greek sport in the nineteenth century and deal with (a) the neohumanist gymnasium and (b) the attempt to bring new vitality to the Olympic Games. These two institutions were organized by two influential middle-class innovators who made major contributions to European sport in a century that can be described as the formative phase of sport. Innovation was borne exclusively by individual men, giving rise to the expression 'history is the work of men (*Männer machen die Geschichte*)'.[6] These innovators reacted to the social, national and ideological changes resulting from the Industrial Revolution, the Enlightenment and the French Revolution but, above all, it was Johann

Joachim Winckelmann's aesthetic and philological Romantic Philhellenism of the second half of the eighteenth century that influenced the educational curriculum of the classical gymnasium and the German middle class in the nineteenth and early twentieth centuries. For the German *Bildungsbürger*, confrontation with the sport of the ancient Hellenes was primarily intellectual. It is curious that Suzanne L. Marchand, in her commendable study *Down from Olympus*, has not taken this into account in period studies of the Greek agonistics and gymnastics.[7]

Although school sport and physical training achieved great importance through the strictly pedagogical arguments of various philanthropists in the German-speaking world after Johann Bernhard Basedow (1724–90) and Johann Christoph Friedrich GutsMuths (1759–1839), there was also a conscious turning for inspiration to models from Greek Antiquity. The neohumanist gymnasium, as conceived by Wilhelm von Humboldt (1767–1835) for the great educational reforms under King Friedrich Wilhelm III (1779–1840) in 1809, for example, concentrated almost exclusively on the cultivation of the classical Latin and Greek languages. An early interest in these languages was already apparent in his *Über das Studium des Altertums, und des griechischen insbesondere* (1793). The characteristics of the Greeks, outlined there, take their point of departure from four component elements:

1. science and art;
2. versatility and uniformity;
3. perception of external cultural influence;
4. affinity with human nature in general.

Despite having a holistic, anthropological perspective, Humboldt saw a special primary educational value in the intellectual dialogue with Antiquity[8] and often touched upon the ideas of Winckelmann (1717–68). The aesthetic sensibilities, language, poetry and philosophy of the Greeks were in the forefront of Humboldt's reflections: 'an utterly vast receptivity for all of the beauty of nature and art, a finely wrought rhythm and this refined taste'[9] distinguished, in his view, not only the lives of some individuals, such qualities were the marks of the Hellenes as a whole:

> In his first babbling the Greek reveals fine and proper feeling; and in the mature age of his manhood he does not completely lose his

initial childish simplicity. In this, methinks, lies a larger part of the real national characteristic.[10]

This picture of the Greeks also included attitudes to the body and to the physical education of the Hellenes but Humboldt addressed them only briefly. In concrete pedagogic practice, in which the number of hours given to the classic disciplines taught each week are proportionally high, sport in reality remained almost unconsidered by Humboldt although some sports theory was provided. Humboldt was of the opinion that the Greeks knew so specifically how to harmoniously combine art, nature and culture 'that they always, and always more than any other people, knew how to cultivate the training of physical strength, agility and beauty'.[11] He thus came to the logical conclusion 'that the cultivation of physical and intellectual education in Greece was very great and that they were especially moved by the ideas of beauty'.[12]

Yet Humboldt was not uncritical of Hellenistic values. As Friedrich Engels was later to do, Humboldt argued against the institution of slavery, which made it possible for the free Greek to spend his life largely removed from the working class. 'He then had the leisure to spend time in the training of his body through gymnastics, to form his mind through art and science, his character utterly given to active participation in the State constitution, in his dealings and his own reflection.'[13] Nevertheless, adulatory studies of the ancient Hellenes were to contribute to their imitation. When it came to the realization of Humboldt's plans for reform – in 1806 in Prussia, in 1830 in Bavaria and very soon after in Austria – the new school of a neohumanist gymnasium was brought into being. Tuition in the old languages initially took pride of place and, together with the other disciplines of Antiquity, comprised at least half of the educational programme in terms of hours per week.[14] In view of this, the question why Greek sport played such a marginal role in the neohumanist gymnasium school system is not easy to answer. However, several reasons, which do not necessarily contradict each other, do present themselves as possible answers: the neohumanist educational canon was directed to general knowledge (*Allgemeinbildung*); it incorporated 'Greco–Roman culture, its mythology, art, literature and history'[15] and after completion of a gymnasium education gave access to the university. The predominantly intellectual educational ideal of the middle-class citizenry and its preference for a literary–aesthetic education and its dominant Grecocentrism in philological–historical and humanitarian aims was enshrined in this approach. At the same time, theory and practice were often widely separate. Despite a pedagogical plea for humanitarian thought, the ethical consideration of the slavery question was hardly touched upon in the gymnasiums – Marxist historical studies first brought the matter to general attention, invariably with a somewhat blunt emphasis. The unfortunate neglect of humanistic ideals is manifest not only in an uncritical acceptance of Antiquity but also in an ignorance of the catastrophic conditions in the industrial world of the nineteenth century. The classical gymnasium and the ideas of neohumanism gave little consideration to this grave contemporary social situation.

The conscious turning here to the physical training of Antiquity (contests in running, jumping, wrestling, javelin and discus) in the Philanthropinum of Dessau and Schnepfenthal, which were conceived for a middle-class citizenry, shows a strong utilitarian nuance.[16] Outdoor activities, archery, walking, swimming and exercises to maintain mental and physical equilibrium now became important. Daily sport classes, including Greek gymnastics with contests similar to the pentathlon and the Olympic Games, were to be found in these middle-class institutes of education. GutsMuths advocated the harmony of body and mind as a pedagogical aim, as described by authors of Antiquity and Jean Jacques Rousseau (1712–78), and argued this involved reciprocation:[17]

1. bodily health – lightness of mind;
2. hardening – in a manly sense;
3. physical activity – mental activity;
4. good education – beauty of the soul;
5. sharpness of the senses – sharpness of mental power.

This philanthropic physical education, which conjoined with the ideal of harmony, had as its aim the conscious cultivation of health and the strengthening of the body to ensure a successful professional life, appears to have had little effect in the school curriculum of the neohumanist gymnasium. Effectiveness was more likely achieved by means of Jahn's gymnastics. The *Turnvater* considered physical efficiency extremely important, albeit for nationalistic reasons. In Jahn's view his utilitarian concept of gymnastics was the answer to Napoleon's European ambitions. Implementation, however, did not take place in the schools, but after school in the open air.[18] The implementation of Jahn's *Turnen* in the school curriculum remained the preserve of other sports

pedagogues, above all, Adolf Spieß (1810–58). After the equipping of
the first *Turnplatz* on the Hasenheide (1811) in Berlin, with similar
gymnastic centres quickly opening in many other cities, with the
founding of the first *Turnverein* and of the first *Turnfest*, Jahn took a
different road. However, his efforts to make nationalistic gymnastics
popular met with resistance. Many people found the militaristic
mentality of the German *Turner*, as can be shown by the words of the
marching song, off-putting:

> When for the people's old and sacred rights,
> Bravely the *Turnmeister*, Friedrich Jahn,
> Strode to the field where man for freedom fights,
> A warlike generation followed on.
> Hey, how the youths leapt after him,
> Fresh and joyful, godly, free!
> Hey how the youths sang after him:
> Hurrah!

Following the murder of the dramatist August von Kotzebue
(1761–1819), a popular critic of Jahn during the time of Goethe, by the
Burschenschaft-member Karl Ludwig Sand (executed in 1820), the
Prussian and Austrian Chancellors, Hardenberg and Metternich, issued
the Carlsbad Decree (the so-called *Turnsperre* which lasted from 1819 to
1842) prohibiting the operating of public gymnastic institutes.[19]
Gymnastics were banned and more than 100 *Turnplätze* were closed.
The way was open for the admirers of Antiquity.

Romanticism, patriotic chauvinism and Grecophilia were three of the
important components in the history of ideas characteristic of the
intellectual milieu of the German-speaking world in the nineteenth
century. Karl Christ, one of the outstanding German historians of
classical scholarship, added to this trio when he identified 'the specific
idiosyncrasy of German development' as having three further
characteristics – idealization, a scholarly attitude and the politicizing of
Antiquity.[20] It might be argued that these characteristics can also be seen
in the sports of the ancient Hellenes. At first, the acceptance of Greek
gymnastics and agonistics remained theoretical. Initial scholarly
research into Antiquity failed to lead to the reformation of physical
education in the gymnasium. Nevertheless, after what was certainly the
outcome of an ideological return to Greek culture, individual humanist
scholars completed inquiries into the Panhellenic agones and the

gymnastics of the Classical world. Furthermore, the image of Antiquity was promoted, above all, in France in the eighteenth century in the *Querelle des Anciens et des Modernes*, a movement idealizing Philhellenism and Antiquity, which also found a footing in historical research.[21] This approach was also supported by prominent German poets and scholars.[22] 'Winckelmann was the initiator, Goethe the fulfiller, Wilhelm von Humboldt the theoretician in his linguistic and scholarly educational writings' of the new humanism or Hellenism.[23]

It had already been suggested in the eighteenth century that the Germans understood the Hellenic heritage better than the French and that the Germans had a closer affinity to the Greeks. In the *à-la-mode* period, considered to be physically and morally decadent, there was a desire for a return to a fictitious ideal of the Greek healthy and balanced character. Winckelmann's classic formula of 'noble simplicity and calm magnificence' and the modification by E. Curtius, 'the simple, moderate and sensible' by means of which 'the Hellenes and the Barbarians differed' highlights this fictitious idealism. In addition, there was the illusory idea that the Hellenes were distinguished by complete mental and physical health or, as Friedrich Rückert (1788–1866) expressed in admiration, 'Only the Greeks are completely healthy in body and mind. Our world is a great house of infirmity in comparison.'[24] Only in the twentieth century have historians found the image of healthy and strong Greeks problematic. Sardonically, Robert Flacelière has asked:

> Are we really, as we have been told, to believe with 'a pure heart' that the course of their [Greek] days were marked by the elegantly proportioned clarity of a Sophoclean drama? Must we really praise without distinction the monumental cleanliness and healthy strength of an entire people, which in reality never cleaned its teeth, never knew a handkerchief, wiped its dirty fingers in its hair, spat without scruple on the floor, and in the years of no widespread famine and pest epidemics, died like flies of malaria and tuberculosis?[25]

To return now to the nineteenth century and specifically to the educational canon, the way it was conceived by Classical scholars and implemented in the neohumanist gymnasium. Karl Christ remarked that 'the idealising basic train of thought ... especially in the historic depictions, are predominant'.[26] According to the German-speaking Philhellenists and Classicists of the period, Greek exemplariness embraced all cultural and artistic spheres as well as the areas of agonistics and gymnastics to which individual scholars sought to attribute special value. This German adulation found the most emphatic expression in the second half of the nineteenth century in the writings of Ernst Curtius, Friedrich Nietzsche and Jacob Burckhardt who, with his admiration for the 'agonal Greek', made competitiveness the absolute quality of Greek culture and thus made an indirect contribution to enhancing an appreciation of sport. For this reason the characterization of the Hellenes as an agonistic people deserves particular attention since some nineteenth-century German authors wished to claim a special affinity to Greek sport. Their claim became even stronger in the twentieth century, achieving its clearest expression in the Nazi Olympic Games in Berlin.[27]

The celebration of the body of the Greek athlete, revealed in sculptures such as the *Doryphorus* by Polyclitus or Myron's *Discobolus*, should be added to an adulation of the Hellenic qualities of life. The Greek concept of *kalokagathia* meaning 'nobleness and goodness', or 'bravery and magnanimity', is a composite word from the Greek *kalos kai agathos*, meaning 'beautiful and good', signifying 'physical and moral excellence', as St Miller has argued.[28] Since the eighteenth century this aesthetic ideal has generated great interest among scholars researching the ancient world, especially those of the early Philhellenist and Romantic school of thought. F. Bourriot's *Kalos Kagathos – Kalokagathia* documented not only the adoption and discussion of this theme in writings of the period authorities, it also stressed that the ideal of *kalokagathia*, this 'mythe du miracle grec', was mainly interpreted and taken up by German-speaking scholars such as Humboldt, Jaeger, Burckhardt and Meier.[29] The adoption of the *kalokagathia* ideal in the nineteenth century, and its consequences for the view of humanity in the Third Reich, has been succinctly described by J.A. Mangan, drawing upon H. Glaser:

> The concept of *kalokagathia* (i.e. the harmony of soul and body, the desired accord between a beautiful soul and a beautiful body), which German Classicism inherited from the Enlightenment and then developed further, was already turning into a cult of the physical in the nineteenth century.[30]

German middle-class scholars of the ancient world offered fundamentally important ideological and factographic principles paving the way for this development. Furthermore, several ancient historians, archaeologists and classical philologists helped to lay the foundations of German adulation. They can be counted among those influential innovators of the nineteenth century who helped, at an intellectual level, to prepare the way for the triumphal march of sport in Europe. Let us begin with Karl Otfried Müller (1797–1840), who provides an impressive and relevant example:

> Among all of the branches of the Indo–Germanic tribes the Greeks are those in which their sensorial and intellectual, inner and outer life were most beautifully balanced, for which reason ... they appeared to have been utterly predestined to undertake the independent fashioning of artistic forms.[31]

Müller drew attention to the special intimacy of the Greeks, meaning above all the Dorians, with agon. This intimacy was expressly addressed in his work, *Geschichte Hellenischer Stämme und Städte*.[32] In his own opinion Sparta minted and made noble the picture of Greek sport: 'That the Dorians more than all others among the Hellenes were dedicated to gymnastics' was, for Müller, a given fact.

> The Dorian tribe is ... probably responsible in particular – as they certainly were responsible for the turning of gymnastic festivals into great national festivals – for the introduction of the wreath in place of other prizes. But Homer's gymnastic fighters still had the chance of more concrete rewards. In retrospect, however, the action was wholly appropriate to the level of ancient Hellenic humanity on which we find the Dorians ... to completely purify all that was Philistine. It was to Olympia that the first wreath was given.[33]

Müller considered the exceptional severity in training youths and the abandoning of weakly children, the 'flogging at the altar of Orthia', which is described as the 'triumph of Spartan hardening' and 'the athletic war games', were prerequisites for these special Dorian qualities. Müller posed this rhetorical question a century before the maxims of youth training under the National Socialists were formulated: 'is not victory in war itself only another means to depict in free strength and healthy beauty a perfect life?' He argued that 'Such an ideal will remove all inhibitions in respect of the external ... the Spartans were the most healthy of the Hellenes, and the most beautiful men were found among them'.[34]

In an attempt to capture Müller's endeavour to summarize and make plausible 'the real basic character of the Dorian tribe' in his closing chapter, a few key expressions must suffice: 'the striving for unity as a whole'; 'the sprightly warrior'; 'the Dorian mentality seeks pure and clear harmony everywhere'; 'joy in a clear, physical existence'. These following characteristics of the Dorians are offered as laudable:

> Human nature itself ... bears the mark of the male gender throughout the entire tribe, from which one can assume that the receiving and needing, the following and yearning, the soft and fickle as essential traits of the feminine being were contrary to the Dorian nature, which bore the character of independence and harnessed power.[35]

It would not be out of place to find a biologically racist and sexist component in this picture of the Dorians. That later authors, with reference to Müller, speak of the Spartan 'racial breeding and racial hygiene', which would then recur in National Socialism, is not entirely beyond understanding.[36]

Before the remarkable contribution to the research into Greek sport by Müller's outstanding pupil, Ernst Curtius, is discussed, attention should be given first to Johann Heinrich Krause (1802–82) from Halle an der Saale, one of the great German pioneering scholars of the history of sport and physical education in the ancient world. With *Die Gymnastik und Agonistik der Hellenen* (1841), *Theagenes oder Wissenschaftliche Darstellung der Gymnastik und Festspiele der Hellenen* (1838) and *Die Pythien, Nemeen und Isthmien aus den Schrift- und Bildwerken des Alterthums dargestellt* (1841), for the first time and with stylistic elegance, Krause analysed and systematically presented epigraphical, archaeological and numismatical documents together with historiographical, philosophical and poetical literature following a historio–philological critique of sources from Antiquity.[37] These volumes ensured that standard works were available to an educated circle of readers for later research into the history of sport and for popularizing this knowledge. Using these works as a base, Classical scholars, sports historians and cultural philosophers dealt with questions of the Greek competitions, from Homer onwards, and Greek physical education. Despite the fact that the epigraphical, archaeological and papyrological sources have subsequently greatly increased in number, Krause's monumental depiction of the Greek contests and gymnastics remains a fundamental introduction which is of 'full and inestimable value to this day'.[38]

From the viewpoint of Classical scholarship outside of the German-speaking world, it should be remembered that the prejudices of academics towards sport in the Anglo–Saxon middle-and upper middle-class school system were essentially less marked than they were among their colleagues at German universities and gymnasiums. That latter state of affairs was partly due to the polarization between the English (British) Sport Movement and Jahn's *Turnen*.

The idea that the ancient Hellenes had a very specific attitude to competition arose for the first time from Ernst Curtius (1814–96).[39] At the same time it should not be overlooked that authors of the ancient world, such as Herodot, Platon or Lucian,[40] had already prepared the way. They were convinced, for example, that the Greeks differed from the Barbarians in their attitude to competition. Ernst Curtius wrote of his analytical approach in a letter to his brother:

> My idea is to reveal and unfold the agonistic character of Greek life ... to show how the entirety of Greek life was a competition between tribes and cities, in war and peace, in art and scholarship, contrary to the life of pleasure in the Orient, with an overestimation of possessions and the desire to possess.[41]

For Curtius, Greek gymnastics and this competitive attitude to health had both a political and a religious dimension which was also partly bound up with the educational concept of the neohumanist gymnasium. The German excavators at Olympia called this attitude to competition a 'basic characteristic trait of the Aryan people', which 'is revealed to us in the greatest purity and in its exemplary meaning by the Hellenes'.[42] Curtius gave his lecture about the Greek *Wettkampf* (1856) more than two decades before the start of excavations at Olympia and in it made his plea for an 'Aryan understanding of history'.[43] In a graphic description of the Semites and other Orientals, who were apparently 'ruled by lower lusts' and lived in 'mindless delusion', any enthusiasm for competition was denied:

> While the son of Sem, looking back, is still absorbed in the sight of the living God ... the eyes of the Japhetids are directed only forward; in strength released by joyous feeling they hurry on the road with a thirst for competitive action. They soon leave the other ethnological groups far behind ... These tribes have all inherited the masculine urge of a thirst for action.[44]

While 'Barbarians' of an Oriental provenance, such as Persians and Semites, had no wish to acquire the 'characteristics' or 'principles of Hellenic life', Curtius is of the opinion that this was not true of the Germans of his time:

> The Germans had certainly been honoured by the suggestion that they had a special understanding of the Hellenic being. The histories of both peoples have not only grown out of their own tribes, but have the character of a history enduring longer than is the case among other peoples. In Hellas, as in Germany, national unity remained an intellectual and inner attribute, an idea that transcended individual tribes and states. Their intellectual realisation has become all the more a matter of competitiveness, and that which is healthy and beautifully successful in this great competition of powers, has become a total possession of the people, among the Germans as among the Greeks, and who can deny how much our education and our literature owes to this competitiveness. Participation in this competitiveness, which guarantees the fresh flow and richness of the inner life of the people, is above all the calling of all of our universities in the *Vaterland*; yes, they should depict this battle in its purest form, in the fullness of its idealism.[45]

In his summary Curtius pleaded for German excavations at Olympia, based on Winckelmann's excavation plans and in response to the special intellectual affinity of the Germans to the Greeks.[46] Marchand commentated on this ambition:

> Curtius developed a plan ... to do homage to the great Winckelmann, and to reveal once more the great works of the ancients to the light of day. Blending together religious and humanistic rhetoric, he called on his countrymen to support his quest to revive the admirable ancient model. 'What lies there in those dark depths', he intoned, 'is life of our life. If other missionaries of God have gone out in the world and preached greater forms of peace than the Olympic truces, Olympia remains for us today a holy place, and we ought to take up, in our world, illuminated by pure light, [Olympia's] flights of inspiration, unselfish patriotism, devotion to art, and joyful energy that endures despite all life's cares.' Duty – to God and Antiquity – called German scholars to realise Winckelmann's dream.[47]

At the end of the first six extensive excavations at Olympia (1875–81), the excavators asked questions both rhetorical and patriotic:

> Should other norms be pertinent then for the unity of the people, for the State and Reich? Had Prussia not always seen it as an honour to devote its energies to matters of the ideal? That the German people had accompanied the five years of work in all stages with joyful agreement, and it will not remain forgotten in history that following the bloody victories justified by the Reich, the impetus given by its imperial house for the discovery of Olympia was a peace initiative of lasting importance, and was instigated for the benefit of all educated nations.[48]

The visionary interpretation of the Olympic Games, which 'rested upon two foundations ... on the feeling of national context, and on the youthful receptivity of the people', clearly reflected the affinity contemporary Germans felt with the ancient age of the Hellenes.[49]

In his efforts to emphasize the differences between the Hellenes and Barbarians, Curtius wrote:

> The Hellenic is nothing less in its being than a sensible and consequent exposition of human predisposition, the decisive, and under favourable conditions, a wonderfully achieved realisation of that which is symptomatic of human nature; thus everyone, without denying their nationality, can walk in the footsteps of the Hellenes, and then do nothing other than personally take up the fight in which they have preceded us; with all of the armoury borrowed from them, one must take to the field against all one-sidedness, capriciousness and foolishness, against all that is extreme and unnatural, against all opulence and lack of freedom.[50]

In their desire for harmony between the Germanic and the Hellenic the first excavators at Olympia saw not only evidence of the attractive Hellenic agonistic quality; they added a political, practically preservative, outcome for the State:

> To Greek sensibility the thought was utterly foreign that humanity comprised two unequally entitled parts, and that only regarding intellectual talent was there a duty to strengthen and ennoble the powers given to the individual with all care. The Greeks recognised in the construction of the body and the high training capacity of

his organs an equally important and irrefutable demand of the gods: the fresh, physical health, beauty of form, a sure and light step, sprightly elegance and power of momentum in the limbs, endurance in running and in battle, a bright and courageous eye and the level-headedness and presence of mind that is acquired only in the daily presence of danger. These exquisite qualities were no less valued among the Greeks as were mental training, sharp perception and exercise in the arts of the Muses. The balance of physical and mental life, the harmonious training of all natural powers and urges were training tasks for the Hellenes, and for that reason music went hand in hand with gymnastics, to train a youth of healthy body and soul, from generation to generation. The flourishing of the State rested upon it.[51]

From here, of course, it is only a short step into the twentieth century. Hitler's concern at the Berlin Games of 1936 for a resumption of excavations at Olympia could count on a broad positive response in the fertile ground ploughed by earlier idealists such as Curtius.[52]

Ernst Curtius, after Karl Christ, who was also 'within the Winckelmann and Humboldt tradition' with his classical-romantic opinions and who 'was so representative of the *Zeitgeist* of his epoch', presented a completely opposite image 'to the dynamism … of a Jacob Burckhardt' in his most popular Greek history in Germany in the nineteenth century.[53] However, there was a 'curious connecting link' to the Basle cultural historian: a mutual subscription to a belief in the importance of the 'agonal principle'.[54]

The neologism 'agonal', derived from the Greek word *agon*, with which Burckhardt (1818–97) wished to characterize the Greeks of the Dorian migration towards the end of the sixth century BC and thus define them against all other cultures of the ancient world, indicated, in his view, 'a motive power, known by no other peoples'. According to the Basle scholar, the Greeks were unique with respect to competition. Neither the primitives, the Barbarians, the Orientals or the Romans had this agonal attitude.[55] Burckhardt's term 'agonal Greeks' has received considerable attention in German Classical scholarship. Many authors have taken the term and given it new interpretations. To what extent Friedrich Nietzsche (1844–1900), Burckhardt's younger colleague at Basle University, was influenced by him is not easily ascertainable, particularly since Ernst Curtius had already presented similar thoughts.

However, it can be shown that Nietzsche's essay *Homers Wettkampf* (1872) offered similar opinions on the Greeks.[56] In his richly metaphoric language Nietzsche wrote:

> Every great Hellene passes on the torch of competition ... this quality depicts a central characteristic of the Greeks ... The greater and more elevated a Greek person is, the brighter shines the flame of ambition from him, straining every one of them against whom he runs on the same track.

This competitive zeal as 'a source of ... highest power' is the source of Nietzsche's understanding of 'Aryan' Greekness and is underlined by the attempt to present the other side of the coin: 'Let us ... disregard the competitiveness in Greek life, we see immediately in the pre-Homeric abyss an appalling wilderness of hate and desire for devastation.'[57] Nietzsche assumed that these predispositions, which he appeared to believe were collectively present in the Greeks and could only be realized through individual endeavour, clearly differentiated the Greeks from modern people. In the end 'the aim of agonal education' was the welfare of the State.[58]

Nietsche not only contrasted the Greeks in their apparently specific attitude to competition with modern man in general (the idea recurs in Aryan = Greek = competitor). For Nietzsche this competitive characteristic has a special emphasis through the polarization of Jews ('worst of all people'[59]) and Greeks. A bridge was formed from the admirable Greeks to the northern peoples.[60] As H. Cancik was able to show in his subtle analysis of Nietzsche, the 'hyper-boreal, as the *Über-Nordischen*, symbolises the Hellenic heritage in the northern lands'.[61] An early anti-Semitic form of thought takes root here, in the second half of the nineteenth century the Greeks are presented both as an ideal and as Aryans, as the 'representatives of the northern European race'. In the *Origines Ariacae* (1883), dealing with racism and proposing the comparison of Greek = Aryan = northern European, one reads that 'the pure Greeks belong to the Aryan type, are blond, blue-eyed, dolichocephalic and of great stature'.[62] Later praise of Nietzsche, by admirers who sought to give significance to the Aryan ideal of competitiveness espoused by their hero, is discernable not least in the intention to organize the Olympic Games at a temple dedicated to Nietzsche.[63]

The Fascist cornerstone for the ideologizing of Greek sport was undoubtedly laid in the nineteenth century. K.O. Müller, J.H. Krause, E.

Curtius, J. Burckhardt and F. Nietzsche provided the German-speaking world with the appropriate source material and arguments for the National Socialist interpretations that were to follow but they also created the theoretical foundations for the academic aims in German schools and gymnasiums. However, as already mentioned, they appeared to give less emphasis to the practice of the physical. The Jahn *Turnen*, with its Germanophile accentuation, apparently showed a stronger practical concern following the lifting of the *Turnsperre*. This heritage may have been reflected in the debate which the young Emperor Wilhelm I took part in, criticizing the traditional education of the humanistic gymnasium and postulating a German *Bildung*. Marchand's text quotes the emperor:

> 'We want to educate our pupils into young Germans', he affirmed, 'not young Greeks and Romans'. Classical education formed physically inferior, decadent thinkers rather than healthy, patriotic doers; the *Gymnasium* menaced the success of the Reich's *Weltpolitik*.[64]

An example of an attempt to combine the ideal of the Greek with the Germanic was provided by Otto Heinrich Jaeger (1828–1912), a writer and gymnastics teacher, who gave his energies to the fostering of natural *Turnen* and chose the Greeks as the highest example of this. He gave expression to this synthesis in a prize-winning essay entitled *Die Gymnastik der Hellenen in ihrem Einfluß aufs gesamte Altertum und ihre Bedeutung für die deutsche Gegenwart. Ein Versuch zur geschichtsphilosophischen Begründung einer ästhetischen Nationalerziehung* (1848).[65] A second example of this approach is to be found in the person of the Jahn *Turner*, Franz Seitz, in the second half of the nineteenth century. Seitz's *Die Leibesübungen der alten Griechen und ihre Einwirkung auf Geist und Charakter der Nation*, which was read at the end of term celebrations of 1871/72 at the Ansbach Royal Institute of Studies, contains ideas arising out of studies of the ancient world. The timing of this study is not insignificant: in the years following the war between Germany and France, physical education in middle-class schools appear to have received greater consideration. This was certainly made easier by the termination of the *Turnsperre* in 1848. The title adopted by Seitz reveals a familiar vision. The Greeks are also the shining examples here and the Germans measure themselves, after Sedan, against both the Greeks and the French, as the following comparison shows: 'The Greeks were in a similar position to the Romans, as the Germans were in recent times to the French'.[66] Two stereotypes confront each other here; 'the academic Germans' and the 'warlike French', these reach back into the typology of the European nations, as is confirmed by the *Völkertafel* (national stereotypes) of the early eighteenth century.[67]

> The Greeks have shown the right way. Not that we can easily imitate them, because nothing repeats itself in name alone. We can arrange no Olympic or Pythian Games in and through public festivals and games, *Turnen* must certainly become closely and inwardly rooted in the entire life of the people in a better and more communicative way than before, but that can only take place through the associations. It must take place no less throughout education in all institutes and among all age groups, and it must be planned for the education of young people throughout their entire schooling.[68]

In the French defeat there can also, incidentally, be seen the germ of the Olympic education and the reintroduction of the Games, as conceived by Baron Pierre de Coubertin (1863–1936). In those days military efficiency and sports education were seen as having a close causal connection. France could have learned, according to the opinion of contemporaries, from Napoleon's defeat at Waterloo.

> The battle of Waterloo, it has been said and often repeated, was won over Napoleon I on the playing-fields of Eton. The tragedy was that the French *lycées* had an excessively intellectual programme; they had no playing-fields, their pupils played no games and received little physical training. That contrast became almost an obsession with Pierre, Baron de Coubertin, who was only eight years old when Sedan was lost, and he had hardly come of age before he embarked on a campaign to remedy the critical French weakness.[69]

The French aristocrat linked the importance of physical training to military success. He voiced his complaint of the French situation emphatically:

> Oh, the great need to rest that France had after this long outburst of courage, and great heavens! How well one understands that France should go and play dominoes instead of exercising its tired muscles. Sated with victory, France gradually fell asleep while,

beside its black, total, horrible defeat had awakened energies which laboured grimly at the undertaking that you know: the German empire. It was thus that military athletics was born in Berlin. It has often been said in France that on the battlefields of 1866 and 1870, the real winner was the schoolmaster; if it is to this belief that we owe the sight of schools opening across our country and popular education spreading so rapidly, then thank heaven for it. But I think that, in believing this, we are giving the teacher more than his due and rather forgetting his colleague, the gymnastics master. German gymnastics which immediately after Jena found ardent and convinced apostles to preach its gospel, then numerous, docile disciples to follow its precepts, is energetic in its movements, based on strict discipline and, in a word, military in its essence.[70]

For Seitz the 'driving motives' of the agonistics was 'primarily the consideration of efficiency in war, whether for defence or for attack'.[71] For Seitz, as 'a member of a student fraternity [, an] enthusiasm for the German *Vaterland*[72] was to be expected but, in fact, he associated himself – in respect of the sporting and paramilitary education of the youth – with the ancient Hellenes who had the Thracians beside them in the north. In that 'Nordic tribe' Seitz wished to see the progenitors of the Germans. The link was the bridge from the Greeks to the Germans. The gymnastics of the Hellenes were the great pedagogic ideal:

> The Greek raised himself above and beyond all neighbouring peoples, he had autocratically a feeling of unity, and this feeling, in every situation, could only be one of superiority. What that came to, we as Germans are beginning to realise to a certain extent – although the Greeks were of this impression throughout an entire lifetime – and saw it as the noble fruition of their untiring endeavours in physical exercises, and the resulting superiority.[73]

Seitz drew conclusions on behalf of his contemporaries:[74]

1. The German people should imitate the 'beautiful and elevating example' of the Greeks.
2. The 'criminal one-sidedness' of intellectual education should make way for the 'symmetric and harmonic' development of all powers.
3. The new education should not only apply to an élite but should 'penetrate throughout the entire people'.

4. At the same time there should be no simplified imitation of Greek gymnastics and agonistics 'because nothing can be repeated in name alone'. 'We were unable to arrange Olympic or Pythian Games but the idea itself was correct and can and will come to be carried out by us.'

5. 'Public festivals and games' for all of the people and methodical, intellectual and physical education at 'all institutes and for all age groups' should result in health for the nation.

Seitz argued that 'That which a great, noble, highly talented people had once achieved in this respect, and the resulting blessings in the intellectual and physical spheres they then enjoyed' should also be achieved – as wished for by the school teachers – by the Germans. However, while giving due attention to Seitz and others, it should be emphasized that the important impulse for physical education in the national school system took its starting point from Jahn's *Turner*, who had fostered the inclusion and firm establishment of physical education through numerous petitions to State officials.[75]

Of course, the ideas and practices of the ancient Greeks greatly influenced Europe in the nineteenth century. It was therefore not surprising that the archaeologist Ludwig Ross (1806–71) who had travelled several times to Olympia from the 1830s onwards, dreamed of modern Olympic Games long before Pierre de Coubertin, although Ross imagined something of a German variant similar in some respects to the Munich *Oktoberfest*:

> But certainly not to horseracing with colourful stableboys aped at by the English, but to a manly shoot-out, to wrestling matches and foot races, to a proper country race on home-reared horses, and above all to song and dance. With such a local festival we would wish to no longer envy the Greeks their Olympians.[76]

The Tyrolian journalist Jakob Philipp Fallmerayer (1790–1861) also demanded the integration of Olympic ideals in the pedagogical programme. His main goal was physical and moral-political education. His glittering examples were the ancient Hellenes, not the modern Greeks of the nineteenth century, because 'in the veins of the Christian people of Greece today' – according to his racist theory – 'not a drop of authentic and unmixed Hellenic blood' flows. In Fallmerayer's opinion, the modern Greeks derived from the Slavs and Albanians.[77]

The evidence above documents the part that Classical German literature and scholarship of the nineteenth century played in the genesis of an image of ancient Hellenic sport. With the democratization of the schools and the gymnasiums, these ideas became the desirable body of institutional education at a broad middle-class level and, to an extent, the foundation of national and nationalistic ideologies. Their growth in the twentieth century should be viewed in the context of this evolution of historical ideas. On the other hand, it cannot be wholly asserted that a belief in Greece's exemplary effect in general, and the entire agonistics and gymnastics programme in particular, were the privilege or the exclusive domain of Germans. A more important stimulus to European Philhellenism from the second half of the eighteenth century onwards came from Great Britain and France transmitted by the likes of Lord Byron, P.B. Shelley, J. Keats, F.R. de Chateaubriand and E. Delacroix. However, a romantic Grecophilia certainly spread throughout the German-speaking world. In 1935 Eliza May Butler drew attention to 'the obsession of the Schillerian German literature and scholarly élite with the ancient Greeks' and convincingly described the 'German philhellenism's rise and fall' in the nineteenth and twentieth centuries.[78]

John Stuart Mill gave a precise explanation of the significant role of Greece in modern Europe in his famous speculative prognosis:

> The true ancestors of the European nations are not those from whose blood they are sprung, but those from whom they derive the richest portion of their inheritance. The battle of Marathon, even as an event in English history, is more important than the Battle of Hastings. If the issue of that day had been different, the Britons and the Saxons might still have been wandering in the woods.[79]

George Grote's *History of Greece* spoke of a 'progressive spirit of Greece, serving as herald and stimulus to a like spirit in Europe' and compared it to the 'stationary mind of Asia'. In the third edition of *Some Aspects of the Greek Genius*, S.H. Butcher dealt with the Greek unity of science, art and freedom and recognized 'in this union ... the distinctive features of the West. The Greek genius is the European genius in its first and brightest bloom.' Regarding the inner equilibrium of the Greeks, H.O. Taylor maintained that 'There was harmony and union between the love of beauty and the love of knowledge'.[80] However, it is noticeable that in practice the Greek agonistics and gymnastics did not have the valued position attributed to them in German writings. In the chapter *Der Wettkampf (Agon) als Mittelpunkt des griechischen Lebens* of his treatise *Die Anschauung vom Wesen des Griechentums*[81] Billeter quotes only German literature. To draw a conclusion from this fact would be an *argumentum e silentio*. It may be coincidence because otherwise numerous works of British (and naturally French and Italian) studies of Antiquity are quoted in Billeter's book. How otherwise could John P. Mahaffy write in 1879 that 'The English schoolboy is physically so superior to the schoolboys of other European nations that we may count him, with the Greek boy, as almost a distinct animal'.[82] England is given a special position in Mahaffy's point of view. Its middle-class system of physical education differed in principle not only from that of the ancient Greeks but also from the modern concepts of Continental France and Germany:

> The finest English schoolboy is not inferior to the best Greek types in real life ... The Greeks were like the French and the Germans, who always imagine that the games and sports will not prosper or be properly conducted without the supervision of a *Turnlehrer*, or overseer ... If the zealous and learned reformers who write books on the subject in modern Europe would take the trouble to come [to England] and see this for themselves, it might modify both their encomia on Greek training and their suggestions for their own countries.[83]

Here, in an indirect way, is a polemic against the exclusively scholastic preoccupation with the Greek agonistics and gymnastics and – not without a degree of chauvinism – the English system of physical education with its value and effectiveness compared to other approaches, is depicted as being superior. In my opinion, modern sources, such as C.P. Segal, come somewhat closer to the reality:[84]

> Sport is the most immutable and modern aspect of our heritage from the Greeks and, therefore, the stadium door is perhaps the most accessible means of entering the ancient world.

Modern sources pinpoint the influence that ancient Greece exercised on the development of the Olympic Games and on sport and upon physical education in Europe in the nineteenth and twentieth centuries.

In conclusion, there has recently been an attempt to compare sport as it was conceived and practised in Great Britain in the nineteenth century with the sport of Continental Europe and especially of the German-speaking world. Above all, German innovations in European sport, in addition to major contributions to European Winter Sports and Alpinism, involve Jahn's *Turnen*. While the late nineteenth century British Sports Movement in Europe has enjoyed a triumphal march, the influence of *Turnen* goes back even further. However, any analysis of the causes of this state of affairs must consider further and other factors. One impulse, which influenced modern sport and physical culture, is connected to the intellectual discourse of the classical scholars concerning the agonistics and gymnastics of the ancient Hellenes and to the Olympic Games of the late nineteenth century. Among other things, the assumption of the physical aesthetics of the Greeks, the so-called *kalokagathia* and the equation with the German ideal of the body resulted from the studies. The ideological basis for this originated from the nineteenth century, found acceptance in the racist schools of thought then being formed and were given deeper expression in the twentieth century. Hitler may have proclaimed 'that the German and the Greek ideal of beauty must be synonymous' but the contemporary cult of the body and the iconic movie-heroes of our day, such as Clint Eastwood, Charles Bronson, Arnold Schwarzenegger and Sylvester Stallone, remain within this tradition. Thus J.A. Mangan's Epilogue to his recent book, *Shaping the Superman*, refers with complete justification to this living legacy in the late twentieth century.[85]

NOTES

1. R. Kosellek, 'Hinter der tödlichen Linie. Das Zeitalter des Totalen', *Frankfurter Allgemeine Zeitung*, 27 Oct. 1999, 1.
2. Christine Eisenberg, *»English Sports« und Deutsche Bürger. Eine Gesellschaftsgeschichte 1800 bis 1939* (Paderborn: Schöningh, 1999), p.430.
3. H. Ueberhorst, *Zurück zu Jahn? Gab es kein besseres Vorwärts?* (Bochum: Universitätsverlag, 1969); H. Becker, 'War Jahn »Antisemit«', *Stadion*, 4 (1978), 121–35; H. Bernett, 'Das Jahn-Bild in der nationalsozialistischen Anschauung', *Stadion*, 4 (1978), 225–61. On the concept of freedom among Jahn's *Turner*, see S. Goltermann, 'Figuren der Freiheit' in M. Hettling and St.-L. Hoffmann (eds.), *Der bürgerliche Wertehimmel. Innenansichten des 19. Jahrhunderts* (Göttingen: Vandenhoeck & Ruprecht, 2000), pp.149–68.
4. Ibid., p.441.
5. H. Strohmeyer, *Beiträge zur Geschichte des Sports in Österreich. Gesammelte Arbeiten aus vier Jahrzehnten* (Vienna: Österreichischer Bundesverlag, 1999), pp.327–60 (Theorie und Praxis der Leibesübungen, Vol.71).
6. H. von Treitschke, *Deutsche Geschichte im 19. Jahrhundert* (Leipzig: Hirzel, 3rd Edn. 1883), p.28.
7. S.L. Marchand, *Down from Olympus. Archaeology and Philhellenism in Germany, 1750–1970* (Princeton: Princeton University Press, 1996); see also E.M. Butler, *The Tyranny of Greece over Germany* (Boston: Beacon Press, 1935).
8. W. von Humboldt, 'Über das Studium des Altertums, und des griechischen insbesondere' in

W. Nippel (ed.), *Über das Studium der Alten Geschichte* (Munich: Deutscher Taschenbuch Verlag, 1993), pp.34–56, 41–2. For information about the 'Humboldtian principles', see Marchand, *Down from Olympus*, pp.24–35.

9. Marchand, *Down from Olympus*, pp.24–9; G. Billeter, *Die Anschauungen vom Wesen des Griechentums* (Leipzig: Teubner, 1911), p.90.

10. Von Humboldt, 'Über das Studium des Altertums', pp.46–7.

11. Billeter, *Die Anschauungen*, p.189.

12. Von Humboldt, 'Über das Studium des Altertums', pp.46–7.

13. Ibid., p.48.

14. M. Fuhrmann, *Der europäische Bildungskanon des bürgerlichen Zeitalters* (Frankfurt am Main: Insel, 1999), pp.53–68, 60; H. Apel, 'Humanistisches Gymnasium', *Der Neue Pauly*, 14 (2000), 563–7, 564–5. On neohumanism and gymnasium, see Marchand, *Down from Olympus*, pp.24–5.

15. Fuhrmann, *Der europäische Bildungskanon*, p.53.

16. H. Bernett, *Die pädagogische Neugestaltung der bürgerlichen Leibesübungen durch die Philanthropen* (Schorndorf: Hofmann, 2nd Edn. 1965), pp.14–40 (Beiträge zur Lehre und Forschung der Leibeserziehung, Vol.6).

17. J.C.F. GutsMuths, *Gymnastik für die Jugend* (Schnepfenthal: Erziehungs-Anstalt, 1793), p.201; J.N. Schmitz, *Studien zur Didaktik der Leibeserziehung. Voraussetzungen – Analysen – Problemstellung* (Schorndorf: Hofmann, 1966), p.23 (Beiträge zur Lehre und Forschung der Leibeserziehung, Vol.27).

18. Schmitz, *Studien zur Didaktik der Leibeserziehung*, p.32: 'JAHN hatte im Geiste des FICHTEschen Nationalerziehungsplanes die Leibesübungen bewußt außerhalb der Schule gestellt'. Marchand, *Down from Olympus*, p.24, points out the 'disgust for French cultural hegemony in the German-speaking lands'.

19. D. Düding, 'Von der Opposition zur Akklamation: Die Turnbewegung im 19. Jahrhundert als politische Bewegung', *Stadion*, 18 (1992), 209–24. On political conflicts and philhellenism during the *Vormärz*, see Marchand, *Down from Olympus*, pp.32–5.

20. K. Christ, 'Aspekte der Antike-Rezeption in der deutschen Altertumswissenschaft des 19. Jahrhunderts' in K. Christ and A. Momigliano (eds.), *Die Antike im 19. Jahrhundert in Italien und Deutschland* (Berlin: Duncker & Humblot, 1988), pp.21–37.

21. See M. Krüger, 'Die antike Gymnastik und Athletik als Vorbild für Turnen und Sport in Deutschland im 19. Jahrhundert', *Stadion*, 21/22 (1995/96), 86–99.

22. For an outstanding example of German philhellenism, see the late romantic lyricist Wilhelm Müller (1794–1827), the so-called 'Griechen-Müller', and his *Lieder der Griechen*.

23. Christ, 'Aspekte der Antike-Rezeption', p.22.

24. Billeter, *Die Anschauungen*, p.109.

25. R. Flacelière, *Griechenland. Leben und Kultur in klassischer Zeit* (Stuttgart: Reclam, 1977), pp.367–74.

26. Christ, 'Aspekte der Antike-Rezeption', p.25.

27. Among the few authors who strongly plea for a relativism of the 'Agonale principle' and who consider it to be a common anthropological and not a specific element of ancient Greek culture and politics, J. Huizinga might be the most important scholar. See J. Huizinga, *Homo Ludens. Vom Ursprung der Kultur im Spiel* (Hamburg: Rowohlt, 1938), pp.84–9. See also, H. Reinwald, *Mythos und Methode. Zum Verhältnis von Wissenschaft, Kultur und Erkenntnis* (Munich: Fink 1991), pp.204–10, 271–5.

28. S.G. Miller, *Arete. Ancient Writers, Papyri, and Inscriptions on the History and Ideals of Greek Athletics and Games* (Chicago: University of California Press, 2nd Edn., 1991), p.216; and N. Yalouris *et al.*, *The Olympic Games in Ancient Greece. Ancient Olympia and the Olympic Games* (Athen: Ekdotike Athenon, 1976), pp.52–3.

29. F. Bourriot, *Kalos Kagathos – Kalokagathia. D'un terme de propagande de sophistes à une notion sociale et philosophique. Etude d'histoire athénienne* (Hildesheim: Olms, 1995), Vol.1, p.95 and Vol.2, pp.70–71 (Spudasmata, Vol.58.1 and 58.2).

30. J.A. Mangan, 'Blond, Strong and Pure: 'Proto-Fascism', Male Bodies and Political Tradition' in J.A. Mangan (ed.), *Shaping the Superman: Fascist Body as Political Icon – Aryan Fascism* (London and Portland, OR: Frank Cass, 1999), pp.107–27, quoted from H. Glaser, *The Cultural Roots of National Socialism* (London: Croom-Helm, 1978), p.45.

31. Billeter, *Die Anschauungen*, p.192.
32. K.O. Müller, '*Die Dorier*: Vier Bücher' in F.W. Schneidewin (ed.), *Geschichten Hellenischer Stämme und Städte* (Breslau: Max, 2nd Edn. 1844), Vol.2, p.256; H.-J. Gehrke, 'Karl Otfried Müller und das Land der Griechen', *MDAI(A)*, 106 (1991), 9–35, but particularly 18–20. For a detailed analysis of ancient Greek history in nineteenth century German scholarship compare K. Christ, 'Die Entwicklung der Alten Geschichte in Deutschland (1971)' and K. Christ, 'Geschichte des Altertums, Wissenschaftsgeschichte und Ideologiekritik' in K. Christ, *Römische Geschichte und Wissenschaftsgeschichte* (Darmstadt: Wissenschaftliche Buchgesellschaft, 1983), Vol.3, pp.213–27 and pp.228–43. See also M. Fuhrmann, *Europas fremd gewordene Fundamente. Aktuelles zu Themen aus der Antike* (Zurich: Artemis & Winkler, 1995), pp.125–79.
33. Particularly Müller, *Die Dorier*, pp.299–301.
34. Ibid., pp.306–8.
35. Ibid., pp.394–7.
36. V. Losemann, '*Die Dorier* im Deutschland der dreißiger und vierziger Jahre' in W. M. Calder III and R. Schlesier (eds.), *Zwischen Rationalismus und Romantik. Karl Otfried Müller und die antike Kultur* (Hildesheim: Weidmann, 1998), pp.313–48, p.322 refers to L. Schemann, *Die Rasse in den Geisteswissenschaften* (1928–31) (Munich: Lehmann, 2nd Edn. 1943) and A. Rosenberg, *Der Mythus des 20. Jahrhunderts* (Munich: Hoheneichen, 1935). See also V. Losemann, *Nationalsozialismus und Antike. Studien zur Entwicklung des Faches Alte Geschichte 1933–45* (Hamburg: Hoffmann & Campe, 1977), p.191 (Historische Perspektiven, Vol.7); and O. Kustrin, '"Die Dorier" von Karl Otfried Müller. Zur Entwicklung des Spartabildes im Spiegel der deutschen altertumswissenschaftlichen Selbstidentifikation des 19. Jahrhunderts' (Unpublished manuscript, Graz, 2000), 99–101.
37. See especially J. Ebert, 'Johann Heinrich Krause, ein verdienstvoller hallescher Philologe und Archäologe' in M. Hillgruber, R. Jakobi and W. Luppe (eds.), *Joachim Ebert. Agonismata. Kleine philologische Schriften zur Literatur, Geschichte und Kultur der Antike* (Stuttgart: Teubner, 1997), pp.366–88.
38. Ibid., p.379.
39. In *Down from Olympus*, pp.77–91, Marchand refers to the archaeological activities but does not pay any attention to the rank of the Greek *agon* as Curtius (and other authors) did.
40. Herodot 8, 26 f., Platon, *Symposium* 182 a-c; Lucian, *Anacharsis*. The idea that Greek gods and heroes invented the different disciplines of sport and events seems to reflect the special affinity of the ancient Greeks towards sport.
41. E. Curtius, *Alterthum und Gegenwart. Gesammelte Reden und Vorträge* (Stuttgart: Cotta, 5th Edn. 1903), Vol.1, pp.132–47; see Billeter, *Die Anschauungen*, pp.212–13. On Curtius and the 'agonale principle', see K. Christ, *Hellas. Griechische Geschichte und deutsche Geschichtswissenschaft* (Munich: Beck, 1999), pp.32–42, especially 41–2.
42. Curtius, *Alterthum und Gegenwart*, Vol.1, pp.132–47. Curtius' speech 'Olympia' (see *Alterthum und Gegenwart*, Vol.2, pp.129–56) is an important document for the German ideological interpretation of Greekness in the nineteenth century. See also Billeter, *Die Anschauungen*, pp.212–15.
43. Curtius, *Alterthum und Gegenwart*, Vol.1, pp.133–4. H. Cancik, *Nietzsches Antike. Vorlesung* (Stuttgart: Metzler, 1995), p.41, significantly adds: 'so dachte man im 19. Jahrhundert'. See also J. Latacz, *Fruchtbares Ärgernis: Nietzsches 'Geburt der Tragödie' und die gräzistische Tragödienforschung* (Basel: Helbing & Lichtenhahn, 1998), p.7. For a more extensive treatment compare K. von See, *Barbar, Germane, Arier. Die Suche nach der Identität der Deutschen* (Heidelberg: Winter, 1994), pp.207–32, and V. Losemann, 'Aspekte der nationalsozialistischen Germanenideologie' in P. Kneissl and V. Losemann (eds.), *Alte Geschichte und Wissenschaftsgeschichte* (Darmstadt: Wissenschaftliche Buchgesellschaft, 1988), pp.256–84.
44. Curtius, *Alterthum und Gegenwart*, Vol.1, pp.133–4.
45. Ibid., Vol.1, p.144.
46. Ibid., Vol.2, p.156.
47. Marchand, *Down from Olympus*, pp.80–81.
48. Curtius, *Alterthum und Gegenwart*, Vol.2, p.196.
49. Ibid., p.155.
50. Ibid., pp.7–8.

51. Curtius, *Alterthum und Gegenwart*, Vol.1, p.130.

52. Ibid., p.143: 'This idealisation is the most beautiful priviledge of classical philology'. See Losemann, *Nationalsozialismus*, p.21; A. Krüger, 'Breeding, Rearing and Preparing the Aryan Body: Creating Supermen the Nazi Way' in Mangan, *Shaping the Superman*, pp.42–68.

53. Marchand, *Down from Olympus*, p.80.

54. K. Christ, *Von Gibbon zu Rostovtzeff. Leben und Werk führender Althistoriker der Neuzeit* (Darmstadt: Wissenschaftliche Buchgesellschaft, 2nd Edn. 1979), p.83; see also pp.69, 74–5; and Christ, *Hellas*, pp.77–8.

55. J. Burckhardt, *Griechische Kulturgeschichte* (1898–1902) (Munich: Deutscher Taschenbuch Verlag, 1977), Vol.4, pp.84–5.

56. A different view is presented in Cancik, *Nietzsches Antike*, p.41; on the national Greek character and the typus of the 'agonalen Menschen', see pp.170–72.

57. Nietzsche, 'Homers Wettkampf' p.297. Compare also Cancik, *Nietzsches Antike*, pp.35–49.

58. Nietzsche, 'Homers Wettkampf', pp.296–7.

59. On the antithesis of Hellenic vs. Jewish civilization and religion, see Cancik, *Nietzsches Antike*, pp.100 and 127. See also H.-G. Marten, 'Racism, Social Darwinism, Anti-Semitism and Aryan Supremacy' in Mangan, *Shaping the Superman*, pp.23–41.

60. Cancik, *Nietzsches Antike*, pp.134–49.

61. Ibid., pp.140–41.

62. Billeter, *Die Anschauungen*, p.182 (with further similar quotations).

63. Cancik, *Nietzsches Antike*, p.36. The idea of the Nietzsche-Games at Weimar is attributed to Count Harry Kessler and Henry van de Velde.

64. Marchand, *Down from Olympus*, p.136.

65. Krüger, 'Die antike Gymnastik und Athletik', 92.

66. F. Seitz, *Die Leibesübungen der alten Griechen und ihre Einwirkung auf Geist und Charakter der Nation, Programm zur Schlußfeier des Jahres 1871/72 an der Königlichen Studienanstalt zu Ansbach* (Ansbach: Brügel, 1872), p.18.

67. Concerning methodological problems of stereotyping, see the introduction 'Zur literarischen Imagologie' in F.K. Stanzel (ed.), *Europäischer Völkerspiegel. Imagologisch-ethnographische Studien zu den Völkertafeln des frühen 18. Jahrhunderts* (Heidelberg: Winter, 1999), pp.8–41.

68. Seitz, *Die Leibesübungen der alten Griechen*, pp.23–4.

69. See especially N. Müller, 'Coubertin's Olympism' in N. Müller (ed.), *Pierre de Coubertin 1863–1937. Olympism. Selected Writings* (Lausanne: International Olympic Committee, 2000), pp.33–48.

70. Coubertin, 'Physical Exercises in the Modern World. Lecture Given at the Sorbonne (November 1892)' in ibid., pp.287–97.

71. Seitz, *Die Leibesübungen der alten Griechen*, p.8.

72. Ibid., p.3.

73. Ibid., p.19.

74. Ibid., p.23.

75. See especially M. Krüger, *Körperkultur und Nationsbildung. Die Geschichte des Turnens in der Reichsgründungsära – eine Detailstudie über die Deutschen* (Schorndorf: Hofmann, 1996), pp.138–9 and pp.339–46 (Reihe Sportwissenschaft, Vol.24).

76. L. Ross, 'Olympia' (1851) in W. Hautumm (ed.), *Hellas. Die Wiederentdeckung des klassischen Griechenland* (Cologne: DuMont, 1983), pp.179–82.

77. G.M. Thomas (ed.), 'Jakob Philipp Fallmerayer, Olympia' (1861) in *Gesammelte Werke* (Leipzig: Engelmann, 1861); see also F. Fetz, 'Jakob Philipp Fallmerayer – ein Tiroler als Vorkämpfer der olympischen Idee' in G. Sauser (ed.), *Innsbrucker Universitäts-Almanach auf das Jahr der Winterolympiade 1964* (Innsbruck, 1964), pp.23–40.

78. Concerning Schiller's *Letters on the Aesthetic Education of Mankind* (1793–95), see especially Butler, *The Tyranny of Greece over Germany*, p.180; and Marchand, *Down from Olympus*, p.xviii.

79. John Stuart Mill (1846), *Collected Works* (Toronto: Routledge & Paul, 1978), Vol.11, p.273.

80. Billeter, *Die Anschauungen*, p.116 and pp.321–2.

81. Ibid., pp.212–15.

82. Quoted in D.C. Young, *The Olympic Myth of Greek Amateur Athletics* (Chicago: Ares, 1985), p.50.

83. Ibid.
84. E. Kephalidou, *The Victorious Athlete. A Study on the Iconography of Ancient Greek Athletics* (Thessaloniki: Aristotle University, 1996), p.247 (English summary).
85. J.A. Mangan, 'Icon of Monumental Brutality: Art and the Aryan Man' in Mangan, *Shaping the Superman*, pp.128–52, especially pp.130–31, and 'Epilogue: Continuities', pp.180–95, especially p.181.

2

A Tranquil Transformation: Middle-Class Racing 'Revolutionaries' in Nineteenth-Century England

MIKE HUGGINS

The Victorian period is often seen, in J.A. Mangan's deft phrase, as 'the Age of the First Recreational Revolution'.[1] It was a period when the middle-class scramble for new forms of sport, such as tennis or golf, and the use of sport to delineate the barriers of a class society became strongly marked.[2] Many newly transformed team sports, initially organized by and for the middle classes, became highly commercialized, highly competitive, working-class spectator sports, played by relatively well paid, working-class professionals; potent symbols of local pride.

This transformation in the scale and nature of Britain's sporting culture between the mid-nineteenth century and the outbreak of the First World War has also been described as a 'revolution' that introduced new forms of organized, commercialized and extensive sport.[3] Wray Vamplew also uses the term, this time in an economic sense, when claiming that sport itself underwent 'an industrial revolution' in this period. Social changes, especially in leisure time and earned income, encouraged the injection of production factors and the application of modern technologies into the supply of sport.[4]

But who were the revolutionaries? Historians have largely, and correctly, pointed to the role of the middle classes as the pivotal creators, shapers and participants in this process.[5] Change, culture and class interact within sport, and sport's cultural practices are highly significant in terms of social behaviour. In their use of the term 'revolution', writers like J.A. Mangan and Neil Tranter were clearly employing a similar definition to that adopted by this edition of *ESHR*.[6] But Tranter's use of italics in his chapter title 'The "Revolution" in Sport', is a strong reminder that use of the term is more complex and problematic than it first appears. Tranter makes very clear that the moves towards codification, commercialization and institutionalization varied from sport to sport. There were also significant continuities from the earlier period and some older sports were able to adapt themselves to the requirements of a new age. Historians have yet to really get to the heart of the nature of this sporting 'revolution', largely because some in the wider historical world seem to be using the term in its looser, more popular, sense, simply as a synonym for change, progress or development. As many of us recognize, there are different types of revolution: cultural, intellectual, social, political and theoretical.

In modern political thought the word 'revolution' has a highly specific technical meaning;[7] revolutions occur when a different social group seizes power with associated radical structural change. Whilst the concept is not restricted to highly complex societies, it is considerably more relevant to them. Marxism had long seen revolution as the replacement of one ruling class by another, involving a class struggle which was expected to lead to political change and the triumph of communism. In the 1960s and 1970s both Europe and the USA saw an explosion of writing and the creation of new theories about revolution and political violence, and new structural theories started to emerge in the late 1970s and 1980s. We now understand more clearly that political revolutions arise from a complex blend of state weakness, elite conflicts and urban and rural revolts. We are much clearer on the causes of political revolutions and on their links with social class.[8] Bourgeois revolutions, for example, as in England and France, have tended to produce more democratic forms of government. Successful proletarian revolutions tend to produce communism and dictatorship.[9] The understanding of power and the way it is exercised is therefore not only important for deeper insight into political revolutions; questions of power are quintessential for an understanding of the history of sport.

The exercise of power often requires the exploitation of power relationships. The need to ensure the consent of the governed means that power is supported by a panoply of ideological, ritual and intellectual buttresses. Here the notion of 'hegemony' has been of some use in enlarging the notion of rule beyond overly simplistic notions of social control to include cultural and intellectual aspects. In order to shed light upon the relationship between sports and cultural studies, historians are moving towards more interdisciplinary analysis of history, cultural expression and power. It is easy, and accurate, to argue that it was the British middle classes who played the dominant role in creating modern sport as a cultural, social and geopolitical entity. But was this a revolution in the more technical political sense, a seizure of power by the middle classes? If so, from whom did they seize it? We lack sufficient data to be clear on this point. Much more detailed investigation needs to be done by sports historians of the earlier nineteenth century which was initially conceptualized as one of 'revolutionary' social and economic development.[10] In reality, early leisure historians of this period, such as Robert Malcolmson, tended to focus on detrimental working-class experiences, the disappearances of sporting traditions and the withdrawn patronage of an often ill-defined 'social elite'. Early leisure historians paid far less attention to sports organization than to the way sports were played, subjected to attack or reformed. More recent research has suggested that the changes of the period may have been less 'revolutionary' than had previously been thought. It places more emphasis on continuities.[11] Yet whether this is accurate revisionism or simply fashionable positioning is undecided. There are many examples where it would appear that the upper classes deliberately withdrew from participation as the pace of economic change increased.[12] This hardly constitutes continuity. In such cases the middle classes cannot be seen to have actively seized power by simply moving into a potential power vacuum. In other cases, including such popular spectator sports as cricket, pugilism and curling, upper-class patronage certainly continued through the nineteenth century although the nature of such patronage changed.

The chronology of the processes of change and continuity has to be examined carefully. At the beginning of the nineteenth century some members of the middle classes were already playing a key role in a number of sports through organization, commercial involvement and spectatorship. At this point the upper classes, with their disposable incomes, their conspicuous patterns of consumption and their free time, were obvious sources of funding for sports organizers, early bookmakers and others from further down the social scale with an interest in sport. At the core of this group lay the innkeepers, whose astute recognition of the commercial potential of some members of the elite was coupled with economic, entrepreneurial and social skills.

In pugilism, for example, the boxer 'Gentleman' John Jackson (the soubriquet is indicative) only fought three times for the title and used his winnings to open Jackson's Rooms on Bond Street in 1795. Jackson taught pugilistic skills to the Fancy (well-to-do boxing supporters) and arranged gloved fights in the Fives Courts on St. Martin's Lane. These fights quickly attracted the patronage of the gentry, including such luminaries as Lord Byron. They were 'an attraction in general to the public' but admission prices, which ranged from a guinea to two shillings, suggest that the 'public' must have been relatively wealthy.[13] Jackson was even astute enough to found the exclusive Pugilistic Club, with a wealthy aristocratic membership including the Dukes of York and Clarence. The Club met regularly at Jackson's Rooms, wore a special uniform and provided the purses for the fights he organized – thus generating Jackson's profit.

Likewise, in cricket, Thomas Lord leased a ground in Marylebone in 1786/87, attracting upwards of 2,000 spectators to a match in June (suggesting some cross-class interest) and prevailing on the upper classes to play and subscribe. Lord was able to harness the upper-class fondness for clubs by providing premises for the newly created Marylebone Cricket Club. His profit was not dependent on the team winning since the minimum entrance charge was 6d. for crowds of 4–5,000 for major matches. Lord suffered a temporary setback in 1809 when the club refused to follow him to a new ground but he won back the patronage of the club at a third ground in St. John's Wood. He built a tavern in 1814 which became the home of the Club and its annual dinners and also made himself rich.[14]

Notions of sporting 'revolution' and of the entire process of change are currently, and correctly, under review. We need to ascertain just who possessed the power in Victorian sport and to do this we need to be much clearer about the complex nature of power in different sports at different times and the various ways power could be exercised. Certainly it is quite clear that by the end of the nineteenth century the middle classes played a central role in the administration and patronage of many sports, at least in terms of those clubs with the top players on their books where their power was undoubtedly considerable. We are still less clear of the extent of middle-class penetration into the organization of the less famous, short-lived and, at present, more obscure sporting clubs and teams.

In some aspects of Victorian sport, however, the *leitmotif* of much recent work has been the description of the dominance of amateur forms of sport by a metropolitan elite, triumphing over the more professionally oriented and more working-class sports of the provinces. In many respects this parallels the wider subordination of the industrial middle-classes by a metropolitan-based, imperially-oriented group of landed, commercial and financial elites in Victorian Britain.[15] In a series of post-Marxist analyses of the nature of a class society in Britain since the eighteenth century, David Cannadine has argued that although British society was transformed through a range of shocks including the French Revolution, the Agricultural and Industrial Revolutions, population growth and urbanization, the British upper classes were not vanquished by the middle classes but were able to hold on to power for much of the nineteenth century. Cannadine argues that only the language of class was transformed.[16] It is partly as a result of such arguments, as Simon Dentith has recently pointed out, that 'it is still a matter of disagreement whether the character of hegemony in nineteenth century England should be characterised broadly as "bourgeois" or "aristocratic"'. Dentith argues that 'the cultural dominance of this landed elite remained important through the century, easily defeating the modest cultural challenges of a progressive bourgeoisie even in their urban strongholds'.[17] Hegemony, of course, is maintained by a wide variety of means, not least sport.

Certainly at first sight the upper classes appear to have maintained a key role in some 'elite' sports, such as yachting and field sports, throughout the nineteenth century. Unfortunately research in this area has been sadly neglected in Britain and much more needs to be done. For many historians, a key example of upper-class continuity of control has been horse-racing. Horse-racing has been portrayed as a sport dominated by the upper classes and coupled with taken-for-granted views about almost universal middle-class respectability, ill-considered assumptions about an absence of middle-class involvement in racing and a lack of inclination to look for it. According to Roger Munting, for example, 'the Turf remained principally a gentleman's pursuit, organised for gentlemen by gentlemen'.[18] Richard Holt has seen it as 'the best example of a sport that remained very exclusive in social terms'[19] and Tranter believed it continued to 'rely heavily on the financial support of a landed elite'.[20] Wray Vamplew claimed that there was 'no hard evidence that the middle class attended race meetings' although, to his credit, he accepted that some members of the middle classes did go to the races, either to 'escape the strait-jacket of Victorian class convention' or to take the chance of 'mixing with the aristocracy and landed gentry'.[21] In sum, such assertions must be seen as rather naive.

As a result of this neglect, racing has been portrayed as an industry based on and determinedly clinging to rural values and feudal styles of organization and management. This belief that the organization and consumption of the sport lay largely in the hands of the upper classes has been pervasively powerful in sporting historiography, despite being mainly mistaken, with the putative key organization generally seen as the Jockey Club. For example, Dennis Brailsford has argued that racing's 'aristocratic connections kept it alive' during the middle decades of the nineteenth century when it came under attack by some leisure reformists espousing 'rational recreationist' arguments.[22] Brailsford further argued that racing passed into a modern sporting world without fundamental change thanks largely to the 'vigorous reforming leadership' of Jockey Club leaders such as Lord Bentinck and Admiral Rous, the 'most famous of all Turf administrators and reformers'.[23] To most sports historians this private Club seemed to have (at some generally unspecified time early in the nineteenth century) established arbitrary control over the sport, virtually put itself above the law and secured government intervention whenever it wished. Under these circumstances it might be thought that there was no revolution in racing during the nineteenth century. This has certainly been the dominant view in racing historiography where the favoured term, as in Brailsford's case above, has most commonly been 'reform'.

MIDDLE-CLASS MANAGEMENT OF CULTURAL CHANGE IN RACING

This overly simplistic view of upper-class dominance in the management of cultural change in racing is in need of rigorous reassessment as part of a much more careful, critical and considered re-evaluation of the complexities of the interaction of the various social classes in the sports of Victorian Britain. The changes in racing that ensured its survival as a major spectator sport despite its association with drinking, prostitution, betting and other forms of ludic excess were highly significant for British cultural life. Certainly racing changed significantly during the nineteenth century and it is also true that the sport could not have survived without the upper-class interest (through ownership, breeding and betting).

However, the group that benefited most from racing, here as elsewhere, was the middle classes. Racing did not simply involve transfers of wealth within the upper classes; by and large upper-class participation in racing involved a transfer of wealth from the upper classes to groups within the middle classes. These middle-class groups included administrators, shareholders, bookmakers, trainers and breeders, whilst the sporting press provided further opportunities for profit. Equally, racing officials – judges, starters, handicappers, clerks of the course – all had opportunities to significantly extend their income. One northern clerk of the course, Thomas Craggs, who held several posts from mid-century until his death in 1885, was a former schoolteacher who reputedly left some £40,000.[24] Others who owned horses, betted and/or attended races gained immense cultural capital from their involvement. Those in ancillary occupations – farmers, saddlers, innkeepers, veterinary surgeons, blacksmiths, corn dealers – all had a financial interest in the continuance of the sport, whilst others – hotel keepers, carriage proprietors, printers, shopkeepers – in the towns where racing took place also had the potential to benefit. Had the upper classes withdrawn from racing, it would have had a major and potentially catastrophic impact on the industry and would have led to huge losses of regular middle-class income. Horse owners, for example, provided two-thirds of all prize money in the form of stakes, entry fees and forfeits. So it was in the interest of some groups in middle-class society to maintain the illusion of upper-class power. The involvement of the upper classes provided a screen which sheltered racing from attack from the small, vociferous and potentially powerful middle-class minority of non-conformist, reformist, anti-betting, respectable 'rational recreationists' and their parliamentary representatives. Aristocratic Turfites in both Houses of Parliament were able to protect the sport from potentially harmful legislation. Their attendance at race meetings conferred apparent respectability and significantly increased racing's popularity thanks to the attendance of status-conscious locals. The upper-class consumption was conspicuous in contributions to race subscriptions, purchase of the most expensive yearlings or the top horses, payment of higher training fees and sometimes in rash betting.

But the actual power of the upper classes, as distinct from their influence, was relatively weak and has been consistently over-exaggerated. The British upper class was divided by the impact of social change. Their political power within racing was imperfectly institutionalized, even in respect to the apparent 'governing body of racing', the Jockey Club, which was very much an association of peers and esquires.[25] Recent research has argued that for much of the century the Club had some influence but little power in wider racing.[26] By and large, the Club was simply a club for the convenience of members who enjoyed the 30 or more days racing held annually at Newmarket – a far larger number than were held anywhere else in Britain. As Paul Kahn has demonstrated, the Club's primary function 'was social and not administrative'.[27] Up to the 1870s the Jockey Club had very limited power beyond Newmarket and a few similarly elite courses such as Ascot, Goodwood and Epsom. The majority of Club members had few practical powers. Recent reassessment of the role of Lord Bentinck has also questioned the reality of Jockey Club domination in the first half of the nineteenth century.[28] Admiral Rous, whose dominance of the 1850s and 1860s certainly flattered his talents, largely resisted change. He executed only limited reforms beyond Newmarket and the Club suffered from a 'want of energy' during his reign. The Club's Annual General Meeting of 1865 only attracted 12 members.[29] By and large the Jockey Club was merely a select club for the aristocratic, the autocratic and the intransigent. Even at the end of the nineteenth century, when the Club had achieved wider influence over elite meetings, only a few of its members had any wider interest in racing. Jockey Club stewards like Lord Durham only stood out, as the well-respected racing journalist Sidney Galtrey admitted, because of 'the lack of material ... to compare with him'.[30] The other context where the upper classes apparently controlled racing was at the level of local meetings whose stewards, the final arbiters, were members of the local upper class. They occupied a post of honour and high status but were often ignorant of the rules, ineffective and lacked sufficient knowledge to recognize when dishonesty was being practised.[31]

Yet it was in many people's interests to maintain the illusion of upper-class power. Racing had to respond to a period of rapid social, economic, political and cultural change, whilst preserving the upper-class involvement essential to its survival. It was not an easy task. The modernization of racing needed a revolution but, so long as the abilities of racing's 'legitimate' 'traditional' leaders were weak, there was a potential loss of authority. The revolutionaries were not the upper-class reformers so well described in the standard histories of the Jockey Club.[32] The real revolution was quietly carried out under the noses of the upper classes, a revolution which allowed the upper classes to preserve the illusion of power but allowed middle-class groups to enjoy its fruits.

The following two sections examine some of these key revolutionaries. The approach used is for illustrative purposes only. Any 'great man' approach to the interpretation of the period needs to be tempered with a recognition of the important social and economic changes which ran alongside and especially the major impact of the railways, the electric telegraph, the sporting press and urbanization of the development of racing.[33]

THE REAL ADMINISTRATORS AND CONTROLLERS

In most countries legislatures come and go but the civil service, whose best work is that which usually goes unnoticed, goes on forever. There are instructive parallels in sport and for the last 200 years much of British racing has been shaped and run by a group of middle-class professionals. Their revolutionary role was carried out with limited public acknowledgement and the nineteenth-century press and racing literature much preferred to focus on 'great' horses, 'great' owners, trainers and jockeys and to keep silent about matters of administration. Two dynasties ran horse-racing. The Messrs. Weatherby played a key role yet their role has been quite deliberately underplayed in racing's secondary literature and much more research is needed. The Tattersalls have received more attention but while their dominant role in bloodstock sales has been recognized, much less attention has been paid to their contribution to the development of a betting market and betting arbitration service. Together, these two families provided the infrastructure, the flow of racing information and the continuity that allowed racing to meet the challenges of nineteenth-century change.

James Weatherby, the son of a Tyneside solicitor and a resident of Newmarket, was first appointed Keeper of the Matchbook, Stakeholder and Secretary to the Jockey Club in 1771. So-called *Sporting Calendars* had been published at Newmarket from *c.*1727 and in 1773 Weatherby, with his privileged access to the Matchbook, issued his own *Racing Calendar* in competition. By 1777 he had driven off the opposition and the annually published *Racing Calendar* and a monthly sheet calendar soon became the ex-officio voice of the Jockey Club. The *Calendar*, published from Weatherby's premises near Piccadilly, contained the rules of the Club, although these were clearly only expected to apply to Newmarket. It also contained the results of other important races throughout the British Isles and a short list of 'Colours worn by the Riders of the following Noblemen and Gentlemen'. Thereafter it is likely that Weatherby maintained a presence in both Newmarket and

London. His nephew, another James Weatherby, took over both the post of Keeper of The Matchbook and the publication of the *Calendar*. In 1791 James Weatherby published *An Introduction to the General Stud Book* which was followed two years later by the first edition of the *General Stud Book*, the official genealogical record of all recognized British thoroughbreds. This listed all pedigrees of horses up to that point and all the mares that had had offspring. The year of birth, sex, colour, name and sire of all offspring were appended. Weatherby's had made themselves arbiters of entry and published further updated stud books in 1822, 1832, 1840, 1845, 1849 and every four years thereafter.[34] They were therefore able to act as gatekeepers so far as entry of racehorses for events throughout the country was concerned.

The lucrative dynasty founded by James Weatherby became effectively the secretaries to the Jockey Club; receiving entries to races at Newmarket, Epsom and other elite courses, registering the colours of owners, publishing the *Racing Calendar* and accepting or rejecting thoroughbreds for the *General Stud Book*. By the end of the nineteenth century they were also acting as agents for many owners, dealing with entries, forfeits, winnings and payments to jockeys.[35] Their advice and supportive framework lay behind the Jockey Club and its rules. The long and continuous success of the family as officials for the Jockey Club, their control of the *Racing Calendar*, which could choose whether or not to recognize race meetings throughout the country, and their publication of the *Stud Book*, placed them at the heart of British horse-racing. Jockey Club stewards came and went but the Weatherby family stayed. Their continued advice on matters such as the shaping of the rules of racing was therefore central. The Jockey Club rules had long been in use at Newmarket, alongside more established rules concerning horse-racing in general which had largely predated its establishment. In 1858 a Jockey Club Committee attempted to introduce more up-to-date general rules of racing with limited initial wider effect. In 1870 the Committee followed this up with numerous fresh rules, largely assisted by Edward Weatherby, then head of the firm, who also established a new London base in Old Burlington Street. Thereafter Weatherby's provided the day-to-day experience, expertise and racing knowledge which created the socially-accepted illusion of Jockey Club power over the elite racing calendar in the later nineteenth century.

The other middle-class dynasty who dominated the social and cultural changes in racing over the nineteenth century was the

Tattersalls.[36] Richard Tattersall, the founder of the firm, was the son of a Yorkshire wool stapler. In 1766 he purchased premises at Hyde Park Corner for the sale of horses. Tattersall's crucial act was to provide a special Room and a cook for the exclusive use of members of the Jockey Club. This link with the Club helped to make his fortune. Tattersall was entrusted with the dispersal sales of aristocratic studs and, with auctioneer fees of five per cent for each horse sold, the family soon dominated the sale of bloodstock in the south, while the Rooms became the acknowledged London centre of aristocratic wagering. The close links between the two dynasties are illustrated by Richard Tattersall's will which named 'my friend, James Weatherby, of Newmarket' as one of the executors.

As well as selling hacks, hunters, coaches, carriages and dogs, Tattersalls soon became the greatest bloodstock auction house in the country. By the 1820s they dominated bloodstock auctioneering in London and by the 1830s they were selling horses to the Continent and to America, as well as conducting auctions at Doncaster, Hampton Court, Hyde Park Corner, Newmarket and elsewhere. Almost single-handedly Tattersalls introduced a change of attitude amongst owners and breeders. At the end of the eighteenth century the majority of yearlings, mares and stallions were sold by private treaty between individuals and it was often difficult to obtain a fair price. Middle-class auctioneers were little involved and the potential for profit presented by thoroughbred sales was largely unrealized. Tattersalls' reputation for honesty and fair dealing helped change attitudes; by the second half of the nineteenth century the majority of sales were by auction and a calendar of major auction sales at Newmarket and Doncaster, run by Tattersalls, had emerged to help stabilize expectations.

The growth of sales meant that in the period around 1870 Edmund Tattersall (1816–98) began to lease additional premises. At Doncaster, where the St. Leger week auctions had been held outside the Salutation Inn, he leased the Glasgow Paddocks and at Newmarket he leased land on the McCalmont estate. In 1872 Edmund Tattersall conducted the huge four-day dispersal of the famous Middle Park Stud, which realized 107,000 guineas, and in 1884 he conducted the dispersal sale for Lord Falmouth, which realized 111,790 guineas. Later the same year Tattersalls purchased the land they had leased in Newmarket and built a ring, seating, rostrum, offices and refreshment rooms to serve the annual October sales. The first experiment with a December sale there in 1886 proved sufficiently successful to make it an annual event. Edmund was now at the head of a large, well-to-do, upper-middle-class family. At the end of the century Edmund's will, written in 1895, and proved in 1898, showed the Tattersall partnership to generate net profit income of £30,000 p.a.[37]

In terms of its impact on racing the Tattersall's development of a London-based betting structure was even more revolutionary. By the 1790s a Subscription Room for the striking and payment of bets had joined the offices as well as a dining room and two rooms for the Jockey Club. The Subscription Rooms brought in money and patronage for the auctions. Contemporary reports from the early decades of the nineteenth century indicate a socially-mixed clientele both inside and outside what had become a centre for backing, laying and the exchange of betting information. The courtyard was crammed with what one contemporary writer described as 'Peers, Baronets, Members of Parliament, Turf-gentlemen and Turf-servants, Jockies, Grooms, Horse-dealers, Gamblers and Spies'.[38] Actual members of Tattersalls needed to be able to meet the annual subscription fee and to provide references but Tattersalls was also a meeting place for leviathan bookmakers, betting commissioners and others of more plebeian antecedents from the inner turfite group who were reliable payers of betting debts. It provided an inner cross-class betting market where large sums of money were wagered and betting odds on important races were regularly reported by journalists from sporting papers such as the *Sunday Times* and *Bell's Life*. Tattersalls' actual membership was predominantly upper class and Newmarket-based, totalling around 200 in the 1830s but growing. In 1842 a more spacious room had to be provided, and, in his evidence to the 1844 House of Commons Select Committee on Gaming, Richard Tattersall claimed 350 subscribers, including many commissioners.

When the Stewards of the Jockey Club decided that in future they would not attempt to rule on betting matters, a new way of settling disagreements was informally introduced whereby they would be settled either by referees at the Committee at the Rooms at Newmarket, which met only during Newmarket meetings, or at Tattersalls Committee at the Corner. This made Tattersalls a potential arbiter of betting matters and the Committee's rules of betting a key guide. The then head of the firm, Richard Tattersall (1785–1859), carefully maintained his link with the Club so his 1843 Rules and Regulations still stated that the Rooms would be 'under the sanction of the stewards of the Jockey Club' and the Club was represented on the Room's committee. Growing interest in betting meant that it was Tattersalls who provided the odds to which smaller bookmakers responded; by mid-century it had became the great betting market, the betting equivalent to Lloyds in insurance. Contemporary writers described it as 'The Turf Exchange', at a time when the expansion of 'list betting houses' in London was forcing some members to 'open offices in self-defence'.[39] While members now had to be elected, this was no obstacle to the top bookmakers of the period who dominated the membership. Its key role can be seen in the way less reputable betting associations, such as the Junior Tattersall's Association and Company or Mrs Beeton's Eastern Tattersalls in Cheapside, used the name to legitimate their activities.

Membership grew, although still including betting members of the Jockey Club, and in 1865 the firm moved to much larger premises at Albert Gate. By now the firm was 'one of the institutions of the time'.[40] However, the upper-class interest in heavy wagering was in decline and owners too were increasingly turning to betting with betting commissioners or legal credit bookmakers who were Tattersalls' members rather than with each other. Here again middle-class efforts had led to a change in upper-class practice which allowed an overall shift of wealth into their hands, although in this case the stricter enforcement of the state Acts against ready-money bookmakers in the 1870s also had some, more limited, impact. The 1870s also saw a national move towards starting price betting. In the antepost betting too, Tattersalls was now becoming a less important part of the betting market with the proliferation of big credit bookmaker firms in the provinces. However, wealthy, more respectable credit bookmakers continued to be members of Tattersalls and Tattersalls continued to play a major role in both upper-class betting and in arbitrating on betting matters, especially where there were disputes between bookmakers or between layers and backers. Its revision and strengthening of the Rules on Betting in 1886 made a further major contribution to national betting. Tattersalls' reputation had entered national currency and by the 1880s the more exclusive betting rings on courses were known widely as Tattersalls enclosures.[41] In 1899 Tattersalls Committee absorbed the Newmarket Rooms Committee and thenceforth dominated the settlement of betting disputes nationally.

Together, the Weatherby and Tattersall families provided both the changes and continuity within which fundamental changes in racing could be managed. Their organizations provided the comfortable reassurance that maintained the wealthy upper-class involvement without which the conspicuous consumption which bloodstock ownership required could not be sustained. This was so even in periods such as the 1840s and 1850s when some upper-class owners were suffering stress, anomie and disillusionment thanks to wider social, political and economic changes and when racing had a well-deserved reputation for dishonesty. Wray Vamplew's initial analysis of this period from *c*.1840 to 1870 saw racing as having changed thanks to a 'Railway Revolution', although he has since substantially modified this view.[42] This modification is capable of wider application and the role of the railways in giving shape and growth to the Victorian transformation of sport can be argued to be more generally over-emphasized.[43] The railways certainly had a major impact across almost all sports in allowing top competitors to compete more widely and thus increased professional earnings, visibility and status, but they had little medium-term impact on spectatorship and revenue raising. The Jockey Club had only limited impact on national racing during this period from the 1850s to the beginning of the 1870s. This was less noticeable to the public since the Weatherby and Tattersall dynasties were able to maintain the appearance of continuity through their activities, their publications, their sales and their organizations. Their work lay behind the cultural transformation of racing over the century.

BETTING, BREEDING AND TRAINING: MONEY-MAKING MOTIVATIONS FOR THE MIDDLE CLASSES

Individual bookmakers, trainers and, to a lesser extent, breeders also aided the fundamental changes in the cultural life of racing and had significant impact on its social and economic relationships. In the early nineteenth century gentlemen were already betting between themselves and with less wealthy members of the Fancy. Such off-course betting amongst early turfites, while cross-class, was largely on credit, paid on a settling day after the race. 'Blackleg' bookmakers with working-class origins but middle-class incomes and lifestyles, such as John Gully, Robert Ridsdale and William Crockford, were soon part of this inner group, acting as trusted commissioners for those living out of 'town' and making bets on their own account. Gully made enough money from upper-class wagerers to become an MP for Pontefract and the owner of coal-mines and land in County Durham; he died a rich man.[44] By the early 1840s bookmakers of a similar type had begun to dominate betting at Tattersalls and elsewhere. By 1842 the Jockey Club had abandoned any attempt to control betting and its members in Parliament were instrumental in the passing of the Betting and Gaming Act of 1845 which meant that disputed bets could no longer be dealt with in court.[45] This initially caused a control vacuum with regard to credit betting which, as we have seen, Tattersall helped to fill.

Cash betting was taking place in the 1830s and 1840s in 'list houses' which listed short odds on future races and took cash bets but only on a relatively small scale.[46] A more contemporary revolutionary figure to come to widespread public (that is, upper-class) notice as the first major 'list' bookmaker was William Davis (aka William Davies or 'The Leviathan').[47] Davis was a man of high moral rectitude; an ex-carpenter, who laid bets in the 1840s, both on the courses and at his 'list houses' in London. He had 'a clear head and quick perception, calculating mind and retentive memory', but 'unassuming deportment and probity of conduct during his career on the turf'.[48] He lost over £10,000 on a Newmarket handicap early in his career but paid it all in thousand pound notes.[49] He had a high reputation for honesty and betting integrity. Unlike bookmakers previously, who took bets on word of mouth and offered credit until after the race, Davis expected most of his customers to pay when they made the bet. Such cash payment in advance was illegal following the 1853 Betting Houses Act, although the Act was widely ignored. He sometimes lost money when all the punters backed the favourite but he made large amounts when the favourite lost; such an unbalanced betting book was a feature of early betting. Davis recognized that by building up a large clientele he would gather large sums of money before an event and could move towards the modern notion of a balanced book, where the bookmaker stands to win a small profit no matter which horse comes first. In 1850 it was estimated that at his two London betting list houses, £300,000 was staked in small bets alone. He had shops at the Durham Arms in Serle Street and at Barrs in Long Acre where he exhibited lists and quoted prices for horses, entered bets in a banker's ledger, took cash and gave out tickets.

Davis continued to offer credit to his large numbers of landed clients whose resources were tied up in property and would therefore need time to pay. His approach and behaviour helped to change upper-class attitudes to bookmakers, which had previously been much more negative. Where once the non-titled were looked down on, it was becoming increasingly clear, even to the upper classes, that they were far more likely to pay up a losing bet and were often far more trustworthy. The reputation for probity of bookmakers like Davis and others of his generation meant that the gentry were more likely to bet with them than risk a bet within their class with the possibility of non-payment. Davis also facilitated the further expansion of bookmaking away from the racecourse and into the towns and cities.[50] He was able to adopt an upper-middle-class lifestyle and left c.£150,000 when he died. By the end of the 1850s men of humble backgrounds largely dominated all forms of bookmaking, sometimes with equal success. Fred Swindell, for example, once a Derby engine-cleaner, left £146,000.[51]

By the 1870s the nature of betting was changing further. Up to this time most bets once made could not be cancelled so if a horse was injured or withdrawn prior to the race the better lost the stake money. On the other hand, an early bet could be made at long odds by someone who knew more about the horse than the bookmaker whose listed prices were over-generous. During this decade there was a gradual move by the majority of small punters and small bookmakers towards the modern pattern of relying on starting prices – the odds available on the course when the horses actually start the race. Since far more information was available, thanks to the daily press reports on horses and their current form, the odds were shorter but the starting prices meant that punters knew the horse would run. Starting prices were initially printed in reliable sporting papers such as the *Sporting Life* and the next fundamental change was their use by larger legal credit bookmakers like Valentine and Wright in London circa 1874 to satisfy their more middle-class clients' concerns about potential exploitation. From the 1870s most larger towns were sustaining middle-class credit bookmaking businesses through a mixture of ante-post betting on major races and starting prices for others.[52] Illegal cash bookmakers followed the same track and by the later 1870s the regional press were also printing starting prices, reflecting the wider working-class punters' and street bookmakers' interest in this approach to betting. By the end of the century almost all significant upper-class betting was largely on credit with a bookmaker and often at starting prices. With books now balanced, this almost certainly meant over time that upper-class money was diverted into bookmakers' banks.

In two other areas, training and breeding, racing provided potentially good profits and occasional opportunities for middle-class individuals to effect change in the social and economic relationships of racing. The costs of racehorse ownership meant a wealthy, educated and metropolitan elite possessed a disproportionate number of the best horses. Detailed analysis of ownership has proved extremely difficult, although an analysis of winning 1904 owners shows that 49 per cent were educated at public schools (Eton provided 17.6 per cent of all winning owners), 24 per cent had University degrees and 48 per cent were members of London clubs.[53] However, racehorses have to be bred and trained and this ensured the redistribution of the upper-class largesse.

The work of trainers took place away from public view and, even in the mid-nineteenth century, their names were scarcely known to the public. Early in the eighteenth century most horses were trained by their owners' own grooms but by the 1760s there were already a few trainers in Yorkshire and in Newmarket sufficiently experienced and successful to set themselves up as public trainers, training for several owners at once and charging a fixed fee per horse. This move fundamentally changed class relationships within elite racing including, eventually, the status of trainers, some of whom were already leaving significant sums in the early nineteenth century. From then on, top trainers such as John Scott, John and William Day, John Porter, Robert Peck and Mathew Dawson attracted large strings of horses and, to an extent, were even able to choose between their employers or refuse to train for particular owners. Such successful trainers often controlled the entire management and disposal of an owner's string, prepared them, entered them in races or not as they thought fit and ran them.[54] It is very clear that at times all trainers were prepared to put their own racing interests above that of their employers[55] and were therefore far from being mere servants. They were highly rated professionals, successfully training large numbers of horses to win over a range of distances and courses. The relationship was still largely a business one but trainers like Scott or Dawson were also the friends of racing Prime Ministers such as the fourteenth Earl of Derby and Lord Rosebery. According to Thormanby, 'peers, baronets, barons and Queen's Counsel learned in the law' dined with Scott at his training stables at Whitewall, near Malton in the North Riding.[56] Scott also stayed at country estates like Streatlam Castle, home of John Bowes. As the top trainer of the mid-nineteenth century, he was held in high esteem and some Jockey Club members even abandoned Newmarket in favour of having their horses trained in the north, although they still raced largely in the south. In 1847 Scott was training on behalf of 19 owners, far more than any other trainer, in 1859 the figure rose to 22. Other trainers were not far behind. According to *Ruff's Guide*, in 1854 John Day was training for at least 15 owners and William Day for 11. Later in the century John Porter of Kingsclere in Hampshire, an even more socially accepted figure, trained for the Duke of Westminster, the Earl of Portsmouth, Lord Alington and Sir Frederick Johnstone. Porter also trained for the Prince of Wales, whose subsequent trainer, Richard Marsh, training and entertaining at the palatial Egerton House Stables in Newmarket, needed £10,000 a year to break even, but did things on the grand scale and mixed freely with the upper set.[57] Such trainers had clearly entered an upper-middle-class world.

As a result of such success and ever-increasing press coverage, one description of Newmarket trainers' houses in 1901 claimed that many had 'fine gardens, trim lawns for croquet and lawn tennis, billiard rooms, and cellars containing choice vintages', while for the trainers themselves it was 'quite the ordinary thing to be tall-hatted, frock coated, kid-gloved, patent-leather booted'.[58] Census data shows that trainers often owned large, comfortable and expensive houses and kept servants. This was a major change in display and status from the breeched and gaitered trainers of a previous age and by 1901 it was the trainer, rather than the owner, who received the reverence of the mass audience when a horse was successful.

The middle classes made a more limited impact in breeding, since the upper classes took a more direct interest in this area of racing. All those interested in ownership and racing success wanted the very best thoroughbreds. The gentry and aristocratic groups either purchased horses from each other, or bred their own from the best stallions. Some, like Bentinck, or the fifth Earl of Glasgow, maintained large studs. Sir Tatton Sykes of Sledmere was one of the largest breeders of bloodstock in England.[59] This limited middle-class opportunities for gainful occupation and/or profit, since it required only a groom and a few stable lads.

As we have already seen, during the nineteenth century the breeding market changed from being dominated by private purchases to auction sales, largely by Tattersalls, which, alongside a major increase in demand, significantly increased prices. At the start of the century middle-class breeders were already in business. Breeding for sale could be financially risky and required real expertise but even then farmers, trainers and innkeepers often kept a mare or two for breeding and some trainers, like the Chifneys at Newmarket and the I'Ansons at Malton, were highly successful. Ownership of a good stallion was a safer route to profit, provided he was potent. One of the sidelines of Richard Tattersall's business in the late eighteenth century had been his Highflyer stud. In the early nineteenth century Mr Theobald, a retired linen draper, astutely purchased top stallions like Mameluke, the 1826 Derby winner, and brood mares of outstanding merit like Pocohontas (purchased in 1841). Theobald's stud remained profitable up to the time of his death in 1850.

The movement to create the breeding industry really gained impetus in the mid-nineteenth century by increasing the size of studs and making economies of scale. In the south of England it was William Blenkiron, the manufacturer son of a farmer, who made a critical shift by using his capital to set up the Middle Park Stud at Eltham. At its peak it owned approximately 200 brood mares and 12 stallions.[60] Blenkiron recognized the power of publicity to attract upper-class buyers; from 1860 he sponsored the Middle Park Produce Stakes at Newmarket in order to encourage prospective Jockey Club purchasers. Blenkiron set out to get the best and most fashionable stock, and saw particularly successful yearling sales between 1864 and 1868. The stud's final sale in 1872 included 103 yearlings, 199 mares, 129 foals and 12 stallions.

English thoroughbreds dominated racing throughout the world and provided middle-class opportunities to purchase horses cheaply and exploit the foreign trade. In northern England, the York breeder Thomas Kirby was a key businessman in creating this market and building up the trade with Europe. Kirby was a central figure from 1791 until the 1850s and traded as far afield as Russia. His trade was mainly through Hull, especially up to the 1850s, when northern English-bred horses were highly successful and his stock was therefore in high demand.[61] Tattersalls were the major firm managing the European trade in southern England and this was a significant aspect of their business. Top-class British horses imported by French breeders helped to provide the foundation of French racing success in the 1860s and 1870s, when French horses proved themselves equal to the British. Indeed, in 1873 the French owner Lefevre was the leading owner in England. In Germany, 37 British stallions had been imported by 1845 and there were further major imports continued until the end of the nineteenth century.[62]

Setting up stud companies was another way of creating opportunities for middle-class profit. Upper-class interest in breeding made this seem an attractive investment option although it was in fact high risk. One of the earliest northern examples, the Rawcliffe Stud Company in York, a joint-stock company owned almost entirely by shareholders of gentry or aristocratic background, maintained its manager in a good lifestyle for over a decade before it went under.[63] The files of failed companies in the Public Record Office are full of later nineteenth century examples. The well-supported Cobham stud, set up in 1872, purchased Middle Park stock with the intention of 'breeding thoroughbred horses for racing and other purposes' and owned over 100 brood mares. It was initially very successful, although its expenses were high, and it maintained its manager at £1,000 per annum for six years before being liquidated in 1879.[64]

MIDDLE-CLASS RACING 'REVOLUTIONARIES'

The analysis of political revolutions has a relatively long history and since the mid-1950s much attention has been devoted to the study of revolutionary leadership.[65] Analysis of the economic status and social origins of European revolutionary leaders, for example, presents a mixed picture although, as in racing, many were of early middle age, with business experience and the social skills necessary to work with both groups and individuals. The middle-class racing 'revolutionaries' were not fanatics or intellectuals who had failed to impress others with their creative ideas. They did not have that sense of failure that wished to destroy a society that failed to recognize them, nor were they revolutionary orators. Racing's 'revolutionaries' were practical men of action who were anxious to get practical tasks carried out. Behind the facade of upper-class power lay the quiet reality of families like the Weatherbys and the Tattersalls whose efforts ensured key changes in racing and betting and the crucial shifts in the organization and administration of the sport. Likewise the ability of bookmakers to meet their debts, and of expert trainers and breeders to produce results, helped to ensure that whilst the upper classes maintained their involvement they did so within a much changed social and economic environment.

By the end of the nineteenth century British racing provided an instructive comparison with racing throughout Europe and the rest of the British Empire in the way that aristocratic wealth was used and exploited. In France, for example, owners contributed less than a quarter of the prize money by the early twentieth century. In England, where the upper classes owned a high proportion of successful horses, owners contributed around two-thirds of all prize money; at Sandown Park, the proportion was 82 per cent. In effect, rich British owners competed for their own money.[66] This allowed more opportunities for middle-class groups to profit from racing.

By the end of the century racing was a cross-class sport and a central leisure activity for much of British society. The naive onlooker might well have seen a sport apparently dominated and run by the upper classes. However, it can be argued that significant and influential middle-class individuals and families, such as the Tattersalls and Weatherbys, played the key roles and ensured that upper-class wealth was redistributed and redirected within the sport. Beneath the surface, the middle classes played a key 'revolutionary' role and made a significant contribution to modern European racing.

NOTES

1. J.A. Mangan, Series Editor's foreword in John Lowerson, *Sport and the English Middle Classes 1870–1914* (Manchester: Manchester University Press, 1993), p.vii.
2. For a detailed consideration of these themes, see Lowerson, *Sport and the English Middle Classes.*
3. Neil Tranter, *Sport, Economy and Society in Britain 1750–1914* (Cambridge: Cambridge University Press, 1998), Ch.3.
4. Wray Vamplew, *Pay up and Play the Game: Professional Sport in Britain, 1875–1914* (Cambridge: Cambridge University Press, 1988), Ch.19.
5. See Mike Huggins, 'Second Class Citizens'? English Middle-Class Culture and Sport, 1850–1910: A Reconsideration', *International Journal of the History of Sport*, 17, 2 (2000), 1–35.
6. Of course, in the case of J.A. Mangan this is hardly surprising as this volume is an extension and elaboration of his earlier reflections on the subject.
7. For example, J.A. Goldstone, *Revolutions: Theoretical, Comparative and Historical Studies* (San Diego: Harcourt Brace Jovanovich, 1986).
8. See, for example, C. Johnson, *Revolutionary Change* (London: Longman, 1983).
9. Barrington Moore, *Social Origins of Dictatorship and Democracy* (Boston: Deacon Press, 1966), pp.413–14.
10. Tranter, *Sport, Economy and Society in Britain*, p.3.
11. Ibid., Ch.2.
12. R.W. Malcolmson, *Popular Recreations in English Society, 1700–1850* (London: Cambridge University Press, 1973), pp.89–117 and 158–71; A. Delves, 'Popular Recreation and Social Conflict in Derby. 1800–1850' in E. Yeo and S. Yeo (eds.), *Popular Culture and Class Conflict, 1560–1914* (Brighton: Harvester Press, 1981), pp.89–127.
13. Derek Birley, *Sport and the Making of Britain* (Manchester: Manchester University Press, 1996), p.156.
14. Birley, *Sport and the Making of Britain*, pp.164–5 and 169.
15. See A. Kidd and D. Nicholls, *The Making of the British Middle Class?* (Stroud: Sutton, 1998), p.xv.
16. David Cannadine, *The Decline and Fall of the British Aristocracy* (London: Yale University Press, 1990); idem., *The Rise and Fall of Class in Britain* (New York: Colombia University Press,

1999). See also J.V. Beckett, *The Aristocracy in England 1660–1914* (Oxford: Oxford University Press, 1986).

17. Simon Dentith, *Sport and Cultural Forms in Nineteenth Century England* (Basingstoke: Macmillan, 1998), pp.6–7.

18. Roger Munting, *Hedges and Ditches: A Social and Economic History of National Hunt Racing* (London: J.A. Allen, 1987), p.21.

19. Richard Holt, *Sport and the British: A Modern History* (Oxford: Clarendon Press, 1989), p.181.

20. Tranter, *Sport, Economy and Society in Britain*, p.19.

21. Wray Vamplew, *The Turf* (London: Allen Lane, 1976), pp.133–4.

22. Dennis Brailsford, *British Sport: A Social History* (Cambridge: Lutterworth Press, 1997 Edn.), pp.72–3.

23. Roger Mortimer, R. Onslow and P. Willett, *Biographical Enclyclopaedia of Flat Racing* (London: McDonald, 1978), p.523.

24. Jack Fairfax-Blakeborough, *Northern Turf History Vol. 3: York and Doncaster* (London: J.A. Allen, 1950), p.246.

25. Vamplew, *The Turf*, p.77.

26. For a more detailed critique and analysis of the Jockey Club and its power, see Mike Huggins, *Flat Racing and British Society 1790–1914* (London and Portland, OR: Frank Cass, 2000), Ch.7.

27. Paul Kahn, 'The Sport of Kings: A study of Traditional Social Structure under Change', Ph.D. thesis, University of Wales, Swansea, 1980, p.27.

28. C.f. the earlier view of Michael Seth Smith, *Lord Paramount of the Turf: Lord George Bentinck 1802–1848* (London: Faber and Faber, 1971) and Mike Huggins, 'Lord Bentinck, the Jockey Club and Racing Morality in mid-Nineteenth Century England', *International Journal of the History of Sport*, 13, 3 (1996), 432–44. Emma C. Eadie, 'The Structure and Organisation of English Horseracing 1830–1860: The Development of a National Sport', D.Phil. thesis, Oxford, 1990, sees the Club's involvement around mid-century as largely one of inertia.

29. Huggins, *Flat Racing and British Society*, p.182.

30. Sidney Galtrey, *Memories of a Racing Journalist* (London: Hutchinson, 1934), p.18.

31. Vamplew, *The Turf*, pp.126–8.

32. Robert Black, *The Jockey Club and its Founders* (London: Smith Elder, 1891); Roger Mortimer, *The Jockey Club* (London: Cassell, 1958).

33. This is developed in some detail in Huggins, *Flat Racing*, Ch.1.

34. For further details, see C.M. Prior, *The History of the Racing Calendar and Stud Book* (London: The Sporting Life, 1926).

35. Vamplew, *The Turf*, p.120

36. The following paragraphs largely rely on Peter Willett, *The Story of Tattersalls* (London: Stanley Paul, 1987) and Vincent Orchard, *Tattersalls: 200 Years of Sporting History* (London: Hutchinson, 1953).

37. Orchard, *Tattersalls*, p.257.

38. Ibid., p.162.

39. Cecil, 'The Turf Exchange', *New Sporting Magazine* (Oct. 1853), 256.

40. Orchard, *Tattersalls*, p.219.

41. Earl of Suffolk and Berkshire and W.G. Craven, *Racing* (London: Longmans Green, 1886), p.249.

42. Vamplew, *The Turf*, Ch.2; J. Tolson and W. Vamplew, 'Derailed: Railways and Horse Racing Revisited', *The Sports Historian*, 18, 2 (Nov. 1998).

43. See M. Huggins and J. Tolson, 'The Railways and Sport in Victorian Britain: A Critical Reassessment', *Journal of Transport History*, 22, 2 (Sept. 2001). John Tolson's recent detailed doctoral work has clearly established the very limited impact of railways on courses and funding for racing. See J. Tolson, 'The Railways and Racing', Ph.D. thesis, De Montfort University, Leicester, 2000.

44. Bernard Darwin, *John Gully and his Times* (London: Cassell, 1935).

45. Eadie, 'The Structure and Organisation of English Horseracing', pp.170–72.

46. See D.C. Itzkowitz, 'Victorian bookmakers and their Customers', *Victorian Studies*, 32, 1 (1988), 12–13.

47. Mark Clapson, *A Bit of a Flutter: Popular Gambling and English Society c.1823–1961* (Manchester: Manchester University Press, 1992), p.26.

48. 'Mr Davies, the Leviathan Betting Man', *Illustrated London News*, 1 June 1850, 386.
49. 'Epsom Races', *Illustrated London News*, 1 June 1850, 385.
50. Carl Chinn, *Better Betting with a Decent Feller: Bookmakers, Betting and the British Working Class 1750–1990* (Hemel Hempstead: Harvester, 1991), p.51.
51. Vamplew, *The Turf*, p.216.
52. Clapson, *A Bit of a Flutter*, p.27.
53. M.P. Filby, 'A Sociology of Horse Racing in Britain', Ph.D. thesis, University of Warwick, 1983, Table 2.
54. See M.J. Huggins, *Kings of the Moor* (Middlesbrough: Teesside Polytechnic, 1991), p.17.
55. Eadie, 'The Structure and Organisation of English Horseracing', pp.163–4.
56. Thormanby, *Kings of the Turf* (London: Hutchinson, 1898), p.92.
57. Richard Marsh, *A Trainer to Two Kings* (London: Cassell, 1925), shows very much an upper-middle-class lifestyle.
58. Charles Richardson, *The English Turf: A Record of Horses and Courses* (London: Methuen, 1901), p.218.
59. 'Thormanby' (W.W. Dixon), *Kings of the Turf*, p.171.
60. *New Sporting Magazine*, May 1861, 330.
61. The Druid, *The Post and the Paddock* (London: Vinton, 1856), pp.71ff, deals with 'Mr Kirby and the Foreigners'.
62. See Peter Willett, *The Classic Racehorse* (London: Stanley Paul, 1989 Edn.), Chs. 7 and 8.
63. M.J. Huggins, 'Thoroughbred Breeding in the North and East Ridings of Yorkshire in the Nineteenth Century', *Agricultural History Review*, 42 (1994), 119.
64. William Allison, *My Kingdom for a Horse* (London: Grant Richards, 1919), p.250.
65. For example, Crane Brinton, *The Anatomy of Revolution* (London: Jonathan Cape, 1953), Ch.4.
66. Vamplew, *The Turf*, pp.182–3.

3

Unrecognized Middle-Class Revolutionary? Michael Cusack, Sport and Cultural Change in Nineteenth-Century Ireland

JOSEPH M. BRADLEY

From Robert Emmett's uprising of 1803, through the years of Daniel O'Connell's Catholic Emancipation campaign, the Young Irelanders, the Fenians, the founding of the Gaelic League and the era of Charles Stuart Parnell, middle-class revolutionaries endeavoured to transform the economic, social and political landscape of Ireland. Likewise, the country's cultural revolutionaries of the late nineteenth century can be considered important in that they created, revived and helped sustain ideologies that contributed to the creation of the Irish Free State in 1922. Such revolutionaries did not change Ireland overnight but they did help to articulate the sense of difference and distinction that demanded expression in the shape of an independent Ireland.

It can be argued that the founding of the Gaelic Athletic Association (GAA) in 1884 was a crucial point in these proceedings. Although it took several decades to develop into a truly all-Ireland institution, apart from the Catholic Church and the Government itself, no single body has impacted on Irish life as has the GAA. It is as a direct result of the existence of the GAA that Gaelic sports developed to become a significant element in defining Ireland and the Irish people.

Although Gaelic 'pastimes' in Ireland have a history going back 2000 years, games involving balls and sticks have similar histories in many countries. Indeed, GAA authors such as De Burca and Mullen have explicitly recognized this. Mullen argues that the British have a vital role in an understanding of modern Irish sport. He opines that: 'Trinity College, Dublin (a Protestant preserve), became a centre for the direct plantation and diffusion of British sport and its amateur ethos'.[1] However, the founding of the GAA revolutionized previous pastimes, Gaelic or otherwise in origin, and made them distinctly Irish. This also made their historical trajectory unique in that such a powerful organization was successfully instituted, endorsed and constituted by the masses and, in the process, became a defining ingredient in understanding modern Ireland.

Ireland had been decimated socially, culturally and economically by the Great Famine of 1845–51: 'amongst the major casualties of the Famine were the field games and other traditional pastimes of rural Ireland, which in many areas suffered an irreversible decline.'[2] Despite the privations of the Famine period there is evidence that Gaelic field games, football and hurling, still survived in a variety of locations around the country. Almost certainly at this point, some individuals and groups of people believed that such games could be organized at a greater level than currently existed. Indeed, De Burca notes a Cork journalist, Denis Holland, as one who advocated such a course.[3] However, the same author believes that Michael Cusack's role in founding the GAA was a crucial one. It was Cusack more than anyone who revolutionized sport in Ireland and laid some of the foundations for the wider social and cultural revolution that was to take place over the next four decades.

BACKGROUND

Michael Cusack was born in 1847 in the Burren region of north Clare, an area most severely affected by the Great Famine. He was one of five children. Cusack's father herded the sheep of a local landlord and in return received rent-free residence and a small plot. His was a largely Irish speaking area well into the latter half of the nineteenth century. Later Cusack also recounted how he engaged in a variety of forms of hurling as he grew up in the Burren.

De Burca records that little is known about Cusack's early education, but educated he clearly was and his tutors recommended him for the teaching profession. Cusack's biographer believes the experience of living his formative years in Clare engendered him with a sense of injustice at the plight of ordinary people. For De Burca, these views would have been regarded as radical at the time, views that eventually 'made Cusack in a certain sense an ardent egalitarian, even a socialist in outlook'.[4] Ultimately, Cusack was an Irish nationalist and he blamed British rule for the poor state of the people.

Cusack was not alone in this analysis and his time spent training to be a teacher in Dublin in 1866 was a highpoint of Fenian activity while British soldiers patrolled the streets of the county's capital. Cusack's first teaching post at Lough Cutra, near Gort, Co. Galway, almost certainly helped form some of his radical opinions concerning education in Ireland: opinions he held until his death several decades later. He probably taught basic elementary subjects during his five years at Lough Cutra whilst he later argued against the failure of the national school system to endorse the Irish language as a medium for learning, the exclusion of Irish history from the curriculum and the almost complete lack of time set aside for physical pastimes.

During this period it seems certain that Cusack became a member of the brotherhood of Irish revolutionaries called the Fenians and it is possible that he took a passive role in the abortive rising in the Corofin area. It was also during this period that he studied for the qualifications that would eventually land him the post of professor at St Colman's College, Newry, an established secondary school. At St Colman's he was viewed as essential to the organization of sport. It was also during this time that he met his future wife whose family were prosperous shopkeepers outside of the town, thus adding to the middle-class nature of his developing social world. In 1874 he finally moved to Dublin as an upwardly mobile middle-class resident. In the capital, Cusack's aptitude for sport began to gain new importance. Outside of academic life he pursued his own sporting pleasures, handball, rowing and athletics being some of his favourite activities. By 1877 Cusack progressed to opening his own school in Dublin. It was also in this year:

> that he made decisions and took the actions for which he deserves to be remembered in modern Irish history ... between October 1877 and November 1887 he made his mark on Irish education, played a decisive role in Irish athletics, revived the national game of hurling, took part in a seminal move to revive the Irish language, edited a new Irish weekly newspaper, and founded what has been for over one hundred years the biggest and most successful of Irish sports bodies.[5]

SOCIAL INCLUSION

Cusack, like Padraic Pearse a few years later, appreciated how important education could be to the formation of a people and a nation: 'A nation's liberty as well as a nation's greatness depends on the education of its people, and that education must be two-fold in character — mental and physical'.[6] In the capital he vigorously pursued sport as both a participant and an organizer and he was eventually offered a seat on the prestigious Irish Champion Athletic Club's council. This role proved an important grounding for his eventual decision to found the GAA. Importantly, this period also marked a revival of athletics in Dublin. Organized sport was taking-off in a variety of ways throughout Britain although many sports and clubs continually suffered setbacks. Models and goals for the planners and organizers of sport were thus being created beyond the context of Gaelic sport: such movements and changes would favour people like Cusack.

Since qualifying as a teacher Cusack had been moving into more prestigious social circles than he might previously have expected. He moved in middle-class circles in relation to his wife's family, his work, his friends and his sporting pursuits. Although fulfilling his educational and social potential, Cusack also seems to have been deliberately negotiating his way to a position of strength. Gaining social standing and influence would enable him to put into effect ideas he espoused in relation to Gaelic sport and its diffusion to wider elements of Irish society, namely the artisans and labourers. Cusack was a believer in what by the early twenty-first century had become known as 'social inclusion'.

Among the many people Cusack met in Dublin was Patrick Nally, a Fenian leader from County Mayo. Both he and Nally were individually responsible for organizing successful sports events for the artisan classes. At his 'people's sports' held in Dundalkin 1881, Cusack made a speech calling for a body to control Gaelic sports. De Burca credits Nally with inspiring Cusack's agitating for Irish athletics and Cusack himself stated some years later that Nally was the most important figure in encouraging him to found a body like the GAA.[7]

By the time he met Nally, it was clear that Cusack sought to revolutionize the ownership, organization of and participation in Irish sport. Cusack was determined to become a vital figure in the shaping of Irish cultural life. He began to articulate his case in a series of articles in *The Irish Sportsman*, a predominately unionist paper. Notably, his articles stated his belief that sport should stay clear of party politics. Within the context of a broad encompassing nationalism and aspiration for an independent Ireland, this belief within the GAA was arguably one of the reasons why it eventually found success and has sustained such a prominent role in modern Irish life.

During the early 1880s Cusack became a supporter and promoter of native Irish industry and the Irish language. Throughout subsequent years he formalized his belief in the Irish language by joining and becoming a highly active member of the Gaelic Union, a pre-cursor of the Gaelic League which was founded in 1893. Cusack's energetic efforts in the Gaelic Union's issuing of the *Gaelic Journal* were recognized by Douglas Hyde as marking the start of 'the modern resurrection of modern Irish'.[8]

De Burca points to Cusack as being the main thinker, planner and force behind the founding of the GAA in Thurles, Co Tipperary, on 1 November 1884. Cusack had moved from desiring a new era in athletics to aspiring towards a revolution in sport throughout Ireland. By this time, his belief in the importance of hurling, combined with Maurice Davin's similar belief in Gaelic football, meant that not only would Irish athletics undergo change but specifically and uniquely Irish sports were to be instigated in a cultural revolution, later linked to political nationalism in Ireland.

Through such outlets as the columns of *The Shamrock*, Cusack campaigned for the inclusion of Irish sports in so-called traditional Irish sporting events as well as the involvement of 'police, soldiers, mechanics and other people who are vulgar enough to be muscular'.[9] For Cusack, Irish sport was to be open and democratic as well as inclusive. Up until this time, Irish sport had been predominantly controlled and enjoyed by exclusive groups.

> The early sporting movement in Ireland, tailored after British norms and subordinated to its attendant rational codes for playing rules and methods of organisation, was initially popularised by a similar hierarchy of occupational elites seen earlier in Britain. It was a network that included military officers, the professions, preprofessional students, and men in the higher ranks of commerce and in the expanding civil service.[10]

The meeting at Thurles revolutionized this situation. For Davin, it was necessary to:

> Form an association which would resuscitate and draft laws for the guidance of those who are patriotic enough to devise schemes of recreation for the bulk of the people, and more especially for the humble and hard-working who seem now to be born to no other inheritance than the everlasting round of labour.[11]

Challenge matches between rural clubs and Cusack's team in Dublin began to be played shortly before the formal founding of the Association. Cusack's focus began to shift towards the country and he began to build networks of influence and support that would be crucial for the first years of the GAA.

Davin's involvement, as was later the case with Archbishop Croke, was also important for the GAA. Davin, a highly successful athlete who was popular amongst the sporting fraternity, had, for several years, similar ideas concerning Irish sport. Cusack also courted Land League and Home Rule leaders in recognition of the nationalist and 'common-man' dimension of the forthcoming GAA and as an appreciation that such support was necessary for success. Cusack's masterpiece of lobbying and conversing was composed for the United Ireland and Irishman of 11 October 1884.

> National pastimes ... were an essential element of a thriving nation, and any neglect of them usually began in urban areas. Not only had this been happening in Ireland but the rot was now also starting to spread to the provinces. The reason for this decline, he believed, was because Irish athletics were controlled by people hostile to national aspirations. Accordingly, the time had come for the masses to take control of their own pastimes and to draft rules for this purpose.[12]

The momentum for this revolutionary period in Irish sport gathered during 1884. Several weeks after the Association was founded Cusack wrote to Charles Stewart Parnell (Irish Parliamentary leader), Archbishop Croke (Bishop of Cashel) and Michael Davitt (leader of the Land League) seeking their formal support. All replied in the affirmative.

> By selecting the representatives of the Irish parliamentary party, the Fenian and land leaguer and the nationalist minded bishop, the GAA, despite barely existing as a functioning organisation, has firmly identified itself with nationalism, and through the choice of Davitt and Croke, with radically minded nationalism.[13]

Croke's reply in particular helped set the stone in which the GAA was to be founded and which has had relevance for the GAA throughout its history:

if we continue travelling for the next score years in the same direction that we have been going in for some time past, condemning the sports that were practised by our forefathers, effacing our national features as though we were ashamed of them ... we had better at once, and publicly, abjure our nationality, clap hands for joy at the sight of the Union Jack and place 'England's bloody red' exultantly above the green.[14]

Croke's letter echoed the words of Cusack just a short time before:

The law is that all athletic meetings shall be held under the rules of the Amateur Athletic Association of England, and any person competing at any meeting not held under these rules should be ineligible to compete elsewhere. The management of nearly all the meetings held in Ireland has been entrusted to persons hostile to the dearest aspirations of the Irish people. Every effort has been made to make the meetings look as English as possible – foot races, betting, and flagrant cheating being their most prominent features. We tell the Irish people to take the management of their games into their own hands, to encourage and promote every form of athletics which is peculiarly Irish and to remove with one sweep everything foreign and injurious in the present system.[15]

The GAA's unequivocal and exclusive identification with the nationalist movement had a revolutionary impact on Irish sport. It also made an important contribution to the success of the new body and the cultural nationalism of the decades leading up to the Irish revolutionary period of 1913–22. It is debatable whether this was the intention of many or any of the founders or patrons of the GAA in 1884. Nonetheless, it does seem certain, especially with the presence of well-known Fenian participation, that the GAA's potential as an important instrument in Ireland's cultural and political revolution was recognized and acknowledged from its early years. Indeed, the Association was racked by infighting and power struggles between many members including, almost to its detriment, constitutional and physical force nationalists.

The evolution of Gaelic sport in Ireland, involving and invoking political issues, could hardly be achieved beyond the context of the economic, social and political conditions Ireland had long since experienced. Not for the last time, and not in any way restricted to Ireland or the Irish, sport in Ireland was to become a repository of national identity and, frequently in the case of the GAA, political national identity. The GAA's alliance with nationalism was a regional variation on an almost universal theme. Two decades before the GAA was born, the Czechoslovakian Sokal Gymnastic Association was formed. The threat of Germanization and the loss of Czech cultural identity motivated leading patriots to revive Czech cultural activities: 'To combine physical education and fitness with specific political objectives – primarily the Czech struggle for national independence … in the face of Austro-Hungarian political and cultural oppression.'[16] The GAA was not unique in the 'sporting' set of rules it implemented in relation to its perceived circumstances. Mandle believes that 'The use of sport to proclaim national distinctiveness was a British invention: imitations might be made in Melbourne or Tokyo, even in Thurles, Co Tipperary, but imitations they were, not originals'.[17]

The revolution in Irish sport formally began in earnest, not only with the organization and codification of sport along new lines, but with a rule being instigated making any athlete who had participated in non-GAA athletics meetings ineligible for GAA meetings held after 17 March 1885.[18] For Cusack, this was in response to the English Amateur Athletic Association's attempts to enforce a similar boycott against Irish athletes unwilling to participate solely under its rules, a ruling that was supported by the Irish Cyclists Association. This was also important for future events and contemporary assessments of the GAA in that the politics of exclusion was introduced into organized Irish sport by an English association. Over the course of time, the GAA faced the hostility of their opponents of the fledgling Amateur Athletic Association (AAA): these very organizations that were themselves exclusive, sectarian and class ridden, pursuing sports that many considered detrimental to native Irish cultural life. However, although it continued to be a debatable issue into the twenty-first century, this first GAA rule excluding certain categories of people from membership was actually revoked as early as 1886.

Despite the early problems and infighting, the GAA spread, in Cusack's words, 'like a prairie fire'. He later stated his belief that:

> Within recent years no popular movement has met with so brilliant a success, in such a remarkably short period of time, as that which had for its objects the revival of our national pastimes and games. The country has every reason to be proud of the enthusiasm with

which the youths throughout the island have caught up the idea of
emulating the prowess of their departed ancestors, and by enrolling
themselves in the ranks of the Gaelic Athletic Association, forming
a vast organisation, whose branches and ramifications have spread
themselves over the whole land, from sea to sea.[19]

Crucial to the future of the GAA's success, and matching the ambitions
of Cusack, Davin and the other protagonists, genuine representatives of
local communities, began to take control of Irish sport and the patronage
of the local landlord or titled member of the landed gentry disappeared
forever. Around the same time, Gaelic football and hurling began to be
revived on a country-wide basis through the playing of inter-club and
inter-parish games, often in association with local athletic meetings.[20]
Life in rural Ireland gained a new meaning and communities where the
social spirit had been decimated in the wake of the Great Famine were
re-invigorated.

'Little more than a year after its foundation the GAA was now
actively involved in athletics, hurling and football in twenty counties
out of thirty-two.'[21] Nonetheless, despite his success in launching the
GAA, Cusack's personality was often dictatorial and his capacity for
attacking opponents made him numerous enemies. After a short debate
and campaign against Cusack on the part of Archbishop Croke and
Edmund Gray MP, proprietor of *The Freeman's Journal*, Cusack's
tenure as the secretary of the GAA ended.[22] Although disapproving of
the manner of Cusack's discharge, De Burca considers his dismissal in
detail and believes it 'fully justified'. In being consumed by arguments
over personalities and styles of management and administration,
Cusack 'neglected what should have been his main concern in 1885 and
1886 – the spread of the GAA throughout the entire nationalist
community'.[23]

Although Cusack found his marginalization from the corridors of
influence in the GAA difficult to accept and understand, he continued
to involve himself with Gaelic games through several clubs and an
unsuccessful concerted attempt to regain influence in GAA affairs. This
attempt coincided with his editing and writing much of the content of
the short-lived *Celtic Times* throughout 1887. Although the paper
continued to be highly critical of elements of GAA officialdom and
replicated Cusack's concern with the cultural development of the
country, particularly in sport, literature and language, for the first time

Cusack also displayed an avid interest in the social and labour problems in Ireland and beyond.

If Arthur Griffith, who founded Sinn Fein in 1905, is considered one of the numerous Irish revolutionaries of his time, then as far as many of Cusack's social arguments are concerned, he can also be viewed in the same light. De Burca claims that 'Almost weekly he argued the case for Irish industry in terms anticipating by over a decade the views of Arthur Griffith'.[24] Cusack's arguments were inspired by a sense of injustice and there is an overwhelming theme of nationalist sentiment running through his protestations in perceiving Britain's rule of the country as the root of Ireland's problems. Cusack recognized that others had been arguing in the same vein for a number of years about the revival of native industries crippled by those 'who robbed us of our industrial occupations and then taunted us with our impoverishment'.[25] Motivated by a sense of injustice, Cusack's affinity with the working man and the sentiments common to most or all nationalists, his political and economic philosophy became increasingly socialist in nature.

> It is somewhat mournful to see the frantic eagerness with which many of our Irish capitalists of late have rushed to embark their money in commercial enterprises across the Channel without a thought as to the benefits which might accrue to themselves and their country by supporting in the same way manufacturing industries in Ireland ... If there were a few more capitalists of this stamp in Ireland things would be e'er long very different.[26]

Although hardly as incisive or rich as the socialist analysis of other Irish figures like James Connolly or James Larkin, when considering the future of the working man, it is evident that by 1886 Cusack's beliefs had clearly begun to take the shape of a more informed socialist idealism.

> Day by day the organisations in question are becoming more numerous and powerful wherever the relations between capital and labour are conducted upon a large scale. The tendency of the present age is to centralise power and capital in the hands of the few, and to increase the numbers of the weak, helpless, and poor ... they see every avenue to work gradually closing against them, and

know that they are being hopelessly crushed out in the fierce struggle for wealth. The system itself is wrong, whatever may be said of the action taken in certain specified instances ... the works of such writers as M Emile (T) Zola, by depicting with startling realism the life of these toilers as it is today, is slowly, but none the less steadily, and surely, – effecting a revolution in the minds of their thousands of readers upon the burning labour question.[27]

Cusack advocated the formation and promotion of trade unions as a means to protect the exploited working man. 'The goal towards which they should direct their attention is the formation of an organisation as far as possible of an international character and the result would be fewer strikes and less poverty and misery.'[28] Such language from Cusack's pen (De Burca believes that he wrote virtually all the content of *The Celtic Times*) represents a kind of politicization that had previously not been evident. Cusack was undoubtedly an educated man with well-established nationalist credentials. He clearly had insight into the experiences of the common man and had long made it clear that he was on their side in terms of sport and the national question.

By the time he began editing *The Celtic Times*, he was probably attending, initially as a reporter, such meetings as the 'Dublin United Trades Council and Labour League', and he appears to have consumed the aspects of socialism that were becoming more popular. This is evidenced in his possible readings of the works of the likes of Emile Zola that he advocated his own readership should address. It is also possible that his thoughts on such matters were being influenced by a 'Scottish socialist' who penned an article entitled 'Human Nature and Socialism' for Cusack's paper in May 1887.[29] Throughout 1887 Cusack argued the case of Irish (and other countries') labour, fisheries, cottage industries and the need to sustain and promote the Irish language. Cusack drew his readers' attention to housing conditions in New York and used this as a means to discuss housing in Dublin in a similar manner to James Connolly's socialist revolutionary analysis a few decades later (although Cusack's was not as informed or as statistically based): 'The condition of the tenement houses in many parts of the city of Dublin is also a public scandal and half of them ought to be razed to the ground.'[30]

Cusack never lost his enthusiasm for a more accessible and widespread education system in Ireland. In addition, he wanted a system that was appropriate to the potential of the pupil and society and reflected the national historical circumstances as conditioned by the dominant colonial system in the country. With regard to the Irish primary system of learning, Cusack argued that 'It, unfortunately, looks at things solely through the schoolmaster's spectacles – it aims at producing scholars, and scarcely troubles itself about the use that the learning the scholar receives will be to him in after life'.[31]

He also believed that education in Ireland should encompass 'mental and physical development', although his gender-restricted thoughts on this matter were reflective of the times he lived in.

> Considering the vast importance of physical training in the education of youth, no school or college should be without its gymnasium or its ball-alley and athletic grounds. In England the physical education of the pupils is carefully provided for and the result is, that when the boy becomes the man and leaves school he has plenty of stamina and vitality in him to baffle his way through life. In Ireland, physical, in conjunction with mental development is not unfortunately so well attended to: but a change must gradually be brought about by the pressure of public-opinion. The change can be wrought by the demands of parents upon the schools to which they send their children, by the influence of trustees and committees in charge of schools, and by the conditions which benefactors and founders could impose upon their gifts and bequests to education.[32]

Cusack continued too on a theme close to his heart: that of an education system that reflected a concern with Irish history. His arguments partly precipitated those put forward by Padraic Pearse, educationalist and leader of the 1916 insurgents, a generation later.

> In our opinion, the most effectual way of dealing with the question is to introduce a system of Irish historical study into out elementary schools. If this were done, we do not think it at all extravagant to assert that a universal knowledge of the history of our fathers is only a mere question of time. An end so desirable from all points of view as this deserves and demands strenuous exertions on the part of those who have the cause of the National education of the Irish people at heart. The object of this article is to aid the good work of making an effort to teach the people the history of their fathers, and, thereby, to keep alive the memory of

the brave and noble deeds of those who fought for the good old cause before them.[33]

On considering some of the British rationale behind the exclusion of Irish history from Irish schools and the belief that there were no 'impartial text-books' that could be depended upon for the proper teaching of the subject, Cusack answered that: 'we will quote the opinion of an old writer, who, on being accused of misrepresenting the conduct of England towards Ireland, wrote that "such misrepresentation would flatter the English, as *only the truth can give them uneasiness*".'[34] Likewise, although hardly revolutionary in arguing for the equality of women, and in what, over 100 years later, can be viewed as a somewhat patronizing tone, Cusack argued appreciatively that married women's traditional role in the home should not be underestimated. Under the title of 'They Never Strike', Cusack wrote that:

> There is one class of labourers who never strike and seldom complain. They get up at five o'clock in the morning, and never go back to bed until ten or eleven o'clock at night They work without ceasing the whole of that time, and receive no other emolument than food and the plainest clothing. No essays or books or poems are written in tribute to their steadfastness ... They are the housekeeping wives of the labouring men.[35]

Despite the fact that much of Cusack's newspaper was taken up by 'political' reporting, there still remained enough space to relay Gaelic Athletic news. A good deal of this news took the form of match reports and a substantial portion also reflected the legacies of previous years' arguments inside and outside of the GAA as well as against the enemies Cusack had attracted over the decades.

CUSACK AS REVOLUTIONARY

After dedicating a great deal of his life to Irish sporting culture, as well as other aspects of the 'national struggle', Michael Cusack faced much difficulty in his final years. His Academy closed and it is likely that he had to rely on the small income from his journalism, although the GAA did present him with a substantial grant. In 1890 his wife and daughter died and his other six children were forced into varying locations to be looked after. Cusack died in 1906 amidst much personal privation.

From humble rural beginnings, Michael Cusack made one of the most significant contributions to culture and sport in late nineteenth-century Ireland. Indeed, the impact of the GAA in Irish cultural and sporting life can be judged to be one of the most significant in the history of modern sport. Regardless of his personal failures, Cusack was one of Ireland's most important sports innovators. From modest roots, he became middle class in his work and in relation to many of the Dublin social circles he moved within. Nonetheless, he used his increasing social status and contacts to further not only his own goals, but also those of many of his contemporaries who lacked the energy, innovation or contacts to establish such a revolution in Irish life. Cusack's social and cultural revolution changed the rules of sport and elements of communal closure in Ireland.

Although Cronin[36] is correct to argue that the nationalistic histories of the GAA have over-dominated to the detriment of other approaches, the GAA provided a context for identity formation and re-inventing as well as a social link for armed revolution when it began seriously in 1916. Cusack's work, whether intentionally or otherwise, was crucial in preparing the ground for the revolution of Ireland during the first years of the twentieth century. At a more local level, the revival and standardization of games that lacked popularity and appeal by the last quarter of the nineteenth century revolutionized Irish rural life. This change was so profound, that it would be impossible to give a considered social or political assessment of Ireland without reference to the Gaelic Athletic Association, the body that was initiated by Michael Cusack.

NOTES

1. M. Mullen, 'Opposition, Social Closure and Sport: The Gaelic Athletic Association in the 19th Century', *Sociology of Sport*, 12 (1995), 268–89.
2. M. De Burca, *The GAA: A History of the Gaelic Athletic Association* (Dublin: Cumann Luthchleas Gael, 1980), p.5.
3. Ibid., p.6.
4. M. De Burca, *Michael Cusack and the GAA* (Dublin: Anvil, 1989), p.15.
5. Ibid., p.36.
6. *The Nation*, 28 Feb. 1891.
7. De Burca, *The GAA*, p.50.
8. Ibid., p.62.
9. *The Shamrock*, 24 Jan. 1884.
10. Mullen, 'Opposition, Social Closure and Sport', 275.
11. T.F.O. Sullivan, *Story of the GAA* (Dublin, 1916), p.7.
12. De Burca, *The GAA*, p.96.
13. M. Cronin, 'Defenders of the Nation', *Irish Political Studies*, 11 (1996), 1–19.

14. GAA Official Guide, 2000.
15. B. MacLua, *The Steadfast Rule, a history of the GAA ban* (Dublin: Press Cuchnlaiim, 1967), p.13.
16. Flanagan, 1991, p.26 in G.A. Carr, 'The Spartakiad: Its Approach and Modification from the Mass Displays of the Sokaol', *The Canadian Journal of History of Sport*, XVIII (May 1987), 87.
17. W.F. Mandle, *The GAA and Irish Nationalist Politics* (Dublin: Helm, Gill and Macmillan, 1987), p.14.
18. De Burca, *The GAA*, p.113.
19. *The Celtic Times*, 26 Feb. 1886.
20. De Burca, *The GAA*, p.120.
21. Ibid., p.122.
22. In all likelihood, his continued opposition to the GAA's proposed linking with the Amateur Athletic Association was another significant reason for his removal.
23. De Burca, *The GAA*, p.138.
24. Ibid., p.152.
25. *The Celtic Times*, 26 Feb. 1887.
26. Ibid., 5 March 1887.
27. Ibid.
28. Ibid.
29. Ibid., 7 May 1887.
30. Ibid., 30 April 1887.
31. Ibid., 9 July 1887.
32. Ibid., 14 May 1887.
33. Ibid., 9 April 1887.
34. Ibid.
35. Ibid., 2 April 1887.
36. Cronin, 'Defenders of the Nation', *passim*.

4

Missing Middle-Class Dimensions: Elementary Schools, Imperialism and Athleticism

J.A. MANGAN and COLM HICKEY

In the Victorian age, as the scope of British economic trading and political interest widened, the term imperialism was increasingly used to categorize, legitimize, justify or otherwise explain Britain's territorial expansion. However, nowadays it is a term to be used with caution. As Winifred Baumgart has observed:

> Imperialism is a vague and imprecise catchword. It is well worn like an old coin, but in contrast to a coin it has more than two sides. It is as many faceted as a crystal, but lacks the crystal's transparency and clearly defined lines ... Broadly speaking, imperialism may be defined as the domination or control of one group over another group. There are widely varying relationships involving such domination and dependence. They may be planned or unplanned, conscious, half conscious, direct or indirect, physical or psychological, open or concealed.[1]

Imperialism is also associated with value judgments. Robert Winks writes, 'With certainty the word is one of abuse, a pejorative term synonymous with economic exploitation, racial prejudice, secret diplomacy and war'.[2] However, he also argues, 'Today the word should be neutral, open to analysis, repair or deconstruction at the hands of the scholar. Broad generalisations about imperialism will be very blunt instruments for such delicate surgery.' Winks continues, in a passage of particular relevance to this study, 'The fact is that – whether Marxist or capitalist – we do not know nearly enough about the process called imperialism to be able, even yet, to arrive at more than tentative conclusions about the causes of imperial growth, the motivation of imperial leaders, or the effects of colonial administrations, either upon the colonial area or upon the imperial power.'[3] While Winks is certainly correct in drawing our attention to the fact that we know very little of the motivation of the imperial leaders and strategists, we know even less about the actual administrators and colonial settlers. As a consequence the very word imperialism, warns C.C. Eldridge, 'should be used with extreme caution. It lacks precise meaning and agreed definition. It meant different things at different times.'[4] Indeed, J.A. Mangan argues that 'whether imperialism was a form of widespread benevolence or an unmitigated evil is beside the point'.[5] Mangan endorses the views of G.H. Nadel and P. Curtis who comment that 'Such judgments belong to the individual conscience'.[6] Imperialism, then, is a reality that needs to be examined objectively.

In view of its multiplicity of meanings and usages, any attempted definition will inevitably fail to satisfy everyone. Yet, as Winks argues, 'the historian must generalise if he is not to remain an antiquarian, a grubber for small bits of string too short to use, but too long to throw away'.[7] Mangan believes that the definition provided by Nadel and Curtis, while incomplete, is perhaps the most useful. For them, imperialism is 'the extension of sovereignty or control, whether direct or indirect, political or economic, by one government, nation or society over another together with the ideas justifying or opposing this process'.[8] Such a definition lacks, for example, a consideration of imperialism as a cultural 'umbilical cord'. Nevertheless, 'This fact should not necessarily be a source of despair, irritation or criticism. Imperialism was an extraordinarily complex phenomenon. Only by acknowledging the multiple meanings attached to it, can a full appreciation of its role in British and overseas affairs – and education – be obtained.'[9] This study will use Curtis and Nadel's definition alongside Mangan's observations as the basis for comment and discussion.

Elementary education generally, and the training of teachers specifically, has received inadequate attention from historians. Furthermore, as Harold Silver has remarked, education has often been ignored by historians of ideas in Victorian society.[10] For example, Norman McCord finds space for only 12 pages dealing with all aspects of education in *British History*[11] while, with regards to imperialism, Mangan has commented that 'Most general histories of British (and English) education can be read without any realization that Britain was an imperial power in the eighteenth, nineteenth and twentieth centuries'.[12] He cites a number of well-known works on the history of education showing the paucity, or indeed absence, of any consideration of imperialism[13] and concludes that the role of education 'in the imperial scheme of things would seem to have received less attention than it merits from British general imperial and educational historians'.[14] Incidentally, it could be argued that some sports historians preoccupied with matters of domestic class still suffer from a similar self-inflicted myopia.

According to John M. MacKenzie, a number of influential British historians have undervalued the importance of imperialism as a factor in British history. He criticizes Henry Pelling who, he claims, 'argued that imperial concerns, with only one or two mild exceptions, seldom played any part in British general elections' and A.J.P. Taylor who 'created a school of "Little Englander" historians which saw imperialism as essentially an irreverence to domestic British history, a view which continues to be reflected in the writings of many historians today'.[15] Furthermore, MacKenzie believes that those historians who have written about imperialism have been concerned with 'the official mind rather than the popular psychology. Thus the centrifugal effects of imperialism have come in for much more attention than the centripetal, and a vacuum has been left in the consideration of its role in British social history.'[16]

Fortunately, with regard to education and imperialism, this is a vacuum that is gradually being filled. A number of recent works have considered the role and function of imperialism and athleticism in British culture both at home and throughout the Empire. In *The Games Ethic and Imperialism: Aspects of the Diffusion of an Ideal*,[17] Mangan considers the ways in which athleticism was introduced, often deliberately and calculatedly, into the public schools of the Empire. Britannia's sons were coaxed, cajoled, coerced or bullied into accepting and adopting two moral certitudes of the age: one of them was athleticism and another was imperialism. The latter underpinned the former allowing it to grow and flourish. The staff in these schools were 'persuasive and persistent propagators of imperialism. Headmasters, for example, espoused British imperialism with a simple-minded, single-minded fervour ... They shared a shallow complacency, attached priority and permanence to the idea of empire, were righteous in their conviction and arrogant in their ethnocentricity.'[18] They were 'forceful disseminators of persuasive propaganda effectively playing the part of "agents of hegemonic persuasion" serving the role of Gramsci's "intellectuals", spreading and legitimising dominant convictions, winning over youth and "creating unity on the contested terrain of ideology"'.[19] Full use was made of every opportunity to reinforce the message, from chapel pulpits and assembly hall podiums to fireside chats.

It is generally accepted that *The Games Ethic and Imperialism* is a major work[20] but our knowledge of the full impact of the relationship between imperialism, athleticism and education remains far from complete. Mangan anticipated this state of affairs when he wrote that he hoped 'in time, others will repair omissions, reveal fresh facets, add subtlety when required and so augment my early and exploratory efforts. Consideration of the diffusion of this influential ideology is long overdue.'[21]

Happily, Mangan's hopes are being gradually fulfilled. Historians have sought recently to illuminate what has otherwise been a dimly lit chamber of historical knowledge and to add to our understanding of the social and cultural developments of other lands.[22] Yet there are still sizeable areas of neglect. We know too little of the public elementary schools and training colleges of Britain and the British Empire. In this context it is necessary to exercise caution when reading Mangan's 1986 analysis claiming that:

> the last quarter of the nineteenth century saw a close relationship established between the system of secondary schooling, propaganda, and the concept of imperialism. It was a relationship substantially restricted to the British public school. Prior to the Balfour Education Act of 1902, and in reality for a long time after, Britain was a nation of two educational systems – the wealthy and well-developed private system of preparatory and public schools, and the poor and under-developed state system of elementary, higher elementary, and state-owned or state subsidised grammar schools.[23]

While Mangan was right to point to the close late nineteenth century relationship between the public schools and imperialism, he was perhaps in danger of underestimating the relationship between elementary education and imperialism.[24] However, his recent work indicates that this too is coming under his analytical scrutiny.[25]

Pamela Horn has recently written of the growth of the imperial ideal from 1880 to the outbreak of the Great War in 1914.[26] In her view there were a number of complementary forces driving the concept of imperialism into elementary schools. The twelfth Earl of Meath, a concerned individual propagandist, was responsible for the introduction of the Empire Day Movement in thousands of elementary schools in England and Wales. In 1907, 12,544 out of a possible 20,541 elementary schools were taking part in the movement. Meath's objectives were clear:

> In an Open Letter first published in 1905 ... Meath stressed that Empire Day promoters wished to inculcate the ideals of good citizenship. These included imperial and national patriotism, loyalty to the monarch, and obedience to authority. He associated them with the Japanese concept of *bushido*, a social and moral code taught in Japanese schools since 1867 and derived from that nation's warrior past. It stressed the importance of loyalty, patriotism and self-sacrifice.[27]

Imperialism received media coverage in the educational press. For example, in September 1900, at the time of the Boer War, an article entitled 'Should not imperialism be taught in our schools?' appeared in *The School Guardian*, the paper that represented the views of the National Society and therefore mainstream Anglican elementary schools. The contributor asserted that 'Children in the more remote parts of the country have felt a thrill as they welcomed the good news' (the relief of Mafeking). He continued, in an outburst of patronizing arrogance, that the children 'in their simple way were proud to belong to a people capable of such heroic deeds ... And if, hereafter, in these eventful days they should be called to bear arms in defence of their country they will feel that the cause is worthy of any sacrifice and spend their last breath fighting for its liberties and possessions.'[28] The message was brutally simple: indoctrinate the young with heroic tales of stirring deeds in a preparation for their own sacrifice.

Imperialistic fervour was further developed through the explicit manipulation of the school curriculum, which was 'achieved in part by the slanting of school syllabuses so as to link them with the idea of colonial expansion'.[29] This manipulation was strengthened by the introduction into the Education Code of 1890 of an 'alternative syllabus' for the upper standards of geography that placed special emphasis on the imperial link. 'It also included, for the first time, the "acquisition and growth of the colonies and foreign possessions of Great Britain" as part of the history syllabus.'[30]

This control of the curriculum was calculated. MacKenzie has drawn our attention to the ways in which history textbooks have helped shape public opinion.[31] One of the most influential historians dealing with imperialism was Sir John Robert Seeley, Regius Professor at Cambridge from 1865 to 1895. 'The great sea change which took place in the writing of popular and school history at the end of the nineteenth century owed most to him.'[32] For Seeley, history:

> was to be deliberately employed as an uplifting moral force, to stimulate exertions, and raise the morale of the nation. History should be treated as a rewarding interaction of past and present, in which imperial expansion should be seen as the moral of British history, ultimately acting as the key to the future. It was a means of uplift from the anxieties of the late nineteenth century, a route to national class and party consensus, enabling the country to escape from the social conflict and political division that seemed to be developing in the 1880s.[33]

In another consideration of Seeley's work,[34] Richard Aldridge points to the potency of Seeley's best-selling textbook *The Expansion of England*, which remained in print from 1883 until 1956. Seeley's vision of Empire 'influenced statesmen, administrators, the general public and students in universities and schools, both within Britain and within the empire as well'.[35] Seeley's thesis was that Britain's Empire was unlike any the world had ever known as it had grown up in sparsely populated areas in which little conquest or domination had taken place. The British Empire could help transform the societies of the Empire into modern ones 'by peace, good government, railways, even sanitation and Christianity'.[36] Seeley's beliefs were influential and spawned a host of acolytes. They included:

> Hugh Egerton, appointed in 1905 as the first Beit Professor of Colonial History at Oxford, and A.P. Newton, the first Rhodes Professor of Imperial History at the University of London in 1919. They, together with Sir Charles Lucas, Chairman of the Royal Colonial Institute from 1915, not only promoted the study of imperial history at university level, but also sought through an imperial studies campaign which included popular lectures, lantern slides and the promotion of Empire Day, to raise the imperial consciousness of the nation as a whole.[37]

Thus citizenship, patriotism, imperialism and militarism became the symbols of a moral imperative expressed through the medium of history teaching. Seeley enjoyed both official and popular acclaim – 80,000 copies of his book sold in the first two years of publication – and many Board of Education pronouncements endorsed his view of Britain, its Empire and the world!

Of course, as MacKenzie reminds us, it is 'very difficult to assess the effect on pupils of all this patriotic history and imperial geography'.[38] However, he directs us to some children's jotters that survive in Lancaster and the research of Stephen Humphries in the hope that an assessment will be attempted. This direction is useful; Humphries has gathered a wealth of material through interviewing people who had been educated in elementary schools.[39] Humphries' ideological standpoint and arguments, as far as athleticism is concerned, remain unconvincing[40] but he is on much firmer ground on the subject of imperialism. He suggests that imperialism was more important 'than either religion or individualism in shaping the content and organisation of school work, especially from the 1900s onwards'[41] and that working-class children were more responsive to lessons inspired by imperialism because they introduced freshness and variety into a narrow and restricted curriculum. 'Most important, however, the ideology of imperialism made a direct appeal to working-class youth because it reflected and reinforced a number of cultural traditions in particular the street gangs' concern with territorial rivalry and the assertion of masculinity.'[42]

Obviously, very few examples of pupils' work remain from this period and we have to rely on reminiscences and autobiographies such as Robert Roberts' *The Classic Slum*,[43] which recalls his schooldays in Salford in the days before the First World War. However, some schools produced their own magazines and a copy of 'The Bellenden', produced by pupils of Bellenden Higher Grade School in 1893, survives. It is appropriate to note that the magazine contains many references to imperial themes. There is, by way of illustration, an article on the history of India that is replete with negative stereotypical images of other peoples and races. Consider the following, for example:

> The great curse of India is opium which destroys hundreds of people. India is also a very productive country and Tea, Coffee and Rice are largely exported. Its wealth was discovered by a company of men who went out there under the name of the 'East India

Company' about 200 years ago. At this time the French were in India and claimed it as their rightful possession. This raised a war and for many years India was one vast battlefield. At last an officer named Clive was sent to drive a native prince called Lurajah Dowlah from his throne. This prince (who sided with the French) had actually imprisoned 126 English people in the Black hole of Calcutta, a small apartment with only two gratings to let in air. When morning came only 23 wretches were left alive ... There had not been any trouble with India until about 40 years ago when a great rioting broke out ... The Sepoys or native soldiers rose on the English everywhere, killing not only men, but women and children. At last, however, an army of men under General Sir Colin Campbell marched to the relief of Lucknow which was besieged by the Sepoys. After a desperate resistance the Sepoys gave way and the British marched into the town in triumph. After this the mutiny was crushed and all went well with India since.[44]

Such xenophobic writing should not surprise. It served only to underline a belief in the British as civilized, benevolent conquerors and the Indians as brutal, dastardly cowards. Elsewhere in the magazine is a crudely drawn cartoon of 'The Smart Foreman'. The illustration shows an Irish worker with a jutting ape-like jaw, dressed in ill-fitting clothes and a bowler hat that is too small for him, asking if there is any chance of work. The foreman replies: 'Well I see there is a man here that hasn't come this morning. If he does not come before breakfast time I'll send him home and give you the job!'[45] The imagery is unflattering and the dialogue derogatory. Simplistic racial images were evidently promoted at the school: the Indians as savages, the Irish as stupid and the British as brave, honourable and, above all, *decent*.

A further element in the promotion of imperialism in public elementary schools was militarism.[46] As early as 1871, the Elementary School Code allowed for military drill as an activity which, it was believed, promoted discipline. In the early twentieth century rampant militarism gave rise to a deep concern about the state of the nation's health and fitness, which in turn had an influence on elementary schools.[47] Peter McIntosh has observed that the Boer War:

> quite apart from its influence on the general educational trend, had a direct impact on physical education. The initial defeats on the field and the rejection of large numbers of recruits at home focused

attention on the physical state of the population of Britain. In Manchester in 1899, out of 11,000 volunteering for enlistment 8,000 were rejected outright and only 1,200 were accepted as fit in all respects.[48]

One of the responses to the problems highlighted by the war was the publication by the Board of Education of a *Model Course of Physical Training for use in the Upper Departments of Public Elementary Schools.* The course was drawn-up in consultation with the War Office and was based on army training methods. McIntosh believes that 'physical training in public elementary schools was given a distinctly military bias'[49] as a result of this development. This bias was strengthened by the fact that schools wishing to extend their physical training were directed to the *Infantry Training 1902* booklet produced by the War Office. The press reaction was favourable. *The Times* supported compulsory military training 'in order to lay the foundations of a military spirit in the nation'.[50] The response from the teaching profession, however, was more critical. McIntosh draws attention to T.J. Macnamara, a Liberal MP, who formerly had been a student at Borough Road College from 1880 to 1882, a teacher, editor of *The Schoolmaster* and President of the National Union of Teachers. McIntosh writes that Macnamara claimed that 'the model course was part of a systemised endeavour to take advantage of the current cry for physical training by making the elementary schools and the Board of Education as sort of antechamber of the War Office'.[51] The same year saw the establishment of the *Interdepartmental Committee on Physical Deterioration* which was set up in response to a letter written to *The Lancet* by Sir Lauder Brunton, Physician at St. Bartholomew's Hospital. One of the committee's recommendations was a call for continuation classes in drill which were to be compulsory for school-leavers. 'By these means,' the committee reasoned, and 'without recourse being had to any suggestion of compulsory military service, the male adolescent population might undergo a species of training that would befit them to bear arms with very little supplementary discipline'.[52] In McIntosh's words, 'as far as physical training went, [the *Report*] was a plea for military training without introducing conscription'.[53] However, such blatant manipulation of the curriculum proved too controversial. An inter-departmental committee reported that the 1902 syllabus was fundamentally flawed, as it had not been drawn up with children in mind, and proposed instead a new syllabus that diluted some of the more militaristic elements of the 1902 course.

Predictably, there was a range of attitudes to the whole question of the extent of military influence in the nation's elementary schools. Opposition came from three main groups. The first group was those with a professional interest in the development of physical education as a curricular subject. McIntosh points to the work of the Ling Physical Education Association which drew up a memorial to the Board of Education containing the signatures of 1,408 professionals arguing that the Model Course was unsuitable as it had been designed for men rather than boys. The second group was those who were much more reluctant to see this development on grounds of conscience. Prominent among this group were the Quakers who were very influential then in the non-conformist community and who rejected any incipient militarism in state schools. In a significant memorandum, they stated that while 'we felt no objection to the inclusion of compulsory drill into the Day School Code ... the system of drill and exercises ... should be determined by gymnastic value alone'. The memorandum concluded witheringly that 'A knowledge of the elements of infantry drill is quite outside the proper scope of such training'.[54] In a stinging rebuke of militarism, totally refuting notions that the country should be actively engaged in preparations for war, the Quakers argued that:

> the greatness of a nation rests, not upon a manhood trained in the use of arms, but upon the strong, free and true hearts of citizens who live in the peaceable spirit of brotherhood, we most earnestly desire to protect our schools from that atmosphere and military training.[55]

The memorandum was published in *The Educational Record*, the journal of the British and Foreign School Society, the leading advocate of non-denominational education. A third group objected on the grounds of class. The fact that the peripatetic instructors of drill were non-commissioned officers (NCOs) hindered the scheme's effectiveness and acceptance since, as McIntosh believes:

> N.C.O.s in those days were ill-educated and when they were projected into schools 'drill' came to be regarded as well beneath the dignity of the trained schoolteacher, and the whole crusade to convince people that the education of a child's body needed a

scientific basis, which should be applied by educated and trained teachers suffered unnecessarily.[56]

It would appear that militarism failed to become an *explicit* part of the curriculum of 20,000 elementary schools of England and Wales. It generated too much controversy. Criticized as it was by so many proponents of alternative systems, ridiculed by the National Union of Teachers as being inefficient, rejected by teachers fearful of being pushed down the ladder of social acceptance, denounced in a plethora of meeting houses, chapels and churches, and resented by those who did not share the typical late Victorian and Edwardian vision of Empire, militarism was replaced by a broader view of physical education, one in which games playing and a diluted version of athleticism was increasingly able to emerge. Ironically, these activities were supposed to promote qualities essential for imperial success. Thus it could be argued that militarism survived in a rather more subtle form than hitherto.

As we have seen, the impetus for this development came with the expansion of athleticism in the public schools, universities and teacher training colleges. However, such progress as there was took place unofficially. This is not to underestimate the scale and scope of athleticism in elementary education, but rather to acknowledge that it was not formally recognized until the 1906 alteration of the elementary school code to allow for the playing of organized games in school time. According to McIntosh[57] the official responsible for this alteration was A.P. Graves, an His Majesty's Inspector (HMI) who had written an article in the *Contemporary Review* in 1904 calling for the introduction of games in school time. At a subsequent meeting with the President of the Board of Education, Augustine Birrell, Graves presented his case with such conviction that within a few days a change in the code had been drafted. Such a heroic account is consonant with McIntosh's interpretation of history; he is like a mid-Victorian landscape painter whose pictures are direct and clear; yet somehow lack the subtlety of the later impressionists. While he is no doubt correct in his sequencing of events he underestimates powerful forces at play in society that made the events he describes possible.

Three main arguments put forward by the Board of Education for the introduction of organized games into the curriculum clearly show the influence of athleticism on official government thinking. First, games were seen to have played a large part in developing the physique and moulding the character of pupils in public schools and in those grammar schools modelled on public schools. Second, it was alleged that both the health and the *esprit de corps* of pupils had improved in elementary schools where games had taken place outside of normal school hours. Third, it was argued that the spirit of discipline, corporate life and fair play was acquired largely through games. Such arguments are of enormous significance. It is evident that the philosophy, if not the facilities, that underpinned athleticism – the belief in games for building physique and character, developing *esprit de corps*, promoting discipline and fair play as well as strengthening the corporate life of the school – were seen to be as desirable for the children of the working classes as they were to the children of the bourgeois, the upper classes and the aristocracy. It is wrong, therefore, to see the alteration of the code in 1906 as marking a sea change in educational thinking, or indeed practice, concerning elementary schools. Rather the alteration was a somewhat belated endorsement of current practice with the careful caveat that no funds were available for its implementation at elementary school level!

Thus, while militarism in its crudest manifestations struggled for acceptance as part of the ethos of the elementary school, the same cannot be said for either athleticism or imperialism. According to the distinguished historian of education, Brian Simon, imperialism had a dual effect on education. On the one hand, there was the demand for more technological and scientific education in response to greater competition from other nations who had developed their industries at a later date than Britain and threatened to outstrip British industry. On the other hand, there was a captive market to support older industries that conversely operated to dampen enthusiasm for scientific education. In Simon's view, this produced 'a demand for more education of the kind provided in the traditional grammar school, and in relation to the schools ... it was the latter demand that clearly predominated'.[58] He further believes that such a development 'dovetailed in with the prevailing desire to curb rather than encourage the extension of educational facilities of the kind that appealed to and were made use of by the working-class.'[59]

The growth of imperialism 'gave rise to the concept of a united nation, led by men of vigour, and comprising a healthy, energetic people capable of extending and exploiting Britain's rule'.[60] Quoting Lord Roseberry, leader of the Liberal Imperialists, who once declared that 'An empire such as ours requires as its first condition an imperial race, a race vigorous and industrous and intrepid. In the rookeries and slums that still survive an imperial race cannot be reared',[61] Simon sees an important link between imperialist expansion and social reform. He believes that 'There was, then, a new interest in promoting health and welfare of the people on the part of those not hitherto concerned with this matter, inspired by an outlook directly opposed to that of the socialists working to the same end'.[62]

By 1900 there was a greater acceptance of the need for greater state intervention in the lives of the population. Liberal views on individualism and *laissez-faire*, once held so passionately by men such as Cobden and Bright, were now seen as outmoded. Imperialism was seen as the means for social betterment in an attempt to foster an imperial race. Belief in imperialism was widespread enough to encompass a broad variety of political opinions.

> Men of various political shades – Conservatives, Liberal Unionists and Liberal Imperialists such as Roseberry, Haldane, Asquith and Grey – lined up behind the imperialist banner, to be followed by such Labour leaders as Blatchford, and, discreetly but no less firmly, by the leading Fabians, Bernard Shaw and Sidney Webb.[63]

We can thus place Pamela Horn's comment that 'Concern over Britain's initial failures in the Boer War and the subsequent pressure for military victory undoubtedly strengthened patriotic sentiment in the early twentieth century'[64] in context. Alongside this patriotic sentiment was a practical attempt by both the Liberals and the Conservatives to improve the health and fitness of the nation's children. Whereas the Conservatives stressed a readiness for a potential 'call to arms' and attempted to give physical training a militaristic flavour (1900–02), the Liberals developed a markedly less overtly militaristic form of physical training and established the Education (Provision of Meals) Act in 1906 and a compulsory School Medical Service in 1907. In addition, McKenna's Education (Administrative Provisions) Act of 1908 empowered Local Education Authorities 'to make such arrangements as may be sanctioned by the board of Education for attending to the health and physical condition of children in Public Elementary Schools'. Therefore, both athleticism and imperialism were served by developments in the elementary school system.

W.J. Wilson, of Oldridge Road Board School, and J.G. Timms, of Rosendale Road Board School, were two London elementary school headmasters who fully subscribed to the ideology of athleticism.[65] They were equally ardent imperialists and, for example, when the London School Board granted a week's holiday to celebrate Queen Victoria's Diamond Jubilee, Wilson recorded in his Log Book: 'At 4 p.m. I assembled all the boys and the staff in the playground. There we all sang verses one and three of the national anthem and gave three cheers for the Queen.'[66] When Queen Victoria died in 1901 he noted:

> On Wednesday January 23rd the school was closed at 2.35 by an order from the Board as a mark of respect to the memory of our late Queen who died in the evening of January 22nd ... every class had references made to them of the incalculable loss sustained by our country. I lost no opportunity of driving home some of the many lessons the boys could learn from the life of our late Queen.[67]

Sadly for us, Wilson does not record what he felt those lessons were!

Notions of patriotism, loyalty and imperialism were also clearly evident at Rosendale Road School. The success of the Earl of Meath's Empire Day Movement had resulted in the celebration of the day by the Education Committee of the London County Council which had replaced the School Board for London in 1904. The Council 'decided that Empire Day should be celebrated in the public elementary schools of the Council with a view to awakening in the minds of the children attending the schools a true sense of the responsibilities attaching to their inheritance as children of the empire, and the close family tie which exists amongst all British subjects'.[68] It is highly unlikely, however, that these colonial subjects would have wanted to be part of the imperial family if they were aware of the way some of their British brothers and sisters were evidently taught!

For a week before Empire Day, the children at Rosendale Road were given lessons about the Empire and extra singing lessons. On the day itself, the school followed the Empire Day programme. The children met in the hall where they were given a talk about the Empire, sang the national anthem and 'other patriotic songs' and recited the Recessional Hymn before listening to a speech on patriotism by the Chairman of the School Managers. This was followed, wrote Timms:

> by an assembly of the whole school in the playground where the national anthem was again given and the National Flag saluted and

cheers given most heartily to His Majesty, King Edward. A march past then took place, the children proceeding in fours between a line of boys carrying the Union Jack. The marching and saluting of the large flag held by two infant scholars and two senior scholars, the youngest and the eldest in the school completed the celebration. Numbers of parents were present and witnessed the proceedings.[69]

Such behaviour was common: 'Most schools joining in the celebrations seem broadly to have followed that pattern'.[70] At Sandhurst School in Catford, South East London, for example, celebrations followed the same format of national songs, speeches and saluting of the flag followed by a half-day holiday.[71]

The imperial ideal was reinforced in elementary schools in three key ways: through the efforts of concerned propagandists and proselytizers; through the manipulation of the curriculum; and through ritualistic and symbolic acts. From the evidence available, this triple assault on the hearts and minds of the nation's school children was concerted and seems to have been successful. It influenced the children both inside and outside the school by corporate and individual approaches. The influence inside the school was through the control of the curriculum; the influence outside was through popular fiction.

> Many educators consciously turned to fiction to solve problems of the [imperial] ideology. Fiction had the advantage of a much more nearly universal availability: anyone educated to the level of basic literacy was accessible through a story. It was also private, enabling the direct messages inculcating imperial ambitions and national and racial pride to be received without a blush; and apparently optional, so that no one need feel repelled by being forced to undergo indoctrination.[72]

As the concept of imperialism became crystallized among administrators and educationalists it entered the training colleges and universities and was diffused downwards to the elementary schools by young, enthusiastic, newly qualified teachers. Imperialism was also successful due to the proliferation of influential magazines, periodicals and novels for both adults and children bought and read by the public at large.

The potency and importance of such imperial fiction should not be underestimated. Mangan has suggested a tendency on the part of historians to ignore the fictional characters of imperial stories. At first sight this may appear to be entirely appropriate as such characters are not part of an empirically valid field. However, Mangan suggests that such neglect is a matter of regret and needs to be remedied: 'It is a basic task of the social historian to consider, certainly within the framework of the education system, the relationship of these culturally constructed stereotypes to their time, to the conventions they symbolize, and to the purposes they serve.'[73] Abdul R. Jan Mohammed argues that 'There is a need to see the ideological functions of colonialist fiction, not just from the perspective of its intended and actual effects on the native, but also as a window through we can look at the imperialist's politics, culture and ideology'.[74] Indeed, 'imperial ideology and fiction formed a symbiotic relationship: ideology shaped the fiction and the fiction, in turn, formed the ideology'.[75]

Imperialism sustained a powerful moral imperative which was transmitted through education. Elementary schools were increasingly influenced by the philosophy of imperialism which in turn created a colonial curriculum which was 'a means of establishing and perpetuating political inequalities. If hegemony in society is the power to shape group consciousness: in education it is the power to define "Valued knowledge" which in turn, also shapes collective awareness.'[76] A firm belief in athleticism marched alongside the imperial ideal in training colleges and elementary schools as an assumed moral ally.

NOTES

1. W. Baumgart, *Imperialism: The Idea and Reality of British and French Colonial Expansion 1880–1914* (Oxford: Oxford University Press, 1982), p.1.
2. R.W. Winks (ed.), *British Imperialism: God, Gold Glory* (New York: Holt, Rinehart and Winston, 1963), p.1.
3. Ibid., pp.2–3.
4. C.C. Eldridge, *Victorian Imperialism* (London: Hodder and Stoughton, 1978), p.3.
5. J.A. Mangan (ed.), *Benefits Bestowed? Education and British Imperialism* (Manchester: Manchester University Press, 1988), p.2.
6. G.H. Nadel and P. Curtis, *Imperialism and Colonialism* (London: Macmillan, 1966), p.25.
7. Winks, *British Imperialism*, p.2.
8. Nadel and Curtis, *Imperialism and Colonialism*, p.vii.
9. Mangan, *Benefits Bestowed?*, p.2.
10. H. Silver, *Education as History* (London: Methuen, 1983), p.23.
11. N. McCord, *British History 1815–1906* (Oxford: Oxford University Press), 1991.
12. Mangan, *Benefits Bestowed?*, pp.3–4.
13. For example, H.C. Barnard, *A History of English Education from 1760* (London: University of London Press, 2nd Edn. 1961), fails to mention imperialism; J.A. Adamson, *English Education 1798–1902* (Cambridge: Cambridge University Press, 1930), mentions internationalism, but not imperialism; and S.J. Curtis, *History of Education in Great Britain* (London: University Tutorial Press, 7th Edn. 1967) refers only to the Imperial College of Science and Technology.

Other texts that ignore the topic include H.C. Dent, *1870–1970: A Century of Growth in English Education* (London: Longman, 1970); S.J. Curtis and M.E.A. Boultwood, *An Introductory History of English Education Since 1800* (London: University Tutorial Press, 4th Edn. 1970); K. Evans, *The Development and Structure of the English Education System* (London: University of London Press, 1975); W.H.G. Armytage, *Four Hundred Years of English Education* (London: Cambridge University Press, 2nd Edn. 1970); and R. Aldrich, *An Introduction to the History of Education* (London: Hodder and Stoughton, 1992).

14. Mangan, *Benefits Bestowed?*, p.4.
15. John MacKenzie (ed.), *Imperialism and Popular Culture* (Manchester: Manchester University Press, 1986), p.2.
16. Ibid.
17. J.A. Mangan, *The Games Ethic and Imperialism: Aspects of the Diffusion of an Ideal* (London: Viking, Penguin, 1986; London and Portland, OR: Frank Cass, 1998), *passim*.
18. J.A. Mangan, '"The Grit of our Forefathers": Invented Traditions, Propaganda and Imperialism' in MacKenzie, *Imperialism and Popular Culture*, p.118.
19. Ibid.
20. The evidence is extensive but see, by way of example, the Foreword by Sheldon Rothblatt and the Introduction by Jeffrey Richards to J.A. Mangan, *Athleticism in the Victorian and Edwardian Public School* (London and Portland, OR: Frank Cass, 2000). See also Mike Huggins, 'Second-Class Citizens? English Middle-Class Culture and Sport 1850–1910: A Reconsideration', *The International Journal of the History of Sport*, 17, 1 (2000), 1–35.
21. Mangan, *The Games Ethic and Imperialism*, p.19.
22. See, for example, J.A. Mangan (ed.), *Pleasure, Profit, Proselytism: British Culture at Home and Abroad 1700–1914* (London and Portland, OR: Frank Cass, 1988); idem (ed.), *Making Imperial Mentalities: Socialisation and British Imperialism* (Manchester: Manchester University Press, 1990); W. Baker and J.A. Mangan (eds.), *Sport in Africa: Essays in Social History* (London: Africana, Holmes and Meir, 1987); and J.A. Mangan and J. Walvin (eds.), *Manliness and Morality: Middle Class Masculinity in Britain and America 1800–1940* (Manchester: Manchester University Press, 1987).
23. Mangan, 'The Grit of our Forefathers', pp.115–16.
24. See, for example, J.A. Mangan and Colm Hickey, 'A Pioneer of the Proletariat: Bert Milnes and the Games Cult in New Zealand' in J.A. Mangan and John Nauright (eds.), *Sport in Australasian Society* (London and Portland, OR: Frank Cass, 2000), pp.31–48.
25. For a comprehensive review of developments in the history of athleticism in the last 20 years, see 'Regression and Progression: Introduction to the New Edition' of J.A. Mangan, *Athleticism in the Victorian and Edwardian Public School* (London and Portland, OR: Frank Cass, 2000), pp.xxvii–lvi. See also J.A. Mangan and Colm Hickey, 'Globalisation, the Games Ethic and Imperialism: Further Aspects of the Diffusion of an Ideal' in J.A. Mangan (ed.), *Europe, Sport, World: Shaping Global Societies* (London and Portland, OR: Frank Cass, 2001), pp.105–31.
26. P. Horn, 'English Elementary Education and the Growth of the Imperial Ideal: 1880–1914' in Mangan, *Benefits Bestowed?*, pp.39–55.
27. Ibid., p.49.
28. 'Should not Imperialism be Taught in Our Schools?', *The School Guardian*, XXV, 1288 (1 Sept. 1900).
29. Horn, 'English Elementary Education', p.40.
30. Ibid., p.41.
31. J.M. MacKenzie, *Propaganda and Empire: The Manipulation of British Public Opinion 1880–1960* (Manchester: Manchester University Press, 1984). See also V. Chancellor, *History For Their Masters* (Bath: Adams and Dart, 1970).
32. MacKenzie, *Propaganda and Empire*, p.179.
33. Ibid.
34. R. Aldrich, 'Imperialism in the Study and Teaching of History' in Mangan, *Benefits Bestowed?*, pp.24–38.
35. Ibid., p.25.
36. Ibid., p.26.
37. Ibid., p.27.

38. MacKenzie, *Propaganda and Empire*, p.193.
39. S. Humphries, '"Hurrah for England", Schooling and the Working Class in Bristol 1870–1914', *Southern History*, 1 (1979), 171–207.
40. See, for example, J.A. Mangan and Colm Hickey, 'English Elementary Education Revisited and Revised: Drill and Athleticism in Tandem' in J.A. Mangan (ed.), *Sport in Europe: Politics, Class, Gender* (London and Portland, OR: Frank Cass, 1998), pp.63–92.
41. Humphries, 'Hurrah for England', 182.
42. S. Humphries, *Hooligans or Rebels? An Oral History of Working-Class Childhood and Youth 1889–1939* (Oxford: Basil Blackwell, 1981), p.41.
43. R. Roberts, *The Classic Slum: Salford Life in the First Quarter of the Century* (Manchester: Manchester University Press, 1971).
44. 'The Bellenden', June 1893, Greater London Record Office, EO/DIV7/BEL/LB1.
45. Ibid.
46. Unfortunately, there has been rather incomplete and ill-informed comment on militarism in late Victorian and later English society by, at least, one sports historian. For a response to the sports historian concerned, which sets the issue in perspective and corrects a tendency to somewhat simplistic analysis, see 'Regression and Progression: Introduction to the New Edition' of Mangan, *Athleticism*, pp.xl–xli.
47. See Horn, 'English Elementary Education', pp.51–2.
48. P.C. McIntosh, *P. E. In England since 1800* (London: Bell, 1968), p.148.
49. Ibid.
50. *Times*, 24 Feb. 1903.
51. McIntosh, *P. E. In England*, p.150.
52. 'Report of Interdepartmental Committee on Physical Deterioration 1904', Minute 2430, para.380 in McIntosh, *P. E. In England*, pp.153–4.
53. Ibid.
54. *The Educational Record*, xvi (14 June 1903), 302.
55. Ibid., 303–4.
56. McIntosh, *P. E. In England*, p.149.
57. Ibid., p.147.
58. Brian Simon, *Education and the Labour Movement* (London: Lawrence and Wishart, 1965), p.168.
59. Ibid.
60. Ibid.
61. Ibid., p.169.
62. Ibid.
63. Ibid.
64. Horn, 'English Elementary Education', p.51.
65. Mangan and Hickey, 'English Elementary Education Revisited and Revised', pp.75–89.
66. Oldridge Road Log Book, 4 June 1897, EO/DIV8/OLD/LB/1.
67. Ibid., 24 Jan. 1901.
68. Annual Report of the London County Council, Education Committee Minutes, 15 April 1908, 1419.
69. Rosendale Road Log Book, 27 May 1907, EO/DIV8/ROS/LB/1.
70. Horn, 'English Elementary Education', p.49.
71. Sandhurst Road Log Book, 24 May 1907, EO/DIV6/SAN/LB/1.
72. J.S. Bratton, 'Of England, Home and Duty: The Image of England in Victorian and Edwardian Juvenile Fiction' in Mackenzie, *Propaganda and Empire*, p.76. See also P. Duane, 'Boys literature and the Idea of Empire, 1870–1914', *Victorian Studies*, 24, 1 (1980), 105–23; and L. James, 'Tom Brown's Imperial Sons', *Victorian Studies*, 17, 1 (1973), 89–99.
73. J.A. Mangan, 'Images for Confident Control: Stereotypes in Imperial Discourse' in J.A. Mangan, (ed.), *The Imperial Curriculum: Racial Images and Education in the British Colonial Experience* (London: Routledge, 1993), p.9.
74. Abdul R. Jan Mohammed in Mangan, 'Images for Confident Control', p.9.
75. Mangan, 'Images for Confident Control', p.10.
76. Ibid., p.16.

5

Mostly Middle-Class Cycling Heroes: The *Fin de Siècle* Commercial Obsession with Speed, Distance and Records

ANDREW RITCHIE and RÜDIGER RABENSTEIN

The 1890s were the heyday of sprinting on the track, one of the most important disciplines in bicycle-racing. One thousand metres, equivalent to several laps of typical tracks, was the most common distance covered in these races and the winner was the first rider to cross the finishing line. The racing took place in an enclosed arena, a track or velodrome, around which the spectators were gathered. Tactics, surprise acceleration and a pure burst of speed over the last few hundred metres were the decisive factors and the actual time of the entire race was relatively unimportant. Records were not set in this discipline, but the racing was attractive to an audience which appreciated the subtleties of tactics between a number of evenly matched opponents and the thrill of a close, fast finish. The sport had emerged in the 1870s and 1880s, the era of the high-wheel bicycle. By the 1890s, the 'match race', between two or three rivals, represented the 'classic' form of sprinting. The most famous amateur and professional sprinters regularly attracted huge crowds and were in international demand. The American Arthur Zimmerman, for example, who won the first officially sanctioned world amateur sprint championship in Chicago in 1893, won 110 races in just one year; the German champion Willy Arend collected 137 'Grand Prix' sprinting prizes between 1896 and 1903 and the African-American sprinter Major Taylor raced in France, Belgium, Italy and Germany between 1901 and 1904, where the spectators were amazed by his performances.[1]

However, as the sport of cycling broadened and diversified in the later 1890s and in the first years of the new century, these 'aristocrats' of track cycling lost some of their earlier pre-eminence. With the introduction of the diamond-framed 'safety' bicycle and the pneumatic tyre, the high-wheel bicycle quickly became outmoded. Through the 1890s, the years of the first consumer bicycle 'boom', bicycle-racing underwent a dramatic character shift as improvements in equipment and pneumatic tyre technology made racing bicycles faster and lighter. The first generation of purpose-built banked and surfaced velodromes, which effectively corralled a paying audience, provided the arenas and economic basis for well-advertised events and undoubtedly contributed greatly to the remarkable increase in speeds achieved in the 1890s.[2]

Gas and electric light made evening racing possible. There was increased interest in setting speed records over short distances and in amassing greater mileages in long distance races. An understanding of pacing techniques, in which the cyclist was helped to overcome wind-resistance, increased both speeds and distances achieved. Extreme long-distance events and performances on both road and track became increasingly popular. Crucially, all these changes took place in the context of, and were initiated by, the increasing commercialization and professionalization of the sport. Bicycle and tyre manufacturers and newspaper proprietors became involved in the sponsorship of bicycle-racing, which was quickly understood to be an ideal circulation-boosting publicity vehicle. The bicycle-racing which emerged in the 1890s – new, exciting and fashionably technological – had many of the characteristics of modern sport.[3]

This tendency to promote endurance events and realize extraordinary performances occurred in many different sports. At a time of supreme confidence, improvements in athletic achievement appeared to be limitless. The suggestion, by extension, was that human capacity was without limits.[4] Technology, exemplified by the bicycle and the newly emerging internal combustion engine, served to enhance human physical capacity. Examples of this trend were long-distance pedestrian events and six-day bicycle races.[5] At the first official world cycling championships in Chicago in 1893, the two events contested were a 1,000m sprint and a paced 100km event. During the first Olympic Games, in Athens in 1896, the first modern marathon-running race took place;[6] six-day roller-skating races took place in the United States[7] and the *Berliner Illustrirte Zeitung* reported a six-day race in New York City for the 'Road-skuller', a rowing machine on wheels.[8] During 1892–93, between Vienna and Berlin, long-distance races were promoted for cyclists, marchers on foot and riders on horseback and long-distance events remained fashionable for many years after that.[9]

A new kind of bicycle-racing emerged, with a 'gigantic' character. The demands of this racing placed extraordinary, hitherto unexplored, stresses and strains on the athletes. Four kinds of cycling events typified this new kind of racing: long-distance place-to-place races on the road; stage-races on the road; 'stayer' (paced) races on the track; and six–day races on the track. Long-distance road-races, several of which survive as the 'Classics' of the modern professional cycling calendar, were organized over distances of as much as 500 or 600kms in the 1890s, often between major European cities with Paris and Berlin featuring prominently.[10] The first major international long-distance race from Bordeaux to Paris, held in 1891, was praised by the German Cyclists' Association as an example of 'the bicycle race of the future' and as 'the beginning of a new era for our sport'.[11] A new facet of the sport was introduced and emphasized: physiological and psychological stresses lasting for more than a 24–hour period. During the 1890s, 'stayer' (paced) races on cycling tracks were prolonged and extended from the 100km distance competed for in the first world championships of 1893 to six-, 12-, 24-, 48- and even 72-hour races. Soon, an uninterrupted 1,000kms became a record-breaking objective. Six-day races on the track and stage-races on the road were introduced as further new extreme racing disciplines.

The urge to break records had been an important part of top-level bicycle-racing since its beginnings, posing an athletic challenge to leading riders throughout the high-wheeler period of the 1870s and 1880s. Racing was crucial in stimulating the early technological development of the bicycle and instrumental in defining the high-wheeler as the favoured, most appropriate and efficient kind of bicycle for sport. The quest was to improve times on certain roads, usually well-known place-to-place routes, and to achieve better, faster performances on the track. Two distances were the consistent objective of riders and equipment manufacturers: the easily understood races over one mile (or one km in continental Europe) and over one hour. The first rider to cover 20 miles in an hour, H.L. Cortis, was extravagantly praised.[12] A detailed recording of best times on record became a regular feature of cycling periodicals and yearbooks from the mid-1870s on, with comparative evaluations of British, French and American athletes. Timing procedures and standards for world records were vigorously debated in often chauvinistic exchanges in the press. Thus, faster times and greater distances continued to be the constant objective in all four of the 'gigantic' disciplines up until 1914.

These extreme cycling disciplines have survived for more than a century, although the physical strains have now, in general, been reduced.

Distances of more than 300kms-a-day are now unusual in single-day professional races, as are stages lasting more than 250kms in professional stage-races. 'Stayer' races now usually last a maximum of one hour and the actual daily racing time in six-day races is between six and 12 hours. However, the major stage-races, the Tour de France, the Giro d'Italia and the Vuelta d'Espana are still of 'gigantic' proportions, as is the recently introduced 'Race Across America', in which about 3,000 miles is now regularly covered by the fastest contenders in about eight or nine days.

LONG-DISTANCE RACES ON THE ROAD

Long-distance cycling races were preceded by long-distance competitions for horse-riding, running and marching, where the objective was to cover a significant distance in as short a time as possible. The late 1880s and early 1890s saw the introduction of long-distance road-races in which rest-breaks were not scheduled and 'gigantic' demands were made on the cyclists, who were required to race over distances of 500 or 600kms.[13] Eating, resting, sleeping, coping with mechanical problems, organizing support, were all part of the athletic challenge. Road conditions were bad and bicycle equipment unreliable, it took more than 24-hours to reach the destination and made it inevitable that the fastest athletes would have to ride for at least one night without sleeping.

The earliest international long-distance road-race was the 577km Bordeaux–Paris, first promoted in 1891, which continued as one of the 'Classic' road-races until it was removed from the calendar after 1987. The daily newspapers and the cycling press took a great deal of interest in this new event. Four British athletes with extensive experience of long-distance racing won the first four places, surprising the opposition by riding right through the night.[14] Bordeaux–Paris continued to be heavily publicized throughout the 1890s; in fact, rival newspapers *Le Velo* and *L'Auto* both promoted an event over this route in 1902. The patriotic feelings of the French were so hurt by the British domination of the 1891 race that a second, even longer, race, without British participation, was organized by Pierre Giffard, editor of *Le Petit Journal*, a leading French daily.[15] More than 200 cyclists participated in the 1,196km Paris–Brest–Paris race which was won by the French rider Charles Terront, who rode for three days without sleep.[16]

Paris–Brest–Paris, an unprecedented distance, demonstrated the human capacity for endurance and what it was possible to accomplish on a bicycle. The public could barely comprehend the extraordinary performances of the winners of this race. At the turning point in Brest, the crowd watched with astonishment as Jiel-Laval, in the lead, ate a few pears and some beef soup, took a bath and then got back on his bicycle and set off for Paris. Never before had an athlete ridden 600kms in 33 hours without sleeping – lack of sleep became the decisive factor in the race. With a lead of more than an hour, Jiel-Laval took a sleeping break at Guingamp on the return journey while his manager, De Civry, posted guards to give warning of second-placed Charles Terront's arrival. But spies reported Jiel-Laval's rest to Duncan, Terront's manager, who instructed his rider to make a detour through the backstreets of the town, bypassing Jiel-Laval's hotel. Jiel-Laval awoke to learn that his opponent was two hours ahead of him. But Terront was totally exhausted; he fell off his bicycle and was only persuaded to continue after much urging by his brother. Ultimately, Terront arrived in Paris eight hours ahead of Jiel-Laval after riding more or less non-stop for 71 hours and 16 minutes.[17]

Paris is still the most prominent starting and finishing point for road-race cycling classics, including the now well-established triumphant entry of the Tour de France onto the Champs Elysees for the final sprint and victory celebrations.

The Germans also originated some long-distance races in the 1890s although most of these were later discontinued.[18] In 1891, a Leipzig–Berlin–Leipzig–Dresden–Leipzig race was held over 500kms. Other races included Magdeburg–Cologne (1892, 457kms), Mannheim–Cologne (1892, 250kms) and Basel–Cleve (1893, 620kms).[19] The long-distance race from Vienna to Berlin organized in 1893 created favourable publicity for the sport of cycling and for the utility and practicality of the bicycle in general.[20] This Vienna–Berlin race was inspired by a long-distance ride by soldiers on horseback along the same route in 1892. The fastest horsemen covered the 580kms in 71 hours and 35 minutes.[21] Racing cyclists were intrigued by the possibility of measuring themselves against the military horsemen and demonstrating the viability of the bicycle for military purposes. Joseph Fischer was the first competitor to reach Berlin, recording a time of 31 hours and 22 minutes.[22] He started the race on 29 June 1893 at 6.10 a.m. and finished on 30 June at 1.10 p.m.[23] Storms during the night had created bad conditions for the cyclists. From a field of 117 German and Austrian amateurs, 38 arrived in Berlin within the prescribed 50 hours.[24]

The event was a success for the sport of cycling and the German bicycle industry experienced a strong surge in sales. Several of the many European bicycle road-races initiated in the 1890s still take place on a regular basis, for example, Liège–Bastogne–Liège (first held in 1890), Paris–Roubaix (since 1896), Paris–Tours (since 1896) and 'Rund um Berlin' (since 1896, now held as an 'open' race). The oldest amateur classic still held in Germany is the 'Rund um Köln' race, first held in 1908. The enduring attraction of events of this kind is proved by the fact that new long-distance races continued to be introduced until 1914 and those still held annually include the Tour of Lombardy (1905), Paris–Brussels (1907), Milan–San Remo (1907), the Tour of Flanders (1913) and the Championship of Zurich (1914).

STAGE-RACES ON THE ROAD

The concept of the stage-race can be traced to a military origin, or to long over-land coach journeys, where a stage was a designated location serving as a night-time stop for marching troops or travellers, allowing rest and the provision of fresh supplies. A stage-race in cycling is a race held over several days, consisting of separate daily races with an aggregate finishing order. The idea of stage-racing for cyclists originated specifically in the long-distance rides undertaken by individual pioneers during the 1870s and 1880s. In the mid-1890s, there was a kind of 'touring fever' in which cyclists undertook semi-competitive, long-distance rides of a touring and record-setting nature which were frequently reported in the press.[25]

In 1875, in a very early, pioneering demonstration of the potential of the bicycle, two French riders, Laumaillé and Richard, rode the nearly 700 miles from Paris to Vienna in 12 days – with better weather, they might have made it in nine or ten days.[26] In Britain, the record for the 'End-to-End' ride (approximately 900 miles from Land's End to John o'Groats) was frequently contested although G.P. Mills' 1894 record of three days five hours and 49 minutes stood for many years. Twelve- and 24-hour rides on public roads were frequently organized by British clubs over continually increasing distances. Following his success in Paris–Brest–Paris, Charles Terront, supported by his manager H.O. Duncan, the Paris agent of the Rudge bicycle company, and sponsored by Rudge and the Clincher tyre company, rode from St. Petersburg to Paris in 14 days – a distance of more than 3,000kms. In his account of the event,

Duncan wrote that the ride had introduced the bicycle to a country 'where it is almost completely unknown', that 'man is still a powerful motor' and that 'the word "distance" is only a word'.[27] Robert Louis Jefferson made bicycle trips to Constantinople, to Moscow and back, and a 6,574-mile ride from London to Irkutsk which was reported in *Across Siberia on a Bicycle*.[28] In 1895, Theophile Joyeux and Jean Corre undertook rival tours of the whole of France; Joyeux covered 4,500kms at the rate of 225kms a day, while Corre rode 5,000kms in 25 days, at the rate of 200kms a day.[29] One of the companions who persuaded Joyeux to persist in his 'tour' was Henri Desgrange[30] and it was Desgrange who laid the foundations of the Tour de France in 1903.

The first Tour de France was a calculated publicity vehicle for Desgrange's sporting newspaper, *L'Auto*, which was engaged in a circulation and prestige battle with its rival, Pierre Giffard's *Le Velo*. The race, which consisted of six huge stages and visited Lyon, Marseille, Toulouse, Bordeaux and Nantes before finishing in Paris, was intended to stimulate newspaper sales both in Paris and the provincial stage-cities by keeping the readers in suspense as to the eventual outcome and entertaining them with dramatic stories of the rivalries and ordeals of the 'stars'. It was a well-orchestrated media event, centred in a capital city obsessed with sport, art and modern technology. In *L'Auto*, one of the first Tour's managers, Geo Lefèvre, reported from Bordeaux: 'I saw more than 10,000 peasants looking at their copies of *L'Auto* out in the fields today. Surely this proves that the Tour de France is the finest sporting creation of the century.'[31] In this first event, 2,428kms were ridden in six daily stages, with rest days in between. The winner, Maurice Garin, took a total of 93 hours and 29 minutes to cover the entire course. The average time spent in the saddle during the six days of actual competition was 15 hours and 35 minutes – the 60 competitors were on the road every racing day until nightfall.[32] In the following years, the route, the overall distance and the number of stages changed annually. The demands made on the cyclists were gradually increased, the stages became shorter but there were more of them, with the result that actual competition occurred nearly every day for three weeks. The Tour quickly became, and still remains, the world's most demanding sporting event. The maximum number of stages appeared in 1927 – 24 stages – and the longest distance covered, in 1926, was 5,745kms.[33]

The familiar story of what happened to Eugène Christophe during the 1913 Tour de France illustrates the additional severity of the regulations. Repairs to bicycles had to be done by the cyclists themselves. Christophe had gained a 20-minute lead on the favourite, Thys, at the Tourmalet mountain (2,114 metres high), but his bicycle suffered a broken fork during the descent. Christophe carried his bicycle 14kms to the next village smithy, repaired it himself and reached the day's finish with a four-hour deficit. The Tour jury imposed an additional penalty of 15-minutes because a boy had operated the bellows in the smithy, which qualified as 'outside help'. Despite all this, Christophe managed to finish seventh overall. Such exploits helped to create the myth of the Tour de France as heroes engaged in super-human, 'gigantic' endeavour.[34]

However, strict regulations could not always guarantee honest results in stage and long-distance races. Because of the difficulty of supervising the riders during races, they were sometimes able to cheat by clinging to the rear of motorcars or travelling part of the route by train. Rival bicycle manufacturers and managers not only organized support for their own riders but also arranged unpleasant surprises for other competitors, such as sabotaged bicycle frames or nails on the road.[35] Some competitors even resorted to road blockades and physical attacks on rivals, as in the 1904 race when passions ran high between rival teams supported by manufacturers La Française and Peugeot and alleged infractions of the regulations caused the Union Vélocipédique Française to disqualify the first four riders, including winner Maurice Garin, against the wishes of Henri Desgrange, promoter of the event.

The idea of holding stage-races lasting as long as several weeks became very popular, both as athletic events and as publicity vehicles. Exceptional strength and stamina were demanded from the participants, while spectators and the public were provided with thrills and sensations widely reported in the press and the heroic stature of rival contenders was carefully constructed. The successful formula of the Tour de France stimulated other European countries to introduce their own national tours and thus the Tour of Belgium (1908), the Tour of Holland (1909), the Tour of Italy (1909), the Tour of Germany (1911) and the Tour of Catalonia (1911) were all established before the First World War.[36]

'STAYER' RACES

The phenomenon of 'pacing' – a word used to describe the aerodynamic and athletic process of one cyclist benefiting by riding in the slipstream of another cyclist, a multi-cycle or a motor-driven pacing machine – made it possible for cyclists to ride faster and further and gave rise to the systematic organization of pacing to achieve record speeds and distances. From very early on – even in the high-wheel days – it was understood that overcoming wind-resistance was a crucial factor in bicycle-racing and, to this day, it continues to be the most fundamental technical and tactical aspect of cycling.[37]

The expression 'pace-making' was probably initially derived from horse-racing, where the 'pacemaker' ensured the desired speed. From the early 1890s, human-power, that is other cyclists taking turns, or tandems, triplets and even quadruplets and quintuplets (four- and five-man bicycles), was deployed to pace an individual rider. Photographs from the mid-1890s show small armies of cyclists hired by Dunlop and other manufacturers to pace their sponsored riders to new records. The record-breaking rider required skill and precise technique in switching from a tiring pacing crew to a new, fresh crew. In October 1896, an article headlined 'The Art of Pacemaking, which has Revolutionized Cycling Contests' explained that:

> The pacing of the racing cyclist is at the present day not only a veritable science, but an extensively followed profession. Hundreds of men are earning their living as pacemakers; and the exhibitions of speed and skill given week by week on our faster tracks prove to what a high pitch of perfection the art has now been carried ... In most paced races, the riders go at absolutely top speed all through. Those who can 'stick the pace' set them alone have a chance of success; the man who 'cracks' is out of it ... With the increased speeds attained by the flying multi-cycle there comes a cry for more and still more 'banking' on the bends of the tracks.[38]

Spaldings Official Bicycle Guide for 1898 commented that:

> racing as an art has been practiced more regularly this year than ever before [making] the season just closed the most successful that has ever been known ... The star feature was the middle-distance match racing made popular in this country by the arrival of Jimmy Michael, a diminutive midget, who has revolutionized our races and set the racing and scientific world a-guessing ... Nothing of a sporting nature can begin to compare with a middle distance paced bicycle race for excitement and interest.[39]

Pace-making machines driven by electricity and steam-power followed, but were unreliable. Smooth, consistent power was essential. From 1897 onwards, specially designed one- and two-seater, gasoline-powered motorbikes proved most effective for pacing on velodromes and underwent a rapid technological development. Late in 1896 record-breaker S.F. Edge told one reporter:

> Next year will see mechanical pacemakers at work ... Later on will come the most startling innovation, mechanical pacemakers fitted with wind-shields. The man going against time will ride, drawn along in the vacuum created behind the shield that is being propelled round the track before him.[40]

These mechanical pacing-machines were systematically used to attack short-distance records, but the most impressive gains were realized over longer distances where the prolonged advantage of efficient pacing was most dramatic. Photographs from the period show pacing-machines partially enclosed in leather farings to reduce wind-resistance and pacers sitting bolt upright to create the maximum shelter for their rider. The track races which used such pace-makers were called 'stayer' races because they were contested over longer distances and demanded stamina or 'staying' power. These machines, built with more powerful engines to achieve higher speeds, were a crucial link between the bicycle industry and the emerging motorcycle, automobile and aviation technologies.[41]

Such races were a dramatic new departure of a modern, machine age, a public demonstration of power and technological accomplishment. They were noisy, smelly and dangerous races held within the confines of a banked, cement velodrome where the spectators surrounded the action. Historians of sport have paid little critical attention to the significance and implications of this type of 'gigantic' bicycle-racing, popular at the turn of the century, in which man and machine collaborated in sporting endeavour. Suffice it to say that the spectacle of a racing cyclist 'towed' at high speed for hours on end by a huge, petrol-driven pacing-machine was a most potent and hazardous expression of technological and athletic modernity.

Speeds of as much as 100km/h, and the consequent high risks involved, characterized this new discipline as 'gigantic' and these 'stayer' races experienced a surge of spectatorship in France, Germany and the United States before the First World War, the element of danger adding drama to the sport. The tracks, although steeply banked, were not ideally suited to high speeds; serious accidents were frequent and numerous cyclists and several pace-makers died.[42] A terrible accident in Berlin in 1909, in which a pacing-machine left the Friedenau track and exploded in the crowd killing nine spectators and injuring 52, brought about strict new regulations in Germany.[43]

The 'gigantism' manifested itself not only in high speeds, but also in the ever-increasing distances involved. Between 1886 and 1894, the record for a paced 24-hour ride on English roads increased from 227 miles (G.P. Mills) to 376 miles (C.C. Fontaine).[44] While long-distance races on the track had formerly been held over a maximum of 100kms, from the mid-1890s they were extended to a period of 24-hours. In the early 1890s, mammoth distances were covered using human-powered pacing. The first 'Cuca Cocoa Cup' 24-hour race was held on the Herne Hill Track in London in 1892 when amateur Frank Shorland covered nearly 414 miles, increasing his total to 460 miles in 1894.[45] The first 'Bol d'Or' was held in Paris in 1894, the winner, Constant Huret, covering 756kms in 24-hours behind tandem-pace, maintaining a speed of 30.706km/h for the entire distance! The 'Bol d'Or' subsequently became the pre-eminent annual, 24-hour, paced endurance race, in which world record distances of 800 and 900kms (behind human-powered tandem pace) and, in 1899, 1,020kms (behind a petrol-driven tandem) were accomplished in front of huge crowds.[46]

The dramatic increase in the speed potential of the bicycle is shown in a chart published in 1909 in the French newspaper *L'Auto*, which showed the kilometre distances covered in breaking the one-hour world record (and thus also the average speed) between 1876 and 1909 (see Appendix). On the high-wheel bicycle, 32.707kms had been covered in the hour by 1884. On the solid-tyred safety bicycle, the distance increased to 36.605kms by 1891. After 1892, with the introduction of the pneumatic tyre and increasingly efficient pacing, the speed shot up quickly: 46.711km/h was realized by 1895; 64.673km/h by 1900; 89.904km/h by 1905, and by the date of publication of the list, Paul Guignard had established a record of 101.623km/h, riding behind a powerful pacing-machine on the Milbertshofen velodrome in Munich.[47]

As the 'stayer' races enjoyed their heyday in the two decades preceding the First World War, the excessive stresses of such endurance races were often criticized. The *Berliner Illustrirte Zeitung* protested against a 24-hour race in Berlin in 1898, but was afterwards compelled to admit that 'the race has not completely justified our fears ... nobody fell off his bicycle from exhaustion, nobody suffered delusions and nobody went crazy'.[48] Even in the face of public criticism, this dramatic kind of bicycle-racing continued to attract huge crowds and provided an ideal opportunity for advertisers to market their products.

SIX-DAY RACES

Six-day races were indoor track-races lasting for six days, either for individual participants or a team of two riders. The limitation of six days for an athletic event was imposed historically because of Sunday observance laws in England; racing could begin at 12.01 a.m. on Monday, but had to finish at midnight on Saturday. Six-day bicycle-racing was pioneered in the English Midlands in 1876 as a feat of endurance for a single rider, inspired by the similar, long-distance pedestrian events which were popular at the time. At the Molyneux Grounds, Wolverhampton, 'in the presence of 10,000 spectators, Camille Thuillet, of Paris, the champion bicyclist of France, ended his task of riding 650 miles in six consecutive days, a feat never before accomplished'. At the same time, Frank White, of Wolverhampton, rode 600 miles in six days at the Walsall Arboretum. It therefore made perfect sense for them to race against each other.[49] Six-day bicycle races, on the high-wheel bicycle, came to prominence in a series of indoor events promoted at the Agricultural Hall, London, by entrepreneur Harry Etherington in 1878 and 1879. These races were widely reported in the press. In the 'Long-distance Championship of the World', from 1–6 September 1879, George Waller, from Newcastle, covered the extraordinary total of 1,404 miles. *American Bicycling Journal* reported that the race 'proved from beginning to end to be of the most absorbing interest to the immense crowds of spectators'. On the fifth day, Waller rode from 6 a.m. to 12 midnight without a single stop or dismount and covered 220 miles, 'a performance which speaks volumes both for the endurance of the rider and the perfection of the machine which he bestrode'.[50]

Etherington also introduced six-day bicycle-racing to America in 1879. These early six-day races were literally 24-hour-a-day, 'gigantic' competitions, where sleep had to be snatched at the risk of slipping in the standings, whereas later races were held over six days with agreed rest-periods, but with at least 12 hours a day of actual racing. Six-day races continued to be promoted through the 1880s as genuine athletic spectacles and as an entertaining and lucrative box-office attraction. In 1885, the *Deutsche Illustrirte Zeitung* commented that 'simple competitions in the different sport disciplines don't seem to satisfy the English and the Americans any longer; now the competitions in walking, bicycle riding and ice skating, etc., are being extended to six days'.[51] Two six-day races were held consecutively at the Royal Aquarium: a long-distance walking competition with 12 'pedestrians' and a 'bicycle tournament', on the 160 metre track with eight hours of racing a day, which was won by Birt from Northampton after completing a total of 630.5 miles.[52]

The first of a series of annual six-day races, ridden without formal breaks, took place at Madison Square Garden in New York City in 1891, many of the riders were imported from among the experienced professionals from the north of England and Scotland. In 1892, riders competed for a $1,000 first prize. In December 1896, 40 cyclists from the United States and Great Britain competed, one of whom was the teenager Major Taylor who later became American and World sprint champion.[53] The race proved to be such a popular success that another was held in 1897; Charlie Miller took first place with a total of 3,300kms.[54] Miller established a considerable lead and could therefore afford seven hours of sleep in these six days, which meant that he spent 137 hours on his bicycle. With these exceptional performances, a typically exploitative type of promotion began; including sensational press accounts designed to attract the crowds. Some newspapers reported that 'the cyclists went crazy because of the strains, and they climbed up the columns of the hall, ate leaves or behaved like lunatics'. Among the press comments were reasoned medical objections to the staging of such stressful athletic events. In 1898, urged on by crafty promoters, Miller got married in his racing jersey in the velodrome.[55]

In these six-day races for individual participants, the fastest competitors might develop a substantial lead (several hundred miles was possible) that was almost impossible for lower-placed riders to recover on the small tracks; at the end there was very little suspense or tension in the racing. Hence, the New York race at Madison Square Garden in 1899 was raced with a team of two riders, only one of whom was on the track at a time, thus creating a faster, more exciting competition. The 1899 race was won by Charlie Miller and George Waller with a joint total of 4,400kms. Even though the six-day 'fever' spread throughout the United States from then on, the first modern race in Europe did not take place until 1909. The race was staged in Berlin and was a great success. German promoters had first shown an interest when the German Walter Rütt was victorious in New York in 1907 and 1909.[56] Although the German press protested against the 'mistreatment' of the riders, the trend was unstoppable.[57] Further six-day races were held in the German cities of Kiel, Bremen, Dresden, Hamburg, Mainz and Frankfurt before the neighbouring countries, Belgium (Brussels, 1912) and France (Paris, 1913) followed. Other six-day races were held in Hanover (Germany), in the United States, Canada and Australia before the First World War.[58]

A number of reasons can be advanced to explain the popularity of six-day races as a permanent feature of turn-of-the-century bicycle-racing and the fascination which has endured to the present day. They provided a long and large box-office catchment and pitted competitors against each other in a small arena, with a circus-like ambience. But most crucially, the spectators witnessed incredible physical and psychological performances by the cyclists. The proximity of the audience to their idols and the intense feeling of sharing their suffering, accidents and injuries added intensity to the atmosphere of the small indoor tracks. As the riders strove to gain time and win special evening prizes offered by the promoters, spectators filled the cheap seats after a day's work to cheer on the exhausted riders in their marathon ordeal.

The four extreme racing disciplines described here shared a 'gigantic' character or nature. A parallel development within these disciplines could be seen internationally, although the chronological sequence of events differed from country to country. In England, Germany and France, long-distance road-races first occurred in the early 1890s and were followed by the extreme 'stayer' races around the mid-1890s. Six-day races were not introduced in Germany until 1909 and stage-races until 1911, but in France, the Tour de France stage-race, first held in 1903, preceded the first six-day race by ten years. It should be emphasized that in no other sport did a machine enlarge and expand human capacity to the extent that the bicycle did. The bicycle enabled an intensification, a maximization of human athletic effort and allowed previously unimagined, 'gigantic', physical feats to be accomplished.

PROFESSIONALIZATION AND COMMERCIALIZATION

These 'gigantic' cycling disciplines not only put intensive athletic demands on the cyclists, but also changed their way of life, their incomes and their social status. So it is appropriate to examine here the nature of the relationship between 'gigantism' and its compulsion to break records on the one hand and the growing professionalization and commercialization of the sport on the other.

Professionalism – racing for cash prizes – was intrinsic to bicycle-racing from the beginning of the sport in the late 1860s.[59] A winner riding a particular maker's machine provided a *de facto* endorsement of that product. Amateur clubs were formed as a reaction to the perceived moral undesirability of professionalism. Professionalism was already well established in other sports before the emergence of the first professional cyclists, the high-wheel sprinters. Kaufmann points to the construction and promotion of racing tracks as one of the principle factors which led to the later growth of professionalism in cycling and this seems to be an essentially accurate explanation.[60] Promoters, backed by the advertising revenue of bicycle and tyre manufacturers, were a key ingredient. They booked riders and were able to charge an admission fee for track events, which led the cyclists – the main actors in the racing drama – to demand their share to compete on a regular basis.[61] By the early 1890s, extensive advertising of bicycles and bicycle accessories was occurring as the bicycle boomed and a sophisticated retail distribution system was established for this major consumer product. British, American, German and French cyclists, hired by bicycle and tyre manufacturers, found themselves in demand and were able to channel their athletic ability into a well-paid career in the service of the bicycle industry. According to journalist and historian Fredy Budzinski, 'The propaganda of action had a stronger impact than any of the claims made on paper about the quality of bicycles, and the German industry acted quickly and willingly to use this new promotional technique'; as did the bicycle industry world-wide.[62]

By 1895, obvious changes in the sport had been brought about by the strong movement towards professionalization. C. Rintelen, writing in 1895, maintained that 'It is thanks to the professionalization in cycling brought about and sustained by the industry that we see today the enormous cycling achievements which have contributed so greatly to the popularity of cycling and of the sport of cycling'.[63] Here, it is claimed that it was the bicycle industry which made professionalization possible and in turn made the raised level of performances possible. This is partly true, but this interpretation does not fully explain the complexity of the situation. There was certainly a strong tendency for the best amateurs to get sucked into professionalism and certainly professional cyclists could better adjust to the immense demands of the sport, but there were also amateurs who participated successfully in 'gigantic' races.[64] Another explanation would be to suggest that, at an expansive technological moment in society, there was an urge to push the limits of what was humanly possible in sport and it was inevitable that such physically demanding and stressful work could, on a permanent basis, best be done by full-time specialists.

In fact, a complex web of economic connections and dependencies existed between 'gigantism', the role of the bicycle industry and the professionalization and popularization of the sport of cycling. A further crucial component in the marketing and consumption of professional cycling was the press, which showed an intense interest in the incredible accomplishments achieved, its reporting being sometimes euphoric and sometimes critical. Advances in the sport were reported either as fascinating or threatening and repulsive and the heavy press coverage helped to contribute to the popularization of professional cycling, which played a dominating role within the sport from the mid-1890s.[65] In 1899, the German Cyclists' Association listed 452 professional cyclists among its members. *Spaldings Bicycle Guide* reported in 1898 that 'it is estimated that there are in the United States 1,000 professional racers'. A year later, Albert Mott, the chairman of the racing board of the League of American Wheelmen, reported that 'there are 621 professionals registered and over 20,000 wheelmen engaged in racing either as professionals or amateurs'.[66]

It was not just the official, licensed professionals who took advantage of the financial opportunities. So-called 'maker's amateurs' found ways to turn their prizes into cash and to be compensated for their expenses and their equipment; they were licensed to compete as amateurs but functioned in most other ways as professionals. This trend towards the commercialization of even the amateur sport put the cycling associations in a predicament; 'amateurs' were frequently suspended for taking money or racing against professionals. Perhaps in no other sport was there such a consistent history of disputes and controversy on the amateur/professional question as within cycling. Among the prizes that American world champion Arthur Zimmerman is reported to have won as an amateur were: 35 diamond pins, rings and brooches; 15 bicycles; 12 silver services; six grandfather clocks; eight pocket watches; seven medals; one piano; two tankards; a building site; 12 bronze figures; a

FIGURE 5.1

An illustration by outstanding advertising and journalistic artist, George Moore, captured the spirit of bicycle racing on British roads in the 1890s, a conspicuous activity which attracted increasing opposition from the general public and from those within cycling who saw it as creating a negative impression of the sport (*Cycling*, 23 May 1891).

SUPPLEMENT TO "CYCLING," MAY 23rd, 1891.

ROAD-RIDERS OF 1890.
No. 4.

EDMUND DANGERFIELD,

Winner of both the 100 Miles Open Scratch Road Races, held last year, by the Bath Road and North Road Cycling Clubs.

FIGURE 5.2

Long-distance, place-to-place road racing was popular and expansive in France in the 1890s, when the foundations of the modern 'classics' of cycling were laid. This picture shows the start of the first Bordeaux–Paris race in May 1891, where British road-riders showed themselves as decisively superior to their French opponents, surprising them by riding non-stop through the night (Ritchie Collection).

FIGURE 5.3

Long-distance racing, with its attendant record-breaking and hitherto unprecedented feats of endurance, was seen as an ideal vehicle for the selling of bicycles and cycling accessories to the consuming public. Especially prominent was advertising by the pneumatic tyre companies, whose recently introduced products were competing intensely for a share of the marketplace (*Wheeling*, 22 June 1892).

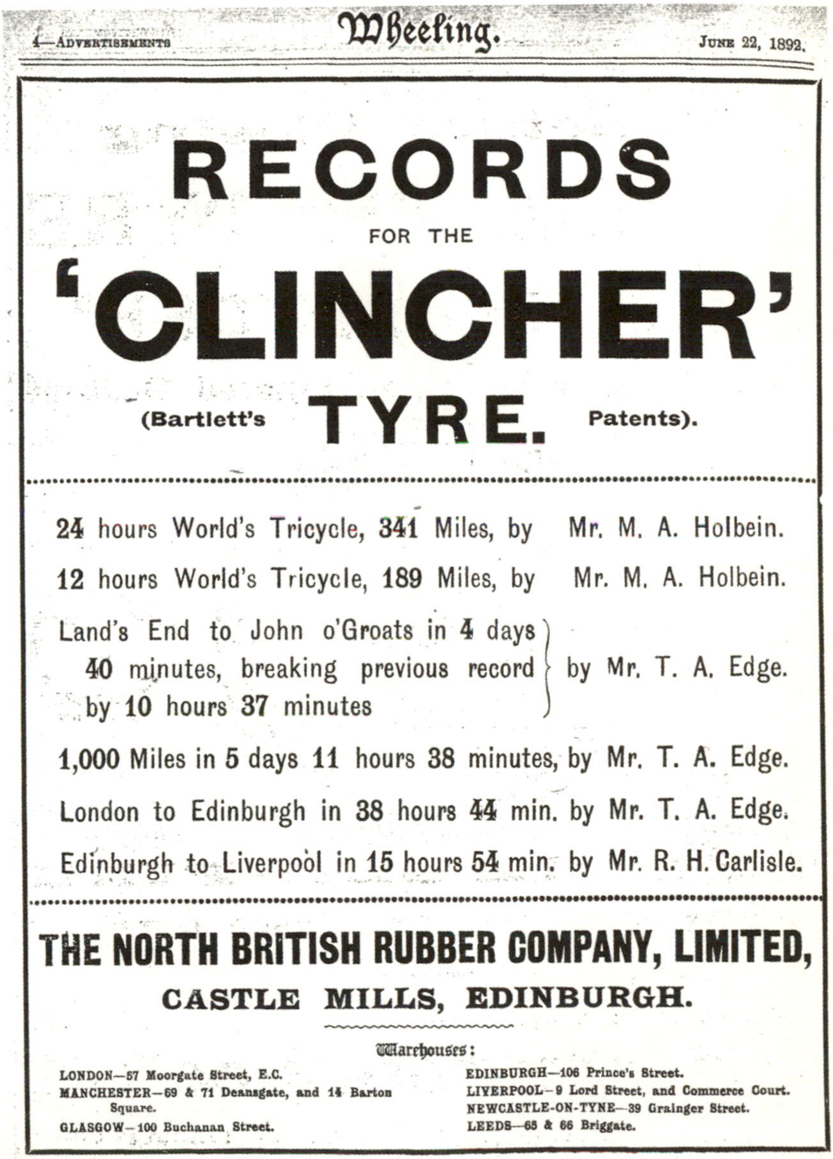

4—ADVERTISEMENTS Wheeling. JUNE 22, 1892.

RECORDS

FOR THE

'CLINCHER'

(Bartlett's **TYRE.** Patents).

24 hours World's Tricycle, 341 Miles, by Mr. M. A. Holbein.

12 hours World's Tricycle, 189 Miles, by Mr. M. A. Holbein.

Land's End to John o'Groats in 4 days 40 minutes, breaking previous record by 10 hours 37 minutes } by Mr. T. A. Edge.

1,000 Miles in 5 days 11 hours 38 minutes, by Mr. T. A. Edge.

London to Edinburgh in 38 hours 44 min. by Mr. T. A. Edge.

Edinburgh to Liverpool in 15 hours 54 min. by Mr. R. H. Carlisle.

THE NORTH BRITISH RUBBER COMPANY, LIMITED,

CASTLE MILLS, EDINBURGH.

Warehouses:

LONDON—57 Moorgate Street, E.C.
MANCHESTER—69 & 71 Deansgate, and 14 Barton Square.
GLASGOW—100 Buchanan Street.
EDINBURGH—106 Prince's Street.
LIVERPOOL—9 Lord Street, and Commerce Court.
NEWCASTLE-ON-TYNE—39 Grainger Street.
LEEDS—65 & 66 Briggate.

FIGURE 5.4

Individual athletic heroes, capable of 'gigantic' feats of speed and endurance, were created by the bicycle racing boom of the mid-1890s. One such was Charles Terront, famous winner of the 1,200 km Paris–Brest–Paris road race in 1891, and of a 1,000km track race against Corre in Paris in 1893 (*Le Véloce-Sport*, 16 March 1893).

FIGURE 5.5

As the principles of 'pacing' were increasingly understood and applied, individual riders were assisted to previously unheard of speeds behind teams of riders on four- or five-man bicycles. Riders switched from team to team to maintain a high speed, a highly technical manoeuvre. Teams were expensively maintained by leading manufacturers, in this case the Dunlop company, whose riders are seen here with record-breaker J. Platts-Betts at Herne Hill, London, in about 1897 (Ritchie Collection).

FIGURE 5.6

Super-endurance long-distance bicycle rides were also undertaken, and made popular in published accounts such as Robert L. Jefferson's *Awheel to Moscow and Back*, published in 1895 (Ritchie Collection).

FIGURE 5.7

The first Tour de France, held in 1903 and won by Maurice Garin, was a potent modern expression of national pride, sporting endurance and the technical accomplishments of French bicycle manufacturers. Garin covered the six daily stages, a total of 2,428km, in 94 hours 33 minutes, at an average speed of more than 25km/h, spending an average of more than 15 hours each day in the saddle (Ritchie Collection).

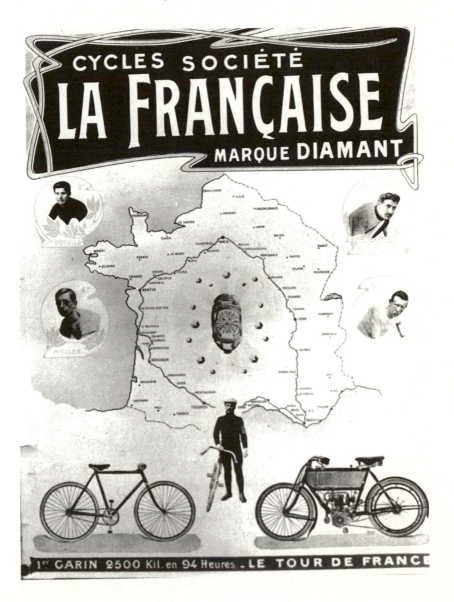

wardrobe; two carriages, one toilet case; a suit; a suitcase; a travelling bag; a gun and many bicycle tyres – worth a total of over $11,000.[67] After he had won three British amateur championships in 1892 riding a Raleigh bicycle presented to him by Frank Bowden, the chairman of the Raleigh company, in 1893 Zimmerman was declared professional by the National Cyclists Union, excluding him from amateur competition in England, but not from winning the world amateur sprint championship in Chicago the same year. Zimmerman actually turned professional in 1894, enjoyed a brief, two-year international career and was always spoken of with awe.[68]

A top professional's income was far greater than the amount that Zimmerman was able to earn as an amateur. Exact incomes are difficult to estimate since athletes earned money from a variety of sources, but the high earning potential of professional cyclists can be outlined. In 1900, Major Taylor was offered $10,000 to race in Europe for three months. In 1905, the world's best 'stayers' received 2–3,000 German marks as first prize in a major race.[69] On German tracks, world champion 'stayer' Thaddeus Robl earned 26,430 marks in 1903, 39,500 marks in 1904, 27,450 marks in 1905 and 49,250 marks in 1906. Between 1895 and 1905, Robl earned a total of 200,000 marks at home and abroad, four times more than any other German 'stayer'. By comparison, on German tracks German sprinter Willy Arend earned 10,822 marks in 1903, only 5,655 marks in 1904 and 4,620 marks in 1905, emphasizing the increasing popularity of 'stayer' races over sprinting in Germany. However, as a sprinter, Arend still made a lot of money outside Germany; between 1895 and 1905 he earned a total of 125,918 marks, his compatriot sprinter Walter Rütt earned 23,964 marks at home and abroad in 1905.

However, these were the best-paid cyclists in their disciplines and most others made a great deal less. In a list of 66 professional cyclists (both 'stayers' and sprinters) showing total earnings on German tracks between 1896 and 1903, only four earned more than 30,000 marks, four more than 20,000 marks, 22 more than 10,000 marks and the rest less than 10,000 marks.[70] World-class sprinters Ellegaard and Major Taylor reportedly had an annual income of about 100,000 marks at the turn of the century.[71] Contemporaries judged the highest professional cyclists' incomes to be equivalent to those of Cabinet Ministers.[72] The total value of prizes awarded continued to increase, for example, in Germany between 1901 and 1907 from 99,956 marks to 1,101,803 marks, which was an 11 times increase.[73] A middle-level British professional, not employed by a bicycle manufacturer, told a reporter in 1896 that from 1893–95, he had made more than £700 annually and that in 1896 he expected to make £1,200: 'I am paid from the company whose tyre I ride, by the rim-makers, by the machine manufacturers, the people who supply the saddle, and I have just made a contract to use a certain make of shoe.'[74] In the United States, *Spaldings Official Bicycle Guide* agreed that 'it would be hard indeed to estimate the amount of money won in prizes and salary by the average racing man, but it is fair to estimate that their winnings averaged $100 for each first, $75 for each second and $50 for each third, to which must be added their salary, as nearly all the professional riders are employed by makers of bicycles and their accessories'.[75] This growing commercialization was recognized and criticized at the time, in 1907 *Bühne und Sport* commented: 'The heyday of the sport was in the 1890s, whereas today business pushes itself too much to the fore'.[76]

In summary, the strong trend towards professionalization and commercialization, more and more apparent from about 1895 on, and the 'gigantism' in cycling complemented each other. The sensational performances by cyclists in the extreme disciplines – endurance racing on the road, stage-racing, 'stayer' racing and six-day racing – were generously rewarded by their sponsors, a network of manufacturing and press interests, and by the general public who paid to see them race.

'GIGANTISM' AND THE PURSUIT OF RECORDS AS A SOCIAL PHENOMENON

In cycling, there was a strong early interest in breaking records, as evidenced by the large number of record lists which were published in the cycling journals from the 1880s on. 'Gigantism' and the pursuit of records were phenomena which could be seen in the fields of both sports and technology, especially around the turn of the century. Both can be seen as fundamental expressions of an industrialized society in which high qualitative and quantitative achievements were the objective of any enterprise. Such efforts and aspirations were evident, for example, in the building of the Eiffel Tower (1885–89), the undertaking of record-setting attempts in cars, motorcycles, motor-boats and aeroplanes as well as in the building of ever-larger warships and passenger steamers, to mention just a few examples. Record-setting Atlantic Ocean crossings to win the 'Blue Ribbon' were widely publicized and culminated in the hubris of the Titanic disaster.[77] The trend extended to amusement parks as well: huge Ferris wheels between 62 and 110 metres high were erected in London, Chicago, Vienna and Paris between 1884 and 1900. The first skyscrapers also date from the 1880s. Thus, bicycle-racing as a sport was in accord with the contemporary trends and the spirit of the times; there was a belief in absolute progress and the feasibility of everything that man tried to achieve by means of technology and the natural sciences. We can safely assert that 'gigantism' in sport was another manifestation of 'modernism' in society.

An article published in *Scientific American* in 1899 explored the phenomenon of the obsession with breaking records, and offered the following explanation of current developments:

> The craze for 'breaking the record', whether it be on the train, the steamship, or the wheel, is prompted by something more than the mere love of the spectacular; for the world recognizes that every new performance is a further breaking away from that universal stagnation in which all matter lay before its present evolution began – a stagnation which it is the constant effort of our modern arts and sciences to overcome.[78]

A public euphoria with every new technological development and a desire to sweep away perceived barriers surely contributed to the flood of athletic records. The press and the public demanded records and gigantic achievements and wanted to witness them, so the cyclists were driven to make superhuman efforts, to struggle and to suffer. The first cyclists to achieve major feats were often surprised to find they were capable of such performances, for example, Charles Terront and Jiel-Laval's three-day, 1,200km, Paris–Brest–Paris ride in 1891.[79]

This new professionalized quality of sport, characterized by the principle objectives of extreme achievements and record-breaking, appeared earlier and more prominently in bicycle-racing than in other sports. The fact was that bicycle-racing was a technologically-based sport and the bicycle industry contributed significantly to racing trends. The urge towards record-breaking, characterized by professionalism, commercialization and 'gigantic' endurance events, led not only to excessive forms of competition, but also to the formation of a new consciousness and awareness. In 1898, Planck described the shift in consciousness which he saw expressed through cycling:

The real sportsman does not care any more about naturalness of movement, or about beauty and dignity of appearance. The marvelous neck where the full chin contrasts with the finely curved line, is stretched out like an ugly goose's gullet, the upper part of the body is rolled up to look like a hedgehog, the legs compulsively working away at the pedals, in this way the cyclist is whizzing along, a 'god on his machine'. It doesn't matter that the legs and feet work in a way that is exactly the opposite of natural; that the muscles of the heart and lungs, strained to the maximum inside the compacted chest, finally fail and cause severe diseases of the heart and lungs, as long as the opponent is beaten by a fifth of a second! Because a victory has to be won, man becomes part of the machine ... All hail to the record! We don't give a damn about man! Nor do we give a damn whether human nobility can be seen in this expression of power or when on other occasions – perhaps even to our liking – we recognize the ape in man.[80]

Even insiders within the sport fought against the excesses described above. Paul von Salvisberg, under the headline 'Human torture', referred in 1897 to the 'nonsense of Six Day races' and reported that a bill had been introduced in the State of Illinois proposing to limit the legal daily maximum amount of racing to 12 hours.[81] In 1898, the *Monatsschrift für das Turnwesen* (*Turning Monthly*), which espoused the ideal of a many-faceted, general physical education and was the mouthpiece for the German Gymnastics Association, quoted several newspapers which reported the deplorable physical condition of the cyclists at the end of a 72-hour race in Paris.[82] Examples were cited of cyclists being taken to hospital and driven almost insane in long-distance races and the demand for an 'Association for the Protection of Humans' was voiced. Even before the first six-day race in Berlin was held, the *Sport-Album der Rad-Welt* for 1908/09 severely criticized contests of this kind. The six-day race was seen as 'a lucrative speculation which encourages the basest instincts of the masses who watch with brutal insensitivity as half-dead people try to chase their best friends to death' rather than as a sports event.[83]

The criticism of independent, cultural critics was similarly severe but more comprehensive. Eduard Bertz condemned the 'greed for speed' and professionalism and dependence on the industry as 'degenerate'.[84] Professor Boruttau's writings were equally critical; he saw the professional cyclist as a modern 'gladiator' who sacrificed his health and life 'to thrill a brutalized public' and to satisfy 'the commercial interests of the bicycle industry'. This criticism applied in particular to endurance races such as the '6–days–24–hour races: in addition to the huge stress of the events themselves, there is the extreme risk which can be seen in the numerous fatal accidents that have occurred in such events, forming a blot on our culture'.[85] In his own way the surrealist Alfred Jarry, using utopian fables, also denounced commercialization and doping among bicycle–racers.[86]

In spite of emotional criticisms such as these, the advocates of unfettered progress and those who profited from this 'gigantomania' prevailed. Professional and commercial sports complete with all their excesses continued almost unchanged until 1914. Only then were reductions of the stresses gradually implemented. Thus, cycling participated in pursuing 'gigantism' in sports achievements to excess in the dynamic period preceding the First World War. The four new 'gigantic' disciplines certainly helped to popularize bicycle-racing, but they also resulted in a loss of prestige and were rejected by a significant, critical segment of the population.[87]

SENSATIONALISM AND 'GIGANTOMANIA'

Cycling, like other sports, responded to the spirit of the time with its 'gigantomania'. The bicycle was used for many foolhardy tests of courage which were not athletic events *per se*, but can be categorized as spectacular sporting entertainments promoted for the amazement of a paying audience. In 1869, Professor Jenkins, 'the Canadian Blondin,' wearing 'white tights, black velvet knee-breeches, a crown-shaped hat, all profusely bedecked with tinsel and beads', rode a velocipede across the Niagara Falls on a tight-rope.[88] In 1886, a cyclist on a high-wheel bicycle rode across a high bridge railing in the United States.[89] Artistic trick–cycling was popular in Vaudeville theatres, at circus performances and during six-day races. Unusual cycling tricks were presented on stage. Cycling acrobats, for example, rode on circular tracks so small and so steeply banked that they were riding on an almost vertical wall.[90] The so-called 'death slopes', looping tracks on which the cyclist had to perform an upside-down loop, became notorious. The biggest 'death slopes' could only be erected outside.[91] After a steep, fast descent, the cyclist performed a loop, riding for a short time upside-down. Cycle jumps into water, from ramps similar to those of ski jumpers, were performed. It was inevitable that accidents and fatalities occurred in these sensational, daredevil performances.[92]

The attempts to set bicycle speed records behind trains during the years 1896 to 1899 came under the same category of a 'lust for sensation' and an obsessive pursuit of records. These pitted the human athlete against the most powerful, fastest land vehicle. More accurately, perhaps, it should be said that, through an understanding of the benefits of pacing, the power of the train was harnessed collaboratively to extend human athletic ability. In 1896, E.E. Anderson rode a mile in one minute and three second behind a train just outside St. Louis, Missouri, and a sextuplet raced against the famous Empire State Express on the New York Central Railway.[93] The most famous of these publicity-grabbing rides involving trains and cyclists was the record set in June 1899 by Charles 'Mile-a-Minute' Murphy, who rode a measured mile in 57 4/5 seconds behind a train on the Long Island railroad, an event reported in hundreds of American newspapers.[94] This spectacularly dangerous ride was seen as a sensational athletic achievement which was both foolhardy and of scientific interest. *Scientific American* discussed the significance of Murphy's ride in an editorial feature and commented that 'without disparaging in any degree the persistence and pluck of the bicyclist, the most interesting feature of the ride is the impressive object lesson it affords as to the serious nature of atmospheric resistance on moving bodies'. Murphy enjoyed a brief moment of international fame as a media 'star'.[95]

Cyclists thus made a significant contribution to 'gigantomania' in spectacular events which emphasized the controversial image of bicycle-racing as a sensational factor in modern life and mass entertainment. Although these activities took place outside formal, sanctioned competition, the distinction between sport and entertainment was not always scrupulously recognized by audiences. To a large extent, of course, it was the spectators, hungry for sensation, who financed both the legitimate 'gigantic' racing achievements and the more unconventional, foolhardy exploits of athletes and performers with their ticket purchases.[96]

PRESTIGE, SOCIAL STATUS AND OCCUPATIONAL
STRATIFICATION OF RIDERS

In investigating the phenomenon of 'gigantism' and the obsession with record-breaking, it is important to ask who the bicycle-racers that achieved these accomplishments were. Their social status and prestige is of interest here. 'Heroic' performances by professional cyclists were not only praised and approved of but were also widely criticized on health and moral grounds. This criticism was not only found in literary or cultural newspapers; even Adolph Schulze, the editor of the leading German cycling paper *Rad-Welt* (*Cycling World*), who might have been expected to look favourably on most cycling events, thought that 'the original distinguished character' of cycling had declined because of the heavy professionalization of the sport. He thought that the 'better elements' had pulled out of the sport because of the severity of bicycle-racing as a way of life. As active racers they did not wish 'to spend all their time training', he thought, and as spectators they considered 'the social contact with inferior elements undesirable'.[97]

Professionalization itself is a simple explanation for the perceived decline of prestige within cycling, namely accepting money to work and perform on the bicycle. Top-level amateur sports were possible only for athletes who were financially independent and therefore amateurism gained an upper-class character. The term 'professional' tended to carry a pejorative meaning, a kind of social stigma, indicating an undesirable, lower middle-class social background. As early as 1890, the journal of the Chemnitz 'R.C. Diamant' Cycling Club wrote that 'the Deutscher Radfahrer-Bund judged every cyclist who accepted money to be a professional, which was equivalent to relegation to an inferior social class'.[98] Some writers carried the criticism even further and put professional cyclists on the same level as high-wire performers, stunt riders, acrobats and travelling entertainers.[99] Thus another reason for the declining interest of 'the better elements' was that they were afraid of the circus-like atmosphere associated with professional racing and preferred to limit their entertainment to within their own social circle.

In order to determine which social strata the bicycle-racers originated in, data on their occupations either before, during or after their athletic careers has been collected and collated. In addition, possible shifts in the proportions of different occupational groups among the bicycle-riders will be examined for the period from 1867 to 1914.

An evaluation of cyclists' occupations from the starting list of the first German velocipede race in Altona on 10 September 1869 reveals that the majority of participants were from the merchant and technical classes, although a lawyer and an artist were also included in this group.[100]

TABLE 5.1

OCCUPATIONAL DATA FOR CYCLISTS PARTICIPATING IN THE FIRST GERMAN VELOCIPEDE RACE IN ALTONA, 10 SEPTEMBER 1869

11 merchants
4 factory owners
4 mechanics
3 university students
1 artist
1 mechanical engineer
1 lawyer
1 director of an institution

Source: R. Höfer, *Zwanzig Jahre Deutscher Rad-Rennsport* (Berlin: Rad-Welt, 1901).

From the 1890s onward, it is more difficult to define the occupations of well-known professional bicycle-racers since many of them had interrupted their vocational training to take up their racing careers. In 1908, the writer Fredy Budzinski listed the occupations of 223 top-level European and American cyclists – mainly professionals – for the years between 1880 and 1908; in 175 of these cases, the occupation noted was that practised prior to the sports career.[101]

It is striking that the predominance of the merchant class in the 1880s gradually decreases, giving way to a greater variety of occupations. A change in the main trends is evident: technical professions and those in skilled trades were increasingly represented, while the percentage of merchants decreased. There was a striking decrease in those employed in administration, for example, in the post office, railway, police, army or banks. There were hardly any representatives from agriculture or forestry, or minor employees from the service sector. It should also be noted that few people with a university education numbered among the successful bicycle-racers. Before the turn of the century, engineers, a dentist, an architect, a chemist and some university students were included, but after 1900 only a single university student appeared in the list.

In the same analysis, Budzinski also gave information on the careers of 46 cyclists after retirement from their sports careers, which at that time often lasted less than ten years. Because top-level cyclists had frequently not finished their vocational training before becoming

TABLE 5.2
OCCUPATIONS OF 175 INTERNATIONAL BICYCLE RACERS BEFORE THEIR
SPORTS CAREERS

1880s	1890s	1900s
(total – 16)	(total – 106)	(total – 48)
11 merchants (64.7%)	41 merchants (38.7%)	16 merchants (33.3%)
1 mechanic (5.9%)	15 mechanics (14.1%)	9 mechanics (18.8%)
2 artisans (11.8%)	17 artisans (16.0%)	10 artisans (20.8%)
1 engineer (5.9%)	6 engineers (5.7%)	3 technicians (6.3%)
1 print-maker	4 technicians (3.8%)	1 vineyard proprietor
	4 university students	1 travelling salesman
	3 mine workers	1 university student
	2 seamen	1 pharmacist
	2 traders	1 farmer
	2 civil servants	1 farm worker
	1 dentist	1 trade employee
	1 architect	1 building expert
	1 bicycle performer	1 hotel employee
	1 journalist	1 volunteer
	1 chemist	
	1 correspondent	
	1 restaurant owner	
	1 telegram deliverer	
	1 hotel employee	
	1 building expert	

Source: Fredy Budzinski, *Taschen-Radwelt – Ein radsportliches Lexikon* (Berlin: Verlag Rad-Welt, 1908–9).

professional athletes, it is difficult to compare them with those who continued to work in their respective occupations. The occupations which they adopted after their sports career show that some of the cyclists turned to the bicycle and motor industry, some rose to prominent positions and others returned to their old occupations or to other occupations in show business related to their bicycle careers. It is difficult to pinpoint obvious trends in the percentage changes of particular occupational categories because of the small sample used in the survey.

Another, more extensive, collection of information on internationally-known cyclists was published by George Hogenkamp in 1916.[102] The occupations of 353 racing-cyclists, before or after their sporting careers, were noted. There was a larger percentage of amateurs in this survey than in Budzinski's. Several riders appeared in both lists. Hogenkamp listed cyclists from almost the entire history of the sport, including some who had been active as early as the 1870s. Percentage changes of certain groups of occupations can be determined from this table although the

TABLE 5.3

OCCUPATIONS OF 46 INTERNATIONAL BICYCLE RACERS AFTER THEIR SPORTS
CAREERS

1880s (total – 10)	1890s (total – 32)	1900s (total – 4)
3 merchants	11 merchants	2 merchants
1 motor-car manufacturer	2 directors	1 bicycle dealer
1 bicycle manufacturer	2 engineers	1 mayor
1 director	3 bicycle and car dealers	
1 bicycle dealer	1 dentist	
1 dentist	4 hotel/restaurant owners	
1 print maker	1 draughtsman	
1 gardener	1 manager	
	1 massage-parlour owner	
	1 opera singer	
	1 artist	
	1 wrestler	
	1 motor-car racer	
	1 trainer	
	1 chauffeur	

Source: Fredy Budzinski, *Taschen-Radwelt – Ein radsportliches Lexikon* (Berlin: Verlag Rad-Welt, 1908–9).

way this data is divided into individual occupational groups is somewhat arbitrary. In the designation of the categories and the sometimes difficult classification of jobs, the priority was given to clarity and lack of ambiguity, in case of doubt, a separate category was created.

An overall view of this survey shows that more than 70 per cent of the cyclists originated from the business, technical or skilled-trade occupations or established themselves in those fields after their sports careers. So a representative cross-section of the population is not reflected here. At this period, bicycle-racers were dynamic and courageous when it came to their occupational lives. The high percentage of self-employed people suggests that the cyclists represented an enterprising and prestigious segment of the population, even allowing for the fact that their high income was certainly an advantageous starting point. Another noteworthy point is the low percentage of labourers and people employed in administration. Only lawyers and doctors are to be found as representatives of those with a university education. Also notable is the high percentage of visual artists and former cyclists working as professionals in other sports. Taking the step to become a bicycle-racer evidently required a higher degree of acceptance of an ideology that glorified technology, progress, records and 'gigantism' than bicycle-riding in public generally. Thus, bicycle-

TABLE 5.4
ANALYSIS OF A GROUP OF 353 INTERNATIONAL PROFESSIONAL BICYCLE
RACERS IN 1916

1. Wholesalers and retailers	108	(= 30.6%)
2. Industrialists, factory owners	39	(= 11.0%)
3. Managers in motorcar and bicycle factories	38	(= 10.8%)
4. Manual workers	31	(= 8.8%)
5. Clerical employees in post office, railway, banks and other offices	28	(= 7.9%)
6. Representatives and travelling salesmen	22	(= 6.2%)
7. Civil servants employed by banks, post office, police and local government	13	(= 3.7%)
8. Judges, lawyers, solicitors	11	(= 3.1%)
9. Servants, including chauffeurs	9	(= 2.5%)
10. Hotel and restaurant owners	8	(= 2.3%)
11. Professional sportsmen (wrestler, billiard player, automobile and bicycle racers)	6	(= 1.7%)
12. Artists	6	(= 1.7%)
13. Authors, journalists, editors	5	(= 1.4%)
14. Owners, entrepreneurs (of plantation, fashion magazine and building contractor)	4	(= 1.1%)
15. Labourers	4	(= 1.1%)
16. Mayors	3	(= 0.8%)
17. Realtors	3	(= 0.8%)
18. Engineers	3	(= 0.8%)
19. Technicians	3	(= 0.8%)
20. Army or navy officers		(= 0.8%)
21. Physicians, dentists	3	(= 0.8%)
22. Teachers	1	(= 0.3%)
23. Theologist	1	(= 0.3%)
24. Soldier	1	(= 0.3%)

Source: Hogenkamp, *Een halve eeuw wielersport.*

racers came mainly from a social stratum whose thinking and actions were dominated by technology and business.

In summary, it can be observed that a large proportion of the bicycle-racers in Hogenkamp's study entered technical and business careers. Because of the movement towards professionalization, cycling as a sport became more and more accessible to those who were less well-off. Thus, the percentage of labourers and skilled manual workers gradually increased. With regard to the groups of occupations, a distinct trend cannot be determined by means of the surveys presented here. The slight shifts of trend found in Budzinski's survey are inconclusive, but they do agree with the loss of prestige of cycling as a sport and the withdrawal of the 'better elements' described by several other writers.

NOTES

This article originated as Section 1.4, 'Gigantismus und Rekordsucht' in Rüdiger Rabenstein, *Radsport und Gesellschaft – Ihre sozialgeschichtlichen Zusammenhänge in der Zeit von 1867 bis 1914* (Munich and Zürich: Weidmann and Hildesheim, 1991). It was translated from German and then edited and revised in English, with the addition of a significant amount of British, American and French material, as a collaboration between Rüdiger Rabenstein and Andrew Ritchie. We appreciate very much the help of Rob van der Plas with translation of the technical German.

Distances and average speeds are expressed in both miles and kilometres. No attempt has been made to convert them because of conversion anomalies. Most of the distances listed in the Appendix, for example, have already been converted into kilometres from miles and re-conversion would create inaccuracies. If necessary, miles may be converted into kilometres and kilometres into miles using the values: 1 mile = 1.6kms and 1km = 0.63 miles. Money and salary amounts are difficult to assess.

1. *Sport-Album der Rad-Welt* (Berlin: Verlag Rad-Welt, 1904), p.124; J.-M. Erwin and A.A. Zimmerman, *Conseils d'Entrainement et Relation de son voyage en Europe* (Paris: Librairie du Velo, 1894); *Berliner Illustrirte Zeitung*, 13, 199 and 16, 241.
2. Tracks were built in the 1890s in all the countries where cycling was popular: Britain, France, Germany, Italy and the United States. Herne Hill track was described as 'the nursery of the majority of our leading riders of the present day'. It was conveniently located in London and 'possesses rare facilities for the successful attacking of records'. It was 'fringed by a belt of trees on one side, and beneath the shelter of a tall railway viaduct on another, and it is seldom indeed that a breeze is blowing in sufficient force to seriously interfere with the comfort of riders'. Most importantly, the track was resurfaced in 1893 with 'the then newly invented and now well-known 'battens', strips of wood laid upon a substratum of concrete and cement, and banked at each end sufficiently to allow of its successful negotiation at even the highest rate of speed'. The cost of the new facility was believed to be in the region of £5–6,000. See 'The cost of a famous racing track', *The Hub*, 22 Aug. 1896. New tracks were also built in London at Wood Green and Catford and the one at Putney was improved. The Wood Green track cost a total of £18,000, including £3,000 for the cement track itself and £3,600 for the grandstand. See 'Famous racing tracks', *The Hub*, 29 Aug. 1896, 147. In Paris and Berlin, new tracks were generally constructed of cement. By 1903, *Sport-Album der Rad-Welt* listed 19 leading continental tracks outside Germany, including Amsterdam, Antwerp, Brussels, Copenhagen, Florence, Rome, Turin, Zurich and three in Paris. The 1904 edition of the same publication lists 54 tracks in Germany!
3. *New York Times*, 2 Jan. 1898, ran the headline 'Innovations in Cycle Racing Threaten to Change the Character of the Sport' and reported that 'There is reason to believe that a year hence cycle racing will be an altogether changed sport from that which America, England and the continent have followed hitherto. Middle distance events are promised as the pièce de résistance at every race meet worth attending, and the short distance contests must sink to the level of introductory features, or fillers between the longer races'. Half a dozen tracks had been built in the New York area and, 'to secure a paying "gate", attractions of a high order must be presented at each track, and the result should be a continuous series of big matches, novel features, and assemblages of racing notables from all parts of the world'.
4. See 'Let him ride to death – The Crazy Fringe' in Robert A. Smith, *A Social History of the Bicycle* (New York: American Heritage Press, 1972), Ch.7, pp.127–41.
5. Jan Daniel Georgens, *Illustrirtes Sport-Buch* (Leipzig and Berlin: Verlag Otto Spamer, 1883); *Illustrirte Zeitung*, 2373 (1888), 675; *Deutsche Turn-Zeitung* (1888), 706.
6. Richard D. Mandell, *Die ersten Olympischen Spiele der Neuzeit* (Kastellaun: Aloys Henn Verlag, 1976).
7. *Deutsche Illustrirte Zeitung*, 48 (1884–85), 470.
8. *Illustrirte Zeitung*, 2366 (1888).
9. Ibid. (1893), 2598, 408; 2607, 660 and 2608, 688; J.R. de Bruycker, *Das Abenteuer der grossen Distanzritte* (Kiel: Moby Dick Verlag, 1985).
10. The oldest of these 'classics' are Bordeaux–Paris (1891), Paris–Roubaix (1896), Paris–Tours (1896) and Paris–Brussels (1896).

11. *Deutscher Radfahrer-Bund* (1891), 510.
12. The record was set on 27 July 1882 at Crystal Palace, London: 20 miles in 59 minutes 31 4/5 seconds, or 20 miles 300yds in the hour. See G. Lacy Hillier, 'A Succinct and Critical History of the One Hour's Cycle Path Record from the Earliest Authenticated Record to the Present Day', *The Cyclist Annual and Year Book for 1892* (London: Illiffe and Sons, 1892).
13. Robert Höfer, *Zwanzig Jahre Deutscher Rad-Rennsport – Geschichte des Deutschen Rennsports von 1881 bis 1901* (Berlin: Verlag der Rad-Welt, 1901), p.43.
14. *Deutscher Radfahrer-Bund* (1891), 312. Journalist Victor Breyer recollected that 'this race was an eye-opener for the masses ... That human beings had been capable of riding nearly 400 miles on their frail machines, almost without a dismount, filled everybody with admiration. It came as a tremendous revelation'. See 'How G. P. Mills won the first Bordeaux–Paris', *Cycling*, 19 March 1947. The North Road Cycling Club had promoted 12-hour and 24-hour time trials since its foundation in 1885, having been formed specifically to take advantage of the fine condition of the Great North Road and its suitability for bicycle-racing. The first North Road C.C. 24-hour race was held in 1886 and won on an ordinary bicycle by G.P. Mills (227 miles), the same rider who won the Bordeaux–Paris race in 1891.
15. A. Versnick, *Parijs–Brest–Parijs: Geschiedenis-Wetenswaardigheden* (Bruges: Excelsior, 1931).
16. See Andrew Ritchie, 'Charles Terront and Paris-Brest-Paris in 1891', *The Boneshaker*, 150 (1999), 9–20; and idem, 'The French Classics and British opposition to road racing in the 1890s', *The Boneshaker*, 151 (1999), 4–13.
17. Philippe Tissié, *Guide du Velocipediste pour l'Entrainement, la Course et le Tourisme* (Paris: Octave Doin Editeur, 1893); H.O. Duncan, *The World on Wheels* (Paris: self, *c*.1926); Versnick, *Parijs-Brest-Parijs*; L. Baudry de Saunier, *Les mémoires de Terront* (Paris: Prosport, 1980 – Original Edn. 1893).
18. *Sport-Album der Rad-Welt* (1903); Fredy Budzinski, *Taschen-Radwelt – Ein radsportliches Lexikon* (Berlin: Rad-Welt, 1908/9).
19. Höfer, *Zwanzig Jahre Deutscher Rad-Rennsport*, p.43.
20. Ibid., pp.50 and 58.
21. Ibid., p.53; Detlev Sierck, 'Das Tourenfahren' in Paul von Salvisberg, *Der Radfahrsport in Bild und Wort* (Munich: Academischer Verlag, 1897).
22. *Illustrirte Zeitung*, 2810 (1893), 45; *Deutscher Radfahrer-Bund* (1893), 424.
23. *Vossische Zeitung*, 30 June 1893.
24. *Illustrirte Zeitung*, 2610 (1893), 46.
25. *De Kampioen* (1890); Leonard de Vries, *De dolle entrée van automobiel en velocipee* (Holland: Bussum, 1973).
26. *Morning Advertiser*, 26 Oct. 1875. Laumaillé and Richard, from the club Vélo-Sport of Paris, encountered terrible weather conditions, but still beat the record time of Lieutenant Count von Zubowitz and his mare Caradoc, which 'inspired the members of the Paris club with the ambition of rivalling it', by nearly three days. They rode bicycles made by the Coventry Machinists Company. 'All along the route the light machines were the admiration and the envy of the people who had hitherto known of no other bicycles than the wooden-wheeled "boneshakers" which are now abandoned in this country'. See also *Bicycling: Its Rise and Development, A Text Book for Riders* (London: Tinsley Bros., 1876), pp.34–40.
27. H.O. Duncan and Pierre Lafitte, *En Suivant Terront de St. Petersburg à Paris à Bicyclette* (Paris: Flammarion, 1894).
28. See Robert Louis Jefferson, *To Constantinople on a Bicycle* (1894), *Roughing it in Siberia* (1895), *A Wheel to Moscow and Back* (London: Sampson, Low, Martin, 1895), *Across Siberia on a Bicycle* (London: Cycle Press, 1896) and *A New Ride to Khiva* (London: Methuen, 1899). See also Thomas Allen and William Sachleben, *Across Asia on a Bicycle* (New York: Century, 1894).
29. Jacques Seray, *1904 – Ce Tour de France qui faillit être le dernier* (Abbeville: self published, 1994).
30. *Radfahr-Humor*, 8 (24 July 1895), 1863.
31. *L'Auto*, date unknown, quoted in Seray, *1904*, p.118.
32. George Hogenkamp, *Een halve eeuw wielersport* (Amsterdam, 1916), p.382.
33. Rene Jacobs, *Velo* (Oudegem: Editions Velo, 1980), p.290.
34. Karel van Wijnendaele, *Mensen en Dingen uit de ronde van Frankrijk* (Belgium: Tielt, 1948), p.36.

35. *Deutsche Turn-Zeitung* (Leipzig, 1904), p.647; W. Gronen and W. Lemke, *Geschichte des Radsports und des Fahrrades* (Eupen: Edition Doepgen Verlag, 1978), p.239.

36. Hogenkamp, *Een halve eeuw wielersport*, p.437; Jacobs, *Velo* (1978), p.285; Gronen and Lemke, *Geschichte des Radsports*, p.239.

37. G. Lacy Hillier, 'A Succinct and Critical History of the One Hour's Cycle Path Record from the Earliest Authenticated Record to the Present Day' claims that the 2 September 1880 attempt of H.L. Cortis to break the 20mph time for the hour was 'the earliest recorded instance of pacemakers being used in an attempt to make good time'. Hillier was one of the four pacers. An analysis of psychological aspects of pacing was conducted in 1898 by Norman Triplett and published as 'The Dynamogenic Factors in Pacemaking and Competition', *American Journal of Psychology*, IX (July 1898).

38. 'The Art of Pacemaking, which has revolutionized cycling contests', *The Hub*, 10 Oct. 1896, 363. The article continues: 'To get good results out of a multi-cycle, the men riding it must, as it is termed, "nick" perfectly together, that is to say, they must work with that mechanical unison of movement that alone brings out the highest speed. For this reason it is that the "professionals" are most to be relied upon. They are men specially picked on account of an ability to ride best in particular company, just in the same way as a university eight is selected.'

39. 'The Year 1897 in Cycling', *Spaldings Official Bicycle Guide for 1898*. Spaldings goes on to comment that Jimmy Michael 'is the most marvellous athlete the world has ever seen, for with his diminutive size he combines a power and an ability that is gigantic, and during the last season has duplicated in this country his record in England, France and Germany. He has been the bright particular star of the match racing season. He has met defeat only once during the entire season, and he met all who were brave enough to face him in a race.'

40. 'Record-breaking as a science', *The Hub*, 7 Nov. 1896, 3. Another article, 'Motor pacing possibilities', *Cycling*, 13 Feb. 1897, stated: 'That mechanical pace-making machines will soon be receiving attention from several quarters is pretty evident. No one who has watched recent developments in this direction can help seeing what possibilities are open to a tireless pacer that can keep up a perfectly even pace for an hour or so without flagging.' The article explores the various sources of power available and emphasizes the huge disadvantage of gasoline-powered pacing machines: the exhaust, which the rider had to inhale.

41. Gronen and Lemke, *Geschichte des Radsports*, includes many interesting photographs of pacing-machines from the period. The link between bicycle-racing and the emerging automobile and aviation industries was both in the technology of large, powerful gasoline-powered engines and the skilled personnel with experience in working with them. Many of the bicycle-racers went into the automobile and aviation industries after their cycling careers were over. This issue still needs to be systematically researched.

42. On 30 May 1903, 24-year-old Harry Elkes was run over and killed by a heavy pacing-machine on the opening day of the Charles River Track, Cambridge, MA, in front of a crowd of 10,000 people. Elkes was on schedule for a world record at 20 miles. *Bicycling World* (8 June 1903), commented that 'It was a baptism of blood for the record-making course, and the bright, particular star of the record-breaking firmament was snuffed out while in the act of setting new figures for the emulation of the riders of the world'. Belgian star Verbist was also killed during a race and British star Jimmy Michael died of a brain hemorrhage while crossing the Atlantic after a serious accident. Gronen and Lemke, *Geschichte des Radsports*, estimate that 33 riders and 14 pace-makers were killed on European and American tracks between 1899 and 1928. *Sport-Album der Rad-Welt* listed the deaths of 'stayers' almost routinely between 1903 and 1905, the toll included Alfred Gornemann, Paul Albert, Harry Elkes and Edouard Taylor in 1903, Karl Kaser and Paul Dangla in 1904 and Charles Brecy, George Leander, Jimmy Michael, Hubert Sevenich and Willy Schmitter in 1905.

43. Hogenkamp, *Een halve eeuw wielersport*, p.387; *Sport-Album der Rad-Welt*, 8 (1910) printed an article on the accident, entitled 'Die Rennbahnkatastrophe und ihre Folgen', which Rabenstein excerpts on p.295 of *Radsport und Gesellschaft*. At a meeting between ministers and representatives of bicycle-racing organizations on 17 August 1909, a complete ban was lifted on the condition that windshields were not used and that a roller had to be installed 40cm from the back wheel of the pacing-machine, to slow the cyclist. See Gronen and Lemke, *Geschichte des Radsports*, p.223.

44. S.H. Moxham, *Fifty Years of Road Riding, the North Road Cycling Club, 1885 – 1935* (Bedford: Diemer and Reynolds, 1935).

45. Cuca Cocoa races were as follows: 1892, Shorland, 414 miles; 1893, Shorland, 426 1/4 miles; 1894, Shorland, 460 miles 1296 yards; 1895, George Hunt, 450 miles 1459 yards; 1896, F.R. Goodwin, 476 miles 1702 yards.

46. Hogenkamp, *Een halve eeuw wielersport*, p.180; photograph in Gronen and Lemke, *Geschichte des Radsports*, p.216.

47. *L'Auto*, 16 Sept. 1909; see also Gronen and Lemke, *Geschichte des Radsports*, p.228. Guignard's world record, set on 15 September 1909, was the reason for the publication of the retrospective record list.

48. *Berliner Illustrierte Zeitung*, 38 (1898), 5.

49. *The Athletic News* (Manchester), 30 Sept. 1876 and 21 Oct. 1876. At the first event, Camille Thuillet 'was accompanied by his friend Keen, the long-distance champion, and the enthusiasm of the spectators rose to a great pitch as the race drew near the end, for the champions were running at the astonishing pace of 16 miles an hour'.

50. The young Charles Terront, who has already been mentioned in the context of the 1891 Paris–Brest–Paris and the ride from St. Petersburg to Paris, was one of the leading contenders in these contests. See Andrew Ritchie, 'The Beginnings of Trans-Atlantic Bicycle Racing: Harry Etherington and the Anglo–French Team in America, 1879–80', *International Journal of the History of Sport*, 15, 3 (1998), 125–41; *Cycle-Clips, A History of Cycling in the North-East* (Newcastle: Tyne and Wear County Museums, 1985).

51. *Deutsche Illustrirte Zeitung*, 28, 2 (1884–85), 47.

52. Ibid., *supra*.

53. Ernest Kaufmann, *Der Radrennsport – Fliegerrennen* (Leipzig und Zurich, *c.* 1923), p.67; Andrew Ritchie, *Major Taylor* (San Francisco: Bicycle Books, 1989).

54. Kaufmann, *Der Radrennsport*, p.76; Gronen and Lemke, *Geschichte des Radsports*, p.163; Budzinski, *Taschen-Radwelt – Ein radsportliches Lexikon* (Berlin: Verlag der Rad-Welt, 1908–09).

55. Kaufmann, *Der Radrennsport*, p.69.

56. Ibid., p.71 and 76.

57. *Bühne und Sport*, 29 (1907), 15.

58. Kaufmann, *Der Radrennsport*, pp.72 and 76; Hogenkamp, *Een halve eeuw wielersport*, pp.462 and 472; *Sport-Album der Rad-Welt* (Berlin: Verlag Rad-Welt, 1912, 1913 and 1914).

59. See Andrew Ritchie, 'The Origins of Bicycle Racing in England: Technology, Entertainment, Sponsorship and Advertising in the Early History of the Sport', *Journal of Sport History*, 26, 3 (1999), 489–520.

60. Kaufmann, *Der Radrennsport*, p.66.

61. Cycling was certainly progressive in its creation of this new type of sports promoters and managers whose tasks included the provision and maintenance of racing facilities and the personal management of the athletes. H.O. Duncan, working in Paris in the 1890s, managed a stable of riders, liaising between them and manufacturers, arranging their racing schedules and personally supervising their training and travel.

62. Fredy Budzinski, 'Radsport und Turnen' in Edmund Neuendorf, *Die deutschen Leibesübungen* (Berlin-Essen: W. Andermann Verlag, 1928), p.665.

63. C. Rintelen, 'Sport und Industrie' in *Amtliche Fest-Schrift zum 12. Bundestage des DRB* (1895), p.49.

64. For example, in the Vienna–Berlin long-distance race in 1893. See *Deutscher Radfahrer-Bund* (1893), p.351.

65. Thaddäus Robl, *Der Radrennsport* (Leipzig: Verlag Grethlein, 1905), p.18.

66. *Amtliche Liste der Deutschen Berufsfahrer* (1899); *Spaldings Official Bicycle Guide for 1898*, p.5; *The Cycle Age and Trade Review*, 16 Feb. 1899, 488. *Spaldings* said 'There are perhaps 25,000 amateur and professional racing men in the United States'.

67. *Deutsche Turn-Zeitung* (1894), p.204.

68. J.M. Erwin and A.A. Zimmerman, *Conseils d'Entrainement et Relation de son Voyage en Europe* (Paris: Librairie du Vélo, 1894).

69. H. Naundorf, 'Radfahren' in C. Diem, H. Sippel and F. Breithaupt, *Stadion, Das Buch von Sport und Turnen – Gymnastik und Spiel* (Berlin: Neufeld and Henius Verlag, 1928), p.272.

70. *Sport-Album der Rad-Welt* (1903, 1904, 1905 and 1907).
71. *Bühne und Sport*, 5 (1907), 8.
72. Eduard Bertz, *Die Philosophie des Fahrrads* (Dresden: Verlag Reissner, 1900), p.86.
73. Adolph Schulze, 'Radfahren' in H. Richard, *Sport und Körperpflege* (Leipzig: Verlag J.J. Arnd, 1908), p.580.
74. 'Popular professionals and their salaries', *The Hub*, 7 Nov. 1896.
75. *Spaldings Official Bicycle Guide for 1898.*
76. *Bühne und Sport* (1907).
77. Hermann Glaser, *Die Kultur der Wilhelminischen Zeit – Topographie einer Epoche* (Frankfurt: S. Fischer Verlag, 1984), p.104.
78. *Scientific American*, 361 (1899), 292.
79. Joseph Jiel-Laval, 'Une course a bicyclette: Paris-Brest et retour' (Bordeaux, 1892) in Tissié, *Guide du Velocipediste pour l'Entrainement*, p.227.
80. Karl Planck, *Fusslümmelei. Über Stauchballspiel und englische Krankheit* (Stuttgart, 1898), p.15.
81. von Salvisberg, *Der Radfahrsport in Bild und Wort*, p.260.
82. *Monatsschrift für das Turnwesen* (1898), 247.
83. *Sport-Album der Rad-Welt* (1909), 6.
84. Bertz, *Die Philosophie des Fahrrads*, 84.
85. H. Boruttau, 'Radfahren und Automobilsport' in Siegfried Weissbein, *Hygiene des Sports* (Leipzig: Verlag Grethlein, *c.*1911), p.184.
86. Jim McGurn, *On Your Bicycle* (London: John Murray, 1987), p.122.
87. Schulze, 'Radfahren', p.574.
88. The event was reported in both the *Buffalo Express*, 26 Aug. 1869 and *New York Times*, 27 Aug. 1869 and imaginatively illustrated in *L'Illustration*, 25 Aug. 1869.
89. Viscount Bury and George Lacy Hillier, *Badminton Cycling* (London: Longman, Green and Co., 1891), p.17.
90. *Berliner Illustrierte Zeitung* (1900), 695.
91. *Sport-Album der Rad-Welt* (1906), 34.
92. *Deutsche Turn-Zeitung* (1889), 336.
93. 'Nearly a Mile a Minute',*Bearings*, 13 April 1896; 'Express Train versus Sextuplet – An Exciting race', *The Hub*, 3 Oct. 1896.
94. Among them: *New York Times*, 1 July 1899; *Chicago Daily Tribune*, 1 July 1899; *Louisville Courier Journal*, 1 July 1899; *San Francisco Examiner*, 1 July 1899. See also Bertz, *Die Philosophie des Fahrrads*, p.90; photographs in Gronen and Lemke, *Geschichte des Radsports*, pp.132 and 174; Andrew Ritchie, *Major Taylor*, pp.118–20.
95. 'Murphy's Bicycle Ride a Hint to the Railroads' and 'A Mile in Less than a Minute on a Bicycle', *Scientific American*, 15 July 1899, 34 and 41.
96. See Rüdiger Rabenstein, 'Sensational Bicycle Acts Around 1900', *Proceedings of the 9th International Cycle History Conference* (San Francisco: Van der Plas, 1999), pp.62–8.
97. Schulze, 'Radfahren', p.574.
98. Max Lange, 'Chemnitzer Radsport-Geschichte' in *R.C. Diamant Chemnitz* (1928), p.60.
99. Bertz, *Die Philosophie des Fahrrads*, p.86.
100. Quoted in Höfer, *Zwanzig Jahre Deutscher Rad-Rennsport*, p.6.
101. Fredy Budzinski, *Taschen-Radwelt – Ein radsportliches Lexikon* (Berlin: Verlag Rad-Welt, 1908–09), pp.17–81.
102. Hogenkamp, *Een halve eeuw wielersport*, pp.535–681.

APPENDIX 1
ONE HOUR BICYCLE WORLD RECORDS ON THE TRACK,
IN KILOMETRES, FROM 1870 TO 1909

1870	Johnson (GB)	21.470	Velocipede
1873	Moore (GB)	22.933	Transitional velocipede
1876	Dodds (GB)	25.508	Ordinary bicycle
1876	Keen (GB)	29.414	Ordinary bicycle (professional)
1877	Shoppee (GB)	26.960	Ordinary bicycle
1878	Weir (GB)	28.542	Ordinary bicycle
1879	Christie (GB)	30.374	Ordinary bicycle
1880	Cortis (GB)	31.896	Ordinary bicycle
1882	Cortis (GB)	32.453	Ordinary bicycle
1882	Cortis (GB)	32.474	Ordinary bicycle
1884	English (GB)	32.699	Ordinary bicycle
1885	Rowe (USA)	33.112	Ordinary bicycle
1886	Rowe (USA)	35.542	Ordinary bicycle
1888	Laurie (GB)	33.910	Solid-tyred safety
1890	Turner (GB)	34.008	Solid-tyred tricycle
1890	Mecredy (GB)	34.601	Pneumatic safety, human-paced
1890	Lloyd (GB)	34.847	Pneumatic safety, human-paced
1890	Parsons (GB)	35.972	Pneumatic safety, human-paced
1891	Ede (GB)	36.682	Pneumatic safety, human-paced
1891	J. Osmond (GB)	38.167	Pneumatic safety, human-paced
1892	Ede (GB)	38.405	Pneumatic safety, human-paced
1892	Fournier (F)	39.323	Pneumatic safety, human-paced
1892	Dubois (F)	39.707	Pneumatic safety, human-paced
1893	E. Osmond (GB)	40.193	Pneumatic safety, human-paced
1893	Stocks (GB)	40.563	Pneumatic safety, human-paced
1893	Meintjes (SA)	41.939	Pneumatic safety, human-paced
1894	A. Linton (GB)	41.949	Pneumatic safety, human-paced
1894	Dubois (F)	43.32	Pneumatic safety, human-paced
1894	Bouhours (F)	44.183	Pneumatic safety, human-paced
1894	A. Linton (GB)	45.445	Pneumatic safety, human-paced
1895	Lesna (F)	45.673	Pneumatic safety, human-paced
1895	Michael (GB)	46.003	Pneumatic safety, human-paced
1895	Bouhours (F)	46.440	Pneumatic safety, human-paced
1895	Stocks (GB)	46.711	Pneumatic safety, human-paced
1896	Chase (GB)	46.944	Pneumatic safety, human-paced
1896	T. Linton (G)	47.258	Pneumatic safety, human-paced
1896	Huret (F)	47.493	Pneumatic safety, human-paced
1896	T. Linton (GB)	48.455	Pneumatic safety, human-paced
1896	T. Linton (GB)	49.894	Pneumatic safety, human-paced
1896	Stocks (GB)	50.390	Pneumatic safety, human-paced
1896	T. Linton (GB)	50.420	Pneumatic safety, human-paced
1897	Stocks (GB)	51.909	Pneumatic safety, human-paced
1897	Stocks (GB)	52.491	Pneumatic safety, human-paced
1898	Ed. Taylore (F)	54.044	Motorized pacing-machine
1898	Elkes (USA)	55.839	Motorized pacing-machine
1899	Ed. Taylore (F)	56.966	Motorized pacing-machine
1899	Bor (F)	58.053	Motorized pacing-machine
1899	Ed. Taylore (F)	58.980	Motorized pacing-machine
1900	Ed. Taylore (F)	62.313	Motorized pacing-machine
1900	Bouhours (F)	62.333	Motorized pacing-machine
1900	Bauge (F)	63.800	Motorized pacing-machine
1900	Bauge (F)	64.350	Motorized pacing-machine

1900	Stinson (USA)	64.673	Motorized pacing-machine
1901	Robl (D)	65.512	Motorized pacing-machine
1901	Dickentmann (Nl)	65.621	Motorized pacing-machine
1901	Robl (D)	65.742	Motorized pacing-machine
1901	Robl (D)	67.353	Motorized pacing-machine
1902	T. Linton (GB)	68.410	Motorized pacing-machine
1902	T.Linton (GB)	71.660	Motorized pacing-machine
1902	Robl (D)	72.560	Motorized pacing-machine
1902	T. Linton (GB)	73.355	Motorized pacing-machine
1902	Michael (GB)	75.274	Motorized pacing-machine
1902	Contenet (F)	77.903	Motorized pacing-machine
1903	Contenet (F)	78.360	Motorized pacing-machine
1903	Monroe (USA)	79.050	Motorized pacing-machine
1903	Robl (D)	80.663	Motorized pacing-machine
1903	Dangla (F)	81.108	Motorized pacing-machine
1903	T. Hall (GB)	84.140	Motorized pacing-machine
1903	Dangla (F)	84.577	Motorized pacing-machine
1903	T. Hall (GB)	87.393	Motorized pacing-machine
1904	Bruni (I)	87.579	Motorized pacing-machine
1904	Darragon (F)	87.850	Motorized pacing-machine
1905	Guignard (F)	89.904	Motorized pacing-machine
1905	Robl (D)	91.303	Motorized pacing-machine
1906	Guignard (F)	95.026	Motorized pacing-machine
1908	Wills (GB)	99.057	Motorized pacing-machine
1909	Guignard (F)	101.623	Motorized pacing-machine

Source: *L'Auto*, 16 September 1909, plus additional records inserted by the authors of this article.

Note: From 1890 onwards, these speed records were all paced, at first by human-pace and then by motor-pace. Unpaced hour records, authorized by the International Cyclists Association after its foundation in 1893, began with Henri Desgrange's 1893 ride of 35.325 kms and culminated with Chris Boardman's 1996 record of 56.375 kms, which still stands.

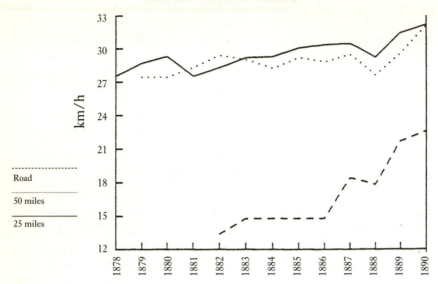

Bicycle racing speeds

a) Increase in racing speeds from 1878 to 1890, showing average speeds of annual 24 hour road rides organized by North Road Cycling Club and 25 and 50 mile championship organized by the National Cyclists' Union (source: *Deutscher Radfahrer-Bund*, 1891, pp.176 and 519).

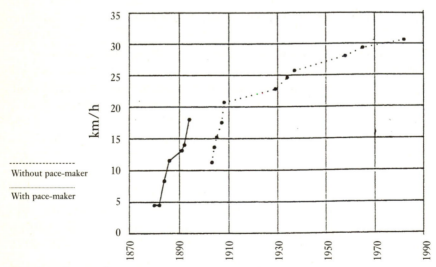

Bicycle racing speeds

b) Average speeds of the British 'End-to-End' record; the black dots show the actual records as they stood at the end of each year in which record was set (from various sources).

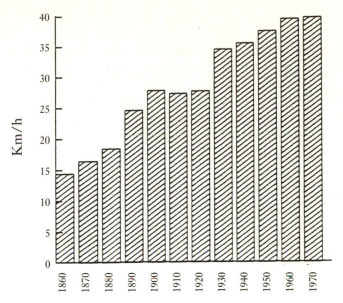

Bicycle racing speeds
c) Average speed of major road races for each decade from 1860 to 1970. (Numbers of races included for analysis for each decade as follows: 1860s – 5; 1870s – 6; 1880s – 9; 1890s – 25; 1900s – 30; 1910s – 48; 1920s – 75; 1930s – 82; 1940s – 65; 1950s – 90; 1960s – 86; 1970s – 57. From various sources.)

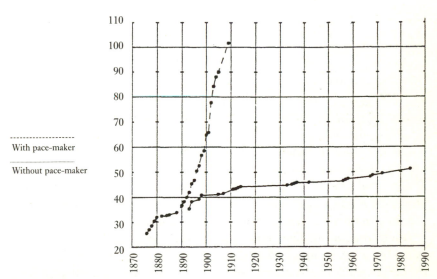

Bicycle racing speeds
d) World hour record on the track with and without pace-makers; the black dots show the actual records as they stood at the end of each year in which a record was set (from various sources).

6

'Golden Boys' of Playing Field and Battlefield: Celebrating Heroes – 'Lost' Middle-Class Women Versifiers of the Great War

J.A. MANGAN

Deeply moved by the events of the Great War certainly hundreds and possibly thousands of women between 1914 and 1919 published short lyrical verses in newspapers, weeklies, pamphlets and small volumes of poetry. A smaller number wrote in later years of the war. If they are not to be found in later Great War anthologies, they were well represented in the publications of the Great War years.

For the most part these women were far removed in both experience and expression from the war poets such as Siegfried Sassoon, Wilfred Owen and Robert Graves. They wrote more of pennants and banners than of mud and blood. They idealized their soldier heroes: they first urged martial patriotism, then depicted them as latter day Christs crucified and finally they mourned them as vanished ghosts. It is broadly possible to trace an unfolding of expression born of their experience: first trumpeted words of strident patriotism and chivalric romance, then stunned cadences of sad sacrifice, followed by horrified lines of bloody realism and, finally, poignant stanzas of lost love.

In their way these women were middle-class 'revolutionaries'. They forced their way, by intensity of feeling, in quite considerable numbers onto the pages of newspapers and weeklies and into collected volumes of poetry. They constituted a minor cultural revolution: they were published female voices heard in greater numbers than ever before, commenting on life, love and death – and they faithfully reflected the values of their time. They especially admired, respected and cherished, as did the wider society, 'the golden boys' of Edwardian summer playing fields. They saw them as heroic exponents of the virtues inculcated, as it seemed to them, in the middle-class public schools, that had played such a significant part in England's admired imperial pre-eminence:

Twelve months ago at school, a merry-hearted boy,
With sunny, golden hair, his mother's pride and joy;
But now his country calls, and so, within a year,
He's serving at the front, a blue-eyed volunteer.[1]

Most of these women were middle class like their lauded soldier lovers, fathers, brothers, friends or neighbours. In a real sense, therefore, their verse is a verse of middle-class Edwardian womanhood forced out by the intensity of events and the pain of circumstance. It is seldom great poetry; nevertheless, it is often greatly moving. More to the point, it is a record of a tragedy; it is the collective voice of a tragic generation. It is also a social record. It is social history in verse that has been mostly ignored and it is time to adequately acknowledge this. Acknowledgement has already been attempted but insufficiently. These women should be more fully and more widely heard. This essay allows them to speak for themselves in order that their period voices reveal themselves through themselves.

In her tribute to these women in the Preface to Catherine Reilly's *Scars Upon My Heart* (Reilly's short collection of these women's verse and her own tribute to them), Judith Kazantzis writes: 'we know of the male agony of the war from the poetry of Sassoon and Owen. We know little in poetry of what that agony and its millions of deaths meant to the millions of English women who had to endure them.'[2] This is true. However, there is more than agony, terrible though it was, in the war verse of these women. There is a great deal more. Consequently, it is a mistake to take Sassoon and his peers as the poetic 'voice' of the Great War.[3] As Alan Judd has recently written, while he greatly admires the War Poets, 'Plato was right to mistrust the artists. Not because the experiences they evoke are untrue, but because often other things are also and equally true, and some of them are even more important.'[4] There were hundreds of lesser and largely unknown versifiers, both women and men, who have a place in history: 'they are not to be dismissed by virtue of their crude metre, stilted language or conventional expression. Whatever their literary qualities, they are the genuine voices of period idealism. It can only be understood through them and others like them.'[5]

The poetess May Wedderburn Cannan was one of many, if not most women, who did not share Sassoon's view of war: 'like many other women of the time, [she] believed that war was right and that her pain and loss, like that of many others, was for a greater cause. She did believe that men were sacrificing their lives for the good of their country.[6] She stated of 1916:

> Siegfried Sassoon wrote to the Press from France saying that the war was now a war of conquest and without justification, and declared himself to be a conscientious objector. He was rescued from trouble by Robert Graves and his friends who claimed a break-down. C.E. Montague wrote *Disenchantment* and Wilfred Owen was much influenced by him. A saying went round, 'Went to war with Rupert Brooke and came home with Siegfried Sassoon'. I had much admired some of Sassoon's verse but I was not coming home with him. Someone must go on writing for those who were still convinced of the right of the cause for which they had taken up arms.[7]

Women versifiers, who made up a large part of the 'unknown' versifiers, did not, incidentally, as Kazantzis suggests, 'first and foremost ... mourn for the dead'.[8] They mourned terribly – eventually – but they also celebrated patriotic war, they cursed the Hun as monstrous, they romanticized youthful death, they equated war with sport, they dressed their khaki warriors in chivalric armour, they depicted the battlefield as a bannered joust. They wrote martial verses filled with images of proud chauvinism, romantic sacrifice, chivalric guardians and sub–human enemies. Even in Reilly's relatively slim collection *Scars Upon My Heart*, as Kazantzis actually admits: 'the orthodox Great War belief in the English cause against the Germans and the backing of an English God and great gratitude to the protagonists of all this, the English fighting men – is the essence of many of the poems.'[9] This chapter goes well beyond Reilly's selection of women versifiers and offers a great deal more evidence of this – and yet it is only a proverbial drop in the ocean. It is not unreasonable to call Kazantzis to task. There is a need to set the versifiers correctly within their period and to note their militant patriotism, their escapist romanticism and their nationalistic fervour, as well as their personal suffering. The simplistic feminist protestation 'that repudiates war as the outcome of compulsive male aggressiveness or, anyway, of the patriarchal mode'[10] is revealed in the verse of the women of the Great War for what it is: naive and polemical rather than profound and analytical. It might be added that even a cursory reading of Ben Shephard's *A War of Nerves* shows such assertions to be inadequate and unacceptable.[11] Indeed, as even Catherine Reilly herself pointed out, 'some feminism runs the other way – a wish to be with the men'.[12]

Where there should be complete agreement with Kazentzis is in her bewilderment at 'the near-as maybe non-presence of women in modern Great War anthologies'.[13] Much of the verse of these mostly middle-class versifiers, most of it not available in *Scars Upon My Heart*, was not poetry of lamentation but, to quote Kazantzis herself writing of May Wedderburn Cannan's verse 'Rouen', was 'the poetry of England, inalienable from Honour, Duty, God, Christ and Sacrifice. This poetry sees as glorious, not war, but certainly the sacrifice of youth.'[14] This is well said. Kazantzis continues, equally well: 'All flowed from Duty. That duty is the world task of keeping alive English values and their guarding of the sanctity of the English hearth and homeland against the militaristic enemy that threatens this.'[15]

This attitude is nowhere better described than in Katharine Tynan's 'High Summer':

> Pinks and syringa in the garden closes
> And the sweet privet hedge and golden roses.
> The pines hot in the sun, the drone of the bee;
> They die in Flanders to keep these for me.
>
> The long sunny days and the still weather,
> The cuckoo and the blackbird shouting together,
> The lambs calling their mothers out on the lea;
> They die in Flanders to keep these for me.
>
> Daisies leaping in foam on the green grasses,
> The dappled sky and the stream that sings as it passes –
> These are bought with a price, a bitter fee –
> They die in Flanders to keep these for me.[16]

Scars Upon My Heart contains little of the jingoistic female verse of the early years of the war and no example of the paranoiac verse full of loathing of Nina Macdonald's *War-Time Nursery Rhymes* to be taught to infants and praised in a Foreword by Geo. R. Sims for the fact that 'it is good that the children should remember certain features of the great World War in which their fathers are fighting so gallantly'.[17] Two examples of verses Macdonald wrote for the nursery:

> I do not like you, Kaiser Bill,
> The deeds you do, the blood you spill,
> And fill me with disgust, until
> I feel I hate you, Kaiser Bill.[18]

And:

> Ding, dong, bell
> Piggy's in the well,
> Who let him sink?
> Johnny Bull, I think.
> Who'll pull him out?
> 'Leave him in!' they shout,
> Johnny Bull is not a fool,
> And knows what he's about,
> Besides, he was a horrid pig,
> A greedy, cruel beast,
> So, let's be thankful there is one
> Less brute on earth, at least.[19]

Kazantzis makes only passing mention of the chauvinism of Jessie Pope and nothing of a similar jingoism of C.A. Renshaw, who won fulsome praise from *The Scotsman* for her militaristic tone: 'The keynote again is martial, and the book has many charming and inspiring poems like those which made the success of its writer's earlier volume, *England's Boys*.'[20] Renshaw, at times, gloried in a perceived heroic lust for battle:

> He tossed his shield in the bleak face of Fate;
> He dreamed of riding out on splendid quests,
> Threading dim forests towards untranquil wests,
> Thundering at some foeman's stubborn gate.
> His heart throbbed like a sea. Romance was great
> In him; his soul was lustful of red war;
> He craved the highest height, the lonest star;
> His blood ran riot like a mountain spate![21]

Genteel middle-class women of the time could be strident in their chauvinism, pitiless in their patriotism, intense in their hatred and without mercy for their enemy:

And the children of men went forth to the fight,
With the sword of the Lord, and the armour of light,
Glory to God –
With the sword of the Lord they will smite, *they will smite.*

Then Hate strode forth; as a giant strong
The arch fiend strode:
He cursed great Love with his poisoned breath,
He cursed sweet Peace to an anguished death –
And the demons of hell: they followed along,
And they chanted their country's national song
In conventional mode,
Since they to the father of lies belong.[22]

For most women versifiers the justice of the cause, the nobility of the struggle and the manliness of their warriors were beyond question. Their patriotism was often proudly uncomplicated as in 'England' by 'C.C.' in *Triumph and Other Poems*:

England! thou place of my birth!
England! thou pride of my heart!
England! thou joy upon earth,
Fighting and doing thy part.

Thou art arisen in might,
Ready to help and to save.
Fighting for honour and right,
Freedom and truth or – the grave.

Tender to fallen and weak,
Mighty, yet true to thy vow,
Proud and yet gentle and meek,
This, O! my England, art thou.[23]

And Anita Moor's 'For England' in *Roundels and Rhymes*:

The Union Jack of England,
The banner of the free,
The emblem of our Empire

Will wave o'er land and sea,
And lead us on to victory,
To break all tyrant might,
To win the war for England.
For Freedom and for Right![24]

On occasion, metaphorical 'white feathers' can be sensed, if not seen, as in Mary M. Alexander's 'Old Flag':

Oh, valiant Sons of Britain, rise!
Let no man lag behind,
But hasten where the Old Flag flies,
Wide waving in the wind:
Proud, proud, that all the world behold
That Flag of Britain's Might,
With, blazoned on each splendid fold,
'For Liberty and Right'.[25]

And in her *The Country's Call*:

Hark! Our Country's Voice is calling,
And its accents clear are falling
To the cadence of a brave old Battle-Song;
'Tis a matter of oppression,
Of deception and aggression,
And she summons all her Sons to right the Wrong.

Chorus

And the answer's coming steady:
'Every man is up and ready
To fight the foe and *never* turn his back;
For his Country – Blessings on her –
For Great Britain's Pride and Honour,
He will face grim death beneath the Union Jack'.[26]

For some of these women the Great War, in its early moments, was neither reprehensible nor abhorrent, but the crucible in which manhood was made: In *The Making of a Hero*, Mary M. Alexander wrote:

To a man – at War's Alarms
Britons all, are up in arms.
Each among them strangely knows
How the Hero in him grows;
Snatched from common lot and fate
Throbs to feel his spirit great;
Thrills to know his soul expand
To conceptions wide and grand ...
Heaving 'neath Life's commonplace
Surges instincts of his race,
Reaching up to sight and sound,
Struggling forth, till, breaking bound,
He awakes, new born to Life,
Hero – eager for the strife.[27]

While C.A. Renshaw recorded of *My Mate*:

God gave him manhood when the trumpets cried;
He leapt into the azure; his boy's face
Took on the light of seas and windy space;
He gloried in this strength; his mounting pride
Challenged the world, flung fears and doubts aside,
And made him Man.
Youth's idle dreams gave place
To red desires of battle's fever-pace,
Of pain and blood and many a reckless ride.[28]

More commonly, many women versifiers welcomed the high adventure of a new moment of chivalry:

O Let the days of Chivalry
And Knighthood come again!
O let us gird our armour on
And fare us forth amain,
Till Sloth, Disease and Ugliness –
The triple fiend – be slain.

This quest is yours: your arms – a mind
Fearless and clear, a flame
Lighting a body which a Greek
Might not have scorned to claim;
A soul that does not know defeat;
Then venture, in Love's name.[29]

The Great War as the 'Quest' became a symbolic Holy Grail in which savage reality became exotic romanticism:

This time last year the dreams of Youth were his;
He loved, made songs, knew laughter and fierce Joy,
Ran with the winds, a straight-limbed English boy,
Glimpsed God behind those veiled Infinities,
Where strange things stir, and passionate Beauty is.
He saw wild War, a luring wild decoy,
And took it childlike for his latest toy,
– A child astray in grim immensities.

This time last year he held the reeking trench,
His dim soul questing for the Holy Grail
Among the mud of Flanders. In a hail
Of lead he fell, and I who loved him so
Knew sudden anguish and the deep heart-wrench.
... And Spring was on the world – a year ago![30]

Or spiritual fulfilment:

But the wise lads, the dear lads, the pathway's dewy green,
For the little Knights of Paradise of eighteen and nineteen;
They run the road to Heaven, they are singing as they go,
And the blood of their sacrifice has washed them white as snow.[31]

The period before the Great War was arguably the Golden Age of English Athleticism – that curious games cult of the English middle class – that had such an immediate as well as subsequent impact on the whole world. Much has been written about Athleticism elsewhere[32] and there is no need here to discuss it further. The point to be made here is simply that in the light of the influence of the cult it is not surprising to find women writing with admiration of the athletic schoolboy now transferred from playing field to battlefield. Joyce Kilmer does this, and indeed more, in 'The New School':

> For many a youthful shoulder now is gay with an epaulette,
> And the hand that was deft with a cricket-bat is defter with a
>   sword,
> And some of the lads will laugh today where the trench is red and
>   wet,
> And some will win on the bloody field the accolade of the Lord.[33]

Kilmer, like a number of these women, depicted gilded youth carrying its gaiety, grace and courage from cricket square to front-line. She also wrote poignantly of 'the haunting silence of studies, river and pitches as boys who had learnt to live now learnt to die'[34] with a well-mannered cheerfulness.

In *The Spires of Oxford*, W.M. Letts offers a reminder, incidentally, that pre-war young men played as enthusiastically at Edwardian Oxford and Cambridge as they did in Edwardian public schools and then, in her words, 'gave their merry youth away' with enthusiastic patriotism:

> I saw the spires of Oxford
> As I was passing by,
> The grey spires of Oxford
> Against a pearl-grey sky;
> My heart was with the Oxford men
> Who went abroad to die.
>
> The years go fast in Oxford,
> The golden years and gay;
> The hoary colleges look down
> On careless boys at play,
> But when the bugles sounded – War!
> They put their games away.
>
> They left the peaceful river,
> The cricket field, the quad,
> The shaven lawns of Oxford
> To seek a bloody sod.
> They gave their merry youth away
> For country and for God.[35]

More brazenly, and far less sensitively, in *Roll of Honour and Other Poems*, May Aldington trilled a rather silly song about upping stumps and 'playing the game' – to the unusual musical accompaniment of the 'roaring of guns' rather than the usual loud cheers of the assembled school, this time on Flanders 'playing fields'.

> Come over here and play the game!
> Summer or Winter, 'tis the same.
> Just leave our women to keep the score,
> They'll help us to make it – six to four!
>
> The Surrey's kick off was really fine,
> Thousands were playing all the time!
> What if the Band is a roar of guns.
> They *must* have our music, the German Huns!
>
> Come over here and play the game.
> Did you say Cricket? It's all the same.
> The Band's still playing, 'Watch on the Rhine,'
> Come along, lads, you're just in time![36]

It was not long before death intruded directly and inescapably on these images of the Flanders 'playing field' and another 'games field' became the deserved destiny of the boy heroes – in Heaven. In *The Holy War*, Katharine Tynan, the most mystical and the most prolific of the women versifiers of the Great War, wished that for Ivo Alan Charteris killed in action in October 1915,

> Many a game and a goal be given
> To you in the playing-fields of Heaven;
> Be as you were, a light shape of joy,
> Glad in the strength and the grace of a boy.[37]

In 'Golden Boys', Letts expressed much the same sentiment:

> Not harps and palms for these, O God,
> Nor endless rest within the courts of Heaven, –
> These happy boys who left the football field,
> The hockey ground, the river, the eleven,
> In a grimmer game, the high elated souls
> To score their goals.

Let these, O God, still test their manhood's strength,
Wrestle and leap and run,
Feel sea and wind and sun;
With Cherubim contend;
The timeless morning spend
In great celestial games.
Let there be laughter and a merry noise
Now that the fields of Heaven shine
With all these golden boys.'[38]

For a number of other women versifiers the relationship between playing field and battlefield was a close one. Another prolific 'poetess' of the great War, C.A. Renshaw, drew a direct parallel between the playing field and the battlefield in a verse simply entitled 'Out', which owes much to Sir Henry Newbolt's more famous 'Vitaë Lampada':

Ten years ago, straight-limbed and eager-eyed,
With all the zest of battle in his soul,
He captained his eleven – took his toll
Of enemy-wickets – swung, his bat with pride,
Stood firm 'fore demon-balls, legs planted wide,
Hair lifting in the wind, pads gleaming white,
Brown arms held taut, eyes full of battle-light.
... Ten years ago, the champion of his side!

Now lies he wounded in a field of France,
Cheering his men with many a feeble shout.
His last stern match is played. Unfavouring
Chance
Has hurled his wickets down. A khaki mass,
He lies heart-heavy on the crimson grass,
– Game to the last – a fearless Champion – out![39]

There is no desperate mourning here. This is a paean to 'a fearless champion' who dies 'heart-heavy' on the 'crimson grass' while Renshaw rejoices proudly in his (and her) stoical acceptance of the 'last stern match' well played!

Another who offers bellicose opposition to mourning and preaches the morality of a war death, 'to keep England safe and warm', is Jessie

Pope in 'Play the Game' – once the relationship between sport and war one of moral association, as well as martial preparation, for 'muscular boys on the ball, is clear'.[40]

> Twenty-two stalwarts in stripes and shorts
> Kicking a ball along,
> Set in a square of leather-lunged sports
> Twenty-two thousand strong,
> Some of them shabby, some of them spruce,
> Savagely clamorous all,
> Hurling endearments, advice or abuse,
> At the muscular boys on the ball.
>
> Stark and stiff 'neath a stranger's sky
> A few hundred miles away,
> War-worn, khaki-clad figures lie,
> Their faces rigid and grey –
> Stagger and drop where the bullets swarm,
> Where the shrapnel is bursting loud,
> Die, to keep England safe and warm –
> For a vigorous football crowd!
>
> Football's a sport, and a rare sport too,
> Don't make it a source of shame.
> To-day there are worthier things to do.
> Englishmen, play the game!
> A truce to the League, a truce to the Cup,
> Get to work with a *gun*.
> When our country's at war we must all back up –
> It's the only thing to be done![41]

In 'Cricket – 1915' she then provides hearty encouragement for the summer sportsmen of Edwardian England now 'on tour' in Flanders where 'thunder bursts in crash and flame':

> The cricket pitch is lush and rank,
> Meek daisies lift their heads, and swank,
> And golden dandelion clumps
> Annex the place reserved for stumps.

The wandering zephyrs pause and pass
Like silver waves across the grass,
And rustics nod their heads and say,
''Twill be a proper crop o' hay.'

Where are those hefty sporting lads
Who donned the flannels, gloves and pads?
They play a new and deadly game
Where thunder bursts in crash and flame.
Our cricketers have gone 'on tour,'
To make their country's triumph sure.
They'll take the Kaiser's middle wicket
And smash it by clean British cricket.[42]

There are other aspects of the verse of the women of the period that deserve greater consideration than they have hitherto received. The widely and firmly held late Victorian and Edwardian belief in sport as preparation for war, for example, is nowhere better described than in Letts' moving verse 'To a Soldier in Hospital' who 'month by weary month' faced each painful day, 'A Merry Stoic, patient, chivalrous'.[43] Letts was convinced that this stoically endured suffering was the outcome of an athletic boyhood.

Courage came to you with your boyhood's grace
Of ardent life and limb.
Each day new dangers steeled you to the test,
To ride, to climb, to swim.
Your hot blood taught you carelessness of death
With every breath.

So when you went to play another game
You could not but be brave:
An Empire's team, a rougher football field,
The end – who knew? – your grave.
What matter? On the winning of a goal
You stake your soul.[44]

As death became an everyday reality on the battlefields of the Western Front and athletic schoolboys became rotting corpses, May

Wedderburn Cannan recorded a pathetic 'awakening' in 'A Ballad of June, 1915':

> I made a garden for my love
> With roses white and roses red,
> And I must gather rosemary,
> For my love lieth dead.
>
> I planned to plunder all the stars
> To make a chaplet for his head;
> The rain beats on the window bars,
> And my love lieth dead.
>
> I meant to make a dream of days
> With life by love and laughter led;
> I stumble over stony ways,
> And my love lieth dead.
>
> I made a garden for my love
> With roses white and roses red,
> And I must gather rosemary,
> For my love lieth dead.[45]

Nora Griffiths too, in her verse 'The Wykhamist' about a Winchester schoolboy, reflected this 'awakening' and caught, with quiet, understated pathos, a sudden terrible transition from classroom and playing field, books and balls, to trenches and no man's land, bullets, shells and premature death.

> ... A year ago you heard Cathedral's chime,
> You hurried up to books – a year ago;
> – Shouted for 'Houses' in New Field below.
> ... You ... 'died of wounds' ... they told me
>
> ... yet your feet
> Pass with the others down the twilit street.[46]

With 'The Wykhamist' the mood is changed. Letts' sombre 'Spring the Cheat' captures the disillusioned suffering that women of the Great War

struggled to put into words as the hideous consequences of the
battlefield became terribly apparent.

> The wych-elm shakes its sequins to the ground,
> With every wind the chestnut blooms fall:
> Down by the stream the willow-warblers sing,
> And in the garden to a merry sound
> The mown grass flies. The fantail pigeons call
> And sidle on the roof; a murmuring
> Of bees about the woodbine-covered wall,
> A child's sweet chime of laughter – this is spring.
>
> Luminous evenings when the blackbird sways
> Upon the rose and tunes his flageolet,
> A sea of bluebells down the woodland ways, –
> O exquisite spring, all this – and yet – and yet –
> Kinder to me the bleak face of December
> Who gives no cheating hopes, but says – 'Remember'.[47]

Before this change, however, the thrilling opening of the Great War had
resulted in a surge of extraordinary romantic chivalric verse on the part
of women versifiers. August 1914 was a month of blazing sunshine; a
romantic moment locked forever in the memory of the survivors. Only
in retrospect was the tragedy to become fully appreciated:

> They called it the Golden Summer afterwards, that last summer
> before our world came to an end .... There were dances on those
> hot summer evenings, and picnics on the river ... and Eights' Week
> with the boats going down to the start and deep voices calling
> 'touch her bow and two' ... and then Term was over and there was
> the Magdalen Commemoration Ball. It was very nearly the end of
> our world. Magdalen, some say, is the most beautiful of all Oxford
> Colleges, and though it is always for Trinity that my heart turns
> over, I have kept through my life a great love for Magdalen living
> my early years under the shadow of her Tower; walking through
> the cool dark of her cloisters into the sunshine of the garden ...
> Leaning over the bridge that crossed Cherwell to look for the flash
> of kingfishers' wings; wondering along Addison's Walk with my
> head full of poetry, thinking the long, long thoughts of youth ...

What I remember most of that last romantic night is the dew on the roses in the President's garden and saying goodbye in the dawn light in the empty street to my three best friends who were off that same day to camp. They were going down, I think we all knew that we were saying goodbye, not only to each other, but to our youth.[48]

These are the words of May Wedderburn Cannan. Her lithe and graceful boys, who had rowed on the Cam and the Isis and who had elegantly graced the cricket fields in their whites in the seemingly endless sunshine of Edwardian summers, were transformed in verse, as if by Merlin's magic, into Arthurian Knights – errant in pursuit of an early twentieth century Holy Grail.

No one delighted in this exotic knightly imagery, or in images of public schoolboys as Christian crusaders, more than Katharine Tynan – half-mystic and full catholic. For Tynan the Great War became the Holy War of a twentieth century English middle class and public school chivalric new order, as in 'To the Others':

> This was the gleam then that lured from far
> Your son and my son to the Holy War:
> Your son and my son for the accolade
> With the banner of Christ over them, in steel arrayed.
>
> Dreams of knight's armour and the battle shout,
> Fighting and falling at the last redoubt;
> Dreams of long dying on the field if slain:
> This was the dream that lured, nor lured in vain.
>
> Your son and my son, clean as new swords,
> Your man and my man and now the Lord's!
> Your son and my son for the great Crusade,
> With the banner of Christ over them – our knights, new-made.[49]

Such boys became collectively an emblematic Galahad described euphorically in 'The Heart of a Boy':

> The heart of a boy is full of light,
> Naked of self, quite pure and clean,
> No shadows lurk in it: it is bright
> Where God Himself hath been.

The boy's heart now is set on a star,
A sword for the weak against the strong,
A young knight riding forth to the War
Who dies to right the wrong.[50]

Tynan's adulation of her young heroes at times became surreal, as in 'New Heaven':

Paradise now has many a Knight,
Many a lordkin, many lords.
Glimmer of armour, dinted and bright,
The young Knights have put on new swords.

Some have barely the down on the lip,
Smiling yet from the new-won spurs,
Their wounds are rubies, glowing and deep,
Their scars amethyst – glorious scars.[51]

And in 'Riding Home':

As they pass without a sound, there is many a red wound.
Oh, pale they are and faint they are, these warriors renowned!
Yet smiling altogether in the calm sweet weather,
As they ride home together.[52]

In her first two volumes of war verse, *Flowers of Youth: Poems in War Time* (1915) and *The Holy War* (1916), she drew 'images of laughing, graceful [public school] boys ... passing sweetly and seemingly painlessly into paradise'.[53] Tynan was the supreme chantress of war as the source of willing 'sacrificial destiny':[54]

Straight to his death he went,
A smile upon his lips,
All his life's joy unspent,
Into eclipse.[55]

For her middle-class Galahads, soldiering was sport:

He plays the game winning or losing,
As in the playingfields at home,
This picnic's nothing of his choosing,
But since it's started, let it come.[56]

She clung to her belief in beautiful boy Paladins throughout the war. In *Late Songs* (1917), 'Children's War' sang yet again of 'the pure and clean':

> Fresh from the Chrisom waters pure,
> Dear boys, so eager to attain
> To the bright visions that allure,
> The fierce ordeal, the red pain.
>
> The light is yet upon their curls:
> The dream is still within their eyes;
> Their cheeks are silken as a girl's,
> The little Knights of Paradise.
>
> Brown heads with curls all rippled over,
> Young bodies slender as a flame,
> They leap to darkness like a lover;
> To Twenty-One is fall'n the game.
>
> It is the Boys' War. Praise be given
> To Percivale and Galahad
> Who have won earth and taken Heaven.
> By Violence! *Weep not, but be glad.*[57]

Romantic mysticism was not exclusive to Katharine Tynan, although she was, in all probability, its most extravagant proponent. In her third book of verse, *Up to the Hills*, C.A. Renshaw wrote of her 'Lancelot' in 'The Unknown Warrior':

> He went to war, a stumbling Lancelot
> With stainless banner and untarnished plumes
> And dreams that men have died for. The perfumes
> Of Spring were in his soul, and Love begot
> The splendour of adventurous deeds and hot
> Knight-errantry ... But Death has ta'en him now,
> My stainless knight, and left me wondering how
> Beauty and Love can be, now he is not.[58]

Renshaw, it should be added, did attempt to capture the horrors of the front-line in some of her later verses, nevertheless 'Romance', written well into the war, still depicted:

> Boys from battle – battle-stained,
> Chivalry has never waned.
> Heads go up and pulses thrill;
> Hearts grow hot and blue eyes fill,
> ... Dim Romance is potent still![59]

While in 'England's Boys' she had earlier sung grandiloquently of 'moonlight armour', 'mail-clad steeds' and 'strenuous Chivalry':

> When England called, a hundred thousand boys
> Came singing down the roadways of the world.
> The trumpet blared, the banner was unfurled;
> The earth breathed battle and its lusty joys.
> What dreams of mail-clad steeds in prancing poise,
> And flash of moonlit armour near the sea
> Stirred their child-souls to strenuous Chivalry,
> And swept them into battle – from their toys.[60]

Some were strident in their worship of their 'chevaliers sans peur et sans rapproche', others were sombre. In *Triumph and Other Poems*, 'C.C.' composed a gentle elegiac verse in quiet praise of her 'knight':

> Sir Galahad the pure has come again.
> Not glorious, in flashing armour clad,
> But shining with a radiance pure and sweet
> That comes from his great soul. He was not high
> Among the ranks of men, but high in heart,
> Brave to the last, he died away from home,
> Serving his country in a foreign land.
> His life was quiet, peaceful and obscure,
> But when the clash of arms that shook the world
> Came, he arose, and girding on the sword,
> Went forth to serve beneath his country's flag.[61]

In *Daybreak and Other Poems*, Alice M. Buckton sent 'M.C.A.L.' into battle in the role of a Crusader off to Jerusalem:

True knight of God! Before thee lies,
Far under unimagined skies
The bright commanding goal!
Crown of the spirit's fair emprise,
The fadeless home of eager eyes,
The city of the soul![62]

And in 'Girl's Song, 1916', May Wedderburn Cannan wrote of her chivalric guardian:

In heaven there may be many stars
For the glory of the Lord,
But one most bright which is the light
Upon my true love's sword,
To show that he always for me
Keepeth good watch and ward.

In England now few lamps there be
Since Death flies low by night,
But brave behind the lowered blind
Shall mine burn steady bright,
That he may know for him also
Burneth a kindly light.[63]

Such verse was surely self-protective, understandably laudatory, defensively celebratory. In realism lay insanity; in romanticism lay sanity. Be that as it may, whatever the reasons for the outpouring of early chivalric romanticism, ultimately there was only the aching loneliness of loss. The trumpets faded away well before 1918, the drums were silent, the cheering over. A new reflective sadness was caught in May Wedderburn Cannan's 'After the War' in her volume of verse *In War Time* (1917):

After the War perhaps I'll sit again
Out on the terrace where I sat with you,
And see the changeless sky and hills beat blue
And live an afternoon of summer through.

> I shall remember then, and sad at heart
> For the lost day of happiness we knew,
> Wish only that some other man were you
> And spoke my name as once you used to do.[64]

Future lost days of happiness would now be filled with silent ghosts. In a simple verse 'I want to Talk to Thee', Dora Sigerson spoke for thousands of the forlorn:

> I want to talk to thee of many things
> Or sit in silence when the robin sings
> His little song, when comes the winter bleak
> I want to sit beside thee, cheek by cheek.
>
> I want to hear thy voice my name repeat,
> To fill my heart with echoes ever sweet;
> I want to hear thy love come calling me,
> I want to seek and find but thee, but thee.[65]

Ghosts in khaki now haunted numerous homes. 'The Boys of the House' of Katharine Tynan came 'at dawn and gloam':

> Young martyrs of the war,
> Who with your bright eyes star
> The shadows grey;
> Who steal at dawn and gloam
> In each beloved room
> So pale, so gay.
>
> Boys who will not grow old,
> Peach cheek and hair of gold,
> Smile and are flown;
> You will come back again,
> In the darkness and the rain,
> In the dusk, in the dawn.[66]

After the war, May Wedderburn Cannan waited in empty hope for her heroes in 'A Dream House' of her imagination:

I will build me a house some day,
In the days when I am old,
And I will have warm-hearted fires
To keep me from the cold;
And it shall be between the sea
And the lift of the English wold.

And I will have sun-dazzled lawns
With roses on each side,
And roses red and white to climb
My windows opened wide
That I may hear the seagulls call
And the lapping of the tide.

And there shall be quiet garden paths
And lilies at the gate,
And evening primroses to light
Lamps when the hour is late;
Lest in the dark they pass my doors
For whom I watch and wait.[67]

These ghosts were everywhere and most often, it seems, where the beauty of nature brought back the most compelling memories, as in Marion Allen's 'The Wind on the Downs':

I like to think of you as brown and tall,
As strong and living as you used to be,
In khaki tunic, Sam Brown belt and all,
And standing there and laughing down at me.
Because they tell me, dear, that you are dead,
Because I can no longer see your face,
You have not died, it is not true, instead
You seek adventure in some other place.

We walked along the tow-path, you and I,
Beside the sluggish-moving, still canal;
It seemed impossible that you should die;[68]

And as in Lady Ashmore's 'Blue-Bell Time':

> In blue-bell time the woods are fair;
> But now, ah, now I am aware
> Of something different in the blue –
> Not like the colour fresh as dew,
> The woodland glades were wont to wear.
>
> The sunlight has a weary air –
> Not as it shimmered here and there
> The day I roamed the woods with you
> In blue-bell time.
>
> There's something missing everywhere:
> And though I may not seem to care,
> Yet, ever since that last adieu,
> When buds break forth, grief blossoms too,
> And mine is more than I can bear
> In blue-bell time.[69]

The loneliness of loss was for life. In 'The Promise', May Aldington made this heart-rendingly clear:

> If only you could promise me,
> That someday I shall be
> Less lonely through the silent years,
> And through eternity!
>
> If only you could promise me,
> That someday I shall be
> Less lonely through the silent years.
> Oh! Love – just promise me.[70]

As did Vera Brittain in her better known 'Perhaps':

> Perhaps some day the sun will shine again,
> And I shall see that still the skies are blue,
> And feel once more I do not live in vain,
> Although bereft of You.
>
> Perhaps the golden meadows at my feet
> Will make the sunny hours of Spring seem gay,
> And I shall find the white May blossoms sweet,
> Though You have passed away.

Perhaps the summer woods will shimmer bright,
And crimson roses once again be fair,
And autumn harvest fields a rich delight,
Although You are not there.

Perhaps some day I shall not shrink in pain
To see the passing of the dying year,
And listen to the Christmas songs again,
Although You cannot hear.[71]

In retrospect, and in the years after the war, the sharpness of loss became, if anything, sharper for some. In 1919 May Wedderburn Cannan wrote 'Women Demobilized':

Now must we go again back to the world
Full of grey ghosts and voices of men dying,
And in the rain the sounding of Last Posts
And Lovers' crying –
Back to the old, back to the empty world.

Now are put by the bugles and the drums,
And the worn spurs, and the great words they carried,
Now are we made most lonely, proudly, theirs,
The men we married:
Under the dome the long roll of the drums.

Now in our hearts abides always our war,
Time brings, to us, no day for our forgetting,
Never for us is folded War away,
Dawn or sun setting,
Now in our hearts abides always our war.[72]

Four years later, she composed perhaps her most moving poem 'The Echo, 1923' for a generation of women that would live too long:

When we are dead and all the longing's over
We shall have rest from dreams of love of men;
We shall not know the bees are in the clover
Nor weep the Summers of our loving them.

We shall have paid at last our debt to Laughter,
It will not matter then if we are sad,
They will not know, a generation after,
We wept the children that we never had.

We shall go down, a legend of lost sorrow,
We shall endure, a lilt of sunset songs;
The bitterness will all be dead tomorrow –
They will not know we knew we lived too long.[73]

The middle-class women of 1914 sent their admired schoolboy athletes[74] off to war, innocently, excitedly and patriotically 'with flowers in their rifles and patriotic songs on their lips, too young, too innocent to suspect what bloody rites of passage awaited them' and then, in time, saddened and alone, too many became 'wasted women who had become widows before becoming wives'.[75]

Robert Wohl has declared that it is tempting to argue that 'if the war generation is "lost"' it is lost 'because it has no history'.[76] His purpose was to restore the men of 1914 to the realm of history. My purpose has been to help restore the women of 1914 to the realm of history. Their words reveal 'the experience that inspired their authors to produce them'.[77] Thus, they constitute a poignant collective biography; a study of shifting period mentalities; a record of love, loyalty and suffering. Through their verse, arguably, they helped move women closer to the centre of the social stage. They certainly made women more visible, they made them more public and they gave them a common voice. At a personal level, the Great War proved to be a harrowing journey of experience – from romance to reality – for many 'lost' women versifiers whose heroes were firstly boyish athletes on playing fields, then laughing knights in armour and finally and perpetually, silent ghosts in khaki.

NOTES

1. Lily Doyle, 'The Blue-eyed Volunteer' in *Bound in Khaki* (London: Elliot Stock, 1916), p.85.
2. Judith Kazantzis, 'Preface' in Catherine Reilly (ed.), *Scars Upon My Heart* (London: Virago, 1981), p.xv.
3. Incidentally, Catherine Reilly points out that a few women were writing protest poetry well before Owen and Sassoon. See Reilly, *Scars Upon My Heart*, Introduction, p.xxxv.
4. Alan Judd, 'The "futile" First World War was a triumph of ingenuity', *Daily Telegraph*, 20 July 2001, 18.
5. J.A. Mangan, 'Duty unto Death: English Masculinity and Militarism the Age of the New

Imperialism' in J.A. Mangan (ed.), *Tribal Identities: Nationalism, Europe, Sport* (London and Portland, OR: Frank Cass, 1996), p.31.

6. Charlotte Fyfe (ed.), *The Tears of War: The Love Story of a Young Girl and a War Hero – May Cannan, Bevil Quiller-Couch* (London: Cavalier Books, 2000), p.57.

7. Ibid., pp.70–1.

8. Kazantzis, 'Preface', p.xix.

9. Ibid.

10. Ibid.

11. Ben Shephard, *A War of Nerves* (London: Cape, 2000), *passim*.

12. Kazantzis, 'Preface', p.xx.

13. Ibid.

14. Ibid., p.xviii.

15. Ibid.

16. Katharine Tynan, 'High Summer' in idem, *The Holy War* (London: Sidgwick and Jackson, 1916), p.43.

17. See Nina Macdonald, *War-Time Nursery Rhymes* (London: Routledge, 1919).

18. Ibid., p.59.

19. Ibid., p.21.

20. Quoted on the back cover of C.A. Renshaw, *England's Boys* (London: Erskine Macdonald, 1918).

21. C.A. Renshaw, 'The Noblest Height' in idem, *Battle and Beyond* (London: Erskine Macdonald, 1917), p.38.

22. Charlotte E. Paterson, 'From the Watch Tower' in idem, *From the Watch Tower* (London: Allenson 1916), p.10.

23. 'C.C.', *Triumph and Other Poems* (London: Chapman and Hull, 1916), p.13.

24. Anita Moor, 'For England' in idem, *Roundels and Rhymes* (Lausanne: Librairie Anglaise Th. Roussy, 1919), p.71.

25. Madame Henri Curchod (née Mary M. Alexander – a Scot from Glasgow), 'The Old Flag' in *The Union Jack and Other Battle Songs and Poems* (Paisley: Alexander Paisley, 1915), p.29.

26. Ibid., p.60.

27. Ibid., p.72.

28. Renshaw, 'My Mate' in *Battle and Beyond*, p.44.

29. Dorothy Plowman, 'The High Adventure' in idem, *Lyrical Poems* (Oxford: Blackwell, 1916), p.11.

30. Renshaw, 'In Memoriam' in *Battle and Beyond*, p.32.

31. Katharine Tynan, 'The Short Road to Heaven' in idem, *Herb O'Grace* (London: Sidgwick and Jackson, 1918), p.19.

32. See, for example, J.A. Mangan, *Athleticism in the Victorian and Edwardian Public School: The Emergence and Consolidation of an Educational Ideology* (London and Portland, OR: Frank Cass, 2000); and J.A. Mangan, *The Games Ethic and Imperialism: Aspects of the Diffusion of an Ideal* (London and Portland, OR: Frank Cass, 1999).

33. Joyce Kilmer, 'The New School' in George Herbert Clarke (ed.), *A Treasury of War Poetry* (London: Hodder and Stoughton, 1919), p.373.

34. Ibid.

35. W.M. Letts, 'The Spires of Oxford' in idem, *The Spires of Oxford and Other Poems* (New York: Dutton, 1917), p.7.

36. May Aldington, 'Come Over Here' in idem, *Roll of Honour and Other Poems* (Rye: Adams, 1917), p. 12.

37. Tynan, 'Speeding' in *The Holy War*, p.39.

38. W.M. Letts, 'Golden Boys' in idem, *Hallow-e'en and Poems of the War* (London: Murray, 1916), p.16.

39. C.A. Renshaw, 'Out' in idem, *England's Boys and Other Poems* (London, Erskine Macdonald, 1918), p.47.

40. Jessie Pope, 'Play the Game' in idem, *Jessie Pope's War Poems* (London: Grant Richards, 1915), p.11.

41. Ibid., p.47.

42. Ibid., p.47.
43. W.M. Letts, 'To a Soldier in Hospital' in *Hallow-e'en and Poems of the War*, p.15.
44. Ibid.
45. May Wedderburn Cannan, 'A Ballad of June, 1915' in idem, *In War Time: Poems* (Oxford: Blackwell, 1917), p.34.
46. Nora Griffiths, 'The Wykhamist' in Reilly, *Scars Upon My Heart*, p.44.
47. Letts, 'Spring the Cheat' in *Hallow-e'en and Poems of the War*, p.45.
48. Fyfe, *The Tears of War*, p.27.
49. Tynan, 'To the Others', in *The Holy War*, p.15.
50. Ibid., p.19.
51. Ibid., p.48.
52. Ibid., p.49.
53. See J.A. Mangan, 'Gamesfield and Battlefield: A Romantic Alliance in Verse and the Creation of Militaristic Masculinity' in John Nauright and T.J.L. Chandler (eds.), *Making Men: Rugby and Masculine Identity* (London and Portland, OR: Frank Cass, 1998), pp.148–9.
54. Ibid.
55. Ibid.
56. Ibid.
57. Katharine Tynan, 'The Children's War' in idem, *Late Songs* (London: Sidgwick and Jackson, 1917), p.11.
58. Renshaw, 'The Unknown Warrior' in idem, *Up to the Hills* (London: Merton Press, 1922), p.24.
59. Renshaw, 'Romance' in *England's Boys*, p.58.
60. Ibid., p.15.
61. 'C.C.', 'To S.P.C.: On his Death' in *Triumph and Other Poems*, p.16.
62. Alice M. Buckton, 'His Lady's Farewell' in idem, *Daybreak, and Other Poems* (London: Methven, 1918), p.7.
63. Cannan, 'Girls' Song, 1916' in Fyfe, *The Tears of War*, p.55.
64. Cannan, 'After the War' in *In War Time: Poems*, p.79.
65. Dora Sigerson, 'I want to Talk to Thee' in idem., *The Sad Years* (London: Constable, 1918), p.35.
66. Tynan, 'The Boys in the House' in *Herb O'Grace*, p.53.
67. Cannan, 'A Dream House' in *The Tears of War*, p.142.
68. Marian Allen, *The Wind on the Downs and Other Poems* (London: Humphreys, 1918), p.12.
69. Lady Ashmore, *Song of the Camerons and Other Poems* (London: Hodder and Stoughton, 1922), p.76.
70. Aldington, 'The Promise' in *Roll of Honour and Other Poems*, p.21.
71. Vera Brittain, 'Perhaps' in Reilly, *Scars Upon My Heart*, pp.14–15.
72. Cannan, 'Women Demobilized' in *The Tears of War*, p.140.
73. Cannan, 'The Echo, 1923' in *The Tears of War*, p.165.
74. They celebrated, supported and mourned, of course, many who were not athletic heroes of public school playing fields, but it is clear that these 'brave schools bloods' had a special place in many of the writers' hearts.
75. Robert Wohl, *The Generation of 1914* (London: Weidenfeld and Nicolson, 1979), p.1.
76. Ibid., p.2.
77. Ibid., p.4. Wohl, of course, covered Europe. I cover Britain, but mostly England.

7

Modernizing Bulgaria:
Todor Yonchev – Middle-Class Patriot and the Assertion of a Nation

VASSIL GIRGINOV and LOZAN MITEV

A man with vision is worth 100 men with intentions

As we are often reminded, individuals make history. However, any attempt to single out the role of a particular individual presents a major challenge and involves the interdependency between actors and conjunctures of agents and power. This essay is no exception to the rule in that it sets out to investigate the contribution of Todor Yonchev to modern physical education and sport in Bulgaria. What follows from this aim are two methodological considerations: first, an analysis has to account for historical settings in which individuals act and has to examine their deeds both as formed by wider socio-cultural influences and as forming these influences; second, there is a need for clarity when choosing a figure epitomizing a society's striving towards a new identity and a place in the world system. Bulgarian history, as indeed the history of most nations, is not short of examples of great humanitarians and their moral exploits and accomplishments. Three main criteria for assessing the contribution of Todor Yonchev to Bulgarian physical culture have been employed: (1) the originality and universality of his conceptual grounding; (2) the relationship between his vision and implementation; and (3) his relevance to present-day sport.

The essay uses these criteria in an attempt to set the life and work of Yonchev in the context of the shaping of the modern Bulgarian state at the end of the nineteenth century. The first section elaborates on the circumstances that shaped the structure of the society and determined the nature of Yonchev's physical education project. The second section deals with the state–society relations responsible for providing the specific and immediate contexts in which Yonchev developed his visions for modern physical education and worked towards their implementation. The third part discusses his career and spells out the major lasting contributions he made to society. Finally, the essay outlines the main constituents of Yonchev's pioneering work to present-day sport.

LAYING THE FOUNDATIONS OF THE NEW STATE: MODERNIZATION VERSUS CONSERVATISM

The Bulgarian state was created in 681. After centuries of development and prosperity, it lost its independence to the Ottoman Empire in 1369 only to re-emerge in 1878 on its way to sovereignty, though substantially different in terms of territory, population and constitution. The plans of the Great Powers (Great Britain and Russia) for the geo-political mapping of Bulgaria urged the re-evaluation of the preliminary peace Treaty of San Stephan (March 1878) and imposed the Berlin Treaty of September 1878 in its place. The Berlin Treaty reshaped the territorial and ethnic base as well as the organizational and spiritual culture of Bulgarian society. The Bulgarian people refused to accept the Treaty and openly resisted its implementation. As Velev *et al.* asserted, 'restoring the wholeness of the 'San Stephan's Bulgaria' as part of the great Bulgarian national ideal – "for a unified and inseparable Bulgaria" has turned into a national incantation'.[1] Eventually a compromise was reached and Bulgaria was recognized as a sovereign state in 1908.

To return to the 1880s, as a result of a deepening administrative crisis and a local uprising, the country achieved unification in 1885. The Bulgarian nation appeared to be on the road to modern development with the ambition to build a new secular state out of the ruins of the theocratic Ottoman Empire. This project presupposed no continuity. Bulgaria aspired to regain its place as a European nation-state. However, the backwardness of the Ottoman Empire provided no political, economic or social foundations to build on and virtually all the constitutional elements of the new state had to be developed or imported.

Russia, which defeated Turkey in the 1877–78 war, assumed a leading innovatory role and laid the foundations of Bulgaria's constitution, parliament, state administration, laws, judicial system, army, police, banking system, transport, communications network and cultural institutions. It is interesting to note that modernization was accomplished in Bulgaria to a far more advanced degree than in Russia itself. As the then Russian War Minister, Milutin, acknowledged, 'we could not have not admitted that our whole state organisation demands a fundamental reconstruction from top to bottom. As for agricultural self-governance, local, regional and state administration – everything has outlived its time and would have to gain new forms.'[2]

Bulgaria's first constitution, Turnovo (1879), defined it as a bourgeois state lead by a monarch and put the building of a capitalist society at the top of its political-economic agenda. This project, however, had to be pursued by a single party – the Liberal Party, representing the poor and the petit bourgeoisie. The Conservative Party, which was supposed to represent the interests of the wealthiest group (a very small number of people linked closely with German and Austrian financial and economic elites), did not constitute itself until four years after the liberation. It then demonstrated a total lack of interest in the political maturity of the people for some ten years before disintegrating and eventually expiring after 1885.[3] Other political parties emerged as spin-offs of the Liberal Party, triggered by either ideological or leadership differences. The lack of political tradition and the need to appeal to the majority of the population stimulated various interest groups to generate support by identifying themselves with 'the whole people' as opposed to a particular class or group. This approach was typical of the behaviour of sports organizations, which also sought identification with wider social groups.

Clearly the Liberal Party's visions prevailed in society as it promoted the values of independence, unification, modernization, universal and free education and international understanding. It is important to note the role of education in building the new society. The Liberal Party programme of 1880 defined its mission of education:

> the school should prepare worthy servants for the public and state life as well as capable and skillful workers for the private domain. This would enable every member of our society to develop, because the economic situation of the people will depend very much on that. The school should give its students as much real knowledge as possible, or what we would call a 'knowledge for life'.[4]

In the first five decades after its liberation, Bulgaria was economically dominated by small to middle-sized craft production and agricultural smallholdings. Until 1884, there were only 23 factories with more than ten employees, this number increased to 30 by 1904 and to 1,245 by 1930.[5] In comparison, the Cadburys chocolate factory near Birmingham in England had 3,000 employees in 1900. Despite this growth and the state's heavily protectionist policies in the form of special laws for encouraging domestic industry (in 1883, 1895, 1897, 1905 and 1928), the economy remained underdeveloped and poorly structured, with industrial production and craft production contributing respectively only six per cent of GDP in 1926 and still only ten per cent in 1930. The nation's trade balance until 1930 was negative, imports exceeded exports, thus placing an extra burden on small firms. Bulgaria's foreign debt in 1939 (12.6 billion Lev) was twice the value of its annual exports (6.07 billion Lev).[6]

Bulgarian social structure mirrored its economic reality, dominated in its income by an agricultural middle-class, but in its social behaviour by a public servant-intelligentsia class. This class, in the form of a state administration was particularly well represented in the field of education (head teachers, school inspectors and teachers' organizations), and promoted an ill-founded intellectual philosophy hostile to the notion of universal education. The core of this intellectualism was a mysticism that detested pragmatism, discovery and liberalism in education, but was unable to offer a down-to-earth expression of its own pedagogical idealism. Between 1878 and the First World War the educational administration exercised a great deal of influence on social and state affairs. It succeeded in imposing its views on the provision of physical education which it depicted as lacking spirituality and morality and as being degrading and even demoralizing. These views appealed to conservative forces in society and were welcomed by the powerful Orthodox Church, which has been historically associated with a negative attitude towards physical education and all forms of athletic displays as potentially immoral. The combined reactionary forces of pedagogy and theology, coupled with the apathy of the larger part of the population, prevented the creation of proper legislative, material and ideological preconditions for establishing a modern educational system.

Table 1 shows the changing structure of society from the Liberation to the next great transformation – Communism in 1944. This structure presents Bulgaria's towns as the centres for modernizing tendencies, as opposed to the highly conservative villages. The towns' diverse social structure comprised a small wealthy capitalist class (of bankers and entrepreneurs), a mixed middle class and a very powerful group of

TABLE 7.1
ASPECTS OF BULGARIA'S SOCIAL STRUCTURE, 1885–1944

PERIOD	1878	1895	1905	1910	1920	1925	1930	1935	1944
Population (000)	2,853	3,310	4,035	4,337	4,860	5,483	6,000	6,090	6,978
number of towns	535		80	80	92	93	97	97	101
village population	2,317		3,838	3,839	4,216	4,276	4,269	4,261	5,251
hamlet population			1,100	1,099	1,344	1,392	1,397	1,395	
% urban	18.8		19.6	19.1	19.9	20.6		21.5	24
% literacy		15.6	23.8			54.0			66.0
Employment (%)									
Agriculture			75.4			75.7	80.0		
crafts, services			9.9			9.9	8.8		
trade, com'ns			6.6			6.5	4.0		
administration			4.9			5.1	5.1		
Doctors	71	325	559	658		1,011			3,516
Hospitals	8		62	67		99			1,141

Sources: P. Kushev, *Zdravnoto sastojanie na naselenieto v Balgaria 1880–1980* (The Health Status of the Population in Bulgaria 1880–1980) (Sofia: Medicina i Fizkultura, 1986) and various State Statistical Institute (SSI) figures (1970, 1980, 1990).

intelligentsia, which often became politically involved. Naturally, these groups were the bearers of modernization as manifested through industrialization and champions of modern physical education in Bulgaria came from their ranks.

PHYSICAL EDUCATION AND SPORT IN THE CONTEXT OF STATE–SOCIETY RELATIONS

Political, economic and social developments nurtured the emergence of a dominant statist ideology, underpinned by the notion of the state as the most adequate representative of public interests and as the supreme arbiter of the interests of groups. Institutionally, the state's penetration of the affairs of civil society grew from 1879's modest first cabinet with six ministries, to incorporate more and more spheres of state and civil activities (including physical education) and, with varying success, exercised control over relationships and resource distribution. Dragan Tzankov, Bulgaria's Prime Minister (1880 and 1883–84) and one of its most influential early political figures, has neatly summarized this point: 'the state in itself is of extreme importance, gained with many sacrifices and, therefore, the state interest has a natural priority over the civic'.[8]

For many decades, Article 83 of the Turnovo Constitution (1879) remained the only judicial document regulating the establishment of civil organizations. It reflected the struggle between two dominant – Conservative and Liberal – political concepts. The former, promoted by Russian and Bulgarian Conservatives, aimed to confine the freedom of association, while the latter sought more civil freedoms. A compromise was achieved which allowed for association as a civil right, providing it did not jeopardize state and public interests, or religious and moral standards as defined by the state.

Another informative example with clear implications for state–society–sport relationships concerns state legislation in the field of local authority self-governance. The 1886 Town and Village Municipalities Act and the 1909 Public Referendum on Community Issues Act gave the people greater say in crucial public matters, including election of the local assemblies and the mayor.[9] Therefore, the introduction of modern physical education and sport at the end of the nineteenth century could be seen as a challenge and as a testing ground of the extent of Europeanization. It was also a means of stimulating new public needs in an area that was not at the top of society's social and political agenda.

From the very first, physical education and sport reflected state projects and ambitions for nationhood and were bound to the military training of the population, a sphere which the Berlin Treaty banned the state from intervention. In 1878 the theme of military education was borrowed directly from the father of Germany's Turnverein (gymnastics) movement, Friedrich Jahn, by the founders of the first revolutionary Bulgarian 'Edinstvo' (Unity) committees. It was introduced in the form of 'underground' shooting groups which were inspired and controlled by the Russian Army in an attempt to save the country after its partition. However, when these groups no longer reflected the state unification project, efforts were made to reshape them into civil societies aiming 'through organisation, discipline, physical exercise and education to protect the honour and rights of the people, silence and public order in the country'.[10] The period after 1878 saw the proliferation of gymnastics and athletics clubs, mainly in the capital Sofia, offering a range of activities including elements of the German Turnverein and Czech Sokol gymnastics. However, their elitist and exclusive character prevented them from becoming centres for disseminating new ideas and practices.

Clearly then modern physical education and sport in Bulgaria did not emerge as a typical leisure pursuit of an affluent class. Nor was their organization grounded in a wide network of clubs and local provision. Following the political and economic priorities set by the state project to build the new nation, sports organizations inevitably had similar missions. Thus, sport entered the public domain as a military necessity and not as a social issue. Its public image at that time is also instructive: the most common names for clubs and associations were those of Christo Botev and Levski (the brightest revolutionary figures whose deeds were highly inspirational to Yonchev), Boretz (Fighter), Luv (Lion) or Unak (Hero).[11]

The struggle between residual and emergent practices (the former linking present to past, the latter linking present to future) became a main feature of the modernization project. This entailed a clash between conservative traditions and objective conditions on the one hand and the rapid influx of modern ideas and influences from other cultures on the other. These confrontations, and the paradox they presented, determined the nature of Bulgaria's social development. Until the First World War the driving force behind emerging practices was the civil factor in the form of an educational intelligentsia (also referred to as an enlightenment class), whose mission was to find solutions to the challenges presented by the Europeanization project. The difficulty of this task presupposed identification with the post-Ottoman reality and the promotion of ideas and projects aiming at shaping this reality, while at the same time building a bridge between past and present thus preserving and creating a national identity. Subsequently, individuals and groups who proved capable of offering solutions to the conflict between the Oriental and the European were destined to be champions of the new order. In this situation, the concept of physical culture developed by Todor Yonchev provided a measure of continuity between past and present forms of physical education and sport, and the social processes within which they were embedded. By the same token, this concept of physical culture was innovative as it ventured to blend the best of the modern European thinking and practices into a new and nationally-rooted sports form. Individuals, as noted above, have an important role to play in this process and, according to E. Rogers, they fall into two distinct types: 'change agents' and 'opinion leaders'. The former 'introduce change formally within institutions', while the latter 'influence others within the system in an informal way'.[12]

TOWARDS A HOLISTIC APPROACH IN SHAPING THE MODERN CONCEPT OF PHYSICAL CULTURE

Todor Yonchev was a prominent figure in the formative years of the modern Bulgarian state. He was a typical representative of the 'Enlightenment Class' and until he appeared on the public scene as a champion of modern physical culture, his biography was similar to most members of that class. He was born on 2 December 1859 in the town of Lom to a middle-class family. At the time, Lom was Bulgaria's second most important port on the River Danube, which provided the only link with Europe and was an important channel for the cultural and economic promotion of the town and its role in the country. He received his primary and secondary education in one of the most prominent schools of the time, under Nikola Parvanov, a great pedagogue of the Enlightenment. It is worth noting that despite Ottoman domination, Bulgarian people succeeded in creating an exceptional educational system numbering a network of 1,504 schools in 1877, of which 72 were in towns and 1,432 in villages. The whole system was underwritten by the Bulgarians themselves and was largely responsible for preserving their national identity.

FIGURE 7.1

Todor Yonchev

The schoolmaster who sent Yonchev to continue his education in a craft school in Krajova, Romania, appreciated his intellectual curiosity. Like most students, Yonchev had a scholarship from the Bulgarian Council. In 1874 he set out to study at the Pedagogical Institute in Vienna, then part of the Austro–Hungarian Empire, as a grant holder of the Oriental Museum. In 1881 Yonchev continued his education as a chemistry student at the University of Vienna. After a successful first year he was forced to terminate his study due to lack of finance and returned to Bulgaria where he was appointed as a chemistry teacher in his home town. In November 1882 he took up a position in the newly established pedagogical school, later an institute. Here he began laying the foundations of a new physical culture and forging spiritual links with Europe.

Yonchev's stay in the Pedagogical Institute had a major impact on his moral values and principles. '[T]he discovery of the practical values of the body building [gymnastics] art'[13] also had a long-lasting emotional effect on his development. He joined the Vienna men's gymnastics society and became involved in gymnastics, participating in various social and cultural events including, most importantly, the regional gymnastics gathering. During this relatively short period of time, Todor Yonchev discovered the fascinating world of corporal (physical) culture, which up until that time, due to the forms of organization, was completely unknown in his own country.

Under the influence of pedagogical idealism, Yonchev continued to study methodological literature on physical education with great energy and attention to detail. Apart from practising regularly with Austrian Turnverein organizations, he gathered information about various European systems of physical education. Despite the conceptual and practical limitations of Yonchev's visions about physical culture,[14] they were nonetheless responsible for defining his pedagogical ideas as he worked as a chemistry teacher but channelled his talent and energy into the field of physical education. The deliberate choice of physical education as the forum for his public endeavours was illustrated by his sensitivity towards the most pressing needs and weaknesses of Bulgarian cultural life.

At the age of 24 Yonchev made his debut as both a 'change agent' and an 'opinion leader' of the new physical culture in Bulgarian education. He did that at a Teachers Council meeting at the High Pedagogical School in Shoumen and assumed responsibility for delivering the classes. His powerful and persuasive arguments regarding the value of gymnastics convinced the school management to undertake the radical reform of gymnastics through European standards of teaching. Prior to Yonchev's arrival, gymnastics did not exist as an independent subject in the school curricula. Moreover, the limited forms of physical activities on offer represented nothing more than the common practice of mechanically borrowing various alien elements from foreign programmes.

In order to disseminate his view of gymnastics as widely as possible, Yonchev undertook a second major step that proved vital for implementing new physical education in Bulgaria. In 1883 he published a gymnastics textbook which was the first methodological literature in the country. As he noted in his memoirs, he 'wanted to offer support and to assist the young pedagogical staff in their careers as teachers'.[15] However, it should be pointed out that the German school of gymnastics largely influenced this publication and, in that sense, it could be seen as derivative. Nevertheless, the textbook made five major original contributions:

1. Introduced three age groups (7–10 [8–12]-, 10–13 [12–16]- and 13–16 [16–25]-year-olds) and offered three categories of educational activities (gymnastics exercises, drills and games);

2. Offered a range of illustrative and examples of activities (lessons);

3. Adapted various folk games as an element of physical education;

4. Linked the terminology and the practice of gymnastics;

5. Provided theoretical and methodological guidelines and rules and offered extensive information on aspects of education which were in accordance with national conditions.

In summation, this first attempt to introduce gymnastics at the regional centre in Shoumen revealed an advanced system of education for the time and laid the foundations for new attitudes and lasting traditions in physical education.

The versatility of Todor Yonchev extends beyond the field of gymnastics. Acutely aware that the new ideas needed to be actively promoted, he established the 'Teachers Newspaper' in Shoumen. Soon after this newspaper became the flagship of the Bulgarian Pedagogical Guild and a major disseminator of new concepts and experiences.

Yonchev remained in Shoumen until 1885 when he went to study agriculture at the Zurich Polytechnic University in Switzerland. There he published for the first time in local newspapers. Upon graduation he was appointed as an assistant in the Polytechnic's chemical laboratory.

On his arrival in Switzerland, Yonchev became a member of the gymnastic society in Zurich. The excellent organization of many spectacular gymnastics displays captured his imagination and further reinforced his convictions about the educational purpose of gymnastics. He took part in all initiatives of the society, including a cantonal (county) gathering which allowed him to accumulate valuable experiences that he implemented later in Bulgaria. As Yonchev himself stressed later, his love of his motherland had brought him back in Bulgaria. He saw his mission as a promoter of good European practices to enhance the people's cultural and economic wellbeing. Yonchev returned to Bulgaria in 1888 and became a lecturer in the newly established Agricultural School near Plovdiv, the country's main agricultural centre. There he published his first articles on his research into growing plants.

1889 marked a new stage in Yonchev's career. He moved to Sofia as a member of the Ministry of Education Industrial Commission, this position placed him in direct contact with key policy-makers in education. Within the Ministry Yonchev found 'fertile soil' for initiatives aimed at modernizing Bulgarian public life. At the time a liberal government was in office with a very ambitious programme for European integration. The then Prime Minister, Stefan Stambolov, was one of the country's most prominent political figures of the time due to his exceptional style of independent leadership and his politics that put Bulgaria back on the European map. He is still highly regarded today.

When the opportunity presented itself during the debates about national curriculum in 1892–93, Todor Yonchev launched his concept of a national physical culture programme. He envisaged physical education as the cornerstone of a universal, pragmatic and socially active education aiming at developing a new type of citizen. In some respects this programme was similar to the English concept of athleticism[16] which represented a powerful educational ideology based on manliness, training and character formation. Yonchev's concept received full political backing from the then Minister of Education, Goergy Zhivkov, and the Liberal government, which had one of the most pro–active and committed educational policies in the country's history prior to the First

World War. By way of illustration, the Ministry of Education budget grew from 1,974,248 Leva in 1886, to 4,682,260 Leva in 1890 and 8,823,743 Leva in 1894 (the government's last year in office); this represented an increase of more than 300 per cent over eight years. Another illustration of the government's radical educational policy was the Prime Minister's response to the challenge about the effectiveness of study scholarships abroad during the Parliamentary discussions on the Ministry of Education's budget in 1889. Stambolov argued that the country needed well-qualified people in all areas of public life: 'we do not provide funds for the poor, but for the gifted ... the government wants to educate the gifted'.[17]

With two critical preconditions secured – a clear vision of required educational reforms and the political will to implement them – a strategy for the implementation of physical education as an essential part of general education and social life could now go ahead. Yonchev developed and promoted a well-thought-out plan which challenged deeply-rooted patriarchic perceptions about education and suggested that the Ministry of Education should hire 12 Swiss physical education teachers on a two-year contract to help build an efficient system and to lay the foundations of modern physical education in Bulgaria.

The hidden agenda behind this proposal, as Yonchev stated later, was the achievement of his ultimate goal for physical education: to become a truly civil movement. His powers of persuasion ensured that the Minister of Education pursued the idea not through official governmental channels but through the Swiss Gymnastics Union. To assist the government in justifying their decision to hire foreign experts, Yonchev arranged a visit to the cantonal gymnastics gathering in Geneva and took Zhivkov to Switzerland. This episode was significant for two main reasons: first, it set a precedent in diplomatic relations, given that international links in general, and Bulgarian–Swiss contacts in particular, were at an embryonic stage; second, it was an outstanding example of an individual's ability to seize the historical moment and make a great cultural impact.

How revolutionary this act was can be seen from the reaction of the educational establishment. The invitation to foreign teachers to initiate a subject that was not even in the core curriculum and was not widely available was considered scandalous. Nonetheless, in spite of such opposition, the Swiss teachers arrived in Bulgaria in 1894. They were selected by the Swiss Gymnastics Union through a specially organized course for volunteers designed to meet the challenge of this type of missionary work.

In the meantime, radical political action took place, including the assassination of the Prime Minister by the opposition which was tacitly supported by the Prince. Members and collaborators with the Liberal government were stigmatized and politically cast out. In the light of these developments the arrival of the Swiss teachers came under severe attack and was presented as an act of political stupidity and financial irresponsibility. The most vocal critics were the head teachers who published a series of malicious articles about the Ministry of Education. Furthermore, some of them demonstrated extreme hostility and made several Swiss teachers redundant. Unfortunately the dominant political culture judged people according to their political affiliation rather than by their accomplishments and Yonchev found himself politically isolated. His inability to participate in making educational policy and helping promote physical education presented a huge threat to everything that he stood for and all that had been achieved under the previous government.

Yonchev took a teaching job in the oldest and most prestigious establishment in Sofia, the First Boys High School founded during the Ottoman domination in 1842. Ironically, it was there that he met Charles Champaud, one of the Swiss teachers, for the first time. Irrespective of political and social hostility, Yonchev decided to pursue his grand visions further. He assumed that in the previous two years the Swiss teachers had created the preconditions for establishing a general public movement along the lines achieved in other European countries. This was Yonchev's second attempt to set up a general movement. As he fully appreciated, the first attempt in 1883 failed because it lacked proper public and political support and technical expertise.

Yonchev offered Champaud the opportunity to set up a gymnastics society as an initial step in the creation of a general physical education movement. Initially, Champaud declined the invitation so as to honour his commitment to the state authorities not to get involved in any public or political movements. This restriction could be attributed to the escalating political struggles in the country. Subsequently, Yonchev continued lobbying amongst like-minded teachers, university professors, students, intellectuals and state officials. Further talks with Champaud resulted in his agreeing to co-operate and in 1895 they called the founding meeting of the first Bulgarian gymnastics society, Unak

(Hero). Todor Yonchev was elected president and Champaud technical instructor, two critical positions for the success of the enterprise.

The ideology of the gymnastics movement as developed by Yonchev revolved around the notion of patriotism, the most appealing and unifying idea in Bulgarian society. The emphasis on patriotism was critical for overcoming all the major hurdles that stood in the way of a new social movement aimed at instilling a modern physical culture. Patriotism was charged with deep social meaning and a powerful catalyst for creating social solidarity. The idea was to portray gymnastics both as a politically and socially unifying force with important educational functions, both civic and personal, bringing people together from all walks of life. In this respect, Yonchev's concept of physical culture represented a marked shift from the military forms of physical education and what Foucault (1980)[18] termed 'corporeal power'.[19] Notably in this regard Yonchev extended the meaning of the term 'gymnastics' by gradually substituting the regimented forms of practice with more liberal forms of team games. This process had both ideological purposes and political implications as it promoted mass participation in universal school physical education and therefore eliminated the class-specific practices in existence elsewhere in Western Europe. These wider social functions were tied to a belief in the values of physical education for personal development and self-fulfilment. In short, the patriotic ideal representing national aspirations and identity was linked with modern forms of physical culture representing personal aspirations and self-evaluation. This ideological combination, together with mass involvement, provided a valuable resource able to mobilize large groups of society and young people in particular.

Sound educational principles, complemented by a series of successful public displays, quickly gained popularity for Unak and had a positive social impact widely reported by the media. The next stage of Yonchev's plan envisaged the creation of a nation-wide network of gymnastics societies. In order to achieve this, he arranged visits to major towns and stimulated public enthusiasm for the success of the movement. Unak also encouraged the rest of the Swiss teachers to set up similar gymnastics societies. Two years of active campaigning resulted in the establishment of 27 'Unak' societies around the country.

Before sending out an invitation to the founding congress of a nation-wide organization, Yonchev needed to develop the key constituents of the new social movement. This was achieved through three interrelated processes of establishing values, institutions and practices which signalled the beginning of the codification and regulation of physical activity and sport as highly visible public elements. First, he established the principles of the Bulgarian gymnastics system, according to which it was universal and holistic by character and included *all* types of gymnastics, athletics and games. Second, he formulated the key values of physical culture – aesthetic development, good citizenship and self-fulfilment – which were later adopted by the whole sports movement. Third, he introduced an organizational structure to the movement based on federalism, the independence of all units and equal rights. These actions underpinned the development of a national sports movement until they were discarded by the advance of the authoritarian regimes of the late 1930s and 1940s. Fourth, Yonchev initiated the publishing of a magazine entitled *Health and Strength* (Zdrave i Sila), the first of its kind. The magazine served three important purposes: the active promotion of Unak's mission; the cultivation of new social values for physical culture in society; and the availability of methodological assistance, thus enhancing the professional skills of Bulgarian specialists. Yonchev also designed those most powerful elements of physical education, its rituals and symbols, in a way that preserved its national identity. This was not all. He was also responsible for diversifying the social base of Unak by inviting prominent public and academic figures as honourable members, thus ensuring greater independence and public acceptance. Despite political and social changes, all these elements remained the guiding principles of the national sport system for generations.

Three years after the creation of the first gymnastics society in 1895, Yonchev founded the Union of Bulgarian Gymnastic Unak Societies. His efforts were assisted by a 1897 Directive of the then Minister of Education, Konstantin Velichkov, who called on all school authorities to consider establishing similar societies because of the benefits they offered for the moral and physical education of youth. Two interesting points deserve mention here. First, in contrast to all other Slav states, which established their gymnastics movements on the lines of the Czech Sokol's (Falcon) model, the form and the practices of Unak remained largely unique and national in character. This uniqueness becomes even more striking given Russia's political and cultural hegemony. It showed quite clearly that the practices promoted by the Union Unak did not simply imitate the Swiss model; there was one significant difference which was well captured in the report by Lui Eyer,[20] one of the Swiss teachers, presented at Unak's fifth congress in 1907. Eyer noted that most gymnastics societies had made a systematic move towards games and events as opposed to repetitive exercises with equipment. This move did not produce quick results in terms of gaining particular skills and was more time consuming, but did enhance the overall development of the individual. This difference is also supported by the publication of another Swiss teacher, Daniel Blanchud (see Figure 7.2). Blanchud's handbook was critical of the rigidity of Swiss gymnastics, endorsed national and other European forms of education and was instrumental in opening up the Swiss model to outside influences. Second, the founding congress of Unak rejected the competitive principle as one of the guiding principles of the Union on the grounds that it should be concerned with promoting gymnastics, not with testing its members' agility.

This episode from the end of the nineteenth century reveals an emerging tension between two competing cultural trends: a Western European striving to assert the competitive element as a dominant feature of modern sport and a Eastern European preference for a social movement promoting wider cultural and educational values.[21] This tension, in various guises, was to dominate sport throughout the twentieth century. Since the 1990s, however, there has been growing evidence to suggest a Western European, Australian and North American tendency to reconsider and resurrect this latter notion of physical culture. David Kirk recently argued for preserving this concept on the grounds that it 'implied that systems of exercise were more than mere movements, but instead were embedded in beliefs, knowledge and broader individual and social practices'.[22] In similar vein, other writers have revived the debate by advocating the concept of wellness.[23]

Todor Yonchev's comprehensive vision embraced the universal character of the movement which, by virtue of the popularity of the term and in order to ensure comprehensiveness and public acceptance, was called 'gymnastics'. His basic idea, as he put it in the Union's constitution, was to call the movement 'body-enhancing' or 'body-building'. This was not merely an issue of linguistics. The actual meaning embedded in those words entails an understanding about universalism in terms of methods, means and forms used for physical education. Table 7.2 shows the key principles, means and forms employed by the Unak Union. It was precisely that principle of universalism which prompted the Ministry of Education to entrust it with the responsibility of developing school physical education programmes and providing

FIGURE 7.2
The front cover of Daniel Blanchud's Complete Handbook of Gymnastics (1901) including in-and-out of school, military and other sports, 54 gymnastics games and over 2,500 illustrations

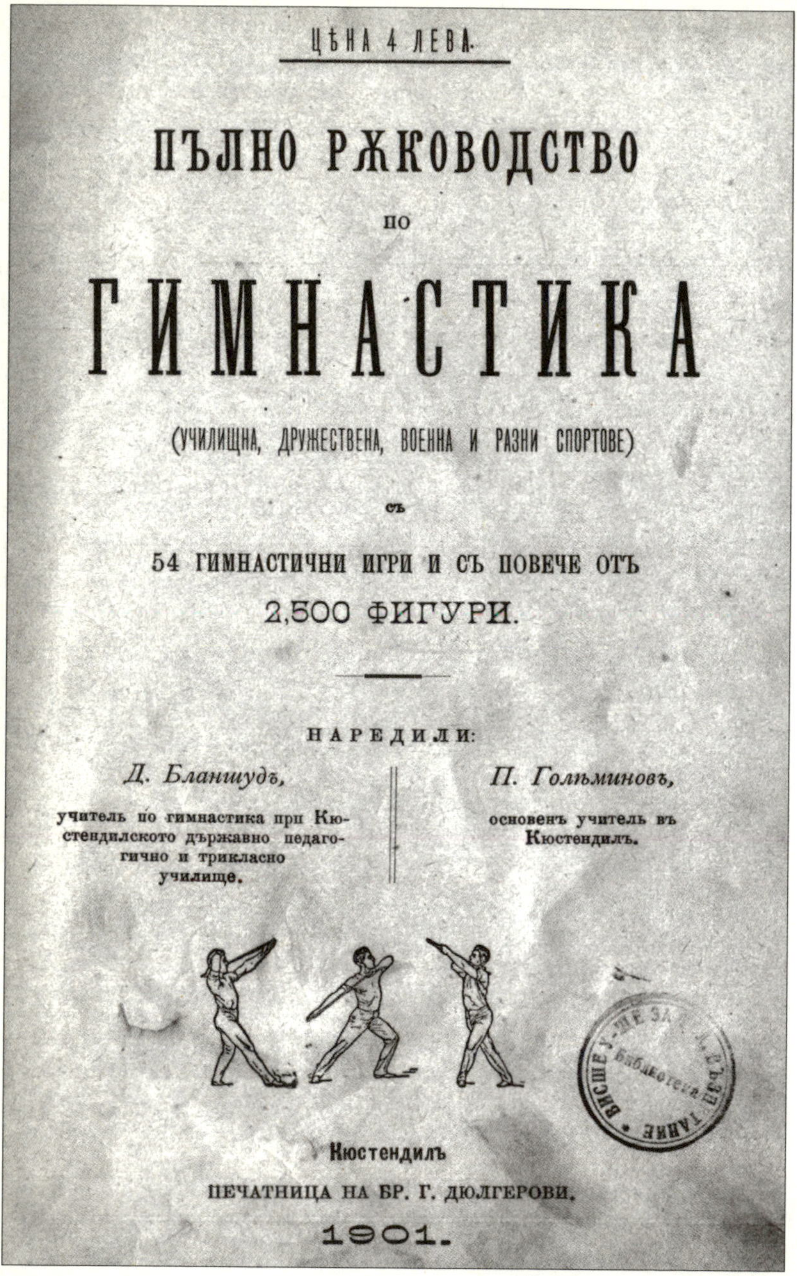

ЦѢНА 4 ЛЕВА.

ПЪЛНО РѪКОВОДСТВО

ПО

ГИМНАСТИКА

(УЧИЛИЩНА, ДРУЖЕСТВЕНА, ВОЕННА И РАЗНИ СПОРТОВЕ)

съ

54 ГИМНАСТИЧНИ ИГРИ И СЪ ПОВЕЧЕ ОТЪ
2,500 ФИГУРИ.

НАРЕДИЛИ:

Д. Бланшудъ,
учитель по гимнастика при Кюстендилското държавно педагогично и трикласно училище.

П. Голѣминовъ,
основенъ учитель въ Кюстендилъ.

Кюстендилъ

ПЕЧАТНИЦА НА БР. Г. ДЮЛГЕРОВИ.

1901.

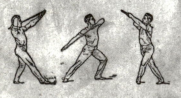

TABLE 7.2
MAIN PRINCIPLES, AIMS AND FORMS OF DELIVERY EMPLOYED
BY UNAK UNION, 1895

Key principles
- Harmonic development of the body
- Exercises should be based on sound physiological and hygienic principles
- Practice should aim at aesthetic and mental development
- Avoidance of exercises contributing to one-sided development

Aims
- To develop and enhance its members physically and morally
- To cultivate a spirit of friendship and sportsmanship
- To promote love of country and its traditions, and keep its members' spirit up

Forms
- Regular gymnastics exercises, athletics, weightlifting, folk games and sport games
- Special sports – winter, water, equestrian and shooting
- Outdoor activities and camps
- Public displays and events/competitions
- Educational workshops

Sources: N. Petrova, *Ucilishtnoto fizicesko vazpitanie v Balgaria prez capitalizma (1878–1944)* (School Physical Education in Bulgaria during capitalism (1878–1944)) (Sofia: VIF 'G. Dimitrov', 1983), p.50; and R. Bardareva, *Organisaciite za fiziceska kultura v Balgaria 1878–1944* (Organisations for Physical Culture in Bulgaria 1878–1944) (Sofia: NSA, 1995).

training for teachers. In that respect, in contrast to culture, education and art, Unak appeared to be the only independent national organization working in partnership with the state. Table 7.3 presents Unak's strategic orientation until the Balkan Wars and the First World War, as defined by its congresses and Yonchev's leadership.

Apart from creating the ideology, the foundations and the strategy of modern physical culture in Bulgaria, Todor Yonchev made another major contribution to Bulgarian sport. His vision and drive were instrumental to linking Bulgarian sport to the emerging modern Olympism. He foresaw the significance of the first Olympic Games in Athens in 1896 and persuaded the Ministers of Education and Foreign Affairs and Religions to accept the invitation to participate. The ministers also approved the delegation and underwrote the cost of participation. Thus Bulgaria became one of the 13 countries taking part in the first Olympic Games of the modern era. It is significant that Todor Yonchev was appointed head of the Bulgarian state delegation for the Games. Four athletes from the Union Unak took also part.

Yonchev's versatility included a range of theoretical, educational, legislative and international projects. In 1900 he initiated and lectured at

TABLE 7.3

UNION UNAK CONGRESSES AND STRATEGIC DECISIONS, 1898–1911

Union Unak Congresses	Strategic Decisions
1st 1898	• Adopting a holistic approach to physical education and sport accounting for members overall wellbeing and not only for their physical development • Developing junior sections and invite all youngsters to join in • Launching of Union's own literature – *Health and Strength* magazine
2nd 1900	• Setting the rules and regulations of the Union • Making regulations concerning the participation of women • Making regulations concerning shooting ranges and practices
3rd 1902	• Suggesting policies for international co-operation and participation in events
4th 1905	• Proposing measures for increasing membership • Setting up training courses for PE teachers • Making a presentation to the Ministry of Education to raise PE teachers' salaries • Making a presentation to the Ministry of Education to ensure two scholarships annually for study abroad
5th 1907	• Proposing measures for increasing membership • Proposing measures concerning dissemination of gymnastics in education
6th 1911	• Ensuring all students become members of gymnastics societies • Making a presentation to the Ministry of Education to introduce gymnastics in all schools • Making a presentation to the Ministry of Education to set up an Inspectorate in Physical Education

the first institutions for training physical education teachers endorsed by the Ministry of Education. In addition, he negotiated scholarships for young Bulgarians to study in Austria and Hungary (Czech, Croatia and Slovenia). After the Olympic Games in 1896, he was also responsible for Unak's first international contacts with sports organizations from Nish, Belgrade, Romania and Russia. In an effort to ensure a sound legislative base for the new physical education movement, he drafted the first Physical Education Act in 1907 although, due to unfortunate political events, it never materialized.

The endeavours of Todor Yonchev were not confined to physical education. He published several handbooks on chemistry and agriculture and was a regular consultant on agricultural problems to various newspapers. In one scientific paper Yonchev even ventured to challenge Einstein's theory of relativity. In 1926 he published his major work *Theory and Truth* as well as various articles on history and culture. Over the years he meticulously collected all materials documenting the history of Unak and donated them to the Union in 1921. Unfortunately these materials, together with the Union's entire archives, were destroyed on ideological grounds by the Communist regime in 1945. Yonchev continued to work in Unak until his retirement at the beginning of the First World War, although he continued to collaborate on various issues. He died on 3 November 1940 in his hometown, Lom.

TODOR YONCHEV'S LEGACY FOR SPORT TODAY

The history of the modern Bulgarian state can be divided into three main periods: capitalist (1878–1944); Communist (1944–89); and democratic (1989–). Each of these periods has been dominated by specific state projects and related ideologies and social and economic strategies. The conceptual grounding and structures of physical culture and sport were largely determined by the nature of state projects. Yonchev emerged on the cultural, political and sports scenes at the dawn of the modern Bulgarian state as an outstanding figure with great vision and enormous energy. He was crucial for laying the foundations of the national sports system and establishing physical education and sport as a legitimate social and political issue.

The Unak Union's policies asserted the importance of gymnastics as both an in-school and out-of-school activity for the physical and moral education of youth. An inspection of present values, structures and relations suggests that there are five main features of the physical culture system established by Yonchev that can be found in each of the three periods of the country's development:

- A holistic approach to physical culture and sport. Despite the ideological justifications attached to sports strategies promoted during the Communist and the democratic periods, sport was largely seen as a major contributor to personal development and enhancement. Subsequently, Communist and post-Communist sports administrations considered it as a joint venture between sport, health and education authorities, although its pursuit was seen as a collective matter by the former and as a matter of individual choice by the latter.

• The importance of pedagogy. From its onset, sport was defined as a pedagogical tool for moral and physical education which could be used either independently or as part of other programmes. This view did not change, as ample evidence from the three periods demonstrates.

• Physical Education as a cornerstone of general education. Putting physical education at the centre of young people's education has always been an ambitious aim and a controversial issue and no administration has ever been complacent about it. However, the main point here is the continuing belief that physical education deserves its central place and has the potential to inspire all other activities. Similarly the assertion of the central place of sport in society has gained it recognition as a service equal to those of education and health. This is arguably Yonchev's greatest accomplishment; he made a notable contribution to both beliefs.

• Relations between public and voluntary organizations. The Unak Union was a model for co-operation between a voluntary organization and a major state agency, the Ministry of Education. However, this model was never taken for granted, as it involved struggles between the two sectors, and thus it was adopted with varying success. During the Communist period, the Ministry of Education's main partner was the Bulgarian Sports Union (BSFS), a quasi-voluntary organization, while at present it is the School Sports Federation. Such links reflect a concept of state–society relations in which voluntary organizations are supposed to play an important social role, both as representatives of their members' interests and as a watchdog preventing the state from advantaging some groups and disadvantaging others. In that respect the nature of state–voluntary sport organizations' relations demands a more thorough analysis and is open to interpretation.

• International linkages. The end of the nineteenth century signalled the emergence of a global society in which nation-states have to compete to assert their identities. In 1896 the Unak Union built the first bridge between Bulgaria and world sport. Communist-led sport was quick to capitalize on the advantages offered by international sport and achieved an impressive presence in its performance rankings and administrative structures. This presence has diminished over the past ten years, but there is evidence now to suggest that international competition is once again the top priority of the Bulgarian sports administration.

In conclusion, the life and work of Todor Yonchev have left a visible mark on Bulgarian physical culture and, indeed, society. Yonchev was responsible for the creation and diffusion of the 'bones' of modern physical culture and shaping the main features that still form the backbone of the national sports system. Yonchev's ideas and deeds define him as an outstanding revolutionary, a change agent, an opinion leader and a major constructive force in the Europeanization of Bulgarian culture. Specific historical circumstances and personal traits resulted in the development of a strong personality with the determination and the will to pursue high moral values and their implementation in politics, society and education. Yonchev's cosmopolitan view of the world combined with his acute sense of national identity and worth have earned him a lasting place in Bulgarian and European culture.

NOTES

Our appreciative thanks are extended to Professor J.A. Mangan for assistance with the presentation of this chapter.

1. G. Velev *et al.*, *Balgaria prez dvadeset i parvi vek – Balgarska natzionalna doctrina, parva cast* (Bulgaria in the Twenty First Century – Bulgarian National Doctrine, Part One) (Sofia: Znanie, 1997), p.75.
2. M. Manolova, *Istorija na darzhavata i pravoto: Treta Balgarska darzhava 1878–1944* (History of the State and the Law: Third Bulgarian State 1878–1944) (Blagoevgrad: UZU 'N. Rilski', 1994), p.11.
3. See V. Nicolova and D. Sazdov (eds.), *Programni documenti i ustavi na burzhoaznite partii v Balgaria – 1879–1918* (Programmes and Charts of Bourgeoisie Parties in Bulgaria – 1879–1918) (Sofia: Nauka i Lzkustvo, 1992).
4. Ibid., p.23.
5. I. Hadjijski, 'Balgarskoto stopanstvo neposredstveno sled osvobozdenieto' ('Bulgarian Industry After the Liberation') in M. Hadjijska (ed.), *Inav Hadjijski – Neizvestnoto ot nego, neizvestnoto za nego* (Inav Hadjijski – the unknown from him, the unknown for him) (Sofia: Otecest ven Front, 1989).
6. I. Tzvetkov, *Balgaria i Evropa during 1939 i 1989 – statisticeski godishnici* (Bulgaria and Europe during 1939 and 1989 – Statistical Comparisons) (Sofia: Ch. Botev, 1994), p.47.
7. P. Kushev, *Zdravnoto sastojanie na naselenieto v Balgaria 1880–1980* (The Health Status of the Population in Bulgaria 1880–1980) (Sofia: Medicina i Fizkultura, 1986).
8. Quoted in R. Gavrilova and I. Elenkov, *Kam istoriata na grazhdanskija sektor v Balgaria* (Towards the History of the Third Sector in Bulgaria), Foundation for the Development of Civic Society, 2 (1998), 75.

9. See Manolova, *History of the State and the Law*, pp.189–97.
10. N. Petrova, *100 Godini obshtestveni fizkulturni organisazii v Balgaria* (100 Years of Voluntary Sports Organizations in Bulgaria) (Sofia: Medicina i Fizkultura, 1978), p.45.
11. See V. Tzonkov, *Balgaria v Olympijskoto dvizhenie do 9.IX. 1994* (Bulgaria in the Olympic Movement until 9.9.1944) (Sofia: Medicina i Fizkultura, 1981).
12. Quoted in J.A. Mangan and C. McKenzie, 'The Other Side of the Coin: Victorian Masculinity, Field Sports and English Elite Education' in J.A. Mangan (ed.), *Making European Masculinities: Sport, Europe, Gender* (London and Portland, OR: Frank Cass, 2000), p.115.
13. Quoted from Yonchev's personal diary, which his daughter's family kindly made available to one of the authors.
14. Yonchev has an ambiguous attitude towards sport. In fact, the word 'sport' can hardly be found in his vocabulary.
15. Quoted from Yonchev's personal diary, which his daughter's family kindly made available to one of the authors.
16. For the authoritative study of athleticism, see J.A. Mangan, *Athleticism in the Victorian and Edwardian Public School: The Emergence and Consolidation of an Educational Ideology* (London and Portland, OR: Frank Cass, 2000).
17. N. Petrova, *Ucilishtnoto fizicesko vazpitanie v Balgaria prez apitalizma (1878–1944)* (School Physical Education in Bulgaria during Capitalism [1878–1944]) (Sofia: VIF 'G. Dimitrov', 1983), p.50.
18. M. Foucault, *Power Knowledge: Selected Interviews and Other Writing* (Brighton: Harvester Press, 1980).
19. It should be noted that the terms 'corporal education' and 'gymnastics' were very popular in Bulgarian vocabulary and had been used interchangeably before they were gradually replaced by the term 'physical Education'. Both terms had wider connotations than their Western European meaning and implied a complex moral and physical education with the use of various forms and methods.
20. L. Eyer, 'Report at the 5th Congress of Unak, 1905', Central State Historical Archive, fund 262, 1/3, 40.
21. For a more elaborate discussion on the origins and the nature of Eastern European (Slav) views on physical culture and sport and their relation to Western sport, see W. Liponski, 'Sport in the Slavic World before Communism: Cultural Traditions and National Functions' in J.A. Mangan (ed.), *Sport in Europe: Politics, Class, Gender* (London and Portland, OR: Frank Cass, 1999), pp.203–50.
22. D. Kirk, 'Physical Culture, Physical Education and Relational Analysis', *Sport, Education and Society*, 4, 1 (1999), 65.
23. L. Seiger *et al.*, *Fitness and Wellness Strategies* (Dubuque, 1995); D. Anspaugh *et al.*, *Wellness: Concepts and Applications* (Boston: McGraw Hill, 2000).

8

Radical Conservatives: Middle-Class Masculinity, the Shikar Club and Big-Game Hunting

J.A. MANGAN and CALLUM McKENZIE

In Britain during the last quarter of the nineteenth century and the first decade of the twentieth century, a number of essentially middle-class organizations were marshalled to protect, encourage or celebrate the killing of wildlife for sport.[1] One such organization, the Shikar Club, symbolized 'the virility' of British imperial big-game hunting, a recreation which was increasingly contrasted with 'the emasculated sport' to be had either in the *battue*[2] or by fox-hunting in Britain, sports which, in the view of Shikar Club purists, were suffering from varying degrees of plutocratic excess, urban decadence, industrial encroachment and, for some, the debilitating presence of women.

The Club was emphatically and strenuously male and middle class. The idea of an international sporting club of this kind had been mooted during the 1850s to provide a forum for 'comrades to discuss exploits in the field'[3] but nothing came of it. The emergence of the Shikar Club in 1907 may have reflected the difficulty of virile, individualistic men conforming to the restrictive club mentality.[4] However, although historians have portrayed big-game hunting as an essentially solitary sport,[5] 'fraternal' bonding was an important element in men's sporting clubs.[6] Furthermore, the simultaneous establishment of the Shikar Club and the Wildfowlers Association of Great Britain and Ireland, for 'manly types' who pursued wildfowl on estuaries and foreshore, may have been a defensive reaction, reflecting perceived liberal threats to big-game hunting and wildfowl shooting, sports which demonstrated mainstream middle-class masculine qualities at this time. This essay examines the middle-class big-game hunting tradition, its rationale and the related masculine moral imperatives as exemplified by some members of the Shikar Club.

THE SHIKAR CLUB AND THE BIG-GAME HUNTING
TRADITION

The Shikar Club was founded by Charles Edward Radclyffe, P.B. Vanderbyl,[7] both pupils at Eton during the 1870s, and Frederick Courtney Selous, a pupil at Rugby during the 1860s.[8] All three men attained the rank of Captain in the British army and, in keeping with military convention, married in later life after concentrating as young officers on soldiering and big-game shooting.[9] The Club was a focus for military men until the 1930s and even then about half of the members were drawn from high-ranking officers, as typified by father and son Brigadier-General Claude De Crespigny and Major Vivian De Crespigny of Champion Lodge, Heybridge, Essex.[10] Sir Claude de Crespigny excelled in a variety of sports and remained fit into late middle age and beyond, 'one of the hardest and pluckiest men in England ... ready to box, ride, walk, run, shoot (at birds for preference now), fence, sail or swim with any one of over fifty years on equal terms'.[11] He lived according to spartan values and took the proverbial 'cold tub before breakfast'.[12] De Crespigny approached the most challenging situations with the same deliberate toughness he brought to his sports and was once observed by fellow club member and imperialist, Alfred Pease,[13] 'assisting' in the hanging of three criminals because 'he would not care to ask a man to do what he himself was afraid of doing himself'.[14]

Upper-middle-class sporting pleasures and military duties, according to De Crespigny, went hand in hand. He argued that every able-bodied Briton had an obligation to defend his country and could not be considered a 'man' until he had done so. De Crespigny practised what he preached: in fact he served in both the Royal Navy (1860–65) and the Army (1866–70) and, later, despite his advancing years, was keen to play an active part in the Boer War. For De Crespigny, field sports were an ideal training for war. More than this, effeminacy, in his view, was put to route by field sports. He likened 'feather-bed aristocrats', particularly those who declined duty, to the effeminate French aristocracy and, in his view, they had no place in the British social hierarchy.[15] His son's military success in the Great War was, in his certain view, the result of the family's predilection for field sports and riding: 'men who have been good sportsmen at home are the men who will do best and show the greatest amount of resource when on active service'.[16] Field sports ensured more than just military training for war, they assisted military advancement and De Crespigny used them as a means of consolidating friendships with other high-ranking military establishing officials.[17]

Field sports might have promoted army careers, but they provoked condemnation from humanitarians opposed to both.[18] However, such criticism of soldier and huntsman in a climate of exuberant imperialism,[19] undermined the credibility of the reformers. Henry Salt, for example, handicapped the effectiveness of his animal welfare programme by challenging the underlying ethos of 'murderous masculinity' upon which field sports rested.[20] Advocates of gun and hound took their opportunity and protested that the opposition to manly pursuits was led by urban-based pacifists and the likes of Salt who led 'effeminate and aesthetic lives' and had acquired a 'righteous horror' of anything involving the death of an animal.[21] Such 'morbid enthusiasts' the advocates sneered, were highly vociferous – an affliction which, according to *Baily's Magazine*, had 'the emasculation of British manhood, the denial of nationalism and the eschewing of patriotic wars' as its 'ultimate objectives'.[22]

Effeminacy was the hunter's incubus. To the initiated in pursuit of the antidote to effeminacy, Scottish deer-stalking was close at hand and, for some, was a major source of 'masculine virtue'.[23] Sir Ian Colquhoun,[24] a noted authority on Scottish deer-stalking, saw the sport as the ultimate test of masculinity.[25] Regrettably, in his view, too many of the young failed the test. He lamented that contemporary youth had lost the tradition of hardihood, were 'fundamentally soft and entirely unashamed of it. If they are tired, they say so with disarming frankness; if they are wet and cold and unwilling to suffer discomfort, they do not hesitate to let the stalker know.'[26] Colquhoun had his supporters: Henry Seton-Karr[27] argued that those 'unpatriotically' seeking to limit deer preservation in Scotland lacked 'virility and robustness'.[28] Seton-Karr, like many others of the upper-middle classes, believed hunting was linked to virility and virility was bound to nationhood and that:

> no race of men possess this desire more strongly than the Anglo-Saxons of the British Isles. This passion is an inherited instinct, which civilisation cannot eradicate, of a virile and dominant race, and it forms a healthy natural antidote to the enervating refinements of modern life.[29]

Virility with the gun was pursued well beyond Scotland. Shibboleths emphasizing personal and national regeneration through imperial hunting echoed through the dining rooms and drawing rooms of the Shikar Club members. One member, in hot pursuit of virility, argued that British discovery and exploration should not be inhibited out of deference to the 'delicate feelings' of the anti-imperialists.[30] Hunting, shooting, coursing and fishing were 'natural outlets for masculine energy' which, according to Hugh Cecil Lowther,[31] the Shikar Club's first chairman, mimicking Colquhoun and Seton-Karr, maintained Britain's reputation as a virile and martial nation.[32]

The Shikar Club institutionalized this confident chauvinism which, unsurprisingly given its upper-middle-class membership, embraced the concept of 'fair-play' as a peculiarly noble British invention and as applicable to the hunting field as to the games field. Abel Chapman,[33] an early member of the Shikar Club, for example, expressed the view, held by many upper-middle-class men, that the 'Boers did not understand the elementary significance of our British term, "sport". No sense of respect for game, no admiration of its grace and beauty ever penetrated minds debased by decades of slaughter.'[34]

Lowther backed Chapman to the hilt; 'proud of tradition in all its forms' he felt that 'sportsmanship' was a vital part of tradition and character formation.[35] Sports which deviated from the Club's sporting code, such as trap-pigeon-shooting, were officially denounced by Lowther and others.[36] Driven-game-shooting was similarly condemned. Their Club considered itself an arbiter of 'fair play' in field sports, committed as it was to maintaining 'sportsmanship which has been *handed down from the past*', and which included restraint in the killing of game and other wildlife.[37] In short, the role of arbiter of 'fair play' derived from the chivalric tradition of the elite British hunter-naturalist. Humanitarians, of course, viewed this interpretation of 'fair play' in a very different light. Henry Salt, for example, sardonically noted the amount of 'sheer, untempered barbarism' that characterized the sporting elite, adding that the 'trouble is not so much that they are in reality savage, as that they suppose themselves to be civilised'.[38]

It is clear from the contemporary sporting literature that by the mid-nineteenth century elite shots cherished their unique identities as 'pioneering' men. By the 1860s, travelling shots were boasting of the challenge of overseas sport, especially in America. In 1861, one hunter advised adventurous and hardy sportsmen to visit 'brother sportsmen in

America', whilst others described their American sporting peers in terms of a ' united freemasonry of true friends'.[39] A mass of sporting literature eventually appeared aiming to attract hunters to the Americas. Parker Gillmore's *Experiences of a Sportsman in North America* (1869) was written to 'encourage British sportsmen to America, provided they were of the right stamp, and didn't mind roughing it in search of sport'.[40] Toughening sports in the New World fitted into prevailing notions of robust upper-middle-class masculinity. Shooting there was unsuitable for the:

> feather-bed sportsman, or the shirker of hard work ... [but] provided you have the constitution, make a try, and on your return, you will recall with pleasure the hardships and misadventures you have gone through, for without an odd contretemps, we should become a very unimaginative, unambitious, namby-pamby lot, unfit for wear and tear, bustle and excitement, that all must endure before their course is run.[41]

Captain Flack's *Hunters' Experiences in the Southern States of America* (1866), made it clear that supreme challenges to hunting provided physical and mental endurance and enabled the hunter to face extreme dangers and difficulties which would discourage 'men of weaker mould'.[42] Grantley Berkeley[43] travelled from Liverpool to the United States in August 1859 but returned in December in order to reveal to the 'rich and rising, adventurous and hardy sportsmen' the limitless hunting opportunities available to English sportsmen.[44] Growing public fascination with big-game hunting strengthened the myths associated with the virile stereotype of the frontiersman and the new sporting opportunities in the US allowed 'frontiersman' hunters to display superlative male qualities of physical and psychological prowess.

That Britain had ample sportsmen ready to take up the challenge of sport in the US was cited as evidence of the moral and physical superiority of the 'established over the newer civilisations'.[45] Some historians have noted a mid-Victorian development of new and more compassionate attitudes towards wildlife in Britain led by the urban middle-class.[46] Others have argued that in consequence, the more savage aspects of fox-hunting were ameliorated by a change in emphasis from killing the quarry to the chase and the performance of the dogs.[47] In fact, changes in the nature of fox-hunting were accompanied by a gradual dissatisfaction with sporting opportunities in England on the part of some members of the middle classes, as industrial and urban encroachment and 'plutocratic' game-shooting threatened to 'desex' the more traditional aspects of shooting and hunting with dogs.[48] Strong protest at this state of affairs was aired. Driven-game-shooting, for example, was stigmatized as 'un-British, humiliating, effeminate and selfish'.[49] The 60 per cent increase in the number of gamekeepers between 1860 and 1900 was claimed to be evidence of the now controlled and artificial nature of shooting as well as the influence of the plutocrat in the countryside.[50] Advocates of more demanding sport stated that shooting in England had become 'artificial' and failed to provide real 'satisfaction' in comparison to the hunting of 'wild beasts and birds'.[51]

Thus, for true shooters, in the disgusting wake of the 'feminization' of fox-hunting and the despicable growth of driven-game-shooting in Britain, Africa, India and parts of Asia, as well as North America, provided new, testing and exciting locations for British middle-class sportsmen of proper masculinity after the 1850s. Overseas hunting was labelled 'real sport', in which the pursuit of wild animals on their own 'primeval and ancestral ground, as yet unannexed and unappropriated in any way by man', assumed a primitive challenge which required masculine skills to overcome.[52] Accordingly, 'to find true wild pagan sport, such as stirs the blood and brings to the top the hardiest and manliest instincts in human nature, one must go to the hills of Northern India or the wildernesses of tropical Africa'.[53] Clearly the urban restrictions of England were unknown in these wild places. The sportsman had the space to leave 'at least 25 miles between himself and the next hunter'.[54]

Therefore, the Shikar Club became an institutional focus for middle-class males who upheld the traditions of 'true' masculine shooting in which merit was derived from strenuous effort and careful respect for game and habitat. The Club members rejected 'squandered bullets and swollen bags', for in their view, a more romantic, moral and spiritual approach to hunting which revelled in 'a love of forest, mountain and desert' and gloried 'in acquired knowledge of the habits of animals; in the strenuous pursuit of an active and dangerous quarry; in the instinct for a well-devised approach to a fair shooting distance'.[55] As far as they were concerned, it was this 'clean sport', based on 'pluck and chivalry', which had made the British Empire and consequently those domestic field sports which did not demand these qualities were to be derided.[56] Trout-fishing, 'amused the ladies'; grouse-shooting was 'a picnic on the moor';[57]

effortless, indiscriminate shooting of game accompanied by hot luncheons and servile gun-loaders was hardly the way to acquire 'fieldcraft'[58] – a requirement of all reputable shots and a valuable asset in war.[59]

For Club men, 'real sport' was a release of 'blood-lust' which represented an innate masculinity. According to one Club stalwart, this lust to kill was certainly not a product of social advantage, but rather an instinctive manifestation of 'real' men rebutting the emasculating tendencies of 'civilisation'.[60] It was not emphatically a class phenomenon. This 'community of blood', united by 'sporting blood-lust', embraced all classes of men.[61] For Henry Seton-Karr, the desire to obtain a 'good head' resulted from man's predatory instincts in which the pursuit and 'slaughter' of wild game was a 'perfectly natural healthy and widespread trait of humanity, even necessary in some cases, for health and happiness and probably intended as an antidote to the purple and fine linen and sumptuous fare of refined civilisations'.[62] However, whatever the egalitarian claims of well-heeled sportsmen, the reality was that they were the only ones with the resources to indulge their male 'instincts'. Assertions of classlessness were one thing; instances of classlessness quite another!

Aesthetics and science were means by which the hunter could distance himself and his sport from the moral criticisms of 'civilisation'. Maurice Egerton[63] 'stalked an 'old ram', on which one horn measured 33 inches, 'so I decided to have him set up whole. What a difference to pheasant shooting this 1st of October!'[64] Two days later, he killed another ram at 130 yards, 'shot through the spine and kidney ... small head, 22 inches, still very pretty and symmetrical'.[65] Abel Chapman, in combat with a much coveted big beast, extolled the virtues of his new express rifle:

> with head and neck exposed at 80 yards, his white ruff gave a splendid mark ... I dwelt on the aim. The express bullet struck to an inch of where I intended, the beast staggered and I saw he was mine. I spotted a second big buck. I planted the second barrel ball in his shoulder ... when next I looked he was dead ... a right and left for the first shots of my new express!![66]

By clothing big-game hunting in the trappings of exquisite technology, killing was distanced from its brutal reality.

Other defence mechanisms were usefully employed. Shikar hunting was distinguished from mere barbarism by an erudite understanding of wildlife habitats and environments, an attribute which all capable and educated shooting men were expected to possess. Then again, linking hunting with sporting art enhanced its reputation as artistic in action and image. Furthermore, the Club's promotion of shooting at various international sporting exhibitions throughout Europe was a deliberate statement about the powerful international respectability of big-game hunting.[67] The plethora of international sporting exhibitions at this time was a clear expression of the importance of big-game hunting within legitimate class and national 'identities'.[68] Lord Desborough, Lonsdale, President of the Shikar Club, and T.L. Fairholme, along with C.E. Fagan of the British Museum, comprised the British delegation which competed against the Austrian and German Empires in 1910.[69]

Such sporting exhibitions occasionally provided the opportunity for open antagonism between national cultures! The Glasgow Exhibition of 1901, for example, was sardonically described as a 'testament to the skill of the Englishman in Scotland's sporting grounds'.[70]

In the pantheon of 'pioneering' hunting heroes of the period, a hierarchy emerged in which shots who took most risks in challenging more dangerous quarry species were singled out for special praise.[71] The veneration of audacious big-game shots was assured by numerous written accounts of big-game hunting which emphasized courageous contests between strong men and wild beasts. Dennis Lyell,[72] for example, extolled the peerless virtues of Captain Charles Hugh Stigand, who narrowly escaped death from rhinos lion and elephant during various safaris and who once punched a rogue lion who had him in an apparent death grip![73] Heroic hunting hierarchies were constructed from an expertise in killing particular beasts and the use and type and calibre of weapon used. Samuel Baker, for example, was revered for his criticism of 'easy' sport and even more so for lamenting that shooting had become a 'safe luxury' with the introduction of the breech-loading rifle and the demise of the muzzle-loading gun.[74] Denis Lyell and Charles Stigand won great respect for only using the .256 Mannlicher and .318 rifles for elephant hunting, thereby fulfilling the requirements of 'true' hunting which required fieldcraft to get sufficiently close to the beast before killing it with an accurate shot to the vital organs.[75]

TYPICAL CLUB MEN

Alfred Edward Pease was one of a number of Shikar Club members who rejected urban life in favour of rural life and its sports despite depending on industrial capitalism to support their lifestyle.[76] Pease's family was Quaker and closely associated with iron-mining near Middlesbrough.[77] While dancing, novels and music were proscribed to the Quaker child, field sports were not! This allowed Pease to fish, shoot and hunt throughout his youth;[78] he took his sporting proclivities to Eton and Trinity College, Cambridge, where he excelled at football, athletics, cricket and hunting.[79] Fellow Club member, Robert Lyons Scott,[80] also drew on his industrial income to devote himself to big-game hunting. Such was his dedication that he single-handedly furnished Greenock's Natural History Museum with trophies between 1890 and his death in 1939.[81] Some club members seem to have been wedded to their sport; they certainly never married. Robert Lyons Scott, Maurice Egerton and Abel Chapman were three such examples. In addition, they were all heavily influenced by their fathers who were energetic travellers in search of sport and adventure.[82] In pursuit of their obsession, nothing would stand in their way. Despite the restrictions of the First World War, Scott, for example, shot, fished and collected in every continent of the world throughout 1914 and 1915.

However, not all big-game hunters were made from the same mould. Whilst Scott's personal image was enhanced by his successful conventional hunting, Pease's unconventional views on the Empire, Africa and shooting diminished his personal image. *The Spectator*, for example, found 'no fault with Mr Pease provided he keeps himself to his role of sportsman and traveller. When he leaves this as he is fond of doing, to instruct us in the grave matters of conduct and belief, he is less to be admired.'[83] By advocating the colonization of Africa for outdoor pursuits well away from the unwholesome influence of the plutocrat and asserting that the working-classes could shoot big-game by diverting drinking expenditure towards travel and recreation, Pease gave a new and often unwelcome meaning to notions of self-help.[84] Furthermore, his enlightened admiration for native cultures irritated those of unsympathetic and prejudiced conservative opinion who were convinced of the primitiveness of the 'savage'; a conviction which hunting reinforced.[85] A belief in the idle, undisciplined native was part and parcel of upper-middle-class Victorian and Edwardian conservative thought. It was an unshakeable belief made rigid by the imposition of ethnocentric negative values onto 'lower races'.[86] Abel Chapman, for example, was able to assert with absolute confidence that the 'mob of savages' required to service a safari needed strong discipline to ensure a successful hunt.[87] His further observation that natives were unalterably lazy sanctioned the notion of hunting as a benign feature of European colonization – a protection for those who would not protect themselves – and, of course, to such Europeans it was something more – a clear manifestation of the gap between 'strong' superior and 'weak' inferior.

Many Shikarians attacked the utilitarian killing of wildlife by natives because it lacked the 'training and testing' so essential to a display of middle-class masculinity.[88] Native shots inexcusably preferred to shoot game-birds sitting because they were easier to kill: 'skill and the exercise of it present no advantages. When [a native] goes to shoot, he tries to kill as many birds as possible.'[89] African 'field sports' were described by one Victorian observer as savage, uncivilized and ignorant, lacking in both refinement and 'enlightenment'.[90] More than this, the native inability to dominate the environment and the dangerous animals within it was construed as evidence of feebleness and lack of male control.[91] Physical skills, such as effective 'running from beasts', as noted by one shot, were trivialized and dismissed because they had no moral value – quite the reverse.[92] Flawed African manhood was contrasted with the European version which had mastered the physical environment and its inherent dangers – an achievement based on scientific rationality, moral superiority and innate intelligence. A native's fear in the face of wild beasts was seized upon by many European shots eager to promote their role as guardians of the vulnerable. Richard Arkwright,[93] for example, was 'amused when a rogue elephant ran amok amongst the kaffirs, and I watched them running up trees to hide. I eventually shot the beast, much to the delight of the kaffirs, and left them to the fat, abounding in their glory.'[94] This paternalism was to have a long life. It was not until the early twentieth century that the African received recognition for his skill with the gun[95] and belief in his maturity took even longer to materialize. Ethnocentric absolutism was woven into the fabric of colonial ideology.[96] It was the essential mental baggage of most big-game hunters.

Although European shots readily criticized the moral and physical deficiencies of 'inferior races', they themselves were not perfect. While shooting big game in Norway in 1897, for example, Abel Chapman lost his 'level head and fired too quick ... both eyes open ... fatal ... an ignominious miss-disgrace. Oh Abel, is nerve and eye beginning to fail? If so farewell to the rifle! But may God forbid!'[97] Chapman required a steady nerve and sound vision as he devoted himself entirely to shooting, and fishing and natural history after selling the family brewery-business in 1897.[98] In terms of self-esteem he had put all his eggs in one basket.

Like all Shikar hunting men, Chapman basked in the glory of the pioneer 'frontiersman' image. His trophies represented a 'long-series of the most strenuous endeavour, of tremendous hard work, plus the risk of adventuring into unknown regions, where we had no certainty of success or failure'.[99] 'Searching' for red deer, wild boar, lynx and other game, Chapman travelled to the 'distant Sierras and other remote areas of Spain' which took him into 'wholly unknown districts, wherein [so far as Englishmen were concerned], we were actually *pioneers*'.[100] Chapman's rhetoric was far from fanciful. He made 23 hunting trips to Spain and Portugal and 46 trips to Scandinavia, including Spitzbergen, as well as forays into France, Morocco, Scotland, the Shetlands and Outer Hebrides and occasional visits to the North American continent.[101] Others were cast in the same self-assured, obsessed, masculine middle-class mould.[102] The noted Club member John G. Millais stated in 1919 that it was the 'sporting pioneer' who had established the British Empire, since his 'initial spearhead of courage and noble conduct was the apex of all future advancement'. He added that 'if these men were not our very best gentlemen, progress would have been lost to other nations'.[103]

Be that as it may, these men were certainly reactionary 'revolutionaries'. They were unrepentant conservative 'radicals' – confident, contemptuous and certain in the correctness of their own certainties. They formed a closed circle of conservative nonconformists. The Shikar Club, which was made up of these 'pioneers', provided a wide range of middle-class men with the opportunity to be 'campfire chums, to cement friendships and revive memories of golden-days'. [104] In a very real sense, for many of them it extended the camaraderie of their schooldays into adulthood.

Many members of the Club, including C.W.L. Bulpett, C.V.A. Peel, H.C. Maydon and H.A. Bryden, published large amounts of shooting literature[105] which enabled the exploits of the field to be relived and retold and was a means of reinforcing chosen gender roles, clear gender identities and the security of superior separateness. (Female experience in big-game hunting, such as it was, had not received sanction through any recognized association.[106]) It could be argued that this writing allowed Shikarians to recreate their most emotional experiences, share them with others of like inclination, affirm an unambiguous masculinity, define a superior distinctive membership and maintain a secure distance from inferior femininity. At this time big-game hunting was emphatically for men. Henry Seton-Karr, for example, asserted that his sporting articles were aimed at the 'fraternity' of fishing and shooting men and that they had been 'well-received by brother sportsmen'. He noted that writing them was 'pleasant work, since we all like to fight our battles over again'.[107] Records, reports and reminiscences were also an important means of bringing the young into hunting. Unsurprisingly, the aged Sir Arthur Vivian rejoiced to see so many young sportsmen at the Club's second annual meet, 'ready to testify to the joys of a hunter's life and to the blessing of health which resulted from the pursuit'.[108] Shikar fathers had a special paternal responsibility to lay the foundations of a proper lifestyle. Sir Robert Loder, an expert rider-to-hounds and exponent of the sporting gun, was seen as a fine example of the Victorian country gentleman: emotionally undemonstrative; a good husband and father, who 'exact[ed] good conduct and regular habits from those over whom he was placed'.[109]

Imperial bonding and the strengthening of the imperial brotherhood was a crucial aspect of big-game hunting. Lowther declared that the principal objective of the Shikar Club was the unification of 'hunting men, young and old, with the *Empire-maker*, whether soldier or civilian, and the humble globe-trotter who carries a gun'.[110]

Hunting also created early and lasting male-friendships which fitted well into contemporary notions of male-bonding.[111] Henry Seton-Karr, for example, remained close to many of his shooting colleagues throughout his life. In his view, shooting produced a union with other men unequalled in any other social interaction.[112] Abel Chapman recorded his 'close, constant and faithful' friendship with Walter Buck and his son, Bertie, which lasted 'without break or wrong-thought' between March 1872 and April 1917.[113] Similarly, after first meeting at Eton, Alfred Pease and Edmund G. Loder remained lifelong friends and often met in some outpost when hunting.[114] Affection between 'guns' was a consequence of a shared set of values and attributes of physically competent men who combined an understanding of wildlife and the environment with technical killing skill, emotional self-control and personal courage. They were self-isolated and self-designated icons. According to Pease, Edmund Loder and his six brothers represented the ideal of Victorian manhood, distinguishable by their ardour, vitality and attainment in outdoor pursuits, particularly shooting and athletics.[115]

In their own eyes, big-game hunters represented the moral superiority of a male, chivalric tradition which comprised values crucial for social, political and moral leadership. The gentleman 'shot' reinforced his hegemony by confronting the wilderness and its animals and demonstrating behaviour suitable for leadership. However, some of these hunters were more than hearty 'frontiersmen': Maurice Egerton balanced his sporting trips to the frontier with frequent visits to the theatre, music halls and church;[116] Lord Lonsdale shot at Malakand but made sure that he enjoyed the cultural pleasures of India and China.[117]

Of course, the Shikar Club was not a wholly homogeneous association, but a striking similarity existed between most of its members. They all possessed a clear idea of the nature of 'true' masculinity. In effect, and in reality, it was a class masculinity which depended on adequate financial resources for travel, guns and trophies.[118] No one has set down the requirements of this masculinity better than Richard Burton, a well-known hunter-explorer.[119] Burton (educated at Eton, Sandhurst and the College of Agriculture, Cheltenham) was described as 'a crack shot, a fine boxer, afraid of nothing that either walked, flew or swam'[120] and is said to have once remarked that 'every region is a strong man's home'.[121] The essence of Burton's philosophy is captured in this extract from his biography:

> Wanted: Men.
> Not systems fit and wise,
> Not faiths with rigid eyes,
> Not wealth in mountain piles,
> Not power with gracious smiles,
> Not even the potent pen;
> Wanted, Men.
>
> Wanted: Deeds.
> Not words of winning note,
> Not thoughts from life remote,
> Not fond religious airs,
> Not sweetly languid prayers,
> Not love of scent and creeds;
> Wanted: Deeds.
>
> Men and Deeds.
> Men that can dare and do;

Not longing for the new,
Not pratings of the old:
Good life and action bold –
These the occasion needs,
Men and Deeds.[122]

No one better exemplified the Club's values than Maurice Egerton. Egerton developed a passion for shooting under the influence of his father, Alan Egerton, an enthusiastic shot and traveller. Both father and son were in South Africa hunting big game during the 1890s and were also involved in military action against the Matebele tribe in 1896.[123] They were both hunters and warriors! Maurice's preoccupation with masculinity manifested itself in a paternal welfare programme for boys, notable for its complete exclusion of girls. However, he was not class conscious: boys from *all* classes were instructed in activities similar to the manly activities practised in the Edwardian Scout movement.[124] One contemporary claimed that Egerton's programme relied on:

> military and moral discipline and sheer fun ... it takes the zest of fishing, birds-nesting, collecting and all field sports and joins to them the delight of games and the romance of adventure stories. Close observation of the countryside includes knowing how to stalk and take cover. The boys trained in this way are by way of becoming an aristocracy, morally, physically and intellectually, with the added charm of brotherhood.[125]

Egerton no doubt considered it appropriate that he supervised his programme himself as, according to a period maxim, manliness for boys should be taught by 'men, not half men'.[126] The lessons of woodcraft and tracking were widely seen as an essential prerequisite for the future shot. A noted 'shot' of the time once asserted that such training encouraged the young to search out 'foreign countries' in order to 'experience the exhilaration of nobler sports than we can find at home'.[127] Unsurprisingly then, Egerton insisted that instruction was given in rabbit-shooting, how to use firearms, canoeing and swimming and stalking on the estate. Boys from less wealthy backgrounds could now learn the values of 'fair play' in relation to field sports. Training was idealistic as well as practical. When rabbit-shooting, for example, Egerton asserted that his young charges used only a .22 rifle to give the quarry a reasonable chance of escape without being ruined by small shot.[128] Academically-able boys from the lower classes were helped towards specific occupations and university. A fortunate few were sent overseas for holidays. Egerton gave a great deal of his time and generous amounts of his money to further his concept of masculinity. Salford Lads Club, the Cheshire Association of Boys Clubs and Knutsford Town Hall were to be redeveloped into educational centres to be used by the boys of Cheshire. Viewing and studying Egerton's collection of bows, arrows and knives, rare birds eggs and natural history specimens which he had acquired on his hunting trips, were an integral part of the programme.[129]

Egerton's 'patriarchal' programme continued the tradition of welfare which had been a feature of Tatton estate life during the nineteenth century. The programme was not wholly altruistic: the Rostherne Boys School was owned and financed by his father, Alan Egerton. Control over the school was useful. Field sports on the estate were sometime allowed to interrupt the boys' schooling. In March 1878, for example, the boys were allowed holidays to assist with the Cheshire Hounds meet at Bucklow Hill, while in December 1884, the boys' attendance at school was 'poor' as many were needed to beat 'the covers' for two days.[130] Egerton also maintained links with Knutsford Grammar School, where he oversaw the Rifle and Drill Corps – an essential part of training into masculinity – in the years prior to 1914.[131]

Matthew Egerton's superior 'manly' approach to life was reflected in his approach to overseas hunting. Northern hunting trips were invariably physically demanding and required early starts often in freezing temperatures and inclement weather. Egerton's preoccupation with early morning starts was important. It was seen by 'traditionalists' as a bulwark against moral and physical decadence.[132] Careful scientific observation by means of barometer and telescope reflected the seriousness of the hunt and distanced it from the leisurely frivolity of the popular *battue* or fox-hunting in Britain. Egerton, like many big-game shots, sometimes used local men as hunting guides. This demonstrated both conscientious attention to detail and the seriousness of the endeavour. In the battle of man against beast, local knowledge was to be suitably employed against local prey to ensure a 'fair fight'.[133]

Egerton's quest for game began in earnest in Sardinia in 1900, chasing unusual quarry not yet acquired by himself or other shots.[134] Rising at about 6 a.m. for a number of weeks, assisted by local shooting guides, Egerton killed a number of hill sheep. Subsequently, in Canada he shot in the Klondyke and fished in the Campbell River for moose, mule deer, muflon, elk and salmon which were not available in such numbers on the Continent.[135] Egerton kept detailed 'scientific' records of the best heads from any area in which he hunted, specifying owner, location and size of quarry. Moose antlers were measured and recorded by circumference, greatest width, points and length from tip to tip.[136]

Egerton was fanatical in his passion for big-game hunting. Not content with ordinary animals, he made a point of seeking out unusual game. In a letter to the curator at South Kensington Museum in 1931, he remarked that he was the first to shoot a Harvey's Duiker on Mount Elgon in Kenya.[137] This killing of the first of a new game species brought special distinction, although disputed kills sometimes provoked acrimonious debate, as in the case of Abel Chapman and Francis Issacs over ownership of the first Bongo[138] to be shot in Central Africa.[139] The quality of the kill also brought merit. Of his first Scottish stag, Abel Chapman wrote 'curiously, this was the first, and at the time, the ONLY stag I had shot in a Scottish forest, yet it comes within the first dozen among the thousands of stags that have been shot in Scotland'.[140] Chapman also recorded that his African trophies comprised 'fine examples of all the grandest game-beasts, which stand first on earth'.[141] His performance did not go unnoticed or unapplauded. He was widely considered as an outstanding hunter for his special achievements.[142]

Other members of the Shikar Club travelled the world in search of both ordinary and unusual game. However, North American locations such as Upper Stickeen, the Yukon and Alaska, were all especially popular with its members.[143] P. Vanderbyl, Captain Radclyffe, J.G. Millais, F.C. Selous and Edmund Loder established records in these localities. The potential for trophies or memorable sport justified the expense and distance of these hunting trips, factors which deterred those with insufficient time or means and the mere 'dilettante'. However, there were few geographical limitations in the search for adventure and the pursuit of new trophies.[144] Some travelled well beyond North America. Chapman, in particular, travelled extensively in search of records, describing as 'unique' his acquisition of rare deer species from the Sierra Morena in Spain.[145] He shot Norwegian Elk, Newfoundland Caribou, Scottish and Spanish deer during the early 1890s and acquired some of the 'best' trophies ever taken in Africa.[146]

Africa was Egerton's first choice as a shooting destination. He purchased a number of farms and plantations at Njora in Kenya, to complement his hunting activities.[147] From July 1921 to October 1939, Egerton shot about 600 head of game on the African Continent.[148] In Kenya, he developed close ties with Ewart Scott Grogan[149] and Hugh Delamere,[150] both members of the Shikar Club. Grogan had four declared ambitions as a child: to slay a lion, rhinoceros and an elephant and to see Tanganyika. He subsequently described his first lion-hunt as the 'defining moment' in his life.[151] Delamere was Egerton's neighbour at Vale Royal in Cheshire, but disliked the restrictions of English upper-class life.[152] He found financial security in East Africa through farming and big-game hunting. Delamere's pioneering reflected the Shikar Club's spirit of imperial 'frontierism'. In 1903, he had spearheaded the movement of English aristocrats, including Ewart Grogan, to Africa in order to create a feudal lifestyle and develop the economic possibilities of East Africa. However, the Shikar Club's sporting code seems to have been flaunted by Delamere, who used live donkeys as bait for lion-shooting at night, accrued £14,000 worth of elephant ivory from Kenya in one year and established the Masara Pack, a 'proper hunt, complete with English foxhounds, redcoats, huntsman's caps'.[153] He was far from a symbol of Shikar purity!

More generally, the ethical shortcomings of big-game hunters were increasingly questioned after 1918.[154] Although the cult of shooting and collecting survived between the wars, by this time there was a greater emphasis on conservation. Pressures on game habitat generally meant that hunters were forced to take greater responsibility for wildlife management. Consequently, the Shikar Club increasingly sought the patronage of politically influential sportsmen such as Robert Coryndon, Alfred Sharpe and A.L. Butler, all prominent members of the Society for the Preservation of the (Wild) Fauna of the Empire (SPFE). By 1926, a number of distinguished members belonging to the SPFE had joined the Shikar Club, including Lord Elphinstone and Major Wigram of the Kashmir Game Preservation Department.[155] During the 1920s, the Club, anxious to publicize its role within the burgeoning conservation movement, condemned public films showing 'unethical' practices, including hunting from motor cars and the filming of wounded and dying animals.[156] The Club complained that such practices were 'utterly opposed to all ethics of good sportsmanship, and are liable to give uninitiated members of the public an entirely erroneous view of how real sportsmen behave on shooting expeditions'.[157] The unprincipled actions of Delamere and his ilk found no allies. Re-emphasis of the morality of big-game hunting was clearly a defensive measure and for one good reason – this form of middle-class masculine assertion was falling out of favour. Major Radclyffe-Dugmore's film *The Wonderland of Big-Game* presented shooting in a skilful and artistic way emphasizing 'fair play' towards game and ecological awareness: the test of the true hunter lay in his 'love of forest, mountain and desert; in acquired knowledge of the habits of animals; in the strenuous pursuit of a wary and dangerous quarry; in the instinct for a well-devised approach to a fair shooting distance; and in the patient retrieval of a wounded animal'.[158] However, despite these gestures to conservation, many observers remained sceptical about the Club. In February 1925, for example, Lonsdale looked to formalize ties with the SPFE in order to widen the Club's sphere of influence in conservation politics. This prospect was greeted with alarm by many members of the Preservation Society. This, together with Lonsdales' ultimate failure to incorporate the Club into the Society, cast serious doubt on the intentions of those who ostensibly embraced conservation whilst at the same time representing themselves as guardians of the masculine tradition through big-game hunting.[159]

CONCLUSION

The establishment of the Shikar Club during a period of transition for mainstream masculinity allows certain conclusions to be drawn about the relationship between culture, masculine identity and field sports.[160] The Club grew out of the nineteenth-century emphatically middle-class masculine tradition of British big-game hunting. Although many 'shots' saw their sport as an extension of man's role as a natural predator,[161] the club was clearly the product and celebration of period cultural values reflecting the political, social and economic power and corresponding confidence of advantaged men. Big-game hunting enabled privileged men to indulge in a sport which they sanctioned, legitimized and propagated as a moral education in true masculinity – a masculinity of successful survival. Prowess with the gun symbolized national, personal, political, economic and moral superiority over others. Membership of the Shikar Club demonstrated and confirmed access to those cultural activities which conferred unquestionable manhood, since the unequivocal definition of manhood was closely connected to these activities. To the initiated, successful hunters were the apotheosis of an ideal manhood.[162] Those who were 'civilized' but unable or unwilling to participate in such hunting were castigated. According to Dennis Lyell, civilization, with its 'false policy of nurturing the diseased and unfit', was upsetting the balance of nature and threatening British virility.[163] H. Anderson Bryden[164] was of the view that big-game hunting was the antidote to the degeneracy of the times which allowed for the celebration of great men, warriors as well as sportsmen.[165]

In effect, the Shikar Club was a privileged patriarchy[166] which perpetuated an elite through the killing of wildlife. The Club was an exclusive masculine organization. To the initiated, membership signified an advanced degree of manhood based on both achievement in the field and political, economic and social status. The men who made up the Shikar Club viewed hunting as way of transcending the mediocrity of urban, artificial values. This elite was not to be restricted by the urban work ethic, subservient to the requirements of the marketplace or handicapped by limited resources. In its own eyes it achieved the dignity of a privileged 'manhood' through challenge in the natural world. The dispensing of superfluous luxuries in the wild was a rejection of the cosmopolitan values of the metropolitan plutocrat. In the words of Abel Chapman, 'one reads of pounds sterling being paid for antiques or curios and those articles may be worth it too. But we nature lovers enjoy our exquisite design, all pure and fresh, without cost.'[167] Of course, this was all illusion. In reality, big-game hunting was an expensive affair, clearly dependent upon those materialistic circumstances so readily dismissed by the gentleman shot.

According to one eminent historian, 'imperialism was a habit of mind, a dominant idea in the era of European world supremacy, which had widespread intellectual, cultural and technical expressions'.[168] The Shikar Club was all these things encapsulated in ritualistic, rationalized, moralistic hunting and was thus a manifestation of the assumed superiority of select middle-class English males in a period of high imperialism. And it was more. It was a curious form of regressive 'revolution', a Canute-like attempt to hold back the lapping waves of gender and class emancipation in order to reassert a 'pure' form of masculinity – privileged, controlled and in control.

NOTES

1. For example: the National Sports Defence Association (1885); the Society for the Preservation of the Wild Fauna of the Empire (1903); the Wildfowlers Association of Great Britain and Ireland (1908); the Salmon and Trout Association (1903).

2. The *battue* was a term for the shooting of driven-game as distinct from 'walking-up' game.

3. H.A. Levenson, 'An Old Shekarry' and 'The Algerian Sporting Expedition', *The Field*, 8 (21 Nov. 1857), 353.

4. Membership of the Shikar Club required that the hunter have corroborated proof that he had killed game on three separate continents. The authors have been unable to locate any formal record books, but are grateful to Henry North of Clifford Hall, Yealand Conyers, Carnforth, whose family have been well-represented in the Club. The Club was administered by a Committee led by P.B. Vanderbyl and the chairman, Hugh Cecil Lowther, and organized from their respective houses. The Club met for a formal annual dinner at various London hotels, but met informally at the Savoy Hotel.

5. See, for example, J.M. MacKenzie, *The Empire of Nature* (Manchester: Manchester University Press, 1988); and H. Ritvo, *The Animal Estate* (New York: Harvard University Press, 1989).

6. Note John Lowerson's observation in *Sport and the English Middle-Classes, 1870–1914* (Manchester: Manchester University Press, 1992), pp.21–3.

7. Charles Edward Radclyffe (1864–1915) served with the Rifle Brigade from the mid-1880s and was wounded in both the Burmese War (1885–87) and the South African Campaign, for which he received the DSO. P.B. Vanderbyl (1867–1930), educated Pembroke College, Cambridge, served in the Boer Wars and First World War at the rank of Captain. See *The Field*, CXLII (15 Nov. 1923), 717. Vanderbyl eventually married at the age of 60.

8. For details of Frederick Courtney Selous at Rugby School, see the Rugby School magazine *The Meteor* (10 June 1897), 58–61.

9. See R. Hyam, *Britain's Imperial Century, 1850–1914* (London: Batsford, 1976), pp.50–51.

10. Archival sources for the De Crespigny family obtained from Essex County Record Office, Chelmsford.

11. 'Essex Portraits, VIII', *Essex Review*, 13 (1904), 241–2; see also *Essex Review*, 44 (1935), 192; *Who's Who in Essex* (Worcester: Baylis and Son, 1935), p.58; *Essex Leaders, Social and Political* (Exeter); and J. Grant (ed.), *Essex: Historical Biographical and Personal* (London, 1913). The multitalented aristocratic sportsman, of course, exemplified by the likes of George Osbaldeston and Thomas Ashetton Smith, was appreciated and respected by many Victorian observers. De Crespigny was continuing the tradition of the competent 'all-round' sportsman.

12. C.C. De Crespigny, *Forty Years of a Sportsman's Life* (London: Mills and Boon, 1925), pp.274–5.

13. Alfred Edward Pease of Guisborough, 2nd Bart. (1857–1939).

14. A.E. Pease, *Half a Century of Sport* (London: John Murray, 1932), p.100.

15. *Essex Review*, 13 (1904); and De Crespigny, *Forty Years of a Sportsman's Life*, pp.230–32.

16. De Crespigny, *Forty Years of a Sportsman's Life*, pp.238 and 240–41.

17. *Essex Review*, 13 (1904).

18. Henry Salt (1851–1939), son of Colonel T. Salt, was educated at Eton and King's College, Cambridge. He was an assistant Master of Eton from 1875 to 1884. Salt was the catalyst for the Humanitarian League and particularly disapproved of blood sports. See Henry Salt (ed.), *Killing for Sport* (London: G. Bell and Sons, 1914), pp.152–5; and idem, *Seventy Years Among the Savages* (London: Allen and Unwin, 1921).

19. 'Epilogue: Continuities', *Shaping the Superman: Fascist Body as Political Icon – Aryan Fascism* (London and Portland, OR: Frank Cass, 2000), pp.180–95.

20. Salt, *Seventy Years Among the Savages*, p.11.

21. 'The Defence of Field Sports', *Baily's Magazine* (Aug. 1885), 318–26.

22. Ibid.

23. See Henry Seton-Karr, *My Sporting Holidays* (London: Edward Arnold, 1904), pp.44, 68, 91–2.

24. Iain Colquhoun, Bart., DSO, Lord-Lieutenant of Dunbartonshire and a Major in the Scots Guards served in The Great War. He owned a Scottish deer-forest and was an authority on the sport.

25. See William John Arthur Charles James Cavendish Bentinck, 6th Duke of Portland, *Fifty Years and More of Sport in Scotland* (London: Faber and Faber, 1933), p.41.

26. Colquhoun, 'The Future of Deerstalking' in J. Ross and H. Gunn (eds.), *The Book of the Red Deer and Empire Big Game* (London: Simkin and Marshall, 1925), p.111.

27. Henry Seton-Karr, CMG, MP, was the son of George Berkeley Seton-Karr, an Indian Civil Servant, and was educated at Harrow and Oxford. He was a barrister and Conservative MP for St. Helens from 1885 to 1906 and JP for Roxburghshire. Author of *A Call to Arms* (London: Longman, 1901), *My Sporting Holidays* (London: Edward Arnold, 1904), and contributor to *Baily's Magazine* and the *Badminton Series*.

28. Seton-Karr, *My Sporting Holidays*, pp.44, 68, 91–2.

29. Ibid., pp.5–6; see also H. Salt, 'The Sportsman at Bay', *International Journal of Ethics*, XVI (1906), 491.

30. F.C. Selous, *Travel and Adventure in South East Africa* (London: Rowland Ward, 1893), p.91.

31. Hugh Cecil Lowther (1857–1944) was the son of Henry Lowther and was educated at Eton. See *Who's Who in Cumberland and Westmoreland* (London, 1937), pp.147–8. Hugh Cecil Lowther was an enthusiastic sportsman, a big game shot and Master of the Cottesmore and Quorn Hounds. See L. Dawson, *Lonsdale: The Authorised Life of Hugh Lowther* (London: Odhams Press, 1946).

32. J.O. Thompson, *Dr. Salter of Tolleshunt D'Arcy* (London: Hamilton and Company, 1933), Preface.

33. Abel Chapman (1851–1929) was the eldest son of T.E. Chapman of Silksworth Hall, Sunderland. Abel was educated at Rugby, after which he became a partner in the family firm of brewers and wine merchants. See George Bolam, 'Memoir' in A. Chapman, *Four Score Years Less Two* (London: London and Counties Press Association, 1929). Chapman became a prolific writer and shot, the results of both careers are currently held at the Hancock Museum, Newcastle University, administered by Les Jessop, whose kind and authoritative assistance was invaluable in compiling a greater understanding of Chapman's emphatic 'masculinity'!

34. Abel Chapman, *On Safari* (London: Edward Arnold, 1908), p.4.

35. Lonsdale, *The Field*, 122 (14 June 1923), 900.

36. Salt, *Seventy Years Among the Savages*, pp.14–15.

37. Dawson, *Lonsdale*, pp.21 and 58.

38. Lonsdale, *The Field*, 900.

39. Grantley Berkeley, *The English Sportsman in the Western Prairies* (London: Hurst and Blackett, 1861), p.2; and Samuel W. Baker, *The Rifle and Hound in Ceylon* (London: Longman, 1890), pp.xi–xii.

40. Parker Gillmore, *Experiences of a Sportsman in North America* (London: no record of publisher, 1869), Preface.

41. Ibid., pp.2–3.

42. Captain Flack, *Hunters' Experiences in the Southern States of America* (London: no record of publisher, 1866), p.1.

43. C. Kirby, *The English Country Gentleman: A Study of Nineteenth-Century Types* (London: J. Clarke, 1937), p.42 describes Grantley Berkeley (1800–81) as an 'aristocrat in his own opinion but unable to convince the world to agree with him'. See also, *Baily's Magazine*, X (June 1865), 10–19, X (Aug. 1865), 118–24, and XXXVII (April 1881), 71–3.

44. Berkeley, *The English Sportsman in the Western Prairies*, pp.1–2.

45. Hon. F. Lawley, 'Phasianus Colchicus', *Baily's Magazine*, LXIII (Jan. 1895), 10.

46. K. Thomas, *Man and the Natural World* (London: Allen Lane, 1986).

47. See N. Elias and E. Dunning, *The Quest for Excitement: Sport and Leisure in the Civilising Process* (Oxford: Oxford University Press, 1986), p.160.

48. See 'Englishmen's Sport in the Future', *Baily's Magazine*, 85 (Jan.–June 1906), 347; 'The Decadence of Sport', *Baily's Magazine*, 83 (Jan.–June, 1095), 198–202; 'The Future of Wildlife in England', *The Field*, 113 (29 May 1909), 895.

49. See *The Field*, XX (2 Aug. 1862), 101; and *Times* (4 Aug. 1862), 8. Surtees called driven-game-shooting the 'old womanly sport of battuing', see A. Steel, *Jorrock's England* (London: Methuen, 1932), p.167.

50. See T.H.S. Escott, *Society in London* (London: Chatto and Windus, 1886), p.22; and F.M.L. Thompson, 'Landowners and the Rural Community' in G. Mingay (ed.), *The Victorian Countryside*, Vol.2 (London: Routledge and Kegan Paul, 1981), pp.457–75.

51. Felix, 'Sport in England', *Baily's Magazine*, 90 (July–Dec. 1908), pp.417–20. (Felix was his pseudonym).

52. W. Bromley-Davenport quoted in H.H. Prichard, *Hunting Camps* (London: William Heinemann, 1910), pp.3–4.

53. Selous, *Travel and Adventure in South East Africa*, p.91.

54. Capt. C.H. Stigand and D.D. Lyell, *Central African Game and its Spoor* (London: Seeley, 1906), p.4.

55. 'The Shikar Club' in Dawson, *Lonsdale*, pp.205–6.

56. 'A Record of Clean Sport', *The Field*, 140 (28 Oct. 1922), 648 – a review of Major-General N. Woodyatt, *My Sporting Memories, Forty Years with Note book and Gun* (London: Herbert Jenkins, 1923).

57. Seton-Karr, *My Sporting Holidays*, pp.66–7.

58. Fieldcraft remains the gauge by which true sportsmen are measured, and indicates their knowledge of the natural environment as well as skill with the gun.

59. Abel Chapman, 'On the Ethics of Sport', 'Records', MS., 3, p.10.

60. H. Seton-Karr, 'Reminiscences of the Rockies', *The Badminton Magazine*, VIII (1897), 256–9. See also Seton-Karr, *My Sporting Holidays*, p.145.

61. T.D. Claye-Shawe, 'What Game Shall I Play and What Sport Shall I Take Up?', *Baily's Magazine*, 98 (Sept. 1912), 170.

62. Seton-Karr, *My Sporting Holidays*, p.145.

63. Maurice Egerton of Tatton Hall, Cheshire (1874–1958).

64. Chester Record Office, Egerton Archives, DET/3229/60/2.

65. Ibid.

66. Abel Chapman, 'Houxty Records and Results', M.S., H 130–8, held at Hancock Museum, Newcastle University.

67. See, for example, 'The Vienna Sports Exhibition', *The Field*, 115, 1 (1910), p.480.

68. Ibid.

69. For a wider treatment of national identity, see J.A. Mangan, *Tribal Identities: Nationalism, Europe, Sport* (London and Portland, OR: Frank Cass, 1995); and G. Jarvie (ed.), *Sport in the Making of Celtic Cultures* (London: Lancaster University Press, 2000).

70. 'The Glasgow Exhibition', *The Field*, 97 (27 April 1901), 564.

71. See, for example, R.S. Baden-Powell, *Pigsticking or Hoghunting* (London: C.A. Pearson, 1924), pp.29–30.

72. Dennis Lyell of Eastwood, Broughty Ferry, Forfarshire, Scotland.

73. Stigand and Lyell, *Central African Game and its Spoor*, pp.142–3. See also D.D. Lyell, *The African Elephant and its Hunters* (London: Horace Cox, 1924), p.140.

74. See S.W. Baker, *Rifle and Hound in Ceylon* (London: Longman, 1890), Preface. For a wider treatment of sporting guns, see R. Riling, *Guns and Shooting, A Selected Chronological Bibliography* (New York: Macmillan, 1951).

75. Lyell, *The African Elephant and its Hunters*, p.147.

76. See M. Weiner, *English Culture and the Decline of the Industrial Spirit, 1850–1980* (Cambridge: Cambridge University Press, 1981); and Thorsten Veblen, *Theory of the Leisure Class* (New York: Macmillan, 1899), p.2.

77. See A.E. Pease, *The Diaries of A. E. Pease* (London: Headley Brothers, 1907).

78. Pease, *The Diaries of A.E. Pease*, p.29. See also 'Alfred Edward Pease', *Baily's Magazine*, CL (March 1914), 161–3.

79. 'Alfred Edward Pease', *Baily's Magazine*, CL (March 1914), 161–2.

80. Robert Lyons Scott (1871–1939), Chairman of Scott's Shipbuilding at Greenock from 1916 to 1939.

81. Information from Valerie Bough, Curator, Mclean Museum, Greenock.

82. Robert's father, John (1830–1903), was a devoted shot and an Honorary Colonel of the Dumbarton Royal Garrison. Robert was educated at Wellington College and developed his shooting skills at an early age. The authors are grateful for the assistance given by Johnstone Robb, Greenock, an ex-employee of Scott's.

83. *The Spectator, a review of Travel and Sport in Africa*, 59 (1903), 536.

84. See A.E. Pease, *The Book of the Lion* (London: John Murray, 1913), Ch.1.

85. See, for example, D.P. Blaine, *An Encyclopaedia of Rural Sports* (London: Longman, 1840).

86. J.A. Hobson, *Imperialism* (Michigan: University of Michigan Press, 1902, reprinted 1972), pp.223–4. See also F. Russell, *The Hunting Animal* (London: Hutchinson, 1984), p.28; and M. Cartmill, *A View to a Death in the Morning* (New York: Harvard University Press, 1993), pp.136–7.

87. Chapman, *On Safari*, pp.284–5.

88. See J.A. Mangan (ed.), *The Cultural Bond: Sport, Empire, Society* (London and Portland, OR: Frank Cass, 1986), pp.15–23.

89. E.L.S., 'The West Indian as a Sportsman', *The Field*, 103 (28 May 1904), 86.

90. Blaine, *An Encyclopaedia of Rural Sports*, Ch.2, 'The Progress of Field Sports in Africa', p.45.

91. Ibid.

92. C.H. Stigand, *Elephant in Africa* (New York: Macmillan, 1913), pp.210 and 535–6.

93. Richard William Arkwright (1822–89), Captain in the British Army in South Africa.

94. R.W. Arkwright, 'Diary, Four Years Campaigning in South Africa, 1843–47', p.89, T/B, 577, at Essex Record Office. See also Stigand, *Elephant in Africa*, p.205; and C.W.L. Bulpett, *A Picnic Party in Wildest Africa* (London: Horace Cox, 1907), p.10.

95. See An Officer, 'The African Native as Sportsmen', *Baily's Magazine*, 112 (July–Dec. 1919), 115–20.

96. E. Said, *Culture and Imperialism* (London: Vintage, 1993), p.296.

97. Abel Chapman, 'Diary, Hunting in Norway', M.S. (1897), available from the Hancock Museum, Newcastle, AS/C3/S2, NEWHM, H9, H130/13.

98. See Abel Chapman, *Savage Sudan, Its Wild Tribes, Big-game and Bird Life* (1921), *On Safari* (1908), *Unexplored Spain* (1910), *Wild Norway* (1897) and *Wild Spain* (1910) and 'Houxty Records and Results' M.S.

99. Abel Chapman, 'African Big-Game' in 'Houxty Records and Results', p.27.

100. Chapman, 'Houxty Records and Results', p.8. See also J.G. Millais, *Newfoundland and its Untrodden Ways* (London: Longman, 1907).

101. Chapman, 'Houxty Records and Results', p.8.

102. Letters to Oldfield Thomas, Natural History Museum, Ref. DF232/6, p.342.

103. J.G. Millais, *Wanderings and Memories* (London: Longman, 1919), p.167. See also Gunn and Ross (eds.), *The Book of the Red Deer and Empire Big Game*, pp.137–8.

104. 'The Shikar Club', *The Field*, 147 (17 June 1926), 952.

105. See, for example, Bulpett, *A Picnic in Africa* (1908); Anderson Bryden, *Great and Small Game of Africa* (1899), *Animals of Africa* (1900) and *Nature and Sport in Africa* (1897).

106. For a wider discussion of male identity in sport, see J. Nauright and T.L. Chandler (eds.), *Making Men: Rugby and Masculine Identity* (London and Portland, OR: Frank Cass, 1999); and J.A. Mangan (ed.), *Making Masculinities: Sport, Europe, Gender* (London and Portland, OR: Frank Cass, 2000).

107. Seton-Karr, *My Sporting Holidays*, Preface.

108. 'The Shikar Club', *The Field*, 111 (13 June 1908), 1006.

109. A.E. Pease, *Edmund Loder* (London: John Murray, 1923), pp.54–5.

110. 'The Shikar Club', *The Field*, 147 (17 June 1926), 952. See also Dawson, *Lonsdale*, pp.205–6.

111. See Jeffrey Richards, 'Passing the Love of Women: Manly Love and Victorian Society' in J.A. Mangan and J. Walvin (eds.), *Manliness and Morality: Middle-Class Masculinity in Britain and America, 1800–1940* (Manchester: Manchester University Press, 1987), Ch.5, pp.180–95.

112. Seton-Karr, *My Sporting Holidays*, p.97.

113. Chapman, 'Houxty Records and Results'.

114. Edmund Loder, b. 7 August 1849, d. 14 April 1920. See Pease, *Edmund Loder*.

115. Pease, *Edmund Loder*, pp.54–5.

116. This information is derived mainly from the 'Egerton Diaries', DET, Chester County

Records Office, and details from Tatton Hall, Cheshire. The authors are grateful for help provided by Margaret Mckean, archivist at Tatton.

117. Dawson, *Lonsdale*, p.182.
118. The 'African Adventure Notes' (n.d.), held at Tatton, and 'Egerton Diaries' illustrate some of the expenses involved in hunting.
119. 'African Adventure Notes', p.3.
120. C.W. Monkton, *Experiences of a New Guinea President Magistrate* (London: John Lane, 1921), p.111.
121. Burton, *The Life of Capt. Richard Burton* (London: Henry and Company, 1893), p.17.
122. Ibid.
123. For a full and detailed account of Maurice Egerton in South Africa, see 'Egerton Diaries' and 'African Adventure Notes', p.6.
124. See J. Springhall, 'Youth and Empire: A Study of the Propagation of Imperialism to the Young in Edwardian Britain', D.Phil. thesis, Sussex University, 1968.
125. 'Scouting for Boys', *The Spectator*, 103 (25 Sept. 1909), pp.463–4.
126. See R.S. Baden-Powell, *Scouting for Boys* (London: C.A. Pearson, 1908), p.266.
127. Stigand and Lyell, *Central African Game and its Spoor*, p.2.
128. Egerton, 'Biographical Notes' (n.d.), held at Tatton Park.
129. From *Personal Jottings, 1939*, held at Tatton Park. See also *Knutsford Guardian*, 18 May 1958, and 8 Aug. 1997, p.6.
130. Egerton, 'Biographical Notes'.
131. 'Manuscript Notes from Rostherne Boys School Log, 1863–1912', Cheshire Records Office.
132. See Blaine, *An Encyclopaedia of Rural Sports*, p.155; and Harry Hieover, *Sporting Facts and Fancies* (London: no record of publisher, 1853), p.203.
133. See R. Connell, *Masculinities* (Cambridge: Polity, 1995).
134. DET/3229/60/2.
135. Ibid.
136. The location and holder of the 'best' moose were given in 'Egerton's Diaries'. W.W. Hart and F.B. Tolhurst held the record for Alaska with beasts of over 20 points. See DET/3229/60/2, Chester Records Office.
137. Letter from Lord Egerton, 10 Jan. 1925, DET/3229/107, N-R, Chester Records Office.
138. The Bongo provoked a great deal of excitement amongst elite shots, probably owing to the difficulty of locating and acquiring it. It was described as 'rare with a red coat, with ten, vertical silver stripes'. See 'Bongo Safari', *The Field*, 141 (10 May 1928), 710.
139. See *Times*, 4 Oct. 1901, 4; and Chapman, *On Safari*, p.288.
140. Chapman, ' Catalogue of My Collections', p.3; idem, 'Houxty Records and Results'.
141. 'African Big-Game', 'Houxty Records and Results', pp.27–8.
142. See 'Knutsford Journal' (July 1958), 10; *Knutsford Guardian* (Aug. 1997), 7.
143. Chapman, 'Houxty Records and Results', H130–15.
144. See S. Hall and B. Gieben (eds.), *Formations of Modernity* (Cambridge: Cambridge University Press, 1992), pp.177–228.
145. Chapman, 'Houxty Records and Results', H139, p.3.
146. Chapman, 'Norwegian Pocket Book', AS-C£-S2 (1892); idem, 'Houxty Records and Results', H130–8, NEW-H130 11, 1894, and No.3, M.S., pp.27–8.
147. Egerton, 'Notes', pp.19–20.
148. Egerton, 'Big-game Book', DET, 3229/123.
149. Ewart Scott-Grogan (1874–1950). Educated Trinity College, Cambridge (1891–94). See J. Venn, *Allumni Canabrigienses From Earliest Times to 1900* (Cambridge: Cambridge University Press, 1922), p.54.
150. Hugh Cholomondeley, Barton Delamere of Vale Royal, Cheshire (b. 1870, d. 1946), settled in Eincuteita, near Nairobi, British East Africa, in 1900, thus marking the beginning of aristocratic 'settlement' in the region. See *Times*, 5 Sept. 1912, 1. See also Venn, *Allumni Canabrigienses From Earliest Times to 1900*. Ewart Scott-Grogan travelled from the Cape to Cairo during the 1890s when on 'vacation' from Cambridge.
151. E.S. Grogan and A. Sharpe, *From the Cape to Cairo* (London: Hurst and Blackett, 1900), pp.xv and 12.

152. See E. Huxley, *White Man's Country, Lord Delamere and the Making of Kenya*, 2 Vols. (London: Macmillan, 1935).

153. Col. T. St.Clair, 'Night Shooting', *Badminton Magazine*, II (1896), pp.597–609; and R. Oliver, *Sir Harry Johnson and the Scramble For Africa* (London: Chatto and Windus, 1957), p.295.

154. Huxley, *White Man's Country*, pp.257–8.

155. 'The Shikar Club', *The Field*, 147 (17 June 1926), 952.

156. 'The Shikar Club', *The Field*, 142 (23 Aug. 1923), 275.

157. Ibid.

158. 'The Shikar Club,' *The Field*, 147 (17 June 1926).

159. Minutes of Meetings, S.P.F.E., 27 Feb. 1925, pp.16–17.

160. See P.G. Filene, *Him/Her/Self, Sex-Roles in Modern America* (New York: Harvard University Press, 1975).

161. For a wider discussion of this, see R. Lee and I. Vore (eds.), *Man the Hunter* (Chicago: Cambridge University Press, 1968), p.319.

162. See H. Faulkner, *Elephant Haunts, Being a Sportman's Narrative of the Search for Dr. Livingston* (London, 1868), pp.27–8.

163. D. Lyell, *Memories of an African Hunter* (London: T. Fisher Unwin, 1923), p.19.

164. Henry Anderson Bryden (1854–1937). Noted period Hunter-Naturalist. Educated Cheltenham College, distinguished athlete – played football for England.

165. H.A. Bryden, *Nature and Sport in South Africa* (London: Chapman and Hall, 1897), p.281.

166. The term 'patriarchy' in historical context is discussed in J. Tosh and K. Roper, *Manful Assertions, A History of Masculinity in Britain* (London: Routledge, 1995), p.9.

167. Chapman, 'Diaries' (1905), pp.7–8.

168. MacKenzie, *The Empire of Nature*, p.ix.

9

A Dark 'Prince' of Denmark:
Niels Bukh, Twentieth-Century
Middle-Class Propagandist

HANS BONDE

The Danish gymnastics teacher Niels Bukh (1880–1950)[1] was probably the best-internationally-known Dane of the 1930s. From 1912 onwards he was involved in virtually all the Olympic Games and was a regular contributor to world expositions. As early as the 1920s he had successfully promoted Danish culture by travelling each summer to various European countries and in 1923 and 1926 he visited the United States. The culmination of his personal fame came with his world tour in 1931. One outcome was the adoption of his gymnastics system in Japan, where it can still be found today. For the remainder of the 1930s he travelled with unabated energy and embarked on tours to two new continents – South America in 1938 and South Africa in 1939.

Bukh became both the outward and an inward face of Denmark. He demonstrated his version of the Western civilized body to many hundreds of thousands of young people around the world. Everywhere Bukh went, he used song, folk dance and gymnastics to help revive the memory of the motherland for many Danish emigrants who came to his displays. Whatever the political profile of the Danish government in charge in the inter-war years, there was a clear recognition of Bukh's importance for putting Denmark on the international map.[2]

Bukh created images of Danishness that stuck fast in the memory, whether it was 'six men on the plinth' or rural lads who executed perfectly synchronized physical movements. His value as a national symbol was reinforced by the fact that his gymnastics, in marked contrast to the Danish national football team, for example, became clearly known as an original and attractive product of Danish physical culture.

Bukh's gymnastics and other big ultra-nationalist Continental gymnastics movements like the Slavic Sokol movement[3] and the German

Turnverein movement[4] were examples of the way gymnastics in the inter-war years was able to contend with the influential British tradition of competitive sport. There was a mirror-image relationship between Bukh's gymnastics movement and these two other movements. Bukh's view, in fact, was that the gymnastics leaders were the proper ethical leaders in society, in the British-inspired sports movement too, and that the competition of the Olympic Games should be replaced by Olympic rallies organized and led by men such as himself with a gymnastics (not least his own type of gymnastics) of 'peoples' as the most important component.

With such an ambitious view of gymnastics, both abroad and at home, Niels Bukh became involved in politics. He felt he had a right to make comparative political statements because, unlike most Danes, he had visited all the countries he spoke about, although as a rule he had only seen their glittering surface. In reality, his global vision was limited. Without his popular platform in Danish rural culture and his public importance to the image of the nation, Bukh would have had little political impact. His political vision, insight and competence were far too limited.

In support of Bukh's political aspirations, both he and his followers used his reputation as a teacher of gymnastics, his national fame and his international prominence to their advantage. In this regard Niels Bukh serves as a classic example of a functional relationship between sport and politics. The fact that Bukh was able to make his mark politically surprised many. He was no master of the traditional political game of patient negotiation but he played his own political game. He quite consciously rejected the written or unwritten rules of the parliamentary system. He relied on a form of 'charismatic mastery', in the Max Weber sense, and he understood how to dramatize himself via the media in an almost completely modern way.

The fundamental thesis of this essay is that Bukh, as a 'middle-class revolutionary' with his roots in the farming world, attempted to have an impact on both the athletic and the political worlds – in three ways: Niels Bukh revolutionized Danish male gymnastics; he gained greater international importance through displays of his gymnastics than through the dissemination of his gymnastics system; and he used his fame in gymnastics as a platform for political propaganda and revolutionary ideas.

THE PHASES OF BUKH'S GYMNASTICS

To begin at the beginning: before Bukh established his own gymnastics high school[5] in southern Funen, he participated as official leader of the Danish rural gymnastics club team at the Olympic Games in Stockholm in 1912 and at the International Congress for Physical Education in Paris in 1913. Prior to that he had served as a gymnastics teacher in the countryside, gradually becoming the leading exponent of Swedish gymnastics in Denmark. He soon attracted attention and as a result was officially appointed to lead the Danish rural gymnastics team.

Niels Bukh's significance in the history of physical culture beyond Denmark and his success in taking Denmark to the world can be illustrated by the following list of the times and destinations of his tours:

Transcontinental

USA – 1923, 1926, 1931, 1939
Canada – 1931
Soviet Union – 1931
China (Manchuria) – 1931
Korea – 1931
Japan – 1931
Brazil/Uruguay/Argentina – 1938
South Africa – 1939

Europe

Belgium – 1920 (Olympic team), 1930, 1935, 1937, 1950
Austria – 1922, 1930, 1933
Germany – 1922, 1924, 1925, 1927, 1930, (Danzig – 1931), 1933, 1936 (twice), 1938, 1950
France – 1924, 1937, 1950
Czechoslovakia – 1925, 1927, 1930
Holland – 1927
Britain – 1927, 1937
Hungary – 1930, 1933
Poland – 1937
Italy – 1934
Portugal – 1938

Nordic Countries

Sweden – 1923, 1930, 1937, 1940, 1949
Iceland – 1927
Faroes – 1927
Finland – 1929
Norway – 1935, 1948

Bukh's gymnastics can be divided into specific phases. In the 'traditional phase' (1880–1916/17) Bukh was born into the Ling rural gymnastics tradition which he mastered to perfection. In the 'revolutionary phase' (1916/17–19) he created his new gymnastics. In 'the European phase' (1920–30) first he promoted his gymnastics in Denmark and then toured several European countries and the United States. In the period from the world tour of 1931 until the outbreak of the Second World War Bukh's gymnastics were at their high point. This was the 'transcontinental phase' which included tours to several continents. With the limits on international travel imposed by the war, Bukh's gymnastics were limited to a virtually 'national phase' (1940–45). After the war Bukh's attempt to revive the national and international fame of his gymnastics encountered considerable gymnastic and political difficulties; the period from 1945 until his death in 1950 can only be described as the 'decline phase' despite the fact that his total dominance within Danish male gymnastics occurred in this period.

A REVOLUTION IN MALE GYMNASTICS

Throughout his childhood and youth at his Danish folk high school Bukh had been deeply influenced by Swedish gymnastics. Swedish gymnastics were created by Pehr Henrik Ling (1776–1839). In the Danish rural context they were used around 1900 as health gymnastics, the object of which was straightened body. Through the team's joint, synchronized movements, where each participant moved within demarcated sets of movements, the body was to be developed to the greatest possible beauty and strength and health on the basis of correct physiological principles.[6] That Swedish gymnastics were constantly criticized in scientific quarters in Denmark does not alter the fact that they nevertheless sought legitimacy in scientifically-based physiology.

The interpretation of physical culture adopted here is inspired by Pierre Bourdieu's concept 'habitus'.[7] By 'habitus' Bourdieu means the attitudes to the world, as a rule unconscious, of a social class. According to Bourdieu these attitudes result in a number of 'practices', namely bodily actions which signal class identity both inwardly in relation to the social group's own self-perception and outwardly in relation to other social classes.

The straight, tense Swedish team gymnastics in the high schools and in the community house[8] can be said to constitute a habitus that was adequate to the Danish Co-operative Movement's core elements such as collectivism, personal dignity and self-discipline.[9] The Danish Co-operative Movement of the 1880s resulted in the Danish farmers joining forces in matters relating to the manufacturing and marketing of their products. The farms were still individually owned, but the sales and manufacturing organizations were owned communally by farmers.

The drawing power of Bukh's male gymnastics by virtue of its modernization of the Swedish gymnastics aroused international enthusiasm through the dynamism, strength and degree of individualism, especially in the men's leaps. Jump gymnastics had already been cultivated in the Swedish-inspired rural gymnastics in Denmark by the time Bukh developed his version. However, Bukh's ability to encapsulate the modern cult of speed in long series of leaps where the men followed one another in quick succession was innovatory. This gave the Danish farmers a modernity in the field of the physical that corresponded to the economic modernity of the co-operative movement.

Bukh belonged to a group of Scandinavian gymnastics teachers who had adapted the orthodoxy of Swedish gymnastics by adding rhythm, muscle relaxation and movement. The others were Elli Björkstén in Finland, I.P. Müller in Denmark[10] and Elin Falk in Sweden. For his part Niels Bukh revitalized the Swedish gymnastics in terms of its function, its teaching and its motion. Furthermore, with Bukh came a shift from the healthy to the beautiful. Bukh continually looked for scientific validation of his gymnastics, but in practice he was preoccupied by aesthetic perfection.

Swedish gymnastics were egalitarian; they were available to all. Everyone did the same thing at the same time on the command of the leader. Bukh, in contrast, selected a gymnastics elite from his pupils who were already the ablest in their parishes. Then again, with his elite teams of both sexes the choreography was so well practised that Bukh had no need to issue commands and simply stood erect at the edge of the display area.

It should not be overlooked that whereas Bukh developed male gymnastics at a time when Scandinavian gymnastics were increasingly becoming a female activity, he did not seriously challenge the Swedish tradition in women's gymnastics. He was less radical in his insistence on rhythm and muscle relaxation than Elin Falk in Sweden and Elli Björkstén in Finland. Nevertheless, he was innovatory. Bukh's women adopted his revolutionary concept of 'primitive gymnastics', although in a less fast and powerful version than the men. During the inter-war years Bukh often toured with both a women's and a men's team which ensured a more complete demonstration of the abilities of the sexes than the usual single sex demonstrations.

The success of Bukh gymnastics was due in part to the fact that it originally constituted a male youth revolution based on energetic gymnastics which 'masculinized' young men's bodies.[11] In time this revolutionary dimension of Bukh's gymnastic system was institutionalized as a cult of masculinity, as a system where many a young man could cultivate and, in the case of the elite, display the masculinity rites full potency in comradeship with other men.

In male gymnastics Bukh broke with the Swedish gymnastics. Apart from his gymnastics no important new aesthetic forms of expression were developed in men's gymnastics in Scandinavia during the inter-war years. The dynamic, 'primitive gymnastics' with their fluid, powerful physical floor exercises constituted a brand new gymnastic concept. 'Primitive gymnastics' stressed flexibility; indeed suppleness was viewed as essential to an erect body. Then there was Bukh's display gymnastics in which the men, in the so-called 'double work', lifted, pulled and supported one another in fluid actions that combined grace and power. In 'double work', and indeed in his male gymnastics as a whole, Bukh developed entirely new stylistic elements.

All in all Bukh created a new male gymnastics system. There was the 'primitive gymnastics', the double work, the development of a new repertoire of movements and a new clothing style whereby the upper body was left naked. In short, Bukh revolutionized style, movement and clothing. Bukh created exercises that expressed male emotions; indeed, from the perspective of Swedish gymnastics, his gymnastics could be regarded as too 'feminine'. Bukh's system clearly had roots in Swedish gymnastics. His fundamental idea was Swedish: the idea that a team of people executed the same movements at the same time. However, as already stated, he deviated from the Swedish model with its display forms where groups of gymnasts formed different patterns in one great choreography.

Was Bukh indebted to gymnastics systems other than the Swedish? He was inspired by the Finn Elli Björkstén's stress on rhythm and a certain freedom of movement, by the power and dynamism of the male gymnastics that had been created by the French gymnastics teacher Hébert and not least by the limbering-up exercises that had been developed by the Danish physiotherapist and remedial gymnastics teacher Kaare Teilmann. However, Bukh's indisputable originality lay in the fact that he grafted the rhythmic qualities of women's gymnastics on to men's gymnastics. He also adapted the remedial gymnastics principle of physical flexibility to general gymnastics, thus creating 'primitive gymnastics' with its genuinely original repertoire of movements. Finally, Bukh introduced brand new aesthetic forms of expression in his 'double work' and in his men's gymnastic routines.

Bukh's women's gymnastics must be said to be a variant of the Swedish type with added inspiration from Björkstén. Bukh's men's gymnastics, on the other hand, must be characterized as an original Danish gymnastics form with roots in Swedish gymnastics and added inspiration from French military, Finnish women's and Danish remedial gymnastics. Bukh participated in the evolution of women's gymnastics, but his men's gymnastics were based on his own revolutionary concepts and approaches.

BUKH AND SWEDISH GYMNASTICS

Swedish gymnastics were a strong part of Swedish national self-identity[12] so the Danish upstart from southern Funen was viewed with a mixture of scepticism and pride from this quarter. On the one hand Bukh was able, like no Swede of the inter-war period, to display Swedish-inspired gymnastics to the world. On the other hand Bukh's displays deviated, from 1912 until 1930, more and more from the Swedish type and he created a higher and higher profile for himself in his insistence on having created a true Danish system.

In 1922 Bukh declared that his gymnastics were just a new 'way of working' within the Swedish system,[13] whereas in 1936 he labelled his gymnastics 'Danish gymnastics' – a firm declaration of the creation of a new form of gymnastics. Bukh's shifts were a reflection of the politics of Scandinavian physical culture. In the 1920s it was unwise to provoke a break with the Swedish gymnastics in its stronghold in rural Denmark. Furthermore, in the early period Bukh gymnastics saw plenty of Danish resistance. In this situation, some believed that Swedish gymnastics gave Bukh's gymnastics a certain legitimacy in terms of a physiological rationale. In 1936, on the other hand, Bukh had consolidated his position as a national figure and as a physical culture teacher was almost sacrosanct in Denmark. This prompted him to represent his gymnastics as something originally Danish and, more exaggeratedly, also as characteristic of all Danish gymnastics.

The attitudes of the advocates of Swedish gymnastics towards Niels Bukh strongly fluctuated and contrasted over time. The dilemma was whether to look at Bukh's gymnastics with pride as a dynamic variant of Swedish gymnastics or whether to reject it as a heretical deviation and risk his gymnastics being recognized as an original Danish system. This battle of the gymnastics formed part of the struggle for national identity and honour and was part of the almost constant face-offs between the Swedish and the Danish press about which nation best carried the Scandinavian gymnastics tradition. This was part of a long legacy of political confrontation. In 1912 at the Olympic Games in Stockholm, the capital of Swedish gymnastics, conflict arose between Bukh and the Swedish spokesmen. On the one hand, although Bukh officially represented Denmark in the competition in Swedish gymnastics he had already by this time changed his gymnastics programme so radically that the Swedes raised doubts about whether it was really pure Swedish gymnastics. On the other hand, it could not be accepted that Bukh had developed a 'new Danish' gymnastics. Perhaps because of the deviations, Bukh's team came second to the Swedish team, although of course the Swedish team was virtually destined to win in Ling's native country.[14]

Bukh did not have it all his own way in Denmark either. The development of Bukh's own concept of men's gymnastics (from 1916 on) led to protests from orthodox Danish 'Lingians' who considered his training too demanding and the pace too fast. The physical contact, the degree of nakedness and the tightness of the costume around the genitals also gave offence.[15] Despite Bukh's indisputable reputation as a gymnastics teacher, he was not invulnerable to such attacks within his own field. He also faced other challenges. As early as 1917 he came under strong fire from some of sports doctors and physiologists[16] and his Danish opponents within Swedish gymnastics lost no time in exploiting the situation.

As Bukh's international fame grew, manifested especially at the time of his world tour in 1931, there was unquestionably some annoyance in Swedish circles over the fact that Niels Bukh and his teams, not Swedish gymnastics teams, were attracting attention from faraway lands.[17]

Bukh's 'Nordic Olympiad' in Denmark in 1935 could be considered both as an outstretched hand of friendship to the birthplace of Swedish gymnastics and as an attempt to take the lead in Nordic gymnastics. Bukh was now an undoubted leading international figure in gymnastics, even in the eyes of the official representatives of Swedish gymnastics. The Swedes were ambivalent in their response to him. In one speech, a Swedish gymnastics director described the 'Olympiad' as the biggest gymnastics rally in the North and paid tribute to Bukh as the great contemporary personality in the field of physical culture but at the same time he criticized Bukh's men's gymnastics for an exaggerated focus on strength and suppleness.[18]

Bukh's participation in the 'Ling Week' in Gothenburg in 1937 led to something of a reconciliation between Niels Bukh and the representatives of Swedish gymnastics.[19] However, Bukh declined to participate in the celebration rally 100 years after the death of Pehr Henrik Ling, the so-called 'Lingiad' in Sweden in 1939, despite the fact that he could easily have managed the visit since his tour of South Africa did not start until several days afterwards. This did not improve relationships between him and the Swedes.

Up to 1940 Bukh's stock rose steadily as an ambassador for Nordic gymnastics throughout the world, despite some competition from the Swedish gymnastics teacher Maja Carlquist's relatively relaxed and rhythmic gymnastics as displayed by her fêted Swedish 'Sofia Girls' who gave 300 displays in Sweden, Denmark, Germany and the USA between 1936 and 1946.[20]

The relative thaw after the Nordic Olympiad continued during the beginning of the Occupation with the participation of the Bukh gymnasts in the Swedish–Danish gymnastics festival in Malmö in 1940.[21] After the rally Bukh was awarded the gold Ling Medal, although there remained a certain amount of criticism of Bukh's men's gymnastics among Swedish specialists for having too much of a feminine emphasis.

After the Occupation Bukh's stock declined in Swedish gymnastics circles because he had collaborated with the Germans. One year before his death, at the second Lingiad in 1949, there was clear discomfort on the part of both the Swedish organizers and the Swedish press about Bukh's participation. The organizers limited the number of his gymnasts[22] and Bukh ended his life under the disapproval of the nation that had nourished his gymnastic roots and whose recognition he needed more than ever.

All in all, Bukh's gymnastics were not, like the emancipatory Swedish gymnastics in Denmark, unequivocally bound up with a political programme favouring parliamentarism and defence against Germany. It was precisely this instability between the gymnastic symbol and its ideological content that made Bukh's gymnastics a disputed political sign in the course of the 1930s and throughout the Occupation of Denmark.

BUKH'S INTERNATIONAL SIGNIFICANCE

In the archives of the Danish Foreign Ministry there is a large body of material about Bukh's travels, not least his world tour of 1931.[23] This archive material provides clear evidence that Bukh was the Danish gymnastics teacher who most conspicuously placed Denmark on the world map and who obtained by far the greatest support from the Foreign Service. By all appearances, Bukh's groundbreaking world tour of 1931 would have been a far smaller format without the support of Danish diplomacy.

In any assessment of Bukh's international significance it is important to distinguish between audiences and activist's training environments that were influenced by his gymnastics. Bukh achieved huge success as a symbol of Denmark abroad. His gymnastics were watched by large numbers of spectators and received massive press coverage in several countries. Against this background it might be thought that his gymnastics gained wide currency internationally but this cannot be unequivocally confirmed. By no means can Bukh's gymnastics be compared to Swedish gymnastics in terms of international impact, not least in educational and military systems in many countries. However, it is not a simple matter to accurately assess his influence, especially when it comes to dissemination beyond public-sector educational systems.

The pupil statistics of Bukh's school, used with caution, provide a picture of the geographical spread of his gymnastics abroad. In all, from 1914 until his death in 1950, he trained over 11,000 pupils, around 6,000 of whom were women.[24] Bukh also trained a large number of foreign gymnastics teachers at his school. In total over five per cent of the pupils came from abroad and over half of these were from Norway which, unlike Sweden and Finland, had no independent gymnastics tradition. From Europe, outside of Scandinavia, it was mostly Germans who visited the school and from beyond Europe his school was mainly frequented by pupils from the United States and Japan – where Bukh had toured. Every year Bukh held separate summer courses for Americans, Britons and Germans. After a tour in 1927 his 'primitive gymnastics' gained currency in Holland as warm-up exercises before sports, his jumping gymnastics were used in clubs and large parts of his gymnastics were introduced to the educational system.[25] The reality appears to be that excluding Germany, Japan, South Africa and Holland, Bukh did not have great influence in other countries like the United States and Britain outside of the school and gymnastics environments to which his co-ordinators belonged. This lack of influence was helped by the German Occupation of Denmark which led to a total halt in foreign pupils, although their numbers began to increase again during the last five years of Bukh's life.

Paradoxically there almost seems to be a 'remoteness principle' at work in the case of the spread of Bukh's gymnastics in the 1930s. The farther away he toured the greater his impact. The overseas fascination with Bukh's gymnastics may have been due to the fact that Bukh's gymnastics represented a striking and appealing new departure, especially since these countries had no direct link to the roots of the European continental gymnastics tradition.

A POLITICAL REVOLUTIONARY

Throughout the 1920s Niels Bukh was dismissive of parliamentary rule. His political attacks on the divisive influence of the party-political system may have been influenced by contact with German and Austrian right-radical so-called völkisch gymnastics circles.[26] However, no direct contact with the Danish radical-Right is evident during the 1920s. Through the 1930s Bukh's critique of democracy was radicalized by his encounter with both right- and left-wing dictatorships. In particular, his encounter with Nazism in 1933 inspired revolutionary ideas about change in Danish society.

Bukh's gymnastics, including particularly his 'primitive gymnastics', were an elitist, hard, demanding form of physical exercises which was not without problems of voluntary dissemination. Bukh's co-operation with various dictatorships can be seen against the background of the fact that help 'from above' provided him with a good chance of achieving diffusion of his gymnastics. Bukh's difficult and, for some people, even potentially dangerous 'primitive gymnastics' could perhaps not be expected to become particularly widespread outside the borders of Denmark as mass gymnastics without the aid of totalitarianism. However, the invitations to Bukh from foreign countries originally came from local gymnastics and educational workers; the interest of the authorities was only aroused later. Bukh's gymnastics, for example, achieved a certain popularity in the youth and gymnastics culture of the Weimar Republic[27] and he was first invited to Japan by an educational worker who had made the acquaintance of his gymnastics during a visit to Ollerup.[28]

The enthusiasm for Bukh's gymnastics in several dictator states lay in the fact that the strong discipline, endurance and strength-radiating appearance of the gymnasts seemed to promise military prowess. This was especially the case in the interest of several South American dictatorships and of the Japanese Navy during the Second World War.[29]

Totalitarian regimes were of the view that Bukh's gymnastics could help create a young generation typified by fitness, dynamism and endurance. The perception that the gymnasts almost merged into one organism in their formally perfect precision gymnastics was also attractive to these regimes, as it gave the promise of order, discipline and unity in countries like Japan, Germany and South Africa. However this was not true in Italy, where the nationalist interest in the country's own youth education quite overshadowed the skills of the Bukh gymnasts.[30] During the war Bukh's gymnastics aroused interest in Axis powers other than Germany. The Romanian military dictatorship, for example, planned to introduce Bukh's gymnastics into the educational system.[31]

For his part, Bukh's fascination with right-wing dictatorships was very much due to their facades of order and purity, whereas the chaos, dirt and stink that greeted him in the Soviet Union in 1931 confirmed his belief in the failure of Communism.

Bukh's world tour of 1931 serves as the perfect example of the inseparability of physical culture and politics in the evolution of his gymnastics. The Soviet authorities first took an interest in Niels Bukh's peasant gymnasts, who looked more like the powerful, dynamic ideal worker of Agitprop art than the worn-out, hungry Soviet representatives of the class that Bukh and the gymnasts met on their tour to the USSR. However, strong disagreements between Bukh and the Soviet authorities may have had an adverse influence on the very limited diffusion of his gymnastics in the Soviet Union.

The Soviet Union confronted Niels Bukh and his troupe with elements of the emergent Stalinist system: the first five-year plans; the kulak persecutions; and the propaganda. Without in-depth understanding of what they saw, Bukh's and the gymnasts' reports to the Danish public may nevertheless have helped to give flesh and blood to the anti-Communism that was widespread, not least in the countryside, and to develop Bukh's anti-Communist image in Denmark.[32]

In 1931 Bukh praised a Japan that was in the process of invading Manchuria. In both Manchuria and occupied Korea he allowed his troupe to be used in the Japanese army's propaganda offensive. On an extended tour around the remainder of the Japanese Island Empire his displays may have functioned as a rallying-point amidst the mixture of militarism and war euphoria that was developing under a prime minister who had abandoned the idea of democratic rule. Japan became the country where Bukh's gymnastics had their greatest quantitative diffusion. There Bukh's gymnastics were disseminated both from above and below. Although to begin with he was invited by Christian, relatively Western-oriented circles, the Ministry of Education, during the growing militarization of the educational system in 1936, saw that it was in its interest to introduce elements of his exercises into gymnastics teaching. Bukh's gymnastics were also used by the navy and in corporate and radio gymnastics.[33]

In 1938 Bukh had the opportunity for yet another overseas journey, as the Danish Embassy in Rio de Janeiro planned a tour to Brazil and Argentina with a troupe of 17 young men in the late summer of 1938.[34] The South American militaries were interested in finding out whether his gymnastics could be used to strengthen the physiques of its soldiers.

In 1939 Bukh's troupe participated in the extreme Rightist revival of the descendants of the Dutch Boer immigrants in South Africa, but due to the liberal political pressure the displays of the troupe came in the end to form part of the pro-British government's unity effort. The recognition of Bukh's gymnastics in the highest political circles helped to ensure that after the tour they became part of the South African educational system. Four Danish teachers who trained at Bukh's gymnastics high school were engaged by the South African educational system to facilitate the process.[35]

BUKH AND NAZI PHYSICAL CULTURE

It was to Nazi Germany that Bukh showed by far his greatest political commitment. Shortly after the seizure of power, the Nazi authorities needed recognition from abroad and a normalization of relations with the outside world. Bukh's demonstration in Berlin in October 1933 became a welcome opportunity for a cultural exchange with a small 'Nordic brother country'. Bukh's appeal to the fascists lay in the fact that he actively backed the Nazi project in Germany and he was able to deliver images of the ideal young 'Aryan' type. His support for 'the new Germany' meant that he and the German *Reichssportführer*, Hans von Tschammer und Osten, developed what Bukh at least saw as a friendship that only ended with von Tschammer und Osten's death in Berlin in 1942. On his return from Berlin in 1933 Bukh lent his support to the glorification of Nazi ideology with its elements of racial theory, anti-Semitism, the cult of the Führer and even suggestions of the legitimacy of violence. In this he certainly overstepped the boundaries of traditional radical conservatism.[36]

In the second half of the 1930s Bukh's co-operation with the Nazis, including participation in the Nuremberg rallies and a meeting with Hitler in 1936, resulted in displays in Germany. Both the display in Berlin in 1933 and the display in Flensborg in 1936 were an odd mix of Danish and Nazi symbols. Bukh's co-operation with Fascism brought other rewards. An attempt was made by the *Reichssportführer* to select Niels Bukh, bypassing all the normal International Olympic Committee regulations, to participate in the Berlin Games of 1936 as a guest of honour. In 1938 an exchange agreement was signed by the Gymnastics High School and the German Reich Academy for Physical Culture; a highly unusual agreement between a private school and a state institution which, if the war had not got in the way, could have meant the Nazi indoctrination of a large part of Bukh's pupils. With the world-famous Norwegian author Knut Hamsun (1859–1952), who also was sympathetic to Nazism, Bukh formed part of the Germans' attempt to create a Nordic–Germanic solidarity, not least through the big joint Nordic events under the auspices of the German propaganda organization Nordische Gesellschaft.

Bukh influenced the development of the Third Reich's cult of the body and aesthetic perception via the *Reichssportführer*. Despite the reserved attitude of the German physical culture authorities towards gymnastics, his gymnastics spread through the German state schools and the leadership training schools of the SA, SS and Kraft durch Freude. *Reichsarbeitsführer* Hierl ensured that Bukh's 'primitive gymnastics' spread through the *Reichsarbeitsdienst*. Thus Bukh influenced the attempt to develop, in Pierre Bourdieu's words, a new 'habitus' for German male youth.[37]

In short, the Nazis used Bukh's gymnastics as an element in the development of a 'Germanic' physical culture. The incorporation of his gymnastics was however probably justified more by military than by ideological arguments.

Can the sympathy of the Nazi authorities towards Bukh also be seen as grounded in a wish to use Bukh's gymnastics in the building up of a Nordic–Aryan body culture with contributions from Germany and the Nordic countries? Although the Nazi ideology of physical culture was full of rhetoric about the 'cold' (in a positive sense) Nordic racial soul, there is no direct ideological evidence for such a vision from Bukh's primary collaborator, the *Reichssportführer*. It is possible that this was because the idea of a Nordic–Aryan race was taken for granted by von Tschammer, who had close contacts with, was a member of the board of, and contributed actively to Alfred Rosenberg's völkisch-inspired[38] Nordische Gesellschaft, that he did not feel a need to make it explicit. However, even for Rosenberg and other 'idealists', the idea of 'Nordic man' was a relatively empty concept with only a limited impact in Germany. Bukh himself, at least on one occasion in 1938, in a letter to von Tschammer, advocated that his gymnastics should be seen as a contribution to 'the united Nordic race, that is also for German youth'.[39]

There are thus indications that Bukh imagined that his gymnastics could contribute to the development of a common Germanic–Nordic culture, but it is unlikely that such a culture would have been approved by the Nazis, who saw Bukh's gymnastics mainly as a means of strengthening German male physical culture and who took a relatively pragmatic line in their international sports policy, so that in practice they relied on traditional competitive sport, the Olympic Games and international matches as a way of achieving international good will.[40] During the German Occupation of Denmark (9 April 1940–5 May 1945) the question was whether Bukh would dissociate himself from the occupying power or continue his collaboration, perhaps on a less equivocal political basis. Bukh was certainly not the only person in Denmark to go 'weak at the knees' at the impressive German victories, but he did actively collaborate with the Nazi authorities. During the first part of the Occupation Bukh believed and hoped that the victory of the Axis powers would form the best possible background for the survival and resurgence of Europe. In the wake of this belief his political initiatives became more serious.[41]

Bukh's close relationship with the Nazis was already revealed by the fact that his school was visited during the first year of Occupation by the whole top political and military German leadership in Denmark. He was involved in the Nazi propaganda in Germany through quotations about the necessity of the German Occupation, his praise of the Nazi *Weltanschauung* and all the weight that his international fame gave these words. The occupying power did in fact, although only to a limited extent, succeed in using Bukh's propagandizing statements in Danish public debate, presumably something Bukh was against since it could harm his credibility in the eyes of the general Danish public.

Bukh was certainly part of the Germans' plans for a puppet government. In the autumn of 1940 he was suggested as Minister of Youth in a secret list of ministers drawn up by the German press attaché Gustav Meissner for the German envoy Renthe-Fink. Whether Bukh was aware of this is not clear. Bukh himself, with his proposal for a 'Federation of Danish Youth', developed ambitions to give his previous federal plans a twist in the direction of the unification of large parts of the Danish youth work, including political work, which came to nothing.[42]

CONCLUSION

Bukh revolutionized Swedish gymnastics. His permanent contribution to international sports culture was the idea of using stretching exercises for limbering up, still widespread today, although rarely in his more demanding form. However, it is not possible to quantify the precise extent of this contribution, not least because there are similar types of exercises within other body cultures, for example that of Astanga Yoga. All in all, Bukh's system was not a large export item. Nevertheless his gymnastics were known and practised in many countries. The fact that he could captivate an international public in a time when British sport was sweeping the globe is impressive in itself.[43]

Indisputably, Bukh created an original, new form of masculine aesthetics in international gymnastics. As seen with modern eyes, this was a progressive attempt to make stereotyped male movement more subtle. Although Swedish gymnastics could leave an impression of beauty in masculine action, unlike Bukh's, they were not designed for this, rather to produce good soldiers. Furthermore, there was a tendency in Bukh's gymnastics towards male forms of physical contact and a development of groundbreaking clothing fashion. His gymnasts touched one another to an unheard-of extent, but this was counterbalanced by the fact the rest of the exercise idiom was so decidedly 'masculine' and typified by powerful and dynamic body language.

In reality, Niels Bukh achieved greater international prominence from the displays of his gymnastics than from the diffusion of his actual gymnastics system. The great exceptions to this rule were Germany and, to a lesser extent, Holland in the 1920s as well as Japan, Germany and South Africa in the 1930s and later. His system is extant in Japan today and Bukh's gymnastics still claimed a foothold in the South African educational system in the 1950s. In Scandinavia it was Norwegian gymnasts who especially adopted Bukh's gymnastics. Further detailed examination of the history of the influence of Bukh gymnastics abroad is required if a more complete picture is to be drawn.

Bukh's ambitions in the area of international sport can best be interpreted from his vision from as far back as 1924 of replacing de Coubertin's Olympic Games with a new form of international popular rallies without competition and with his gymnastics as the fundamental element. This idea resurfaced regularly and the Nordic Olympiad of 1935 was only reluctantly limited to Scandinavian countries. The first Lingiad in 1939, however, demonstrated that within the Nordic area the lead in the development of an alternative world olympiad had now been taken by Sweden! The rally involved 7,300 gymnasts from 37 nations.[44] As late as 1943 Bukh worked to organize a wide-ranging international sports festival, now in the form of a 'peace rally' after the expected victory of the Axis powers. After the Allied victory, however, it was the Swedes who repeated their Lingiad in 1949.

There was a profound connection between Bukh's engagement in gymnastics and his political and ideological interpretation of the outside world. The most important examples are the development of Bukh's anti-Communism during the Soviet tour, his sympathy for the imperialist, collectivist Japanese Empire during (and after) the world tour in 1931, his attraction to Nazism after the display in Berlin in 1933, his sympathetic attitude to the Latin American military states where he gave displays in 1938 and his politicized tour to South Africa in 1939 where he identified with the völkisch-inspired Afrikaner movement. This engagement contrasted with his lack of ideological engagement in the democracies he visited.

After the Liberation of Denmark in May 1945 Bukh encountered strong resistance because of his sympathies with the Third Reich. He was criticized for his journeys abroad, not least to South Schleswig and Norway, and he also encountered local resistance from both the labour and sports movements. Even in Germany he was no longer regarded as a brilliant international gymnastics teacher and was not invited to the Olympic Games in London in 1948. By then, Bukh's days as a pace-setting revolutionary ideologue and gymnastics teacher from and of the Danish middle class clearly were over.

NOTES

1. This essay is based on my monograph *Niels Bukh – Danmarks store ungdomsfører* (Copenhagen: Museum Tusculanum, 2001).
2. Danish Foreign Ministry Archives, Rigsarkivet, 42. Dan 16/2, Niels Bukh System, Packages I and II, 42. Dan 26/2, Niels Bukh System, Packages I and II, 45 N. 36 'Gymnastikstævner', Package I, 45.N.94, 'Skytte, Gymnastik- og Idrætsstævne i Ollerup'.
3. The Sokol movement was a pan-Slavic movement which was used to build bridges among the Slavic peoples. However, it was also part of the nation-building of individual states, not least the Czech Republic, which arose in the wake of the First World War, where the Sokol movement grew to become a quasi-governmental mass organization with about one million members.
4. A civilian movement, typified by apparatus gymnastics, which developed throughout the 1920s and the beginning of the 1930s in an increasingly anti-parliamentary and anti-Semitic direction, finally voluntarily trying to join the German Nazi Party.
5. The Danish tradition of the 'folk high school' (*folkehøjskole*) is intended to allow young people to meet at colleges in the countryside where the aim is not to take degrees but to develop oneself in a spirit of community with other young people.
6. Cf. O. Korsgaard, *Kampen om kroppen* (Copenhagen: Gyldendal, 1982), p.82ff; and E. Trangbæk, *Mellem leg og disciplin* (Åbybro: Duo, 1987), *passim*.
7. Cf. P. Bourdieu, *A Social Critique of the Judgement of Taste* (London: Routledge and Kegan Paul, 1984).
8. In the community house farmers could gather to listen to lectures which ranged thematically from 'the technological innovations in agriculture' to 'the importance of the religious spirit in the age of materialism'. The aim was to use information and education to develop the farmers into the core group of an informed and politically mature people.

9. Cf. H. Bonde, 'Farmers' Gymnastics in Denmark in the Late Nineteenth and Early Twentieth Centuries: A Semiotic Analysis of Exercise in Moral Action', *International Journal of the History of Sport*, 10, 2 (1993), 198–214.
10. Cf. H. Bonde, 'I.P. Muller, Danish Apostle of Health', *International Journal of the History of Sport*, 8, 3 (1991), 347–69.
11. Cf. H. Bonde, 'Gymnastics as a Masculinity Rite: Ollerup Danish Gymnastics between the Wars' in J.A. Mangan (ed.), *Making European Masculinities: Sport, Europe, Gender* (London and Portland, OR: Frank Cass, 2000), pp.140–60.
12. On the Swedish gymnastics, see J. Lindroth, *Idrott mellan krigen* (Stockholm: HLS Förlag, 1987); and J. Ljunggren, *Kroppens bildning – Linggymnastikkens manlighetsprojekt 1790–1914* (Stockholm: Brutus Östlings Bokförlag, 1999).
13. N. Bukh, *Grundgymnastik eller primitiv gymnastik* (Ollerup: Gymnastikhøjskolen, 1922).
14. Danish Foreign Ministry Archives, 45. N. 8a 'Olympiske Lege', Package I from 1911–22; *Stockholms Dagblad*, 9 July 1912; *Ungdom og Idræt*, 4 Oct. 1912.
15. Interview with Bukh gymnast C. Nielsen and A1st Team, 1915, 'Vandrebog', Ollerup Archives.
16. J. Lindhard, 'Hr. N. Bukhs Opvisning i Koncertpalæet', *Akademisk Gymnastik* (1917), pp.43–9.
17. *Svenska Dagbladet*, Stockholm Edn., 22 Dec. 1931.
18. H. Bonde, 'National Identity and the Body, The Nordic Olympiad in Denmark in 1935', *Scandinavian Journal of History*, 20 (1995), 295–313.
19. *Göteborgposten*, 21 April 1937.
20. 'Sofia-flickarne', *Nordisk Familjeboks Sportslexikon*, 6 (1946), 438.
21. Cf. H. Meyer, 'Lingiaderna 1939 och 1949 i svensk pressopinion', *Idrott, historia och samhälle* (Stockholm: Svenska idrottshistoriska Föreningen, 1999), p.133.
22. Bukh's letter to the chairman of the organizing committee, Agne Holmstrøm, 21 May 1949; Bukh's letter to the leader of the Danish gymnastics organization De Danske Sytte-log Gymnastikforeninger (DDSG) and I. Arnth-Jensen, 7 July 1949; the Yearbook of the Ollerup Gymnastics High School (1949), Ollerup Gymnastics High School Archives.
23. Cf. Danish Foreign Ministry Archives, Rigsarkivet, 42. Dan 16/2, Niels Bukh System Packages I and II, 42 Dan 26/2, Niels Bukh System, Packages I and II, 45 N. 36 'Gymnastikstævner', Package I, 45.N.94, 'Skytte, Gymnastik- og Idrætsstævne i Ollerup'.
24. Cf. Bonde, *Niels Bukh*, Appendices A and B, Table and Graph A.1.0.
25. V.B.D. Dalen, *A World History of Physical Education* (New York: Prentice Hall, 1953).
26. H. Bonde, 'The Nordic Body, The Vision of an Aryan-Germanic Body Culture', *Sozial- und Zeitgeschichte des Sports*, 2 (1999), 42–5 and 56ff.
27. Ibid., 42f.
28. Cf. H. Bonde, 'Sport und Internationale Politik, Dänische Gymnastik in Japan 1931' in *International Perspectives and Results of Historical Research on Physical Education and Sport* (Tokyo: Tsukuba University Press, 1996), pp.695–705.
29. Ibid.
30. Danish Foreign Ministry Archives, 45.N.36., 'Gymnastikstævner', Package I from 1922–31 Dec. 1947.
31. 'Berlingske Tidende', undated (April 1942), Ollerup Gymnastics High School Archives.
32. H. Bonde, 'Sport og international politik, Dansk gymnastik i stalinismens gennembrudsfase', *Historisk Tidsskrift*, 2 (1995), 342–66; and idem, 'Sport and Anti-Communism: Danish Gymnastics' Encounter with Stalinism in its Formative Years', *International Journal of the History of Sport*, 16, 1 (1999), 137–47.
33. Bonde, 'Sport und Internationale Politik, Dänische Gymnastik in Japan 1931', pp.695–705; ibid.
34. The tour lasted from 11 August until 11 October.
35. H. Bonde, 'The White Man's Body, Danish Gymnasts in South Africa 1939' in F. Merwe (ed.): *Sport as Symbol, Symbols in Sport* (Berlin: Academia Verlag, 1996), pp.81–95.
36. H. Bonde, 'The Iconic Symbolism of Niels Bukh, Aryan Body Culture, Danish Gymnastics and Nordic Tradition', *International Journal of the History of Sport*, 16, 4 (1999), 104–19.
37. H. Bonde, 'The Nordic Body, The Vision of an Aryan-Germanic Body Culture', *Sozial- und Zeitgeschichte des Sports*, 2 (1999), pp.50ff.

38. In the German völkische ideology social classes and political parties were considered 'artificial' and representative democracy was rejected in favour of a 'semi-mystical cult of the elite'. Not only through the link with nature and history, but also increasingly through links with 'scientific' racism, the unity of das Volk was to be ensured.

39. Letter from Bukh to von Tschammer und Osten dated 12 March 1938, Ollerup Gymnastics High School Archives.

40. H.J. Teichler, *Internationale Sportpolitik im Dritten Reich* (Schorndorf: Verlag Karl Hofmann, 1991).

41. See H. Bonde, 'Danmarks Ungdomsforbund – Om højreradikal kontinuitet efter 9. april 1940' in H. Dethlefsen and H. Lundbak (eds.), *Fra mellemkrigstid til efterkrigsstid* (Copenhagen: Gyldendal, 1998), pp.179–204.

42. Ibid.

43. Cf. A. Guttmann, *Games and Empires, Modern Sport and Cultural Imperialism* (New York: Columbia University Press, 1994).

44. Cf. *Dansk Sportsleksikon*, II (1945), 137, 'lingiaden'.

10

The Apostle of Italian Sport:
Angelo Mosso and English Athleticism in Italy

GIGLIOLA GORI

After the political unification of 1861, the Italians experienced a difficult period of transformation and tension under the leadership of the Liberal Party. Illiteracy and illness affected not only the rural families of the south but also the proletariat of the north. Poor hygiene and inadequate nutrition led to high levels of mortality and deformity among children. Many young men (about 42 per cent in 1870 and 52 per cent in 1890) were rejected for military service on medical grounds.[1]

What is more, apart from burning declarations of patriotism and the aspiration to create a powerful nation, the government had to face the fact that the Italians were not one people at all. The Italian people spoke different dialects and possessed different cultures; they did not understand each other, as for centuries they had been divided into a number of small states, governed until only recently by foreign dynasties within the alliance system of the Austro-Hungarian Empire.

To echo the harsh but shrewd judgement of Metternich during the Congress of Vienna in 1815, to an extent, Italy in 1861 remained merely a geographic expression. However, once the country was unified the Italian government, led by the 'Right' until 1876, attempted to blend the Italian people into one nation. There were acute problems including increasing tension between the Vatican and the anti-clerical Italian State and growing conflict between the middle and working classes in a country economically split into the modernized north and backward south.

The second half of the nineteenth century can be considered a dramatic period of nationalization, cultural ideologization and pedagogical socialization. The lower classes and women, who were discriminated against and considered incapable adolescents needing men's protection, fought for their emancipation, demanded their rights at work and in society and called for free access to education and participation in political life. Some joined liberal associations or religious organizations sponsored by the Catholic Church, others supported new radical movements such as Socialism and Marxism which were involved in the promotion of a new utopian society where justice, peace and harmony would triumph at last. In scholastic circles, the educationalist Antonio Labriola, follower of first Herbart and then Marx, was the fiercest protagonist of the people's demands for education.[2]

Understandably, the Italian bourgeoisie sought to retain its political, economic and social power and entrusted its representatives in Parliament with the task of reducing tension and maintaining stability throughout the country. This political class, mainly of positivist conviction, was thus engaged in a dual effort to promote social order and at the same time to build an industrious society where secular and bourgeois capitalist values could be promoted successfully and harmoniously. Consequently, its aim was that the people would receive basic state instruction, learn sound hygiene practices and better their condition step by step as workers and citizens. The Italian positivists,[3] although conservative in disposition, considered popular education to be a necessary instrument of peaceful national revolution. They reflected both a wider European positivistic optimism and a corresponding trust in unbounded social progress.

Educational reform, amended several times, characterized post-unitary Italy up to the beginning of the twentieth century. It was founded on social pedagogy, medical science and a belief in linear progress. The conviction that at least primary schooling should be compulsory for children of all classes and that educational gymnastics should be taught in all schools was broadly accepted as a means of achieving the intellectual, moral and physical improvement of the nation.

However, the educational gymnastics adopted was old-fashioned, too much endowed with martial overtones and lacking in scientific value. Moreover, recreational games and modern sports were omitted completely in growing contrast to the schools of the most advanced European countries, including Germany which, now ironically, in its earlier enthusiasm for gymnastics, was the inspirational model for Italian physical education. The Italian gymnastics programmes were modelled on the paramilitary activities of the *Turnen*, established in Germany by

Friederich L. Jahn as early as 1811 and later adapted by Adolf Spiess for educational purposes. In the 1870s, widespread approval of such militaristic programmes in Italy was the result of the recent past struggle for independence, which had created a martial mass psychology.

Military parades, complicated collective exercises low in physical content and the exaggerated use of acrobatic gymnastics using vaulting-horse, parallel-bars and rings ensured that gymnastics was more military preparation than educational instruction. By 1878 Obermann's gymnastics, imported into Turin by the Swiss Rudolf Obermann in 1833 and disseminated throughout the country in the post-unitary years, had become compulsory for both sexes in the school curriculum under a law introduced in 1878 by Francesco De Sanctis, the Minister of Education.

The 'Left', led by Francesco Crispi, came to power in the last quarter of the century. It leaned more and more towards authoritarian politics in both internal and foreign affairs and adopted an aggressive colonial attitude. In these years, the myth of 'The Armed Nation' produced an emphasis on the iconic importance of military exercises and target-practice, not only for soldiers but also for all male adolescents. Crispi was determined to create a strong military state and encouraged popular gymnastics societies, which were considered a source of future effective soldiers. In 1883, a special law was issued so as to renew the National Target-Practice Federation founded in 1861, and in 1885 about 600 target-practice associations existed in the territory. Following the French model of the *Bataillons Scolaires* (Scholastic Battalions)[4] started in 1882, the Italian Ministry of Education was involved in the militarization of secondary schooling. Its gymnastics teachers now had to organize target-practice competitions for pupils of 14–19-years-old. With this responsibility, a new militaristic spirit animated gymnastics teachers. During their Bologna Congress in 1890, they stated that new *palestre marziali* (martial gymnasia) should be created to support 'The Armed Nation' and the *Lega per la Nazione Armata mediante le Palestre Marziali* (League for the Armed Nation Through Martial Gymnasia) was founded shortly afterwards. A little earlier, in 1888, a commission to reform gymnastics had been set up by the Ministry of Education.

This *fin de siècle* period was a complex and contradictory time. It was characterized by chauvinistic nationalism, but also by social and political disorder that was difficult to control and which favoured the development of new cultural movements – 'crisis-culture' movements. Influenced by Sorel, Nietzsche, Dilthley and Bergson, but also by Kant and Hegel, a number of Italian intellectuals now rejected positivist ideology and its secular myths such as linear progress, the productive work ethic and the cult of the sciences. Positivism had failed to realize its too optimistic objectives and, what is more, the 'Left' had proved disappointing in power. A widespread need for change, combined with a new desperate vitality and an increasing dissatisfaction with the past – in essence – an anxious collective state of mind, opened the way to an individualistic spirit of adventure and the search for new ideals in a heady climate of nationalist ambition.[5]

The boring military gymnastics taught in schools provoked criticism and were berated by progressive teachers, scholars and politicians. The challenge now was to reconstruct physical education by means of the introduction of modern sports into the school curriculum. There was also the further challenge: the working class demanded access to healthy, recreational activities in their spare time. These challenges were mainly faced by experts in education and medical science. Important contributions were made by Doctor Emilio Baumann, 'the Father of Italian Gymnastics', and Professor Angelo Mosso, 'the Apostle of Italian Sport', both strenuous advocates of physical education for the people and sadly sometimes fierce opponents. Both argued their respective cases from strongly middle-class backgrounds and both were militant crusaders in the interests of health and fitness.

Emilio Baumann (1843–1917) was a talented physician, an expert in pedagogy and a teacher of gymnastics. Initially, he was clearly in favour of a modern and rational gymnastics which would explain scientifically the structure and purpose of each physical exercise. Openly in contrast with the educational gymnastics programmes implemented as a result of the De Sanctis' law of 1878, he supported 'natural' physical exercises – walking, running, swimming, jumping and climbing activities which were easily understandable to everyone – rather than 'artificial' exercises invented by 'experts'. 'What interest', Baumann wrote in 1885, 'might people have in watching pupils busy in choreographic actions and movements, or becoming exhausted by having trained with equipment that has nothing in common with practical life?'[6]

Aware of the poor physical condition of most people employed in modern industry, Baumann recognized that 'artificial' exercises could deny the physical regeneration of the workers. The physical recreations, which should be practised in spare time, in his view, should fight efficaciously against the muscular damage of sedentary work and the mental alienation of modern civilization.[7]

Baumann strongly believed in scientific methodology and its practical implementation and stressed the importance of the scientific evaluation of students. He invented medical equipment to periodically test pupils' physical skills. He was a realist, conscious of the cultural and economical backwardness of the country, and he invented rational gymnastics exercises that were easy to teach and to practise virtually anywhere.

Baumann did not overlook the 'weaker sex' and fought for their involvement by arguing that: 'gymnastics should be the same for the two sexes, as only one gymnastics existed for both men and women'. However, he added, 'some circumstances suggest a need for diversity, not in quality and purpose, but in accordance with Italian backward social custom'. He claimed that such backwardness 'did not exist among northern peoples who ... gave women and their freedom better consideration'. Regrettably, he said 'Italian women were not properly considered as people, and women cutting capers or tumbling, lifting weights, [or] handling weapons ... could provoke [only] erotic thoughts among Italian spectators'.[8] In consequence, Baumann believed that in infancy gymnastics should be the same for both sexes, but young women should be taught *callistenia* – a special gymnastics promoting feminine physical beauty through exercise which ensured grace and elegance while at the same time promoted strength and stamina, without compromising women's dignity or modesty and met social proprieties.[9]

Baumann directed the prestigious Normal School of Gymnastics in Rome for men from 1884 and actively participated in all initiatives to find a solution to the problem of improving educational gymnastics. Unfortunately, Baumann missed an important opportunity to promote his rational, 'natural' system in 1885, when he was appointed as one of the state members of a select committee charged with the reformation of educational gymnastics. His ideas were opposed by an inspector of gymnastics, Professor Felice Valletti, who possessed a strong and conservative personality, was an expert in history and pedagogy, but lacked knowledge of the biological sciences. Valletti successfully defended the paramilitary gymnastics programmes then in place. Baumann was crushed by Valletti's will. Valletti never abandoned his belief in the value of paramilitary school gymnastics as a preparation for conscription. In 1891 he published an article on this theme, strongly endorsing the establishment of popular schools of military gymnastics,[10] and later ended an essay on the history of gymnastics with the following famous words:

I do hope that gymnastics is seen more and more extensively to prepare worthy sons for the fatherland, soldiers ready to die for it at any time, but capable to live as well … so that the fatherland can become respected and feared, according to the wishes of King Vittorio Emanuele the Second.[11]

Over the years, Baumann lost much of his innovative spirit. Nevertheless, he had made his mark. His publications included some 40 titles by 1914 and many were re-published.[12] He was held in high repute and considered to be the father of Italian gymnastics. For his part he frequently lamented the fact that the State did not provide sufficient financial support for educational gymnastics. Baumaun enjoyed a high reputation most particularly because he successfully adapted his scientific approach to the financial resources of the poorest Italian schools and the limited training of gymnastics teachers.

In 1893, Baumann was chosen as one of the 29 members of a new state committee together with the physiologist Professor Angelo Mosso and other important physicians, teachers and politicians working on the reform of educational gymnastics programmes. In one respect, their report was an educational milestone. It pressed for reform, but the result of their deliberations was a compromise. On the one hand, the report stated that physical education should produce healthy and robust men of action ready to work for the society and the fatherland in times of danger. On the other hand, it also stated that school physical education should abandon its too militaristic acrobatic and choreographic aspect and sports and games, both Italian and English, should be included.[13]

Apart from this recommendation, the work of the committee then was not audaciously innovative. However, it did draw Italy a little nearer to the most enlightened European countries. None of the recommendations were immediately implemented because of the fall of the government and the appointment of a new Minister of Education. The recommendations were set aside until the passing of Daneo–Credaro law of 1910, which was broadly inspired by them.

In his later years, rather oddly given his earlier radicalism, Baumann became militaristic in his outlook and, for the sake of a new martial patriotism, became rather forgetful of his previous belief in rational and 'natural' gymnastics.[14] As one of the founders of the League for the Armed Nation Through Martial Gymnasia, mentioned earlier, he swayed with the warlike wind blowing from the Establishment.

Baumann eventually withdrew his support for 'natural' physical activity in the open and no longer aimed to improve the Italian's health and national hygiene. He began to concentrate on a strict education for strengthening the will and spirit of the young through his 'psyco-cinesiology' – the art of forging people's character through the strong disciplining of the body from infancy. Now in his opinion, outdoor games and sports could not effectively replace indoor gymnastics. He conceded that Italian traditional games could be practised voluntarily by the most energetic pupils, but only after the gymnastics class.

Opposed to both German and Swedish gymnastics and their 'artificial' equipment, Baumann claimed independence and originality for his gymnastics system based on psycho-kinesiology. In conjunction with this system, he invented cheap gymnastics equipment for schools and created exercises for both primary and high schools that allowed pupils to be taught collectively in the narrow spaces available in classrooms using school benches as basic equipment. In 1907, Baumann proudly affirmed:

> Being so different in its purposes, our gymnastics system is necessarily different in its means and instruments. Since our first principle of education is that pupils should learn discipline, i.e. to obey the teacher, our system starts with gymnastics among primary school benches. This does not exist in Sweden or Germany. As a consequence, often our equipment is substantially different from that already known: it is exclusively Italian – the equipment for collective high and long jumping; the spiro meter; the gymnastics table; the board and basket for equilibrium; the *ceppi* and *appoggi* [small-size tools]; and the *stadio* [a round gymnasium] ... most equipment that constitutes the basis for training ... in foreign countries, such as that used in Swedish and German gymnastics, has no room in our system. Finally, regarding the few pieces of equipment we have in common, it should be made clear that they now look rather different and have different goals.[15]

Baumann's gymnastics system was widely used. It deeply influenced the traditional Italian physical education, as it was seen as an efficacious way of promoting discipline. The later Fascist period with its emphasis on physical education as the basic means of strengthening the frail will of Italians[16] clearly demonstrates Baumann's lasting influence.

Angelo Mosso's work was inspired by completely different ambitions.[17] Angelo Mosso (1846–1910) was born in Turin but spent his youth in Chieri – a little town near Turin – where his father was a joiner and his mother could barely read or write. He was born into the working class but by virtue of his talent eventually became a middle-class proselytizer for fitness and health. Angelo attended primary and junior schools in Chieri. He was far from being a model pupil and was more interested in playing outdoors than in sedentary studies. Consequently, he was considered something of a rebel. Mosso was expelled from school, advised to give up studying and urged to become a joiner like his father. However, convinced of their son's intellectual ability, his parents supported Angelo and he continued his studies. He moved to Asti and attended the lyceum there. He remained academically idle and failed to obtain a grant to undertake advanced studies. His family made further sacrifices for him and from 1864 onwards Mosso studied at the Faculty of Medicine in the University of Turin. Luckily, two of his university teachers discovered that Mosso was a very talented student and offered him a position as a teacher of natural sciences at the lyceum of Chieri. Now 20 years old, Mosso was determined to pay for his studies and took on the roles of both a university student and schoolteacher. This double workload was demanding but satisfying. Early in the morning, regardless of the weather, he walked the 20 kilometres from Chieri to Turin in order to reach his university classes, then he walked back to Chieri to teach his pupils.

Alongside such hard physical demands (in practice, a daily pedestrian marathon race), Mosso also had to concentrate on both teaching and university preparation. Nevertheless, in 1870 he obtained a degree in medicine *cum laude* and had the honour of having his thesis published free of charge. In the same year he became medical officer in Florence, the city of the Renaissance, and was also engaged in the physiology laboratory led by Maurizio Shiff, a famous professor from Holland. Simultaneously, Mosso broadened his education to include the fine arts. Later, he was employed as a military doctor in the battalion of Cava dei Tirreni, a small southern town near Naples, where he came into contact with the *Magna Grecia* (Great Greece) culture that had developed in ancient Italy under the influence of Classical Greece. Mosso was now able to explore the supreme beauty of Greek ruins and came to greatly appreciate the Hellenistic civilization. His artistic experiences of Florence and the *Magna Grecia* greatly influenced his later life.

Between 1871 and 1872, Mosso began a specialist course on physiology in Florence, where his brilliant, unremitting work as a researcher brought him fame and opportunity. He moved to Germany to attend the prestigious school of physiology in Leipzig, directed by the famous scientist Karl Ludwig. Ludwig, together with other scholars Mosso had met earlier in Italy, such as Moleschott, Schiff and Kronecker, provided him with a modern methodology for inquiries based on physics and graphics rather than chemistry. On his return to Italy in 1874, Mosso began his scientific work, which was highly original and the product of both a systematic and intuitive mind. Both the university institutes of physiology at Heidelberg and Kiel had offered Mosso a job, but he decided to leave Germany and spend time with the well known French scientists Marey, Bernard, Brown–Sequard and Ranvier in Paris before returning to Turin.

Jule Marey was not only the President of the French Academy of Sciences, but also of the French League for Physical Education. He stimulated Mosso's subsequent interest both in the application of physiology to sport and the English games cult (athleticism) then dominating English middle–class education. Mosso considered this to be the healthiest and most modern scientific system of school education. He believed it could physically regenerate the Italians, whether rich or poor, men or women, young or old.

From 1875 to 1879, Mosso taught pharmacology at the University of Turin and in 1880, at only 34 years old, he won a prestigious professorship of physiology there, replacing his teacher Professor Moleschott who had been head-hunted by Rome's La Sapienza University.

As a physiologist, Mosso's field of interest covered both somatic and psychic phenomena. He and his followers made use of new scientific instruments invented and made by Mosso himself. Instruments included the *pletismografo* (pletismograph) to measure any volumetric variation of the organs caused by major or minor changes in blood supply, the *ergografo* (ergograph) to depict muscular fatigue and the *miotonometro* (miothonometer) to measure variation of muscular tone.

Firmly convinced that emotions and intellectual faculties influenced the human system, Mosso explored the physical basis of psychic actions and in time this new branch of medicine (now known as psychosomatic medicine), brought him international fame. He published *La paura* (The Fear) and *La fatica* (The Fatigue) in 1884 and 1891 respectively.

Unfortunately his research on physic-psychic phenomena involving dreams, poison and death was not completed in time to be published before his death. Mosso's scientific activity is recorded in some 170 publications in different fields,[18] most of them translated into many foreign languages, kept in the foundation of the Italian Biological Archive (1888) and in the international scientific laboratory built in the Alps (1895) where he spent long periods studying the physiological adaptation of human breathing and blood circulation at high altitude.

In the years 1898 to 1900, the now famous Mosso travelled to the United States where he attended conferences and visited many universities. This experience renewed his interest in physical activity and sports pedagogy and opened the way for a new interest in social and cultural dynamics, in his opinion exemplarily represented by the truly democratic American society. The result was a study of the democratic approach of the United States to religion and science.[19]

Mosso, the polymath, was now a physiologist renowned in the international scientific community and a member of the most important institutions in Italy and Europe. Due to his fame, Mosso became a Senator in the Italian Parliament in 1904, but in the same year he was struck by a severe illness that progressively transformed him into an invalid. Despite this Mosso enthusiastically ventured into totally new fields of study, that is, anthropology and archaeology. He spent long periods in the Mediterranean, where he could protect his delicate health and indulge his early passion for the fine arts. In this sunny climate Mosso excavated archaeological locations, studied their evidence, developed new anthropological theories and finally published important works on the ancient civilizations of Crete, Etruria and Southern Italy.[20]

In the light of his competence in physiology and ancient history and his profound interest in the political and social sciences and his extensive knowledge of educational planning in a range of modern societies, Mosso can be considered the most authoritative proponent of modern physical education and sport in Italy in the late nineteenth and early twentieth centuries. Mosso was too informed, independent and authoritative to accept the uninformed attitudes of the government. He did not fail to fight for his beliefs, freely opposing both the narrow-minded and chauvinistic in education, civil society and the military. His revolutionary mind addressed the physical education programmes in schools and the army, worked to improve working-class hygiene, health and living conditions and provided support for women's emancipation in Italy. On all these subjects he gave speeches, presented bills in Parliament, participated in state commissions and attended conferences, but above all he continually published books addressed to the common people, written in a captivating witty style.

As mentioned above, in the last decades of the nineteenth century the old-fashioned German system of educational gymnastics was compulsory in Italian schools. According to Mosso, this was a mistake for many reasons.[21] The centralization of the programmes, the absurdly poor financial state provision for equipment and facilities, the differing regional climates and varied social and cultural customs meant that to impose the same kind of exercises everywhere was misguided. Furthermore, the poor salaries of the teachers of gymnastics (their income was ten times less than teachers of German[22]) compelled them to find a second job and therefore hampered their work in schools.[23] Consequently, very few teachers were recruited, educational gymnastics was in the non-specialist hands of primary school teachers while in high schools, who were often short of qualified teachers, compulsory educational gymnastics frequently only existed on paper. Mosso sought students' opinions; unsurprisingly pupils found educational gymnastics in the high school boring. About 90 per cent of high schools pupils absconded from gymnastics classes, although they were only taught ten to 20 times per year. Headmasters turned a blind eye.[24] As for modern sport, as mentioned earlier, it did not exist in schools at this time. However, modern sport was available in private sports societies (the first had been founded in 1844 in Turin), where not only traditional gymnastics but also walking, swimming, rowing, mountaineering, tennis, football, sailing and cycling were enjoyed by a number of enthusiastic middle- and lower-class people in the most industrial regions of the country. In particular, according to Mosso, cycling developed spontaneously among young Italian men and women. In spite of government apathy, Italian youth attempted to transform its 'sporting life'.[25]

Mosso and other progressives now stressed the need to extend these sports to schools and argued that militaristic indoor gymnastics should be completely abolished – or at least reduced. Mosso denounced the appalling hygienic conditions of most scholastic gymnasia where humidity, dust and lack of sun brought illness rather than health to pupils. He declared that he had personally visited some such which could not be considered gymnasia – they were dark rooms, corridors, halls or lofts. Some looked like prisons and were so cold that training could result in rheumatism or pneumonia:[26] 'There will soon come a time when the public will consider that breathing the air in such gymnasia and training students among school benches is a crime.'[27]

Mosso also fought against the 'religious' atmosphere which hovered around gymnasia: 'gymnasia are like sacristies and churches, where the "priest" has taken Holy Orders; in contrast, the Americans have secularised their gymnasia, and anyone who demonstrates the capacity, can teach there'.[28]

In the 1890s, Mosso pointed out that Italian pupils spent only five per cent of their time in physical education while the remaining 95 per cent of their time was devoted to intellectual studies, without adequate consideration of the severe harm that mental fatigue could produce:[29]

> In their stupid and blind ambition, governments, professors and teachers compete in stuffing young heads with useless notions that students cannot assimilate; and even if they might learn them, they would forget these things before there came the time to make use of them. We see that workers are preparing a revolution to cut down their shift to eight hours daily, but we constrain our students in their most vulnerable age to curve their back over writing-desks and school benches, for at least ten hours per day![30]

In those same years, English middle–class athleticism had been already included in the schools of most European countries. Mosso, perfectly aware of this, did not fail to insistently inform his readers about what was going on in the rest of Europe. In fact in Germany, always an inspirational model to Italy, the addition of games to educational gymnastics had been discussed as early as 1876 and the idea was implemented by the Minister of Education Gustav Von Gossler, under a new law in 1882.[31] In 1883, the Belgian government organized instructional courses on games which were introduced into schools replacing acrobatic gymnastics. In Austria, Von Gautsch had ordered headteachers to organize skating and swimming in 1891. In Hungary, Von Berzevicz had demanded the reform of motor activities in the schools in 1889.[32]

Even in chauvinist France, Baron Pierre de Coubertin was engaged in a crusade to introduce the *le régime arnoldien* – Thomas Arnold's educational system as romantically represented in the famous story *Tom Brown's Schooldays*.[33] De Coubertin wrote two popular books, *L'éducation en Angleterre* (Education in England) in 1880 and later

L'Education anglaise en France (English Education in France) in 1889, which greatly influenced both experts and public opinion. In consequence, in 1887 a French commission, formed by eminent scientists and others, successfully achieved the introduction of modern sport into French schools.

In the following year, the Italian government recommended that school gymnastics should be again reformed – without success.[34] According to Mosso, the failure was due both to the public, who did not understand the value of modern sport, and parliament which consisted of closed minds: 'It was as unsuccessful as to try climbing an Alpine mountain, with 29 people fastened to one rope; and, what was worse many of them had never climbed before.'[35] In 1893, Mosso found himself and ten other experts yet again charged with the reform of educational gymnastics. Their failure has already been described.

From the earliest moments of his career Mosso had insisted that English sports were essential. He made good use of his reputation as a physiologist sensitive to what was happening in the rest of the world and of his knowledge of the Classical Age to convince the Italians that outdoor activities were not only commonplace in the other modern countries, but that their 'cradle' was Ancient Rome and the Italian Renaissance.[36] Mosso believed that English athleticism had its roots in Italy's glorious past, his hope was that even the most conservative of Italians would agree that this system was the most effective way to improve Italian lives. In *Mens sana in corpore sano*, Mosso played considerably on nationalist feelings. Some 60 pages were devoted to the history of physical education of the ancient Greeks and the Romans and other Italian civilizations. He argued that 'We do everything for our brain, and nothing for our body. We should return to the ideals of the ancient southern Italians, and especially the Sicilian people, whose admiration for beauty and belief in physical perfection, was supreme.'[37]

To cater to the people's nationalist pride, Mosso even proposed to replace the English terms 'sports' and 'games' with the Italian term 'agonistica' ('outdoor recreational athletics') and to replace the expression 'physical education' with 'ginnastica' ('scholastic gymnastics'), meaning indoor physical education.[38]

In *Mens sana in corpore sano*[39] and, more extensively, in *L'Educazione Fisica della Gioventù* (Youth's Physical Education), Mosso wrote that the historical origins of modern English athleticism were also to be found in the glorious period of the Italian Renaissance.[40] At that time, the famous educationalists Vittorino da Feltre and Maffeo Vegio, the scientists Gerolamo Mercuriale and Paolo Cortese and the sports specialist Antonio Scaino recommended all kinds of games for all-round development. In his discussion of the Renaissance, Mosso described the happy times spent by Florentine youth who played ball games and tennis in spring and football in the winter. Somewhat bitterly, Mosso concluded:

> Modern gymnastics comprises a serious evil in our physical education, because all those games demanding natural, fast and dynamic movements, and vigorous skills, have disappeared. At present, when our poor boys risk going out to play ball games in the square, the police chase after them as if they were rabid dogs.[41]

Mosso, distinguished physiologist and political liberal, was a true democrat. From 1884, he suggested that if the government was too weak to act then the municipalities should take the initiative and rent fields and parks on the outskirts of cities, where students and the ordinary public could enjoy games free of charge on Sundays. He argued that modern civilization had produced an artificial habitat that weakened the urbanite's constitution and reduced his resistance to the weather. He stated that:

> modern society provides sad days for the miserable and unfortunate children of the working class ... Modern cities are like monsters growing up in pathological conditions: their brain and muscles, i.e. industries and manufactories, suffocate their breathing organs, i.e. squares and parks. A democratic state should take this problem to itself, and make games in the open known to children and adults. It should oppose increasing air pollution in the industrialised cities. The wealthiest citizens can easily leave the city and breathe deeply pure air of the country, mountain or sea side, but the poor people have to remain where they are.[42]

In the first years of the twentieth century, Giovanni Giolitti's political leadership introduced liberal, reformist and revolutionary social policies in order to solve the growing social conflict between rich and poor gradually and without any heavy-handed control.

In this setting Mosso and other enlightened individuals contributed to Senator Pecile's project to promote physical education, sport and games among the young and the mature of both sexes. Then the

Comitato nazionale centrale per l'educazione fisica ed i giuochi ginnici nelle scuole e nel popolo (National Central Committee for Physical Education and Gymnastic Games in Schools and for the People) was founded. Sport grounds, popular gymnasia, recreational areas for festivities, gymnastic competitions and a variety of sports were provided and maintained by statute[43] by authority of local committees. This action was inspired by an earlier experiment in Germany in 1891.[44] Similar committees had worked well there but the Italians failed in their objectives for a number of reasons. Mosso claimed that, contrary to the Germans, the Italians had not co-operated well and press publicity had left much to be desired.[45]

Mosso conceded that the *Comitato nazionale centrale* had the noblest intentions, but was only too well aware that various difficulties had made its existence precarious and had adversely influenced its work. He suggested further that, as usual, too many parliamentarians were members of the committee and added maliciously:

> Deputies, as well as Senators never draw back wherever patriotic initiatives are concerned, but once they have their names on the list, they do nothing. ... In fact, due also to the indifference of both the Ministry of Education and the nation itself, also the committee died little by little of inertia, since it is much easier to preach than to deliver![46]

Always mindful of his own deprived youth, Mosso never gave up his efforts to promote the democratic well-being of his country. In the future, he said, interest in individual rights would have to increase and society would have to organize physical education better, especially in the case of young workers. In this way the socialist movement might also benefit the middle classes and, especially, their children. Idleness is the worst fault of over-academic youth with the result that the governing class is flabby. On one occasion Mosso wrote:

> We are hopeful that in a democracy this great immorality will disappear, but in any case we should help all young workers who wish to study and escape the humiliating conditions of work that brutalizes people. The workers' technical and professional instruction is a source of national wealth. Intellectual mass education and technical innovations improving production go hand in hand.[47]

Mosso criticized army physical training more than once. The myth of the 'Armed Nation' might need strong and well-trained male bodies but, according to Mosso, the current army programmes were as old-fashioned as those taught in schools and they did not provide sufficient stamina even for marching! In 1883, Mosso challenged the proposed law to reform the National Target-Practice Federation which stated that it would be compulsory for male pupils over 14 years to take part in both pre-military exercises and practise target-shooting. Mosso asked:

> Why should we allow young people to handle rifles precociously. Is it not unnatural? ... Military exercises are the triumph of perfect immobility. Whoever watches soldiers' training cannot but agree that half of the available time is spent standing to attention and listening to the sergeant who explains each exercise, while the second half is spent in the execution of rigid and jerky movements, which are against nature and shake up the human organs without any improvement in health ... with this wrong system in place, Italian schools might be monopolized by former sergeants who, rejecting the life of a soldier, at present are attending the male Normal School of Gymnastics in Rome.[48]

Finally, Mosso affirmed that an ideal civil education should re-establish equilibrium between intellectual and manual work and promote 'natural gymnastics' – enjoyable movements such as games, running, jumping and walking which give mankind grace and strength.[49]

Once he was nominated Senator of the Italian Parliament, Mosso opposed a further bill reforming of a previous law on the National Target-Practice. According to the bill, target-practice in schools should be the responsibility of the War Office. A booklet, *La difesa della patria e il tiro a segno* (Defence of the Fatherland and Target-Practice) containing various Mosso speeches on the matter appeared in 1905. In it he strongly defended the need to prepare future soldiers through physical education in state schools, popular sports institutions and private gymnastics societies, but under civil specialist teachers. In one of these speeches Mosso declared:

> Although the poor country boys who live and work in farms don't have enough time to practise target-shooting, they are sufficiently strong to become good soldiers;[50] on the other hand, the young urban people who can easily practise this activity, are too weak for

marches and heavy knapsacks, due to a too sedentary life and lack of physical exercise in the open air. These citizens should abandon dark and unhealthy urban places and become strong by means of games and athletics in the sunshine.[51]

By way of practical support for his constructive proposals, Mosso asked the Italian Parliament for funds to distribute among these institutions. His appeal was unsuccessful. Instead, Mosso was given a consolation prize by the War Office Minister who promised to give the Ministry of Education the responsibility for the adequate training of pupils with a view to eventual conscription.[52]

As has been previously mentioned, Mosso was not only a proselytizer for modern physical education and recreational sports and games, he was also an advocate of women's rights and opportunities to enjoy these healthy activities. He believed in women's emancipation and fought against the backward attitude toward Italian women which was underpinned by both a well-established paternalism and anti-feminist foreign literature. In 1904, for example, the notorious book by Moebius on the mental inferiority of women was translated and published in Italy with wide success.[53]

Mosso certainly had a good cause. Before the last quarter of the nineteenth century, regular recreational sports were enjoyed only by aristocratic girls and available only sporadically to middle- and working-class women and then only in the most industrialized regions. After 1878, young schoolgirls were at last given educational gymnastic classes along the lines of the early German system which was popular in Italian schools. Pre-military exercises and those involving equipment were adapted to the capacity and modesty of the 'fair sex'. This notwithstanding, at the end of the 1880s, female gymnastics programmes still consisted of exercises allegedly inspiring fitness, energy and courage to ensure that girls became only good mothers and teachers.[54]

German exercises were not the best possible exercises for girls but at least they allowed some, but not all, to escape a totally sedentary life. Fewer young girls were sent to primary schools by their parents than boys of the same age and they were often withdrawn prematurely. As for secondary schools, they were mostly attended by boys. Boys had the possibility of careers; girls waited for a good husband at home. Statistics for 1881 reveal that the percentage of female illiterates was 73.51 compared to 61.03 male illiterates.[55]

In 1892, Mosso was invited to present the concluding speech at an important congress held by the Society for Women's Education in Rome. This speech, which provides the clearest evidence of his endorsement of female physical emancipation, was published in 1893.[56] At the congress, in the presence of eminent personalities and Queen Margherita of Savoy, a talented sportswoman, Mosso stated that physical activities were normal for women in other modern countries and that these women were stronger, more agile and fitter than Italian women. Mosso added that in England, Mrs Henry Sidgwick had recently published detailed information on 562 female students who were involved in sport at the universities of Oxford and Cambridge – these female graduates were physically superior to other English women and more fertile.[57] Mosso drew the following discouraging picture for his audience:

> In English women's colleges, where girls can gather freely, they play various games, and certainly have their rackets and balls with them when they come to visit Italy; in contrast, in our boarding-schools, girls of the same age walk skilfully and quietly ... intimidated by a monastic and numbing surveillance. On my visits to the best Italian schools for girls, I have never seen a lawn-tennis court.[58]

In Italy, Mosso added, Italian young women disdained gymnastics as a business for children and the public failed to understand that exercise is more important for female than male adolescents. These activities did not simply develop muscles, but influenced the internal functions, such as breathing, the circulation of the blood and the nutrition of tissues. Depression and hysterics, both degenerations of the nervous system – a sad feminine prerogative – resulted in a kind of permanent apathy and might be prevented and even cured through exercise in the open air. Of course, female physical activities needed to become more attractive, be practised in new gymnasia and in the open air and include modern sports and games.[59]

The last part of Mosso's speech was dedicated to the demolition of theories arguing the biological and psychological inferiority of women. Mosso was both a true feminist and a Latin man who admired feminine beauty – especially Italian women's beauty.[60] Reminding the audience that in earlier ages the Church even denied that women had a soul, 'Mulier non est facta ad imaginem Dei' ('A woman is not made according to God's image'), Mosso pointed out that since then many philosophers had spoken in derogatory terms about women's natural inferiority. In fact, he pointed out that at that very conference, a presentation by the anthropologist and psychologist Professor Giuseppe Sergi had been couched in these terms.[61] In Mosso's opinion, however, women's alleged and actual inferiority was the product of a social existence where men held women in subjection. Women's weaknesses were the product of an artificial habitat where men brought women into subjection.

Mosso's enthusiastic endorsement of Italian women's emancipation was strongly reinforced by the period that he spent in the United States (1898–1900). There, Mosso found a totally different society where both sexes had the same chances. Mosso devoted the last chapter of *Mens sana in corpore sano* to the American woman's modern education. In it he stressed that the American woman's supremacy was not inherited nor good luck but was the fruit of her tireless study and work.[62] In this advanced nation the new woman was prominent in the arts, literature, education and industry – and even in sport. The emancipated American woman – efficient worker, good wife and prolific mother – impressed him greatly. This new woman reminded Mosso of the 'Golden Age' of ancient Rome and the Renaissance, when women were respected and universally admired as pedagogues, physicians and artists. Mosso ended his apologia for female Americans by affirming forcefully: 'Within the family the American husband is much more submissive than the Latin husband; however, working outside so intensively, he loses the sense of the family, which is firmly held by women. So, while American men provide materially, their wives provide intellectually.'[63]

Mosso's despair at the slow growth of modern sport and games in Italy caused him to frown on the 1908 Olympic Games which were held in Rome.[64] Mosso was enthusiastic about Pierre de Coubertin's work and the rise of the International Olympic Movement and freely quoted the famous Father Pierre Didon for his important speech on the moral influence of athletic sports, presented in France in 1897.[65] Nevertheless, Mosso was pessimistic about his country hosting the Olympics. He did not believe that the Italians could win medals in athletics, nor win honourable places in other games and was depressed by the prospect of world-wide public embarrassment.[66]

The final words of this essay should be spent on the problematic relationship between Mosso and Baumann. In 1906, Baumann was forced to defend his position as Director of the male Normal School of

Gymnastics in Rome, having been savagely criticized in a witty article by Mosso.[67] Mosso argued that the reason for the past and present deficiencies of Italian gymnastics was to be found in the School. He claimed that it was in 'senile' decline and its closure was necessary. In addition, Mosso stated that the School lacked space, equipment and facilities with the result that the teachers who graduated could have no idea of a modern gymnasium.[68] Baumann attempted to answer Mosso immediately in the same magazine but his article was refused. So, Baumann published a booklet at his own expense, entitled *L'educazione fisica italiana e le panzane del prof. Angelo Mosso* (Italian Physical Education and Professor Angelo Mosso's Nonsense).[69] Baumann stated that Mosso's endorsement of modern sports and games had in fact given the *coup de grâce* to physical education. With his inflexible ideas on the best possible physical education, Mosso had become its most effective destroyer. Bitterly, Baumann commented that due to Mosso's unbending convictions and his unwavering espousal of them: 'teachers' reputations were demolished, and people's trust in the discipline [of physical education] totally destroyed'.[70]

There followed a period of great hostility between 'the Apostle of Italian Sport' and 'the Father of Italian Gymnastics' and their followers. Baumann had been terribly hurt by Mosso's attack. Baumann and Mosso were both able men of science strongly determined to modernize Italian gymnastics. Jointly, they fought against the use of unscientific German equipment. Both favoured scientific gymnastics in the open. Both left posterity important contributions in theoretical and applied research. Both supported women's emancipation.[71]

Baumann was a realist. He was acutely aware of the government lack of funds and the miserable condition of teachers and facilities in most schools. Therefore, he attempted to promote his rational gymnastics system whenever possible with the resources available. In contrast, Mosso was an idealist. He was cosmopolitan and an expert in physiology, education and general culture. He was inspired by the concept of democracy, sensitive to social inequalities and thus openly opposed negative government policies in various fields. He confronted the government, the political parties, the Roman Church and whoever was out-of-date. He was a revolutionary – educationally, socially and politically. He wanted to transform a backward society and make it modern, progressive and rational and, above all, healthy.

Mosso and Baumann were conciliated. On the occasion of a

ceremony held in Bologna to celebrate Baumann's 40 years of professional activity, Mosso generously expressed the belief that Baumann's work would be greatly appreciated and highly regarded in the future. Mosso was an accurate prophet. Under Fascism, Italian physical education was moulded according to Baumann's ideas – particularly his emphasis on the strengthening of the people's health and willpower. Mosso's educational subscription to English athleticism found recognition much later – in the democratic end to the twentieth century. Thus, in the final analysis, Mosso's revolutionary liberalism triumphed.

NOTES

I should like to express my appreciation to Helen Hardy for early assistance with this chapter and also to Professor J.A. Mangan for his most helpful and careful editorial assistance.

1. E. Baumann, *Psicocinesia ovvero l'arte di formare il carattere* (hereafter *Psicocinesia*) (Rome: Valle, 1890), p.89. Comparative tables on the rejected conscripts may be found in B. Farolfi, 'L'antropologia negativa degli italiani: i riformati alla leva dal 1862 al 1886' in M.L. Betri and A.G. Marchetti (eds.), *Salute e classi lavoratrici in Italia dall'unità al fascismo* (Milan: Franco Angeli, 1982), pp.165–97.
2. On Labriola, see G. Trebisacce, *Marxismo e educazione in A. Labriola* (Rome: La Goliandica, 1979); S. Poggi, *Introduzione a Labriola* (Rome-Bari: Laterza, 1982).
3. On the Italian positivism, see G. Flores d'Arcais, *Studi sul positivismo italiano* (Padova: Cedam, 1951); A. Saloni, *Il positivismo e Robero Ardigò* (Rome: Armando, 1969); E.R. Papa (ed.), *Il positivismo nella cultura italiana* (Milan: Valle, 1985).
4. E. Baumann, *Programmi di ginnastica vigenti e futuri* (Rome: Franco Angeli, 1885).
5. On this period, consult F. Cambi, *Storia della pedagogia* (Rome-Bari: Laterza, 1995), pp.391–5; and G. Cives (ed.), *La scuola italiana dall' Unità ai nostri giorni* (Florence: La Nuova Italia, 1990), *passim*. It might be interesting to compare these books, which were written in democracy, with others published during the dictatorial fascist era, such as that by G. Arrighi, *Disegno storico della pedagogia* (Florence: Barbera, 1936). Arrighi's book tried to demonstrate that the 'crisis culture', in the educational field, also defined as 'pedagogy of anarchism', was the unavoidable and necessary premise for the next advent of Fascism and its schooling system. On physical education in the years between the nineteenth and twentieth centuries, consult at least S. Giuntini, *Sport, scuola e caserma dal Risorgimento al primo conflitto mondiale* (Padova: Centro grafico editionale, 1988); and G. Bonetta, *Corpo e nazione. L'educazione ginnastica, igienica e razionale nell'Italia liberale* (Milan: Franco Angeli, 1990).
6. Quoted by M. Di Donato in his book *Indirizzi fondamentali dell' educazione fisica moderna* (Rome: Universale Studium, 1962), p.153.
7. Baumann, *Psicocinesia*, p.496.
8. E. Baumann, *Ginnastica e scienza, ovvero la ginnastica italiana e le scienze affini (anatomia, fisiologia, igiene, meccanica umana) con riferimenti alla ginnastica medica, ortopedica e pedagogica* (Rome: Regia Scuola Normale di Ginnastica, 1910), pp.462–3.
9. Ibid., p.464.
10. F. Valletti, 'Ginnastica popolare e militare', *Rivista Militare Italiana* (1891), 413–47.
11. F. Valletti, *Storia della ginnastica* (Milan: Ulrico Hoepli, 1893), p.183.
12. Among Baumann's main publications should be quoted also *La ginnastica nei suoi rapporti con la medicina e l'igiene* (Genova: Artisi Tip., 1870); *Spirometria e ginnastica* (Bologna: Tipografia dei Compositori, 1872); *L'educazione fisica nelle scuole specialmente elementari* (Genova: Tip. Sordo Muti, 1873); *Elementi di ginnastica razionale* (Bologna: Società Tipografica dei

Compositori, 1879); *Ginnastica fuori. Id uso delle scuole elementari maschile e femminile* (hereafter *Ginnastica fuori*) (Bologna: Società Tipografica già Compositori, 1880); *Anatomia applicata alla ginnastica* (Bologna: Società Tipografica già Compositori, 1880); *Ginnastica teorica* (Bologna: Società Tipografica già Compositori, 1880); *Ginnastica fra i banchi* (Bologna: Società Tipografica già Compositori, 1882); *Il fine della ginnastica* (Bologna: Tip. militare, 1882); *Meccanica umana* (Bologna: Valle, 1882); *L'educazione fisica nelle scuole elementari e normali* (Turin: Pararia, 1894); and *Callistenia ovvero la ginnastica della donna pubere* (Rome: Valle, 1901). Finally, a number of gymnastics manuals for different kinds of schools, books on technical equipment with accurate descriptions of relative exercises and booklets on first aid were published.

13. The detailed report written by that committee in 1893 can be found in G. Gori, *Educazione fisica, sport e giornalismo in Italia. Dall' unità alla prima olimpiade dell'era moderna* (Bologna: Pàtron, 1989), pp.100–12.

14. On Baumann's natural gymnastics in the open air, see Baumann, *La ginnastica fuori*.

15. E. Baumann, *La ginnastica italiana* (Rome: Valle, 1907), p.xiii.

16. G. Gori, 'Model of Masculinity: Mussolini, the "New Italian" of the Fascist Era' (hereafter 'Model of Masculinity') in J.A. Mangan (ed.), *Superman Supreme: Fascist Body as Political Icon-Global Fascism* (London and Portland, OR: Frank Cass, 2000), pp.27–61.

17. The biographical details on Mosso are taken from: L. Ferretti, *Angelo Mosso apostolo dello sport* (Milan: Garzanti, 1951); G. Sciutto, 'Biografia di Angelo Mosso', *Società Medico Chirurgica*; A. Mosso (ed.), *Angelo Mosso, fisiologo, pedagogista, archeologo* (Chieri: Annuario of 1958–59); M. Rosso and A. Tedoldi, *Angelo Mosso: Illustre scienziato chierese fisiologo, pedagogo antropologo archeologo* (Chieri: Lions Club n.d.).

18. In the physiologic, educational and sporting ambits should be quoted the following Mosso publications, at least: *La paura* (Milan: Treves, 1884); *La fatica* (Milan: Treves, 1891); 'L'educazione fisica e i giuochi nelle scuole' (hereafter 'Giuochi'), *Nuova Antologia*, 120 (1891); *L'educazione fisica della donna* (Milan: Treves, 1892); and *L'educazione fisica della gioventù* (Milan: Treves, 1893), later collected in one volume entitled *L'educazione fisica della gioventù-della donna* (hereafter *L'educazione fisica*) (Milan: Treves, 1894); *Fisiologia dell' uomo sulle Alpi* (Milan: Treves, 1897); *La riforma dell'educazione* (hereafter *La riforma*) (Milan: Treves, 1898); *Mens sana in corpore sano* (hereafter *Mens sana*) (Milan: Treves, 1903); *Vita moderna degli italiani* (hereafter *Vita moderna*) (Milan: Treves, 1905); *La difesa della patria e il Tiro a Segno* (hereafter *Tiro a Segno*) (Milan: Treves, 1905); 'I Giuochi olimpici a Roma?' (hereafter 'I Giuochi olimpici?'), *Nuova Antologia*, 799 (1905).

19. A. Mosso, *La democrazia nella religione e nella scienza* (hereafter *La democrazia*) (Milan: Treves, 1901).

20. Mosso's important books on archaeology are: *Escursioni nel Mediterraneo e gli scavi di Creta* (Milan: Treves, 1908) and *Le origini della civiltà mediterranea* (Milan: Treves, 1910).

21. Mosso, *Mens sana*, pp.114–15.

22. Ibid., p.118.

23. Ibid., p.116.

24. Mosso, *L'educazione fisica*, p.207.

25. Ibid., p.114.

26. Mosso, *Mens sana*, p.87.

27. Mosso, *L'educazione fisica*, p.117.

28. Mosso, *La riforma*, p.25.

29. Mosso, *Mens sana*, p.89.

30. Mosso, *L'educazione fisica*, p.67.

31. Mosso, *Mens sana*, pp.123–8.

32. Mosso, *L'educazione fisica*, pp.70–71.

33. Ibid., pp.101–7.

34. Mosso, 'Giuochi', 9. See also G. Gori, 'Sports Festivals in Italy between the 19th and 20th Centuries: A Kind of National Olympic Games?' in R. Naul (ed.), *Contemporary Studies in the National Olympic Games Movement* (Frankfurt am Main: Peter Lang, 1997), p.33.

35. Mosso, *L'educazione fisica*, pp.86–7.

36. Besides Mosso, many other intellectuals and patriots of the nineteenth century had previously emphasized the Roman past glories, so as to convince people to fight for their independence.

Indeed, it was nothing new when Mussolini used the ancient culture of Rome to convince people that they could become a grand people again. See Gori, 'Model of Masculinity', *passim*.

37. Mosso, *Mens sana*, p.32.
38. Ibid., pp.97–8.
39. Ibid., pp.67–70.
40. Mosso, *L'educazione fisica*, pp.1–19.
41. Ibid., p.17.
42. Ibid., pp.99–100.
43. Statute and norms of the central and local Committees were publicized by Mosso, who ended *La riforma*, with an appendix, where these were published in total. See Mosso, *La riforma*, pp.209–25.
44. Mosso, *Mens sana*, p.82.
45. Ibid., p.45.
46. Mosso, 'I Giuochi olimpici?', 442.
47. A. Mosso, 'La riforma della ginnastica', *Nuova Antologia*, 237 (1892), 237–67.
48. Mosso, *L'educazione fisica*, pp.158–60.
49. Ibid., p.159.
50 Mosso scientifically demonstrated this through figures and tables. See *Tiro a Segno*, *passim*.
51. Ibid., pp.6–7.
52. Ibid., p.40.
53. P.J. Moebius, *Inferiorità mentale della donna (sulla deficienza mentale fisiologia)* (Turin: Fratelli Bocca Edn., 1904).
54. On the origins and development of scholastic and competitive gymnastics in the nineteenth century, consult P. Ferrara, *L'Italia in palestra. Storia, documenti e immagini della ginnastica dal 1833 al 1973* (Rome: La Meridiana Editori, 1992), pp.29–168. On the specific women's field, see G. Gori, *L'atleta e la nazione. Saggi di storia dello sport* (hereafter *L'atlera e la nazione*) (Rimini: Panozzo, 1996), pp.61–77.
55. G. Genovesi, *Storia della scuola in Italia dal Settecento a oggi* (Rome-Bari: Laterza, 1998), p.226.
56. Mosso, *L'educazione fisica*, pp.213–40.
57. H. Sidgwick, *Health statistics of Women Students of Cambridge and Oxford and their Sisters* (Cambridge, 1890), p.91.
58. Mosso, *L'educazione fisica*, pp.228–9.
59. Ibid., p.221.
60. In *Vita moderna*, p.30, Mosso confessed that by the harbour of New York his heart moved in front of a group of beautiful female emigrants, whose broad forehead, swarthy skin and black eyes recalled the 'pure Italian type'.
61. Mosso, *L'educazione fisica*, pp.230–33. There, Mosso quoted figures by V. Turquan, *Manuel de statistique pratique* (Paris, 1891), p.487.
62. Mosso, *Mens sana*, p.292.
63. Ibid., p.337.
64. Mosso, 'I Giuochi olimpici?', *passim*.
65. Mosso, *La riforma*, pp.168–9.
66. See L. Toschi, 'Romane olimpiadi-giochi frivoli e ludi necessari (1908–1960)', *Lancillotto e Nausica*, 3 (1988), 28–41; A. Lombardo, 'Alle origini del movimento olimpico in Italia (1894–1914)', *Ricerche storiche*, 2 (1989), 297–314; G. Gori, *L'atleta e la nazione*, pp.79–95. (A reviewed research on this story will be soon published in English by Gori, as part of a book edited by Lämmer.)
67. A. Mosso, 'L'educazione del soldato e la guerra russo-giapponese', *Nuova Antologia*, 503 (1906).
68. Ibid.
69. E. Baumann, *L'educazione fisica italiana e le panzane del prof. Mosso* (Rome: Scuola tipografica salesiana, 1906).
70. Ibid.
71. Consult S. Spezia, 'Emilio Baumann, Angelo Mosso e una famosa polemica' in A. Noto and L. Rossi (eds.), *Coroginnica. Saggi sulla ginnastica, lo sport e la cultura del corpo 1861–1991* (Rome: La Meridiana Editori, 1992), p.111; R. Freccero, *Sport e società. La cultura plagiata*, Vol.II (Turin: Levrotto & Bella, 1997), pp.107–18.

Epilogue:
The History of Modern European Sport as a History of Modern European Ideas

J.A. MANGAN

The paradox of the most bourgeois of centuries was that its life-styles became 'bourgeois' only late, that this transformation was pioneered on its fringes rather than at its centre, and that, as a specifically bourgeois way and style of living, it triumphed only momentarily. That is perhaps why the survivors looked back to the era before 1914 so often and so nostalgically as the belle époque.[1]

Eric Hobsbawm remarked in *The Age of Empire* that the everyday culture of modern life is still dominated by three innovations of the period: the advertising industry in its modern form, the modern mass circulation newspaper or periodical and the moving photograph or film.[2] Surely modern sport, also the cultural product of the period, has come close to greatly influencing if not dominating the everyday lives of countless millions in the Europe of the twentieth century.

Hobsbawm asks of the Age of Empire:

[H]ow are we to situate this period? For, after all, the relation of past to present is central to the preoccupations both of those who write and those who read history. Both want, or should want, to understand how the past has become the present, and both want to understand the past, the chief obstacle being that it is *not* like the present.[3]

With his own sharp perspicacity he then answers his own question. The depiction of the nineteenth century contained within his acclaimed trilogy[4] states that the central axis around which he organized the history of the century was 'the triumph and transformation of capitalism in the historically specific forms of bourgeois society in its liberal version'.[5] This triumph and transformation had enormous consequences for modern sport. It allowed it time, space and opportunity.

Those with most time, space and opportunity for reasons too obvious for detailed rehearsal here, were the European middle classes: 'In the century of the conquering bourgeoisie, members of the successful middle classes were sure of their civilization, generally confident and not usually in financial difficulties, but only very late in the century were they physically *comfortable*.'[6] In this late situation of unified certainty and comfort – financial and physical – they created the new forms of sport typical of the era. They drew on the past to an extent but only to an extent. They drew on activities of all 'classes' of the past but only to an extent. Much was new: their present was not like their past! The innovatory public institutions of bourgeois society linked to its theoretical systems shaped the nineteenth century and, by extension, the global phenomenon of late nineteenth- and early twentieth-century sport – and much of its considerable global, political, economic, cultural, social, educational, moral, aesthetic and emotional associations in the later twentieth century. This has still to be fully recognized.

As mentioned in the Prologue, a crucial component of the significant bourgeois social institutions linked to powerful ideological systems was the 'school'.[7] This should never be overlooked. Its part in the successful socialization into belief and action through and beyond modern sport throughout Europe was considerable. In Hobsbawm's words:

> The institution of 'old boys' which developed rapidly from the 1870s on, demonstrated that the products of an educational establishment formed a network which might be national or even international, but it also bonded younger generations to the older. In short, it gave social cohesion to a heterogeneous body of recruits. Here ... *sport provided much of the formal cement.*[8]

There was thus a conquest of Europe (and the globe) by 'the capitalist economy carried by its characteristic class, the "bourgeoisie" and under the banners of its characteristic intellectual expression, the ideology of liberalism'.[9] With respect to Hobsbawm, this was far from the only role sport played in the European middle-class community: it was also an agent of militarism, an instrument of imperialism and a source of moral hegemony. Hobsbawm sees only part, albeit a vital part, of the picture. The late nineteenth century, as stated briefly in the Prologue, was an 'era of unparalleled peace'.[10] During this period advanced industrial economies transformed European societies – their work patterns and their play patterns – in varying degrees of intensity in various places, but to a greater or lesser extent everywhere. Then these economies 'provided the smaller bodies of men who, with almost contemptuous ease, could conquer and rule over vast empires'[11] and who carried around the world their own cultural privileges, pleasures and pastimes and, in time, left them almost everywhere – intact, adapted or transformed.

None of this is to overlook, ignore, or marginalize other great movements and their significant 'revolutionaries' which were also the outcomes of capitalized economies and corresponding liberal ideas, especially, the eventual and responsive, 'massive organized movements of the class of wage-workers created by, and characteristic of industrial capitalism'.[12] They played as far as they were able; they had their sport, increasingly but not wholly given by, or taken from, the middle classes. In time, as the wage workers grew in power and influence, and as the world of bourgeois liberalism, relatively, lost confidence, authority, wealth and power, they would come to participate more, perform better, control more and eventually more than share the advantages, pleasures and privileges of modern sport. But *Reformers, Sport, Modernizers* is not their story. It is the story (in reality, a fragment of the story) of a 'revolution' in sport in the late nineteenth and early twentieth centuries inspired by, lead by and controlled by the European bourgeoisie, who then slowly and steadily gave ground to others as their innovations were increasingly given to, taken over by, or shared by others. This should cause little surprise: 'In itself there is nothing about the historic pattern of reversal, of development undermining its own foundations, which is more or peculiar to the period as distinct from any other. This is how endogenous historical transformations work. And they are still working this way.'[13]

A crucial reminder – a great deal of the innovation in modern European sport was associated with values. In his search for the meaning of Europe in recent history, Mark Mazower has observed that 'ultimately values lie at the heart of this history – the values that caused people to act, which shaped and transformed institutions and underpinned communities, families and individuals'.[14] No one should overlook the fact that *morality* – more than pleasure, leisure or relaxation – was at the centre of the evolution of modern European sport of the late nineteenth and early twentieth centuries. This is a point of fundamental importance which is insufficiently appreciated. And it is one good reason why historians of ideas ignore modern sport at their intellectual peril.

Much of the moral philosophy, preaching and proselytizing at the centre of the introduction, extension and expansion of modern European sport was the 'property' of middle-class moralists. To fail to understand this is to fail to understand the political, social and religious basis of modern sport and to fail to realize its significance for a recent European history of ideas. In its essence, much of the history of modern sport will be found in the history of modern ideas.

Hobsbawm 'surveys the moment in history when it became clear that the society and civilization created by and for the Western liberal bourgeoisie represented not the permanent form of the modern industrial world, but only one phase of its early development'.[15] With regard to the smaller but far from unimportant world of modern sport, the same is true of *Reformers, Sport, Modernizers*. As Hobsbawm states: 'There is no return to the world of liberal bourgeois society … For better or worse, since 1914 the century of the bourgeoisie belongs to history.'[16] The characters and communities of *Reformers, Sport, Modernizers* also belong to history; their influence, however, remains.

NOTES

1. E.J. Hobsbawm, *The Age of Empire, 1875–1914* (London: Weidenfeld and Nicolson, 1987), p.166.
2. Ibid., p.8.
3. Ibid.
4. *The Age of Revolution* (1995), *The Age of Capital* (1975) and *The Age of Empire* (1987).
5. Hobsbawm, *The Age of Empire*, pp.8–9.
6. Ibid., p.165.
7. The term is used here in both the European and American sense to embrace thus primary, secondary and tertiary education.
8. Hobsbawm, *The Age of Empire*, p.179, emphasis added.
9. Ibid., p.9.
10. Ibid.
11. Ibid.
12. Ibid., p.10.
13. Ibid., p.11.
14. M. Mazower, *Dark Continent: Europe's Twentieth Century* (London: Allen Lane, 1998), p.xv.
15. Hobsbawm, *The Age of Empire*, p.11.
16. Ibid., p.12.

Notes on Contributors

Hans Bonde is Associate Professor at the University of Copenhagen. He has recently completed his study of the internationally renowned Danish youth leader Niels Bukh.

Joseph M. Bradley lectures in Sports Studies at the University of Stirling. He has written widely on sport in Scottish society and its links with culture, religion, politics, ethnicity and diaspora. His publications include *Ethnic and Religious Identity in Modern Scotland: Culture, Politics and Football* (1995) and *Sport, Culture, Politics and Scottish Society: Irish Immigrant and the Gaelic Athletic Association* (1998).

Vassil Girginov is Senior Lecturer in Leisure and Sport Studies at Luton Business School, University of Luton. He holds Masters degrees in Sports Management from the National Sports Academy, Sofia and in European Leisure Studies from the Universities of Loughborough, Tilburg, Brussels and Bilbao, as well as a Ph.D. from the University of Loughborough. His research interests include the Olympic movement, sports management and policy analysis and Eastern European sport.

Gigliola Gori has a Ph.D. in Social Sciences from Georg-August-Universität, Göttingen. She is Associate Professor of History of Pedagogy, Physical Education and Sport at the University of Urbino. Her research interests include sport, politics and gender in Italy. She serves on the Council of the International Society for the *European Sports History Review and Acta Kinesiologie Universitatis Tartuensis*. She is also a founding member and fellow of the European Committee for Sport History (CESH).

Colm Hickey is Deputy Headteacher at St. Bernard's Catholic School, High Wycombe. He took his first degree at the former Borough Road College and completed his MA in the History of Education at the University of London, Institute of Education. He has published a number of articles in the fields of athleticism, imperialism and elementary education. He is currently completing his Ph.D. thesis on Athleticism and the London Teacher Training Colleges at the International Research Centre for Sport, Socialisation and Society at the University of Strathclyde.

Mike Huggins is a retired head of post-graduate teacher training at Lancaster University and currently lectures in history at St. Martin's College, Ambleside, Cumbria. He has written widely on the history of sport and leisure in the modern period, most recently *Flat Racing and British Society 1790–1914* (2000). He is currently co-editing, with J.A. Mangan, a volume entitled *Disreputable Pleasures: Vicious Victorians at Play*.

J.A. Mangan is Director of the International Research Centre for Sport, Socialisation and Society at the University of Strathclyde and author and editor of many books. He is founder and General Editor of the Cass series *Sport in the Global Society* and founding and Executive Academic Editor of the following Cass journals: *The International Journal of the History of Sport*; *Culture, Sport, Society*; *Soccer and Society*; and *The European Sports History Review*. His books *Athleticism in the Victorian and Edwardian Public School* and *The Games Ethic and Imperialism* have recently been reprinted by Frank Cass.

Callum McKenzie is currently completing his doctorate at the International Research Centre for Sport, Socialisation and Society, Strathclyde University. He has published articles on the themes of field sports, masculinity, morality and the search for 'order' in the age of imperialism in various international and national academic journals.

Lozan Mitev is Senior Lecturer in the History of Sport at the Department of History and Management of Sport, National Sports Academy, Sofia. His Masters dissertation, for the National Sports Academy, Sofia, was on the creation of the Bulgarian model of totalitarian physical education and sport 1937–49. He is a member of ISHPES. His research interests include the history of Bulgarian sport and the Olympic movement.

Rüdiger Rabenstein is currently a professor at the University of Münster, in Germany. He studied sports science, sociology and history, and his doctoral dissertation, entitled 'Cycling and Society', was later published as *Radsport und Gesellschaft*. He has extensive experience as a competitive athlete, coach and judge, and is also a promoter and announcer for bicycle races.

Andrew Ritchie specializes in the history of the bicycle from the nineteenth century onwards and has published two books on the subject: *King of the Road: An Illustrated History of Cycling* (1975) and *Major Taylor: The Extraordinary Career of a Champion Bicycle Racer* (1988). He is currently working on an in-depth study of early bicycle-racing as it emerged in the nineteenth century and is preparing a revised edition of *King of the Road*. He is Associate Academic Editor of *The International Journal of the History of Sport* as well as co-editing the annual *Proceedings* of the International Cycle History Conference.

Ingomar Weiler has been Professor of Ancient History at the University of Graz, Austria since 1976. He is the author of *Der Agon im Mythos* (Darmstadt, 1974), *Sport bei den Völkern der Alten Welt* (Darmstadt, 2nd edn. 1988), *Griechische Geschichte* (Darmstadt, 2nd edn. 1988), editor of *Quellendokumentation zur Gymnastik and Agonistik im Altertum* (Vienna, Cologne, Weimar, 6 volumes, 1991–98, 7th volume forthcoming) amongst others. His key interests are sports history, the social history of antiquity and the history of scholarship.

Abstracts

The Living Legacy: Classical Sport and Nineteenth-Century Middle-Class Commentators of the German-Speaking Nations
Ingomar Weiler

The German innovations to European sports affect above all Jahn's *Turnen*. Another impulse is connected with the intellectual discourse of the classical scholars concerning the agonistics and gymnastics of the ancient Hellenes and with the Olympic Games of the nineteenth century. Among other things resulting from these studies was the assumption of the physical aesthetics of the Greeks and their equation with the Germanic ideal of the body. The ideological basis for this aspect dates back to the nineteenth century where it found acceptance in the racist schools of contemporary thought; the idea grew into deeper expression during the twentieth century.

A Tranquil Transformation: Middle-Class Racing 'Revolutionaries' in Nineteenth-Century England
Mike Huggins

The Victorian middle classes were key creators, shapers of and participants in many of the major forms of modern sport. Yet the manner in which they seized power from both upper- and lower-class groups during the nineteenth century, and the chronology of the process, is still not entirely clear. In the case of racing, apparently dominated by the upper classes, this revisionist article argues that a quiet middle-class revolution allowed the upper classes to preserve the illusion of power, while middle-class groups increasingly enjoyed the actual fruits. Significant and influential middle-class administrators and organisers, such as the Weatherby and Tattersall families, and major bookmakers, trainers and breeders played key roles in ensuring that upper-class wealth was redistributed and redirected within the sport. In the process they made a significant contribution to modern European racing.

Unrecognized Middle-Class Revolutionary?
Michael Cusack, Sport and Cultural Change in
Nineteenth-Century Ireland
Joseph M. Bradley

Nineteenth-century Ireland experienced several periods of armed insurrection. However, this insurrectionary era was not limited to armed struggle. By the last quarter of the nineteenth century many cultural activists were also fomenting change. Michael Cusack was foremost amongst those seeking cultural revolution. Cusack's ideas became concrete in 1884 with the founding of the Gaelic Athletic Association. The creation of the GAA formalised and institutionalised cultural opposition to the British sporting domination of the country and led to a revolution in Irish sporting pastimes.

Missing Middle-Class Dimensions:
Elementary Schools, Imperialism and Athleticism
J.A. Mangan and Colm Hickey

Elementary education in general, and the training of teachers in particular, has received inadequate attention by historians. Indeed, as Harold Silver has remarked, education has often been ignored by historians of Victorian society. While with regards to imperialism, J. A. Mangan has commented that 'Most general histories of British (and English) education can be read without any realisation that Britain was an imperial power throughout the eighteenth, nineteenth and twentieth centuries'. Yet imperialism sustained a powerful moral imperative which was transmitted by middle-class educationalists. Elementary schools were increasingly influenced by imperialism which in turn created a colonial curriculum as a means of establishing and perpetuating imperial supremacy. A firm belief in athleticism as a relevant morality of middle-class imperialism marched alongside subscription to the imperial curriculum in training colleges and elementary schools.

Mostly Middle-Class Cycling Heroes:
The *Fin de Siècle* Commercial Obsession with Speed,
Distance and Records
Andrew Ritchie and Rüdiger Rabenstein

During the 1890s, the sport of bicycle-racing underwent a spectacular 'boom'; speed and distance records of all kinds, on road and track, were compulsively attacked and established. High speed and long-distance races and rides pushed at the limits of human capability. Newly recruited, well-paid, highly publicized professional riders were employed by bicycle and tyre manufacturers to promote and advertise their products to the consumers and place-to-place races which are now the 'classics' of the sport were first sponsored by competing newspapers. Bicycle-racing was sponsored by the bicycle industry and by the media in a way which was strikingly 'modern' in its social and economic organization and impact. Middle-class heroes of bicycle-racing were thrust into the public arena in one of the most conspicuous turn of the century mass-spectator sports.

'Golden Boys' of Playing Field and Battlefield: Celebrating Heroes – 'Lost' Middle-Class Women Versifiers of the Great War
J.A. Mangan

Deeply moved by the events of the Great War, hundreds, possibly thousands, of women published short lyrical verses in newspapers, weeklies, pamphlets and small volumes between 1914 and 1916. A smaller number wrote during the later years of the war. Although these verses may not now be found in Great War anthologies, they were well represented in the publications of the time. For the most part, these women were far removed in both experience and expression from war poets such as Siegfried Sassoon, Wilfred Owen and Robert Graves. They wrote more of pennants and banners than of mud and blood. These middle-class women versifiers tended to idealise their athletic soldier heroes: they urged on them martial patriotism; they depicted them as latter day Christs crucified; and finally they mourned them as vanished ghosts. It is possible to trace an unfolding of expression born of their experience: first trumpeted words of strident patriotism and chivalric romance, then stunned cadences of sad sacrifice, later horrified lines of bloody realism and finally poignant stanzas of lost love. These women were 'revolutionaries' in their way. They gave women of their class a common voice and in so doing made women more visible.

Modernizing Bulgaria: Todor Yonchev – Middle-Class Patriot and the Assertion of a Nation
Vassil Girginov and Lozan Mitev

The emergence of modern physical culture in Bulgaria in the late nineteenth century is closely related to the project of building a new secular state out of the ruins of the theocratic Ottoman Empire. This process involved struggles between conservative and liberal forces in society and related residual (linking present to past) and emerging (linking present to future) practices. As history evidences, individuals play an important role in promoting new cultural values and experiences. This chapter examines the pioneering patriotic work of Todor Yonchev in shaping modern sport in Bulgaria and in forging links with European and world sport. Attention is given to the originality and universality of Yonchev's conceptual grounding, the relations between his vision and its implementation and the relevance of his contribution to present day sport.

Radical Conservatives: Middle-Class Masculinity, the Shikar Club and Big-Game Hunting

J.A. Mangan and Callum McKenzie

The Shikar Club – an association formed in 1907 for elite big-game hunters – was an upper-middle-class institution for the celebration of manly virtues associated with the sport in foreign lands: fortitude, perseverance, dedication and skill with the rifle. In a post-nineteenth century world of changing attitudes towards hunting, 'masculinity' and colonialism, the Club was more than an upper-middle class 'dining–club' for male 'shots'. As others vacillated, the Club emerged as an emphatic proselytizer of chauvinistic manliness and ethnocentric certainty. In contrast to urbanized, 'emasculated' even 'feminised' hunting and shooting in Britain, the exploits of Club members abroad encapsulated what they saw as the best traditions of 'British' hunting – pioneering, fearlessness, physical prowess and, above all, fair play. That the Club still exists today suggests the tenuous longevity of this hunting and moral code in contemporary society, so different in this modern era from the Shikar Club's 'Golden Age'.

A Dark 'Prince' of Denmark: Niels Bukh, Twentieth-Century Middle-Class Propagandist

Hans Bonde

Neils Bukh, the Danish gymnastics innovator, was probably the best internationally known Dane of the 1930s. Bukh revolutionalized the masculine aesthetics of international gymnastics. He used his gymnastic fame as a popular 'platform' from which to propagate right wing political propaganda and revolutionary ideas. The attraction of Bukh's gymnastics for several twentieth-century dictatorships lay in the discipline, stamina and strength promoted by his gymnastics system which had clear military, psychological and physiological advantages.

The Apostle of Italian Sport:
Angelo Mosso and English Athleticism in Italy
Gigliola Gori

Angelo Mosso was an idealist. He was cosmopolitan and an expert in physiology, education and general culture. He was inspired by the concept of democracy, sensitive to social inequalities and thus openly opposed negative government policies in various fields. He confronted the government, the political parties, the Roman Catholic Church and whoever was out-of-date. He was a revolutionary – educationally, socially and politically. He wanted to transform a backward society and make it modern, progressive, rational and, above all, healthy. Mosso's educational subscription to English athleticism found eventual recognition in the post-fascist twentieth century. Thus, in the final analysis, Mosso's revolutionary liberalism triumphed.

Select Bibliography

The Living Legacy:
Classical Sport and Nineteenth-Century Middle-Class
Commentators of the German-Speaking Nations
Ingomar Weiler

H. Bernett, *Die pädagogische Neugestaltung der bürgerlichen Leibesübungen durch die Philanthropen* (Schorndorf, 2nd Edn. 1965).

F. Bourriot, *Kalos Kagathos – Kalokagathia. D'un terme de propagande de sophistes à une notion sociale et philosophique. Etude d'histoire athénienne* (Hildesheim, 1995, 2 Vols.).

K. Christ, 'Aspekte der Antike-Rezeption in der deutschen Altertumswissenschaft des 19. Jahrhunderts' (Introduction – 2. Part) in K. Christ and A. Momigliano (eds.), *Die Antike im 19. Jahrhundert in Italien und Deutschland* (Bologna and Berlin, 1988), pp.21–37.

C. Eisenberg, *»English Sports« und Deutsche Bürger: Eine Gesellschaftsgeschichte 1800 bis 1939* (Paderborn, 1999).

M. Fuhrmann, *Der europäische Bildungskanon des bürgerlichen Zeitalters* (Frankfurt am Main and Leipzig, 1999).

M. Krüger, *Körperkultur und Nationsbildung: Die Geschichte des Turnens in der Reichsgründungsära – eine Detailstudie über die Deutschen* (Schorndorf, 1996).

V. Losemann, *Nationalsozialismus und Antike: Studien zur Entwicklung des Faches Alte Geschichte 1933–45* (Hamburg, 1977).

J.A. Mangan (ed.), *Shaping the Superman: Fascist Body as Political Icon – Aryan Fascism* (London and Portland OR: Frank Cass, 1999)

S.L. Marchand, *Down from Olympus: Archaeology and Philhellenism in Germany, 1750–1970* (Princeton, NJ, 1996).

N. Müller (ed.), *Pierre de Coubertin 1863–1937: Olympism. Selected Writings* (Lausanne, 2000).

H. Strohmeyer, *Beiträge zur Geschichte des Sports in Österreich. Gesammelte Arbeiten aus vier Jahrzehnten* (Vienna, 1999).

A Tranquil Transformation:
Middle-Class Racing 'Revolutionaries' in
Nineteenth-Century England
Mike Huggins

C. Chinn, *Better Betting with a Decent Feller: Bookmakers, Betting and the British Working Class 1750–1990* (Hemel Hempstead: Harvester, 1991).

M. Huggins, *Flat Racing and British Society 1790–1914* (London and Portland, OR: Frank Cass, 2000).

J. Lowerson, *Sport and the English Middle Classes 1870–1914* (Manchester: Manchester University Press, 1993).

R. Mortimer, *The Jockey Club* (London: Cassell, 1958).

R. Munting, *Hedges and Ditches: A Social and Economic History of National Hunt Racing* (London: J.A. Allen, 1987).

N. Tranter, *Sport, Economy and Society in Britain 1750–1914* (Cambridge: Cambridge University Press, 1998).

W. Vamplew, *The Turf: A Social and Economic History of Horse Racing* (London: Allen Lane, 1976).

W. Vamplew, *Pay up and Play the Game: Professional Sport in Britain, 1875–1914* (Cambridge: Cambridge University Press, 1988).

Unrecognized Middle-Class Revolutionary?
Michael Cusack, Sport and Cultural Change in
Nineteenth-Century Ireland
Joseph M. Bradley

M. De Burca, *Michael Cusack and the GAA* (Dublin: Anvil Books, 1989).

M. De Burca, *The GAA: A History of the Gaelic Athletic Association* (Dublin: Cumann Luthchleas Gael, 1980).

M. Cronin, 'Defenders of the Nation', *Irish Political Studies*, 11 (1996), 1–19.

B. MacLua, *The Steadfast Rule, a History of the GAA Ban* (Dublin: Press Cuchulainn, 1967).

W.F. Mandle, *The GAA and Irish Nationalist Politics* (Dublin: Helm, Gill and Macmillan, 1987).

M. Mullen, 'Opposition, Social Closure, and Sport: The Gaelic Athletic Association in the 19th Century', *Sociology of Sport*, 12 (1995), 268–89.

Missing Middle-Class Dimensions:
Elementary Schools, Imperialism and Athleticism
J. A. Mangan and Colm Hickey

T. Adkins, *The History of St. John's College Battersea: The Story of a Noble Experiment* (London: National Society, 1906).

G.F. Bartle, *A History of Borough Road College* (Kettering: Dalkeith Press, 1976).

J.A. Mangan, *Athleticism in the Victorian and Edwardian Public School* (London and Portland, OR: Frank Cass, 2000).

J.A. Mangan, (ed.), *Benefits Bestowed? Education and British Imperialism* (Manchester: Manchester University Press, 1988).

J. A. Mangan and John Nauright (eds.), *Sport in Australasian Society: Past and Present* (London, Portland OR, 2000).

J.A. Mangan, *The Games Ethic and Imperialism: Aspects of the Diffusion of an Ideal* (London and Portland, OR: Frank Cass, 1998).

J.A. Mangan (ed.), *The Imperial Curriculum: Racial Images and Education in the British Colonial Experience* (London: Routledge, 1993).

J.A. Mangan (ed.), *Making Imperial Mentalities: Socialisation and British Imperialism* (Manchester: Manchester University Press, 1990).

J.A. Mangan (ed.), *The Cultural Bond: Sport Empire, Society* (London and Portland, OR: Frank Cass, 1992).

P.C. McIntosh, *P.E. In England Since 1800* (London: Bell, 1968).

Mostly Middle-Class Cycling Heroes:
The *Fin de Siècle* Commercial Obsession with Speed,
Distance and Records
Andrew Ritchie and Rüdiger Rabenstein

Viscount Bury and G. Lacy Hillier, *Badminton Cycling* (London: Longman, 1887).

P. Chany, *La fabuleuse histoire du cyclisme* (Paris: Antoine Blondin, 1975).

H.O. Duncan, *The World on Wheels* (Paris, 1928).

J. Durry, *La véridique histoire des géants de la route* (Lausanne: Antoine Blondin, 1973).

W. Gronen and W. Lemke, *Geschichte des Radsports und Des Fahrrades* (Eupen: Doepen Verlag, 1978).

R. Rabenstein, *Radsport und Gesellschaft – Ihre sozialgeschichtlichen Zusammenhänge in der Zeit von 1867 bis 1914* (Hildesheim: Weidmann, 1991).

A. Ritchie, *King of the Road* (London: Wildwood House, 1975).

A. Ritchie, *Major Taylor* (Baltimore: Johns Hopkins Press, 1996).

P. Sergent, *A Century of Paris – Roubaix* (London: Bromley Books, 1997).

'Golden Boys' of Playing Field and Battlefield:
Celebrating Heroes – 'Lost' Middle-Class Women Versifiers
of the Great War
J.A. Mangan

C. Fyfe (ed.), *The Tears of War: The Love Story of a Young Poet and a War Hero: May Cannan and Bevis Quiller-Couch* (London: Cavalier Books, 2000).

S. Hynes, *A War Imagined: The First World War and English Culture* (London: The Bodley Head, 1990).

J.A. Mangan, *Athleticism in the Victorian and Edwardian Public School: the Emergence and Consolidation of an Educational Ideology* (London and Portland, OR: Frank Cass, 2000).

J.A. Mangan, 'Duty unto Death: English Masculinity and Militarism in the Age of the New Imperialism' in J.A. Mangan (ed.), *Tribal Identities: Nationalism, Europe, Sport* (London and Portland, OR: Frank Cass, 1996).

J.A. Mangan, 'Muscular, Militaristic and Manly: The British Middle Class Hero as Moral Messenger' in R. Holt, J.A. Mangan and P. Lanfranchi (eds.), *European Heroes: Myth, Identity, Sport* (London and Portland, OR: Frank Cass, 1996).

J.A. Mangan, 'Gamesfield and Battlefield: A Romantic Alliance in Verse and the Creation of Militaristic Masculinity' in J. Nauright and T.J.L. Chandler (eds.), *Making Men: Rugby and Masculine Identity* (London and Portland, OR: Frank Cass, 1998).

C.E. Playne, *The Pre-War Mind in Britain: An Historical Review* (London: Allen and Unwin, 1928).

C.W. Reilly, *Scars Upon My Heart: Women's poetry and verse of the First World War* (London: Virago, 1981).

K. Tynan, *The Holy War* (London: Sidgwick and Jackson, 1916).

R. Wohl, *The Generation of 1914* (London: Weidenfeld and Nicolson, 1997).

Modernizing Bulgaria:
Todor Yonchev – Middle-Class Patriot and the Assertion of a Nation
Vassil Girginov and Lozan Mitev

R. Bardareva, *Sporta v Balgaria – pojava i razvitie* (Sports in Bulgaria – Emergence and Development) (Sofia: NSA, 1991).

R. Crampton, *A Short History of Modern Bulgaria* (Cambridge: Cambridge University Press, 1997).

L. Mitev, 'Fur Bulgarien: Em Schweizer Tumlehrer, in Die Olympisehe Spiele 1896' in A Then (ed.), *Erleuterungen zum Neudruck des Offiziellen Berichtes, Karl Lennartz und Mitarbeiter Hrsg.* (Kolone, 1996).

N. Petrova, *100 Godini Obshtestveni Fizkulturni Organizacii v Balgaria* (100 Years of Voluntary Sports Organisations in Bulgaria) (Sofia: VIF G. Dimitrov', 1978).

N. Petrova *et al.*, *Istoria na Fiziceskata Kultura* (History of Physical Culture) (Sofia: Medicina i Fizkultura, 1985).

Radical Conservatives:
Middle-Class Masculinity, the Shikar Club and Big-Game Hunting
J.A. Mangan and Callum McKenzie

H. Bryden, *Animals of Africa* (London: Ronald Ward, 1900).

A. Chapman, *On Safari* (London: Edward Arnold, 1908).

C. C. De Crespigny, *Forty Years of a Sportsman's Life* (London: Mills and Boon, 1928).

J. Lowerson, *Sport and the English Middle Classes, 1870–1914* (Manchester: Manchester University Press, 1992).

J. MacKenzie, *Empire of Nature* (Manchester: Manchester University Press, 1988).

J.A. Mangan and J. Walvin (eds.), *Middle Class Morality in Britain and America: Manliness and Morality, 1800–1950* (Manchester: Manchester University Press, 1987).

A.E. Pease, *Half a Century of Sport* (London: John Murray, 1932).

J. Ross and H. Gunn, *The Book of the Red Deer and Empire* (London: Simpkin and Marshall, 1925).

F.C. Selous, *Travel and Adventure in South East Africa* (London: Ronald Ward, 1893).

K. Thomas, *Man and the Natural World* (Harmondsworth: Allan Lane, 1986).

A Dark 'Prince' of Denmark:
Niels Bukh, Twentieth-Century Middle-Class Propagandist
Hans Bonde

H. Bonde, 'Farmers' Gymnastics in Denmark in the Late Nineteenth and Early Twentieth Centuries: A Semiotic Analysis of Exercise in Moral Action', *International Journal of the History of Sport*, 10, 2 (1993), 198–214.

H. Bonde, 'Sport and Anti-Communism: Danish Gymnastics Encounter with Stalinism in its Formative Years', *International Journal of the History of Sport*, 16, 1 (1999), 137–47.

H. Bonde, 'Gymnastics as a Masculinity Rite: Ollerup Danish Gymnastics between the Wars', in J.A. Mangan (ed.), *Making European Masculinities: Sport, Europe, Gender* (London and Portland, OR: Frank Cass, 2000), pp.140–60.

P. Bourdieu, *A Social Critique of the Judgement of Taste* (London: Routledge & Kegan Paul, 1984).

A. Guttmann, *Games and Empires, Modern Sport and Cultural Imperialism* (New York: Columbia University Press, 1994).

H.J. Teichler, *Internationale Sportpolitik im Dritten Reich* (Schorndorf, 1991).

The Apostle of Italian Sport:
Angelo Mosso and English Athleticism in Italy
Gigliola Gori

E. Baumann, *Psicocinesia ovvero l'arte di formare il carattere* (Rome: Valle, 1890).

E. Baumann, *Ginnastica e scienza, ovvero la ginnastica italiana e le scienze affini (anatomia, fisiologia, igiene, meccanica umana) con riferimenti alla ginnastica medica, ortopedica e pedagogica* (Rome: Regia Scuola Normale di Ginnastica, 1910).

F. Cambi, *Storia della pedagogia* (Rome-Bari: Laterza, 1995).

G. Cives (ed.), *La scuola italiana dall' Unità ai nostri giorni* (Florence: La Nuova Italia, 1990).

P. Ferrara, *L'Italia in palestra. Storia, documenti e immagini della ginnastica dal 1833 al 1973* (Rome: La Meridiana Editori, 1992).

L. Ferretti, *Angelo Mosso apostolo dello sport* (Milan: Garzanti, 1951).

G. Flores d'Arcais, *Studi sul positivismo italiano* (Padova: Cedam, 1951).

A. Mosso, *La democrazia nella religione e nella scienza* (Milan: Treves, 1901).

A. Mosso, *Mens sana in corpore sano* (Milan: Treves, 1903).

A. Mosso, *L'educazione fisica della donna* (Milan: Treves, 1892).

Index

Africa, big-game hunting 190, 193–4, 200, 201
Age of Enlightenment 9
agonistics, ancient Greeks 16, 22–3, 30, 31n27
Aldington, May 143–4, 157
Aldridge, Richard 78
Alexander, Mary M. 140–1
Allen, Marion 156
Alpinism 10
Amateur Athletic Association (AAA) 65
Ancient Rome, as model 242–3, 251n36
Anderson, E.E. 119
anti-Semitism 23
Arend, Willy 91, 114
Arkwright, Richard 194
Aryan ideal 23, 223–4
Ashmore, Lady 157
athleticism
    in elementary schools 83–4
    English model 241–2
    and First World War 142–3
    and imperialism 75–76
Austria, physical education 241

Badesdow, Johann Bernhard 11
Baker, Samuel 192
Baumann, Emilio 233–6, 248–50
Baumgarat, Winifred 73
Belgium, physical education 241
Bellenden Higher Grade School 79
Bentinck, Lord 40, 42, 52
Berkeley, Grantley 189, 205n43
Bertz, Eduard 117
betting, horse-racing 46–7, 48–50
bicycle-racing
    accidents 101, 127nn42,43
    advertising 109
    Bordeaux–Paris race 93, 94, 108, 126n14
    cheating 98
    'gigantism' 92–4, 100–1, 104, 106, 115–19
    innovations 91–2, 125n3
    long-distance road races 94–6
    pacemaking 98–102, 111, 127nn37,38,40,41,42,43
    Paris–Brest–Paris race 94–5, 116
    professionalization 104–5, 114–15, 120
    promoters 105, 128n61
    record breaking 93, 101, 109, 115–19, 126n12, 130–3

sensationalism 118–19
six-day races 102–4, 117–18
social status of racers 120–4
stage-races 96–8
'stayer' races 94, 100–2
Tour de France 95, 97–8, 113
track sprinting 91–2, 125n2
Vienna–Berlin race 95–6
big-game hunting, Shikar Club 185–203
Billeter 29
Birrell, Augustine 83
Björkstén, Elli 214, 215, 216
Blanchud, Daniel 177, 178
Blenkiron, William 53
body, ideal of 30
Boer War 77, 80–1, 85
Bongo, shooting of 200, 208n138
Bordeaux–Paris bicycle race 93, 94, 108, 126n14
Boruttau, H. 118
Bourdieu, Pierre 214
Bourriot, F. 16
boxing see pugilism
boys, training of 198–9
Brailsford, Dennis 40
Breyer, Victor 126n14
Britain
    bicycle races 96
    English (British) Sports Movement 10, 19, 30
    hunting clubs 185
    imperialism 73–88
    physical education 29, 80–4
British and Foreign School Society 82
Brittain, Vera 157–8
Brunton, Lauder 81
Bryden, H.A. 195, 203, 209n164
Buck, Walter 196
Buckton, Alice M. 153–4
Budzinski, Fredy 105, 121–4
Bukh, Niels
    gymnastics system of 210–11, 214–16, 225–7
    international significance 212–13, 219–20, 226
    and Nazi Germany 223–5
    politics of 211, 220–3, 226–7
    and Swedish gymnastics 216–19

world tour (1931) 219, 222
Bulgaria
  Communist period 181, 182–3
  history 163–6
  physical education 166–83, 184n19
  role of Todor Yonchev 162–3, 169–83
  social structure 165–6
  Unak 174–81
Bulpett, C.W.L. 195
Burckhardt, Jacob 16, 22
Burton, Richard 197–8
Butcher, S.H. 28
Butler, A.L. 201
Butler, Eliza May 28
Byron, Lord 28, 38

Canada, big-game hunting 200
Cancik, H. 23
Cannadine, David 7n18, 39
Cannan, May Wedderburn 135–6, 137, 148,
  154–6, 158–9
Carlquist, Maja 218
Carlsbad Decree 14
'C.C.' 139, 153
Celtic Times 66–7, 68–70
Champaud, Charles 174–5
Chapman, Abel 188, 191, 193–4, 194–5, 196,
  200, 203, 205n33
Charteris, Ivo Alan 144
Chateaubriand, F.R. de 28
Christ, Karl 14, 15
Christophe, Eugène 97–8
class system, nineteenth century 38–9
Cobham Stud 54
Colquhoun, Ian 187, 204n24
commercialization, bicycle-racing 104–5,
  114–15
Communism, Bulgaria 181, 182–3
competition, ancient Greek attitude to 19
Corre, Jean 97
Cortese, Paolo 243
Cortis, H.L. 93, 127n37
Coryndon, Robert 201
Coubertin, Pierre, Baron de 25–6, 241
Craggs, Thomas 41
cricket, Lord's cricket ground 38
Crispi, Francesco 232
Crockford, William 48
Croke, Archbishop 63–4
Cronin, M. 71
Curtis, P. 74
Curtius, Ernest 15, 16, 19–22
Cusack, Michael
  background of 59–60
  dismissal of 66
  founder of Gaelic Athletic Association 60–6

impact of 71
socialism of 67–70
Czech Republic, Sokol movement 227n3

Dangerfield, Edmund 107
Davies, Norman 7n11
Davin, Maurice 62–3
Davis (Davies), William 49–50
Davitt, Michael 63
Dawson, Mathew 51
Day, John and William 51, 52
De Burca, M. 59, 62, 66, 67
De Crespigny, Claude 186–7
Delacroix, E. 28
Delamere, Hugh 201, 208n150
Denmark
  Bukh's gymnastics 214–19
  Cooperative Movement 214
  international gymnastics 212–13, 219–20
  and Nazi Germany 223–5
  physical culture 210–11
  schools 227n5
Dentith, Simon 39
Desgrange, Henri 97
dictatorships, and gymnastics 221
Didon, Pierre 248
Dorians 17–18
Duncan, H.O. 96–7, 128n61
Durham, Lord 42

Edge, S.F. 100
education
  and European development 1–2, 6–7n4
  historiography 74–5
  and imperialism 75–88
  Ireland 60–1
  Italy 231
  neohumanist gymnasium 10–13
  school curriculum 77–8
Egerton, Hugh 78
Egerton, Maurice 191, 193, 197, 198–201
Eiselen, Wilhelm Bernhard 10
Eisenberg, Christiane 9
Eldridge, C.C. 74
elementary schools
  and imperialism 75–88
  physical education 80–4
Elkes, Harry 127n42
Ellegaard, 114
Empire Day Movement 77, 86–7
endurance events 92–4
Engels, Friedrich 12
Enlightenment *see* Age of Enlightenment
Etherington, Harry 102
exercise, attitudes to 2, 5
Eyer, Lui 176–7

Fagan, C.E. 192
Fairholme, T.L. 192
Falk, Elin 214, 215
Fallmerayer, Jakob Philipp 27
Feltre, Vittorino da 243
field sports
    and militarism 186–7
    see also hunting
fieldcraft 191, 192, 206n58
First World War, women poets 134–159
Fischer, Joseph 95
Flacelière, Robert 15
Flack, Captain 189
Fontaine, C.C. 101
fox-hunting 189–190
France
    bicycle races 93–95, 96, 97–98, 108, 113,
        126n26
    and Germany 24–6
    horse-racing 53, 54–5
    interest in Antiquity 15
    physical education 241–2
Friedrich Wilhelm III 11
Friesen, Karl Friedrich 10

Gaelic Athletic Association (GAA)
    Cusack's dismissal 66–7
    exclusionary rule 65
    founding of 58–9, 61–4
    political identity 64–5
    success of 65–6
Gaelic football 66
Galtrey, Sidney 42
Games Movement 10
Garin, Maurice 97, 98, 113
Germany
    athleticism 241
    bicycle races 95–6, 104
    classical Greek influences 9–30
    Nazi physical culture 223–5
Giffard, Pierre 94
Gillmore, Parker 189
Graves, A.P. 83
Gray, Edmund 66
Great War *see* First World War
Greeks, classical influences on German sport
    10–30
Griffith, Arthur 67
Griffiths, Nora 148
Grogan, Ewart Scott 201, 208nn149,150
Grote, George 28
Guignard, Paul 101
Gully, John 48
GutsMuths, Johann Christoph Friedrich 11, 13
gymnastics
    Bukh's system 210–11, 214–27

Bulgaria 167, 170–1
Danish 210–13, 216–19
and dictatorships 221
and masculinity 215, 226
militarization 232–3
and patriotism 175
spread of 10
Swedish 10, 213–19
teachers 240
Turnen 10, 13–14, 24, 30, 211, 227n4, 231–2

Hale, John 2, 6–7n4
Hamsun, Knut 223–4
Herne Hill cycling track 111, 125n2
Hillier, G. Lacy 127n37
history, textbooks 78–9
Hitler, Adolf 22, 30
Hobsbawm, Eric 253, 254, 256
Hogenkamp, George 122–4
Holland, Denis 59
Holt, Richard 39, 90n46
Horn, Pamela 76–7, 85
horse-racing
    betting 46–7, 48–50
    breeders 52–4
    General Stud Book 44
    middle-class control 40–55
    owners 51
    Racing Calendar 43–4
    sale of horses 45–6
    trainers 51–2
    upper-class control 39–40, 41–2, 47–8, 54–5
Humboldt, Wilhelm von 11–12
Humphries, Stephen 79
Hungary, physical education 241
hunting
    and masculinity 186–92, 195–9, 202–3
    and militarism 186–7
    opponents 187
    United States 188–189
    see also Shikar Club
Huret, Constant 101
hurling, Ireland 62, 66
Hyde, Douglas 62

imperialism
    and big-game hunting 193–4
    definition 73–4
    historiography 75
    and schools 75–88, 134–5
India
    British imperialism 79–80
    hunting 190
international events
    big-game hunting 192
    see also Olympic Games

Ireland
  cultural change 58–71
  education 60–1
  Great Famine 59
Irish, racist stereotypes 80
Issacs, Francis 200
Italy
  educational gymnastics 231–50
  militarism in schools 232–3
  National Target-Practice Federation 232, 245
  political history 230–1

Jackson, 'Gentleman' John 37–8
Jaeger, Otto Heinrich 24
Jahn, Friedrich Ludwig 10, 13–14, 24, 30, 167, 232
Japan, Bukh's gymnastics 210, 221, 222, 226
Jarry, Alfred 118
Jefferson, Robert Louis 97, 112
Jenkins, Professor 118
Jessop, Les 205n33
Jiel–Laval, Joseph 95, 116
Jockey Club 40, 41–2, 43–4, 46–7
Joll, James 6
Joyeux, Théophile 97
Judd, Alan 135

Kahn, Paul 42
kalokagathia 16, 30
Kazantzis, Judith 135, 136–7
Keats, J. 28
Kilmer, Joyce 142–3
Kirby, Thomas 53
Kirk, David 177
Kosellek, Reinhart 9
Kotzebue, August von 14
Krause, Johann Heinrich 18

Labriola, Antonio 231
Laumaillé, 96, 126n26
Lefèvre, Geo 97
Letts, W.M. 143, 144–5, 147, 148–9
Ling, Pehr Henrik 213
Ling Physical Education Association 82
Lingiad 218, 226
Loder, Edmund G. 196, 200
Loder, Robert 196
Lonsdale, Lord 192, 197, 202
Lord, Thomas 38
Lowther, Hugh Cecil 188, 204n4, 205n31
Lucas, Charles 78
Ludwig, Karl 238
Lyell, Dennis 192, 203

McCord, Norman 74

Macdonald, Nina 137–8
McIntosh, Peter 80–1, 83
MacKenzie, John M. 7n18, 75, 78, 79
Macnamara, T.J. 81
Mahaffy, John P. 29
Malcolmson, Robert 37
Mangan, J.A. 16, 30, 35, 74, 75–6, 87–8
Marchand, Suzanne L. 11, 20
Marey, Jule 238
Marsh, Richard 52
Marylebone Cricket Club 38
masculinity
  and gymnastics 215, 226
  and hunting 186–92, 195–9, 202–3
Maydon, H.C. 195
Mazower, Mark 255
Meath, Twelfth Earl of 77
Mercuriale, Gerolamo 243
Michael, Jimmy 99, 127nn39,42
Middle Ages, role of education 1, 3
Middle Park Stud 53
militarism
  in elementary schools 80–3, 90n46
  and field sports 186–7
  in Italian schools 232–3
Mill, John Stuart 28
Millais, John G. 195, 200
Miller, Charlie 103
Mills, G.P. 96, 101, 126n14
modernization, impacts of 4–6
Mohammed, Abdul R. Jan 88
Moor, Anita 139–40
Moore, George 107
Mosso, Angelo 233, 235, 237–50
Mott, Albert 106
Mullen, M. 58
Müller, I.P. 214
Müller, Karl Otfried 17–18
Munting, Roger 39
Murphy, Charles 119

Nadel, G.H. 74
Nally, Patrick 61
neohumanist gymnasium 10–13
Newbolt, Henry 145
Newmarket, horse-racing 43–4, 45–6
Newton, A.P. 78
Nietzsche, Friedrich 16, 22–4
nineteenth century
  definition of 9
  'revolution' in sport 2, 35–7, 54–5, 255
Nordic Olympiad (1935) 218, 226
North Road Cycling Club 126n14

Obermann, Rudolf 232
Oldridge Road Board School 86

Olympia, excavations 19–22
Olympic Games
    1908 (Rome) 248
    1912 (Stockholm) 212, 217
    1936 (Berlin) 22
    modern reintroduction of 25, 27, 179
    Niels Bukh 210, 212
Osbaldeston, George 204n11
Owen, Wilfred 134, 135, 136

Paris–Brest–Paris bicycle race 94–5, 116
Parnell, Charles Stewart 63
Parvanov, Nikola 169
patriotism, and gymnastics 175
Pearse, Padraic 60, 69
Pease, Alfred 186, 192–3, 196
Peck, Robert 51
Peel, C.V.A. 195
Pelling, Henry 75
physical culture, concept of 172–3
physical education
    Bulgaria 166–83
    elementary schools 80–4
    Greek model 13
    Italy 231–50
    see also gymnastics
physiology, and sport 238
Planck, Karl 116–17
poetry, by women 134–59
politics, and sport 64–5, 211, 221–2
Pope, Jessie 138, 146–7
Porter, John 51, 52
professionalization, bicycle-racing 104–5,
    114–15, 120
psychosomatic medicine 238–9
psyco-cinesiology 236
public schools, Edwardian heroes 134–5
pugilism 37–8
Pugilistic Club 38

Quakers 82

racing *see* bicycle-racing; horse-racing
Radclyffe, Charles Edward 186, 200, 204n7
Radclyffe-Dugmore, Major 202
railways, influence on sport 48, 56n43
Rawcliffe Stud Company 54
record breaking
    bicycle-racing 93, 101, 109, 115–19,
        126n12, 130–3
    and modernism 115–16
Reilly, Catherine 135, 136–7, 159n3
Renaissance 2, 6–7n4, 242–3
Renshaw, C.A. 138, 141, 145, 152–3
'revolution', nineteenth-century sport 2, 35–7,
    54–5, 255

Richard, 96, 126n26
Ridsdale, Robert 48
Rintelen, C. 105
Roberts, Robert 79
Robl, Thaddeus 114
Rogers, E. 168
Roseberry, Lord 84–5
Rosenberg, Alfred 224
Rosendale Road Board School 86–7
Ross, Ludwig 27
Rous, Admiral 40, 42
Rousseau, Jean Jacques 13
Rückert, Friedrich 15
Russia, and Bulgaria 163–4
Rütt, Walter 104, 114

Salt, Henry 187, 188, 204n18
Sand, Karl Ludwig 14
Sandhurst School 87
Sassoon, Siegfried 134, 135–6
Scaino, Antonio 243
schools
    and imperialism 75–88, 134–5
    influence of 1–2, 254
Schulze, Adolph 120
Scott, John 51–2
Scott, Robert Lyons 193, 206nn80,82
Scout movement 198
Seeley, John Robert 78–9
Segal, C.P. 29
Seitz, Franz 24, 26–7
Selous, Frederick Courtney 186, 200
sensationalism, bicycle-racing 118–19
Sergi, Giuseppe 248
Seton-Karr, Henry 187, 191, 196, 205n27
Sharpe, Alfred 201
Shelley, P.B. 28
Shephard, Ben 136
Shikar Club 185–203
    and conservation 201–2
    'fair play' of 188
    founding of 185, 186
    masculinity 190–2, 195–9, 202–3
    membership 192–202, 204n4
shooting *see* hunting
Shorland, Frank 101
Sidgwick, Mrs Henry 247
Sigerson, Dora 155
Silver, Harold 74
Simon, Brian 84–5
Sims, Geo. R. 137
slavery, and classical gymnasium 12, 13
Smith, Thomas Ashetton 204n11
Society for the Preservation of the (Wild)
    Fauna of the Empire (SPFE) 201–2
Sokol movement 210, 227n3

South Africa, Bukh's gymnastics 222–3, 226, 227
South America, Bukh's gymnastics 222
Southern, R.W. 1
Soviet Union, gymnastics 222
Spartans 17
Spiess, Adolf 14, 232
sport
    analogy with war 142–7
    nineteenth-century 'revolution' 2, 35–7, 54–5, 255
    and politics 64–5, 211, 221–2
sportsmanship, hunting 188
Stambolov, Stefan 172, 173
Stearns, Peter 4, 6
stereotypes, racist 79–80
Stigand, Charles Hugh 192
Sweden, community house 214, 227–8n8
Swedish gymnastics movement 10, 213–16
    and Niels Bukh 216–19, 225–6
Swindell, Fred 50
Swiss Gymnastics Union 173–4
Sykes, Tatton 52

target-practice, Italy 232, 245
Tattersall family 43, 45–8, 52–3, 54–5
Taylor, A.J.P. 75
Taylor, H.O. 28
Taylor, Major 91, 103, 114
technological developments, and bicycle-racing 100, 127nn40,41
Teilmann, Kaare 216
Terront, Charles 94, 95, 96, 110, 116, 128n50
Theobald, Mr 53
Thormanby 51
Thuillet, Camille 102, 128n49
Timms, J.G. 86–7
Tour de France 95, 97–8, 113
Tranter, Neil 35–6, 39
Turnen 10, 13–14, 24, 30, 167, 211, 227n4, 231–2
Tynan, Katharine 137, 144, 150–2, 155
Tzankov, Dragan 166

Unak, Bulgaria 174–81

United States
    bicycle-racing 102–3
    hunting 188–189
    women 248
upper classes, involvement in sport 37–8, 39–40

Valletti, Felice 234
Vamplew, Wray 35, 39, 48
Vanderbyl, P.B. 186, 200, 204nn4,7
Vegio, Maffeo 243
Velev, G. 163
Velichkov, Konstantin 176
velodromes, development of 91–2, 125n2
Victoria, Queen 86
Vienna–Berlin bicycle race 95–6
Vivian, Arthur 196
Von Gossler, Gustav 241
von Salvisberg, Paul 117
von Tschammer und Osten, Hans 223–4

Waller, George 102, 103
war, analogy with sport 142–7
Waterloo, Battle of 25
Weatherby family 43–4, 47–8, 54–5
White, Frank 102
Wildfowlers Association of Great Britain and Ireland 185
Wilhelm I 24
Wilson, W.J. 86
Winckelmann, Johann Joachim 10–11, 15, 20
Winks, Robert 73–4
winter sports, spread of 10
Wohl, Robert 159
women
    gymnastics 215, 216, 234
    Italy 246–8
    middle-class 2
    War poets 134–59
Wood Green cycling track 125n2

Yonchev, Todor 162–3, 169–83

Zhivkov, Goergy 172
Zimmerman, Arthur 91, 106, 114